FamilyFun
VACATION GUIDE
Florida
& The Southeast

By Jill Mross, Anne Dukes, Christy Smith,
Wendy Swat Snyder, and the
experts at FamilyFun Magazine

DISNEP
EDITIONS
New York

FamilyFun
VACATION GUIDE
Florida & The Southeast

Editorial Director
Lois Spritzer

Design & Production
IMPRESS, INC.
Hans Teensma
Pam Glaven
Katie Craig
Lisa Newman
James McDonald
Katie Winger

Disney Editions and *FamilyFun* Book Editors
Alexandra Kennedy
Wendy Lefkon
Lisa Stiepock

Research Editor
Beth Honeyman

Contributing Editors
Jon Adolph
Rani Arbo
Duryan Bhagat
Jodi Butler
Jaqueline Cappuccio
Deanna Cook
Tony Cuen
Ann Hallock
Jessica Hinds
Martha Jenkins
Rich Mintzer
Jody Revenson
David Sokol
Deborah Way

Copy Editors
Diane Hodges
Jenny Langsam
Monica Mayper
Jill Newman

Editorial Assistants
Laura Gomes
Jean Graham

Production
Janet Castiglione
Sue Cole

This book is dedicated to our *FamilyFun* readers, and contributors, and to traveling families everywhere.

WRITER
Jill Mross is an Orlando-based writer who, with her husband and preteen son, has traveled both near and far in search of the ultimate vacation.

WRITERS/RESEARCHERS
Anne Dukes (Georgia) is a writer living in Atlanta, who loves to travel with her son and daughter. Favorite destinations include the North Georgia mountains, the canyons and arches of Utah, and Washington, D.C.

Christy Smith (Florida and Georgia) is a freelance writer living in Altamonte Springs, Florida. She and her family love traveling throughout the South, discovering new favorite places, and visiting old favorite friends.

Wendy Swat Snyder (South Carolina) writes travel and tourism-oriented articles for a variety of Southeast regional publications. A native New Yorker, she now calls Charleston, South Carolina home.

Illustrations by **Kandy Littrell**

FamilyFun Vacation Guide Florida and the Southeast copyright © 2003 Disney Enterprises, Inc. All rights reserved. No part of this book may be reproduced or transmitted in any form or by any means, electronic or mechanical, including photocopying, recording, or by any information storage and retrieval system, without written permission from the publisher.

For information, address Disney Editions, 114 Fifth Avenue, New York, New York 10011-5690.

Printed in the United States of America

First Edition
1 3 5 7 9 10 8 6 4 2
Library of Congress Catalog Card Number: 2001017483
ISBN 0-7868-5301-8

Visit www.disneyeditions.com

Contents

- 5 Dear Parents
- 6 How to Use this Guide
- 8 Introduction to Florida and the Southeast
- 10 Ready, Set, Go!

FLORIDA

- 40 Introduction
- 42 Northeast Florida
- 56 Orlando and the Space Coast
- 74 SeaWorld and Discovery Cove
- 82 Universal Orlando
- 96 Walt Disney World Resort
- 126 South Florida
- 144 Florida Keys and the Everglades
- 158 Southwest Florida
- 168 Florida's West Coast
- 184 Tallahassee and the Florida Panhandle

GEORGIA

- 196 Introduction
- 198 Augusta and Middle Georgia
- 212 Savannah and Coastal Georgia
- 228 Callaway Gardens and Columbus
- 240 Greater Atlanta
- 254 North Georgia

SOUTH CAROLINA

- 266 Introduction
- 268 Charleston Area
- 280 Columbia Area
- 286 Myrtle Beach
- 294 Santee Cooper Country
- 304 South Carolina Low Country
- 314 South Carolina Up Country

NORTH CAROLINA

- 324 Introduction
- 326 Coastal North Carolina
- 348 The Heartland
- 368 North Carolina Mountains

INTRODUCTION

Dear Parents,

A FRIEND OF MINE—a dad—said something recently that rang true to me. "A great childhood," he said, thinking aloud, "is really made up of a thousand small good moments." His comment prompted me to step back and take stock of what those moments might be for my own two young sons. What will be their happiest memories? Topping the list in my mind are the simple but extraordinary pleasures we've had traveling together: the hermit crabs we discovered at a Maine beach, the afternoon spent playing catch on the Mall in Washington, the thrill of a first flight, a first train ride, a first hike to a mountaintop.

As parents, we all work incredibly hard to find the time and money to take our children on vacation. We want to show them the remarkably varied American landscape and introduce them to its many cultures and histories. We want to get away from jobs, homework, and household chores long enough to enjoy one another's company uninterrupted. And most of all, we want to have fun.

The editors at *FamilyFun* and I take great pride in this book and others in the series. They are a culmination of ten years worth of gathering for our readers' the best vacation advice out there. Traveling with children is an art—and our charge is to help with your decisions every step of the way so that you can make the most of every minute of your time away.

Alexandra Kennedy
Alexandra Kennedy
Editorial Director

How to Use This Guide

WELCOME TO THE world of *FamilyFun* magazine's new travel guide series. In our effort to present you with the finest in vacation options, we called on the best experts we know: our hardy group of writers. All are parents who travel with their kids, and all live and work in the area(s) about which they're writing. These are the people who can tell you where to find that teddy bear shop that isn't in the main mall, which restaurant has the best milk shakes, which museum will invite your toddler to roll up his sleeves and create art, and which theme park will give your preteen a good return on the price of admission. With all their recommendations comes the endorsement of their kids: our traveling children have been our best critics.

Since all of the guides in this series cover more than one state, we have divided them into easy-to-use sections. So here's a guide to the guide.

READY, SET, GO!—is a mini-encyclopedia of handy facts, practical advice, what to do/where to go/when to go/how to travel: in other words, all you need to know about planning a successful family vacation.

INTRODUCTION—will give you an overview of the states being covered in this guidebook. Read it—it will whet your appetite, and perhaps give you some new ideas for family activities.

CHAPTERS—States and chapters are presented in geographical order. Chapters represent the regions we think your family will enjoy most. We have omitted those places that we feel would not be family-friendly or are too expensive for what you get in return. We also make note of attractions that appeal only to a certain age range.

FamilyFun has given each entry a rating—stars (★) that range from one to four—to guide you to our favorites. Remember, however, that this guidebook contains nothing that we do not recommend—it's just that we liked some things better than others. We've also assigned a dollar sign rating (**$**)—in high season for a family of four, also ranging from one to four. Check the price range at the start of each chapter as the key changes. We hope that this will help you to decide whether a hotel, restaurant, or attraction will fit in with your budget.

Typically, we start each chapter with an introduction, followed by *FamilyFun*'s Must-See List of up to ten things to try to do while visiting. We've divided attractions into two categories: "Cultural Attractions" (museums, historic sites, and so on) and "Just for Fun" (water parks, zoos, aquariums, roller coasters, and the like). Wherever possible, we've included Web site information.

What more can we say? We hope that this guide helps you to fashion the best possible vacation for your family, one that is a pleasure in the planning, a delight in the doing, and one that will leave every member of your clan with memories that will last a lifetime—or at least until ninth grade.

Bon Voyage!

Florida and the Southeast

FEW REGIONS in the country offer as many popular vacation hot spots for families as Florida, Georgia, and the Carolinas—*FamilyFun*'s top getaway destinations in the southeastern United States. Wonder why? We're glad you asked.

Whether your kids are excitable preschoolers or challenging preteens, budding naturalists or wannabe surfers, these four states serve up some of the most incredible, widely diverse, and way-cool vacation attractions this side of paradise.

If your youngsters dig theme, amusement, and water parks, the Southeast wrote the book on them, with more roller coasters, water slides, and wild rides than a 10-year-old could ever hope for. Not to worry if your troops are a bit younger—they'll find there are a load of rides and activities designed for the mini thrill seeker (Mom and Dad, too). From mega-show biz to hokey-but-fun carnival midways, expect a rip-roaring good time.

And if you're looking for something a little more laid-back, or your kids like hiking and camping, you'll find them throughout our four-state lineup. With hundreds of parks, beaches, and waterways to choose from, your outdoor enthusiasts will truly be in their element. From biking, birding, and beaching to skiing (both water and snow!), shelling, and sailing, Mother Nature has her finest works on display here.

And don't overlook the Southeast's incredible array of knock-your-socks-off museums and learning centers, with lots of hands-on science, history, and nature—all guaranteed to provide some cultural enrichment. If your kids are thinking boring, they're sure to change their tune after visiting family-friendly places that feature cuddly teddy bears, basketball-playing rats, way-cool antique cars—even a museum dedicated to sports legend Michael Jordan!

In addition to the Southeast's action-packed lineup of family fun, the region provides a ton of family-friendly accommodations to suit every budget, pocketbook, and lifestyle. Some resorts offer supervised children's programs, a few of which may rival an attraction or two on the thrill-a-minute meter. For serious outdoors lovers (tents, RVs), camping under the stars in the Southeast provides the ultimate in scenic, fresh-air sleep. If you crave something a bit more upscale, but still close to nature, we've also included some great campgrounds that offer comfy cabins.

One thing is for sure—in this region, your kids will never go hungry. Whether they're into burgers and fries, shrimp and hush puppies, pasta and garlic bread, or eggs and grits, restaurants go out of their way to please young palates. To celebrate that very special occasion while on vacation, consider dining at one of the region's theme restaurants or dinner shows. Not only is the food tasty, there's plenty to keep the kids entertained while they chow down.

Add to all this some little shopping gems where you can buy cool stuff like funky jewelry, good-looking duds, and unusual handmade goods just right for kids and you've got the makings of a memorable vacation. So come on—what are you waiting for?

Let the fun begin!

k up and get
u're o

INTRODUCTION

Ready, Set, Go!

JUST TEN YEARS AGO, *FamilyFun* was a fledgling magazine, and the family travel "industry"—now a booming, $100 billion annual trade—was as much a newcomer as we were. In a way, you could say we have grown up together.

FamilyFun was one of the first national magazines to actively research and publicize travel ideas for families with school-age children (a fun job, we must add). Over the last decade, as the numbers of traveling families increased, so did the business of family travel. These days, there are more resources, opportunities, and means for the vacationing family than ever before—which, in turn, gives *FamilyFun* the chance to be an even more valuable clearinghouse of ideas for you.

Through the years, we have been privileged to work with veteran travel writers and editors who have gone around the world with their kids. We've also taken time to listen to our readers—insightful, creative families from across the United States—and to note (and sometimes publish) their stories, recommendations, and tips on traveling as a family. A combination of those two wisdoms is what awaits you on the following pages.

Although it may not be readily apparent, a lot of trial and error underlies these pages. Each destination, before it reaches this book, undergoes a rigorous investigation, and not all make the grade.

We know that family vacations are a big investment, and we know that's why you're here. You're hoping to sidestep the pitfalls of experimentation and to locate destinations that will be a real hit with your family. Congratulations! You've come to the right place.

FamilyFun **VACATION GUIDE**

First Steps

At the outset, organizing a family vacation can seem as daunting as landing a probe on Mars. Better to stay home and watch the Discovery Channel, you think—maybe toast a few marshmallows in the fireplace.

The truth is that planning an adventurous vacation can be fun, especially if you prepare for it in advance and involve your kids. The onerous part is remembering all the things you have to think about.

That's where we come in. This introductory chapter covers family travel from A to Z, from deciding where to go, to getting there and making the most of your vacation. Some of this may seem like old news to you, but we want to make sure you don't forget a thing.

How much do we spend?

Chances are, you already know approximately what you have to spend on a vacation—and you've already got a modus operandi when it comes to money matters. Maybe you're a family that carefully figures a budget, then finds a vacation to fit it. Or maybe you're the type to set your heart on a once-in-a-lieftime trip, then scrimp and save until you can make it happen.

Determine the type of trip you will take. Before you even start your planning, take a moment to consider: what kind of trip are you taking? Are you splurging on a dream vacation, or conserving on a semi-annual getaway? What aspects of this trip are most important to you?

> **HAVE MODEM, WILL TRAVEL**
> For information on how to research and book travel plans on the Web, turn to page 31.

Budget carefully. Once you know what those broad parameters are, the next step is to think through your vacation budget in detail—if not at the outset of planning, then at an opportune point along the way. When you know what you have to spend, you'll make quicker and less stressful decisions en route and you'll be able to pay the bills without a grimace once you get home. You'll find lots of budget-saving tips in this introductory chapter.

When can we go?

Scheduling your vacation well can make a big difference in everyone's experience of the trip.

Consider each individual. Most likely, tight school and work schedules will decide when you travel — but if possible, aim for a time slot that allows everyone to relax. For instance, an action-packed road trip sounds exciting, but it might be just the wrong medicine for a parent who's squeezing it into a packed work schedule. End-of-summer trips may be tough for kids with back-to-school anxieties, and midyear trips that snatch kids from school sometimes cause more trouble than they're worth.

Where do we go?

In this book (and the others in this travel series), you'll find scores of winning family destinations. By all means, though, don't stop here. Doing your own research is half the fun, and these days, you have a wealth of resources at your disposal.

Make a list of destinations. What hot spots intrigue your clan? What adventures would you like to try? Draw up a big list, and don't worry about coming up with too many ideas—you can return to this list year after year. Here are a few trails you can follow: relatives, friends, and coworkers (who love to report on their own successful trips), a professional travel agent, local chambers of commerce and state tourism boards, and magazines, the Internet (see page 34 for some good family travel sites), and local hotels and outfitters in the geographic areas you're interested in.

Evaluate your family. A good vacation has to accommodate *everyone* in the family, no matter what their ages, limitations, or interests. While no destination will make everyone happy all the time, you should search vigilantly for those that offer a niche for each family member.

Involve your kids. The more involved your kids are in planning—especially during these early, brainstorming stages — the more likely they are to work to make the trip a success.

Experiment wisely. While experimentation can add spice to a trip, too much may overwhelm your kids (and you). If your child has her heart set on horseback riding, for example, make sure she tries it out at home before you put down a deposit on a dude ranch vacation.

Check the season. Be informed about travel conditions for the time of your trip and make sure you're not heading for trouble (hurricane season in Florida, for example, or black-fly season in the Adirondacks). This is especially important if you're cashing in on off-season deals.

FamilyFun VACATION GUIDE

Local Flavor on the Cheap

Don't wait till you arrive at your destination to investigate opportunities for local fun—research a few in advance:

- Check out a regional festival or agricultural fair. For fairs in the western U.S., visit www.fairs net.org and for festivals nationwide, visit www.festivals.com
- Explore a college campus (which may offer green space, bike paths, museums, observatories, and more). To find a list, go to a general Internet search engine like www.yahoo.com, click on education, and search for colleges by state. Then, call the school's information office for a map and a roster of special events.
- Visit a farmers' market. For a list of markets around the U.S., log on to www.ams.usda.gov/farmersmarkets/
- Take in an air show (they're usually free at military bases). For a list of air shows by region, see www.airshows.org
- Find a local nature center or Audubon preserve.

Schedule appropriately. How much time do you need to give this particular destination its due? You don't want to feel like you're rushing through things—but neither do you want to run out of activities that will interest your kids.

Should we have an itinerary?

Drawing up a travel itinerary, whether it's rough or detailed, will ensure that you travel wisely, hit the hot spots, and give everyone in your group a say in what you'll see.

Include something for everyone. No doubt, each member of your family will have his or her own list of must-sees. If a unanimous vote on itinerary stops is out of the question, ask everyone to write down top choices, then create a schedule that guarantees each person at least one or two favorites. If your children span a wide age range, remind them that there will be some patient standing by while siblings (and Mom and Dad) have their moments in the sun.

Involve the kids (again). Once you've got the basic stops down, kids can help research destinations, plan driving routes, locate pit stops, and help plan rainy-day alternatives.

Make a plan, then break it. Don't let your preplanned schedule get in the way of spontaneous delights. What if your kids want to ride that water slide for an extra three hours? One fun moment in hand is usually worth at least two on the itinerary.

Beat the crowds. Remember to head for popular attractions first thing in the morning or in late afternoon and early evening. Save the middle of the day for poolside fun or activities that take you off the beaten path and away from crowds.

Travel in tune with your family's natural rhythms. Preschoolers tend to be at their best early in the day—a good time for structured activities. Many teens, on the other hand, are pictures of grogginess before noon. Adapt your itinerary to suit ingrained family habits—including your usual meal and nap times—and you'll have smoother sailing. When visiting very popular destinations, take the time to find out in advance when their slowest periods are.

Train-your-own tour guides

Guided tours at historic sites and museums are often a snooze (or too sophisticated) for young kids. Instead, create your own tour—have each family member study up on a different attraction by writing or calling for brochures, surfing the Web, and visiting the library. Then, when you arrive, you'll have an expert guide on board.

GETTING THERE

As we all know, the experience of taking kids from point A to point B runs the gamut from uneventful (read: bliss) to miserable. Knowing the ins and outs of your travel options will speed you toward a sane trip.

FamilyFun **READER'S TIP**

Hire Some Junior Travel Agents

When we were planning a summer trip to Louisiana, I overheard one of my kids tell another that they were going to have to do everything Mom and Dad wanted to do. That's when I decided that each family member would get to plan a full day of our trip. I purchased a regional travel guide and told everyone they had $200 for one day's activities, meals, and accommodations, so they would have to budget (a useful exercise for my 10- and 12-year olds). Every night, any money left over from that day was given to the next planner. I am proud to say that everything went well, and the kids proclaimed it the best vacation ever!

Cindy Long, Spring, Texas

By Plane

PROS: It's fast. And if you land a good deal, air travel can actually be affordable.

CONS: If you don't land a good deal, air travel can be prohibitively expensive, especially for a big family. Other pitfalls include flight delays, mounting claustrophobia on long trips, and strict baggage restrictions.

Look for deals. Traveling in off-peak season and taking off-peak flights (very early or very late in the day) may save you money; flying midweek and staying over Saturday night almost always will. You may also wish to research deals at different airports (for instance, T. F. Green Airport in Providence, Rhode Island, often offers cheaper fares than Boston's Logan Airport 45 minutes away). Also, remember that most sale tickets have a cutoff date—you'll have to book two, three, or four weeks ahead of your departure date to get the deal.

Consider using an agent. Booking your own airline reservations on the Web is a cinch these days (see pages 35 and 36), but there are still advantages to using a professional travel agent who knows your family's needs. First of all, for the $10 or $20 per-ticket surcharge you may pay, you'll save Web-surfing time, and you'll be spared the stress of babysitting the fickle airline market. Also, an agent may be able to suggest a Plan B (such as using a smaller airport to get a better deal)—something the Web search engines can't do for you. Try to get a good agent recommendation through friends, coworkers, or relatives; if you need further help, the American Society of Travel Agents (703-739-2782, www.astanet.com) provides a list of members, as well as brochures on travel topics (including one on how to choose a travel agent).

By Car

PROS: Road trips are the cheapest way to get from here to there, and they can also be real adventures. In addition, the car is familiar territory for your kids, so they'll feel right at home (for better or worse) during the trip. And, of course, a road trip affords you priceless flexibility.

CONS: You're in for major advance planning, from making sure your car is in good condition to scheduling regular rest stops and having a dependable cache of road snacks, games, and other diversions. Even with those, the hours of close confinement may quickly erode your family's wanderlust.

Get a good map. If you belong to AAA, request a free "TripTik" map. Otherwise, you can map your route and download printed driving directions on Websites like www.mapquest.com, www.freetrip.com, and www.mapsonus.com

✓ CHECKLIST
Flying with Kids

WHEN YOU BOOK
- Try first for a nonstop flight. If that's not available, fly "direct," which means you'll stop at least once but won't switch planes.
- Book flights that depart early in the day, if possible. If your flight is delayed, you—and the airline—will have time to make other arrangements.
- Specify your ticketing preferences, whether paper or electronic.
- Check to see if a meal will be served in flight. If so, order meals your kids like. Many airlines offer kids' meals or a vegetarian choice that may be pasta. If not, plan accordingly.
- Ask for the seats you'd like, whether they're a window, an aisle, or the bulkhead for legroom.

PACKING TIPS
- Stuff your carry-on for every contingency. Pack all medications, extra clothes for little kids, diapers, baby food, formula, wet wipes, and snacks (they'll also help kids swallow to relieve ear pressure).
- Have each child carry a small backpack with travel toys, a light sweatshirt, and a pair of socks for the flight.

ON THE DAY OF YOUR TRIP
- Call ahead to check for delays.
- Have all photo IDs within easy reach (not necessary for kids under age 18 traveling with their parents on domestic flights; on most international flights, even infants will need a passport).
- If you have heavy bags, check your luggage first and then park.
- If you are early for the flight or run into long delays, don't go straight to the gate. Instead, meander through the airport's diversions: windows onto the runways, children's play areas (many major airports now have these), Web access computers, and, of course, stores where kids can find a treat to tide them over.
- Carry on extra bottled water. It's easy to get dehydrated on a plane, and the drink service may be slow in reaching you.

ON THE PLANE
- Ask if your child can view the cockpit (the best time may be after the flight is over).
- Secure pillows and blankets for family members who may want to nap.
- Take breaks from sitting; occasionally walk the aisles and switch seats.

FLYING FEARS

Most children are fearless fliers—and those who are afraid often can trace their concerns to adults who unintentionally transmit their own fears. If you need help answering your children's questions, you can ask them on-line at www.wic-kid.com

FamilyFun TIP

Bookworms

When you're on the road, there's nothing like a good story to pass the time. For night drives, audio books can be a lifesaver. Try borrowing or renting one from your local library, or visit www.storytapes.com, the Website for Village StoryTapes (800-238-8273). You can either rent or purchase from their excellent selection; three- to four-week tape rentals cost $6 to $17 (for *Harry Potter IV*); to buy, tapes cost $12 to $60.

Be prepared for emergencies, large and small. It goes without saying that your car should be in prime working order before you depart. You should have supplies for road emergencies on board, as well as a good first-aid kit (see page 33 for a list of what to include), and, if you have one, bring a cell phone.

Keep things orderly. We all know what happens to our cars within minutes of the time the kids buckle in; on long road trips, expect the chaos to rise by a factor of ten. In an effort to keep things in check, bring containers to hold trash and toys; pack the children's luggage so it's easiest to reach; divvy up the backseat space so kids know where their boundaries are; and go over basic behavior rules before you leave.

Drive in time with your family's rhythm. Night driving offers less traffic and a chance that young kids will sleep (you can let them ride in their pj's). Alternatively, an early start may avoid late-afternoon, kid-cranky hours. When possible, go with your family's natural flow.

Help prevent motion sickness. Have frequent, small meals during your trip (symptoms are more likely to occur on an empty stomach). Over-the-counter medications such as Dramamine, as well as ginger ale, ginger tea, or ginger candy also can help, but once symptoms begin, it's usually too late for oral medications. Make sure the car is well ventilated, and have sickness-prone travelers take a window seat, which offers

WEATHER WATCHERS Before you leave, assign forecaster duties to one of your kids. Using the Internet, he or she can research and predict the type of weather you'll encounter (and advise everyone on what to pack). Try www.weather.com

fresh air and a view of the road. If a child feels nauseated, have him look straight in front of the car or focus attention on the horizon. If your child becomes carsick, stop the car to give him a break from the motion; having him lie down with his head perfectly still also may help.

By Train

PROS: First of all, trains are just plain cool, for kids and adults alike. Second, there's room to explore, and everyone can kick back and enjoy the view. And third, if you are headed to a major metropolitan area with a good public transit system, you'll avoid the expenses and hassles of city driving and parking.

CONS: There's only one national passenger rail service, Amtrak, and at press time its future was in question. Also, Amtrak's limited network may not be convenient to your destination (ask about connector trains and rental car agencies when you call). In some regions of the United States, Amtrak's city-to-city service rivals car, bus, and plane travel for efficiency; on cross-country hauls, this is not the case. If you're investing in a long train trip, you're in it more for the experience of train travel.

Inquire about special deals. Children ages 2 to 15 usually ride for half fare when accompanied by an adult who pays full fare. Each adult can bring two children at this discounted rate. Amtrak also offers

A Road Trip Survival Kit

A BAG OF TRICKS

♦ mini-puzzles with a backboard
♦ video games, cassette or CD player (with headphones)
♦ paper, pens, pencils, markers
♦ travel versions of board games
♦ stuffed animals
♦ Etch A Sketch
♦ colored pipe cleaners
♦ deck of cards
♦ cookie sheet (a good lap tray)
♦ word puzzles
♦ small action figures or dolls
♦ stickers
♦ Trivial Pursuit cards
♦ cotton string (for cat's cradle games)

A COOLER OF SNACKS

Bring lots of drinks and a cache of snacks like granola bars, trail mix, grapes, carrot sticks, roll-up sandwiches, fruit leather, and popcorn.

Keeping 'Em Busy: 60-Second Solutions

SQUABBLE SOLUTIONS
Give your kids 25 cents in pennies at the start of the trip. Each time they fight or whine, charge them a penny. Offer a reward, such as doubling or tripling their money, if they haven't lost a cent during the ride.

WAGER AND WIN
Kids are natural wagerers—they love to bet how much, how long, how far, how many. If you're in a bind for a moment's entertainment, ask them to guess the number of French fries on your plate or to estimate how many steps it will take to walk to your airport gate. The key here is to be able to verify the guesses—you'll need to wear a watch with a second hand and carry a calculator.

CREATIVE COMPETITION
Kids love challenges. Need to get rid of the trash in the car? See who can smash the trash into the smallest paper ball, then toss it in the wastepaper bag. Want quiet time? Hold a five-minute silence contest. Need to get through errands in a hurry? Challenge your kids to a race against time. You may feel that your motives are transparent, but your kids won't care.

special seasonal rates, other family deals, and Web-only deals.

How to find them. Amtrak's Website, www.amtrak.com, provides information on fares, schedules, reservations, routes and services, station locations, and special offers. You can also call Amtrak at 800-872-7245 for information and reservations. When you book, ask if there is a full-service dining car and ask whether you can reserve a block of seats for your family.

Consider a sleeper car. For overnight trips, sleep-in-your-seat fares are the cheapest, but first-class bedrooms are much more comfortable.

Arrive early. If your train seats are unassigned, get to the station early for the best chance of eveyone's sitting together. You can even have one parent run ahead to grab a group of seats while the other shepherds children and luggage to the platform.

By RV
PROS: It's a home away from home, which means you can eat, sleep, and use the indoor plumbing (as everyone will agree, one of the finest features of RV travel) whenever you want. In an RV, you are free to explore with independence, self-sufficiency, and freedom—three assets that can be priceless when you're traveling with kids.
CONS: It's a home away from home,

READY, SET, GO!

FamilyFun READER'S TIP

Patchwork Pillows

I am 10 years old, and every year my family goes camping. I collect patches from each place we visit, including the Grand Canyon, Yellowstone and Yosemite National Parks; San Francisco; Las Vegas; and, most recently, Santa Fe, New Mexico. I put all the patches I've collected during each year on separate pillows. I keep the pillows on my bed to remind me of our great trips.

Alex Smythe, Tucson, Arizona

which means you face dishes, cooking, and maintenance (generators, water pumps, waste tanks, and the engine, for starters). In addition, RV rentals are not cheap, although they can compare favorably to the cost of a week's lodging, food, and travel (especially for big families).

What they cost. Expect to pay rental fees between $500 and $1,500 per week, depending on location, model, and time of year you'll be traveling, and the luxury factor (RVs can get pretty posh). Gasoline costs will be high, but you'll save considerably on food and accommodations (campground fees average $20 to $40 per night).

How to find them. Rental information is available through auto clubs and through Go RVing (888-GO-RVING, ask for the free video and literature; www.gorving.com). Cruise America (800-327-7799) offers 150 rental centers across the United States and Canada. The RV America Website (www.rvamerica.

com) has listings of dealers, clubs, and resources.

Be a savvy renter. Choose an RV that's big enough for your family, but know that many campgrounds only permit vehicles less than 30 feet long. Before you rent, ask how many people fit comfortably in the RV, what powers the appliances, how much insurance is required, and whether supplies such as linens and kitchen utensils are included in the rental price. Get a demonstration of how to work everything in the vehicle, read the manual, practice a little ahead of time, and you'll be ready to take the plunge.

By Bus

PROS: The major advantages of bus travel are that it's cheap, that it spares you the stress of driving, and that tickets usually can be purchased on the day of your trip, at the station. **CONS:** Unfortunately, traveling by bus often takes longer than by car. What's more, bus travel offers little opportunity for diversion for your

Thinking of Skipping School?

If you are, then according to a recent Travel Industry Association of America poll, you're in lots of company. The TIA survey found that one in five parents allows a child to miss school to gain travel experience (of these, 72 percent, however, missed only one or two days). If you're planning to play hooky on vacation, start by keeping the school well informed of your plans. Discuss with the teachers what work your kids will have to keep up with, and create a regular routine during your vacation when they can do so. To help kids stay in touch with their classmates and to broaden their learning experience, establish a way for them to share their travel adventures with the class, either while they're en route (by e-mailing or posting letters) or once they return to school.

children. And since you're sitting close to other passengers, many lively family games are off-limits (some buses offer a TV movie; ask when you call).

How to find them: Greyhound Lines (800-229-9424) offers service across the United States. In the Northeast, between New Hampshire and Washington, D.C., Peter Pan Bus Lines (800-237-8747) is another option. Both have Websites, www.greyhound.com and www.peterpanbus.com, complete with fare and schedule information. To locate smaller local or regional bus lines, try the local Yellow Pages or the department of travel and tourism in the region you'll be visiting.

By Rental Car

PROS: This isn't exactly a pro, but if you've flown or trained into an area without a safe and dependable public transport system, you'll need a rental to get around. Plus, a rental car is cost-efficient for families (as opposed to solo travelers). Best of all, you won't be putting miles on your own car—and if you rent a minivan, you can have drink-cup slots and elbowroom for every single kid.

CONS: None, really, save the expense and a list of rental and insurance decisions that can be as daunting as a Starbucks menu.

How to find them: Your travel agent can book a car for you, but if you want to do it yourself, you'll find all the major agencies in the 800 directory.

Compare costs. Whether you shop on-line or over the phone, compare costs for as many companies as you can (no one company has the best deals in every city or state). In general, weeklong and weekend rentals are a better deal than per-day rentals. In your research, you may wish to inquire about companies' service records, especially if you're going with a local budget chain.

Ask about discounts. Membership in AAA or other associations, credit cards, entertainment book coupons, and package-deal reservations may net you bargains: ask about potential discounts when you make your reservation.

Ask about services and charges. Rental car companies put a lot of information in fine print. So, before you pay (and before you drive away), ask lots of questions. What are the mileage and one-way drop fees? Is there a fee for early or late car returns? Should you bring the car back with an empty gas tank or a full one to get the best refueling price? Does the company offer 24-hour breakdown service? Do the cars have air-conditioning, a jack, and a spare tire? Is there a fee for extra drivers (married couples are often exempt,

FamilyFun TIP

Compare Quotes

When you book a room at a major hotel chain, call both the hotel's local number as well as the toll-free reservation number; the rates you'll be quoted may differ.

but you should check). Are car seats available at no extra charge? (Even if the answer is yes, your own car seat may be cleaner, and, because it's familiar, more comfortable for your child.)

Pay only for the insurance you need. The car, and any damage to it, will be your responsibility for the duration of your trip. Before you purchase insurance from the rental agency, check to see whether your own auto or liability insurance provides adequate coverage. Some credit card agreements may also include rental protection; call the customer service

FamilyFun READER'S TIP

Tabletop Scrapbook

Here's a fun project my family has long enjoyed while traveling. After we have mapped out our vacation, my kids, and now grandchildren, use a laundry pen to draw our route on a cotton tablecloth. We pack up the cloth along with colored markers, and while on the road, family members take turns marking the name of towns and rivers and noting funny signs. When we stop for picnic lunches, we not only use the cloth but also continue adding drawings of sights we've seen and things we've done. After the trip is over, we have a memory-filled tablecloth to use for years to come.

Janet Askew, Adair, Iowa

FamilyFun **VACATION GUIDE**

number on the back of your card to inquire.

WHERE TO STAY

Where you tuck your kids in at night depends entirely on your family's traveling style and budget—and, of course, on what's available in the area to which you're traveling. There are so many options—hotels, motels, inns, cottages, cabins, condominiums, resorts, time-shares, campgrounds—it can be hard to know where to start.

Lists of local accommodations can be found through tourism boards, the Web, travel books, and the 800 numbers or published directories of major franchises. However, finding the places that really go the extra mile for families isn't easy. This book—and other family travel publications—will be your best bets, as will the time-tested recommendations of friends and acquaintances. Always, always ask your own questions as well: see our checklist on page 25 for some basics.

Hotels, Motels & Lodges

From generic chains, to mom-and-pop operations bursting with character, to ritzy palaces, this category really runs the gamut. If you don't have a dependable recommendation (from a friend, trusted travel agent, or guidebook like this one), you may wish to place your trust in the major chains (budget or no) where you at least know what you're getting.

How to find them: Most major chains can be found in the 800 directory (as well as on the Web) and can provide a list of property locations. Alternatively, you can contact regional travel bureaus or consult a national rating system, such as those in Mobil Travel Guides (available in bookstores or the on-line store at www.mobil.com) or the Automobile Association of America (call your local AAA office to order regional TourBook guides).

PICKY EATERS? If you have picky eaters in the family (or if you suspect a child may not enjoy the food at a certain restaurant), feed them ahead of time—and let them enjoy an appetizer or dessert during your meal.

Inns, B&Bs, and Farm Stays

These have traditionally been the domain of honeymooning couples and retirees. Increasingly, though, they are accommodating a growing family travel market. There are certainly gems out there for your discovery—but do your research rigorously (speak with the owner, if possible) to find out whether kids are *truly* welcome at the destination of your choice. The last thing you want to be doing on vacation is shushing your kids and shooing them away from pricey antiques. Look for inns and B&Bs attached to a working farm—these tend to be more kid-friendly, with animals to watch and feed and plenty of outdoor play space.

How to find them: Try travel magazines, regional chambers of commerce, and two excellent Websites, www.bedandbreakfeast.com and www.bbgetaways.com

Condos and Cottages

These are ideal if your group is staying put for the length of your vacation, since they offer room to spread out and cook your own meals. When you book, ask about amenities: does the condo come with linens, pots and pans, a television, phone, dishwasher, and washer/dryer? Are there extra tax and/or booking fees? If you rent directly from the owner, be even more rigorous in your questioning. Is there

WHAT TO ASK BEFORE YOU BOOK

1. ACCOMMODATIONS: What rooms (or condos or cabins) are available? How many beds are there and what size are they? Are the rooms nonsmoking? What amenities are included (laundry, phone, cable TV, refrigerator, balcony, coffee service, cots, cribs, minibar)? Are the rooms located in the main building? What specific views are available? Is there a charge for kids staying in the same room with parents? Are there family packages? Can guests upgrade rooms upon arrival?

2. DINING: Are there dining facilities on the property? If so, are there restrictions for kids? What are some menu items, and what does the average meal cost? Is there a kids' menu? Is there a complimentary breakfast offered? Are there snack and/or drink machines? If there are no dining facilities on-site, is there a family restaurant nearby?

3. RECREATION: What recreational facilities are available (game rooms, pool, tennis courts, equipment rental, and so on)? At what hours are they available? Are there additional charges for their use? Are there age or time restrictions for any recreation? What recreational options are available in the nearby community (movie theater, minigolf, bowling, and the like)?

25

a cancellation policy if the place is not up to your standards?

How to find them: The Internet has made it easy to connect potential renters with homeowners and rental brokers. Unfortunately, that means there are literally thousands of sites to sift through. Luckily, most sites offer very detailed information on properties, so you can actually make an informed decision on-line to pursue a place.

For starters, here are the Website addresses for a number of national and international vacation rental clearinghouses: www.eLeisure Link.com (888-801-8808); Barclay International Group (800-845-6636; www.bar clayweb.com); and 10,000 Vacation Rentals, Inc. (888-369-7245; www. 10kvacationrentals.com).

To rent directly from a property owner, try Vacation Rentals by Owner at www.vrbo.com. You also can locate condos and cottages by inquiring at local tourism bureaus, local realtors (especially for seaside properties), and major resorts, which often keep lists of rentals on property or nearby.

Campgrounds

These range from the extremely rustic—grassy knolls with fabulous views to the luxurious—complexes with video games, sports areas, and fax and modem hookups.

Depending on where and how you prefer to camp, you'll have your pick of sites in state or national parks, national forests, or private campgrounds. (See "Happy Campers," page 38-39.)

When you book a site, inquire: What are the nightly fees? Does the campground accept reservations? If no, how early should you arrive in order to claim a site? Is there a pool or lake? Lifeguards? Equipment rentals? Laundry facilities, rest rooms, and hot showers? A grocery store nearby? Remember that campgrounds near major tourist attractions fill up early, so make reservations in advance (choice spots in some national parks, for example, fill up months ahead).

Family Hostels

A CHEAP SLEEP

If you think hostels are the exclusive domain of students and backpackers, think again: many of the neatest have private family rooms that can be reserved in advance. Some also offer special programs, such as historic walking tours, natural history programs, and sports activities. Hostels in the Hostelling International/ American Youth Hostels system are as varied as their locations and include registered historic buildings, lighthouses, and a former dude ranch. For the latest edition of *Hostelling Experience North America*, call *202-783-6161* or visit www.hiayh.org

How to find them: In addition to the campgrounds recommended in this book, you can find lists of campgrounds on the Internet: check out About.com's camping section at www.camping.about.com, www.camping-usa.com, and the National Association of RV Parks & Campgrounds at www.gocampingamerica.com. For campgrounds in national parks, visit www.nps.gov and state. For a national directory of KOA campgrounds, visit www.koakampgrounds.com.

Resorts

A resort vacation is a big investment, and up-front research is essential to ensure you get your money's worth. When you are making inquiries, don't be shy about taking up the resort staff's time with questions. Be sure to grill them with the entire housing quiz on page 25. Ask, too, about programming for kids and families. If there is a children's program, what days and times does it run? Is it canceled if not enough kids sign up? What is the ratio of counselors to children? What are the age divisions? What activities does the program offer? What are the facilities? What, if any, is the additional cost? Are there games, programs, or organized recreation especially for families? Baby-sitting services? Assistance for kids who get sick? What are the terms for these? If the resort is "all-inclusive," find out

FamilyFun TIP

Walk it through

When you're booking a room or condo over the phone, ask the reservation specialist to "walk" you through the place, virtually, from the front door to the balcony view (if there is one!). They may think you're going overboard — but you'll really know what you're getting.

FamilyFun READER'S TIP

Invent a Travel Kit

When our family flies, I make travel kits for my two sons, Noah, 8, and Paul, 4. I fill old wipes boxes with a variety of treats: chocolate kisses, fruit snacks, a sealed envelope with a love note inside, stickers, and a small wrapped package such as a pencil sharpener, pencils, and a blank book (I staple together scratch paper). I write the boys' names on the front with a permanent marker, and then, in flight, they decorate the boxes with stickers. The trick is not to give them the travel kits until we're on the plane. After they exhaust their supply of goodies inside, they can refill it with things they collect during the trip.

Kathy Detzer, White River Junction, Vermont

Travel Insurance

It's not for everyone, but some travelers like to invest in this just-in-case insurance. Cancellation policies cover losses if you can't make your trip due to illness or a death in the family (you may wish to consider this if you have to put down a hefty deposit or prepay for your vacation in full). Medical policies provide for some emergency procedures. You can buy travel insurance from a specialty broker (see below), from your travel agent, or directly from an insurance company. Do not buy insurance from the tour operator or cruise line you will be traveling with.

Travel Guard International
(800-826-1300; www.travel-guard.com)

CSA Travel Protection
(www.csatravelprotection.com)

Travel Assistance International (800-821-2828; www.travelassistance.com)

Access America (866-807-3982; www.accessamerica.com)

exactly what is covered. If you will be taking advantage of the services included in the price, it may mean a good deal for your family; if not, you might be better off elsewhere.

How to find them: Travel magazines, travel agents, and family travel Websites (see page 34) will all be able to offer recommendations on family resorts. Also, the Globe Pequot Press (www.globepequot.com) has two good resource books: *100 Best Family Resorts in North America* and *100 Best All-Inclusive Resorts of the World.*

SAVING MONEY

A great vacation balances moments of extravagance with activities that are as enjoyable as they are affordable. The key, then, is to find painless ways to cut costs so that you can feel good about indulging. Here's a host of secrets from budget-savvy travelers.

Stock up at home. Specialty items, such as sunscreen, film, batteries, over-the-counter medications, and first-aid supplies can be outrageously expensive in vacation spots. Buy them in bulk at home and bring them with you.

Travel off-peak. Whether it's a ski resort town in the summertime, or Yosemite National Park in the spring, or the Adirondacks in the winter, off-peak travel is one of the best ways to save, as long as you're primed to enjoy the unique flavor of an off-season trip. Rates for travel and lodging are often slashed considerably—and you can enjoy a different perspective (and fewer crowds) at the destination of your choice.

Don't delay. The sooner you begin planning and booking your vacation (six months to a year or more in advance is not too early), the more deals will be available to you.

Shop around. This is the cardinal rule of vacation planning. Take time to compare prices for every service that you'll be buying, from airfares, hotels, and rental cars to tickets for attractions.

Ask for discounts. Don't be shy about asking for discounts. Call ahead to the attractions that you plan to visit and ask where one finds discount coupons. When making hotel reservations, ask if discounts are available—if not on the room alone, then on a package that may include the room and tickets to a nearby attraction. Coupons are also available on-line: a good place to start is the coupon link at www.about.com

Guided Tours

WHEN DO YOU NEED ONE?

For certain types of specialty travel (technically-challenging outdoor adventures for example), an expert guide is a necessary aid for a safe and enjoyable trip. In addition, using a local guide for day trips (say, fishing or snowmobiling) can be a wonderful way to connect with local lore and culture in the region you're visiting. In general, however, guided tours (especially group tours that include full itineraries and meals) tend to be pricey, tightly scheduled, and lacking the freedom most families value highly.

STRAP A SHOE BAG to the back of the front seat and stuff it with your small kid-entertainment supplies: crayons and coloring books; kids' magazines; craft supplies, such as pipe cleaners, markers, glue sticks, and construction paper; songbooks; paper doll kits; a deck of cards; and a cassette player with story tapes. And don't forget a Frisbee, jump rope, and chalk (to draw hopscotch grids) for rest stops.

FamilyFun VACATION GUIDE

FamilyFun READER'S TIP

Make Your Own Postcards

While traveling by car or plane, my kids entertain themselves by creating their own postcards. Before the trip, I buy blank, prestamped postcards from the post office. Once we are under way, the kids draw pictures on the cards — usually of things they have done on vacation or are looking forward to doing. We address the cards to relatives and friends and drop them in the mail, making sure we send a few home for our own travel journal. This activity has been so successful, we now give friends travel kits of the prestamped cards and crayons as a bon voyage gift.

Lynette Smith, Lake Mills, Wisconsin

Look at package deals. At first blush, packages can seem outrageously expensive. But before you pass them up, compare them carefully to what you'd pay if you bought all the pieces of your vacation separately. Rates for airfare, lodging, and car rentals can be substantially lower when purchased together, especially for popular destinations. Contact your travel agent for information or research deals from travel clubs like AAA (call your local chapter or visit www.aaa.com), American Express Travel Services (800-346-3607; www.americanexpress.com), and from tour agencies affiliated with major airlines.

Use member benefits. Membership in an auto club, professional organization, or Entertainment book club may score you discounts on travel bills—ask before you book. Your credit card company, as well, may offer free services, such as collision-damage and travel-accident insurance, if you use the card to pay for travel expenses (call to request a copy of the company's travel benefits policy). If you travel regularly, the savings you'd garner from Web-saver clubs like www.bestfares.com can be well worth the $50 to $70 annual fee.

Tickets to attractions. Buying tickets to attractions in advance through an association or organization or at the hotel desk often will save you money. Equally important, you'll avoid the ticket line itself. On-line, try www.citypass.com for discount tickets in major metropolitan areas.

Keep your distance. Unless on-site housing offers necessary convenience for your family, consider lodging that's outside the major tourist area or city you're visiting. An extra 15 minutes of travel can considerably reduce lodging expenses, especially if you're staying more than a few days.

Check out kids' deals. Look for hotel deals where kids eat and/or stay free with their parents.

Consider cooking. Dining out is certainly part of the vacation experience, but three meals per person, per day add up quickly. Cooking your own meals can save you lots of money, even if you factor in the expense of a room with a kitchenette. In a regular hotel room, you can probably manage breakfast and/or lunch with a well-stocked cooler.

Pack your own minibar. Those high-priced hotel mini-bars are magnets for kids. Make a list of your kids' favorite treats, then purchase them in bulk as individually wrapped items. Pack a selection in a separate box or bag that can double as the designated minibar once you arrive at the hotel.

Let's do lunch. If you have a yen to try a particular fancy restaurant, head there during lunch. The atmosphere will be the same, and the menu will be similar, but smaller lunchtime portions will be accompanied by lower prices.

Revel in free fun. Remember the birthday when your child spent more time playing with the wrapping paper than with the actual toy? Vacations are filled with similar, low-cost but memorable moments, including hours at the beach, hiking trails, parks, and playgrounds. If you're in a new area, scan the local paper for listings, or call a local travel bureau or chamber of commerce for ideas.

Be savvy about souvenirs. Decide ahead of time how much you're willing to spend on souvenirs. Depending on the age of your kids, give each child his or her own spending money (they'll be stingier with their own funds than they are with yours). As an added incentive, let them keep a portion of any money they don't spend.

USING THE WEB

With the advent of the World Wide Web, individuals now have access to all the tools that travel agents use (and then some). The trick is to know how to use them well.

PROS: Researching travel ideas on the Web may draw in your kids more readily than a guidebook would.

☑ CHECKLIST
Packing With—And For—Kids

Like so much of your family vacation, packing is a balancing act—in this case between including everything you need and making sure you can actually lift your bags. No matter where you're headed, this checklist should cover most of the essentials.

Give the kids a role. Every child has favorite outfits as well as clothing that he or she won't wear (and that you shouldn't bother packing). Young children can select the clothes they'd like to bring and set them aside for you. Older kids can do much of their own packing, especially if you help them write up a checklist of their own.

Don't worry about wrinkles. Like aging, this happens even with the best of precautions. Suggest some folding methods, but don't insist on your kids' finessing this. One surprisingly effective technique for kids is simply to roll everything up.

Make each child responsible for his or her own luggage. A backpack and a soft-sided suitcase for each child will do the trick. Let your kids decorate their bags with stencils and stickers — and remember to attach a name tag.

Separate toiletries in sealed, waterproof bags. Lids on toiletries often pop off or open during travel.

Take precautions in case of lost luggage. If you're flying to your vacation destination, pack at least one complete outfit for each family member in each suitcase. That way, if a piece of luggage is lost, everyone still has a change of clothes. Also, pack medications, eyeglasses, and contact lens solution in carry-ons.

Clothing
Include an outfit for each day of the week, plus extra shirts or blouses in case of spills. If your children are younger, encourage them to choose brightly colored outfits that will make them easier to spot in the crowd.
- Comfortable shoes or sneakers
- Socks and undergarments
- Sleepwear
- Light jackets, sweaters, or sweatshirts for cool weather
- Bathing suits
- Sandals or slip-on shoes for the pool
- Hats or sun visors
- Rain gear, including umbrellas

Toiletries
- Toothbrushes, toothpaste, dental floss, and mouthwash
- Deodorant
- Combs, brushes, hair accessories, blow-dryer
- Soap
- Shampoo and conditioner
- Shaving gear
- Feminine-hygiene items

- Lotions
- Cosmetics
- Nail care kit
- Tweezers
- Cotton balls and/or swabs
- Antibacterial gel for hand washing
- Sunscreens and lip balm
- Insect repellent

Miscellaneous "must-haves"

- Essential papers: identification for adults, health insurance cards, tickets, traveler's checks
- Wallet and/or purse, including cash and credit cards
- Car and house keys (with duplicate set packed in a different bag)
- Eyeglasses and/or contact lenses, plus lens cleaner
- Medications
- Watch
- Camera and film (pack film in your carry-on bag)
- Tote bag or book bag for day use
- Books and magazines for kids and adults
- Toys, playing cards, small games
- Flashlight
- Extra batteries
- Large plastic bags for laundry
- Small plastic bags
- Disposable wipes
- First-aid kit
- Travel alarm
- Sewing kit

Keep Your First-Aid Kit Handy

There's no such thing as a vacation from minor injuries and ailments, so a well-stocked first-aid kit is essential to have on hand. You can buy a pre-packaged kit or make your own by packing the following items in an old lunch box:

- Adhesive bandages in various sizes, adhesive tape, and gauze pads
- Antacid
- Antibacterial gel for washing hands without water
- Antibacterial ointment
- Antidiarrheal medicine
- Antihistamine or allergy medicine
- Antiseptic
- Antiseptic soap
- Pain relief medicine—for children and adults
- Cotton balls and/or swabs
- Cough medicine and/or throat lozenges
- Motion sickness medicine
- Fingernail clippers
- First-aid book or manual
- Ipecac
- Moleskin for blisters
- Ointment for insect bites and sunburn
- Premoistened towelettes
- Thermometer
- Tissues
- Tweezers and needle

FamilyFun VACATION GUIDE

FamilyFun TIP

The Internet Travel Bible

If you're serious about researching (and especially booking) travel plans yourself, consult *Online Travel* by Ed Perkins (Microsoft Press, $19.95). This paperback tome is an invaluable resource on getting the best deals available and navigating the benefits and pitfalls of today's travel market, both on- and off-line.

Plus, when it comes time to book reservations, the Web can be a treasure trove of bargains—if you know how to hunt for them (see "The Internet Travel Bible" above). Why is that so? In essence, the Internet allows travel service providers to change their bargain pricing structures and unload unsold seats and rooms at a moment's notice. Of course, agents are still out to make as much money as they can—but you often can reap the benefits of their last-minute sales. In fact, many of these sales are available only on-line.

CONS: Keeping tabs on the travel market on-line can be extremely time-consuming if you are determined to find the best deal possible. In addition, since Web search engines can't read your mind and ask you questions, they can't ferret out all your options—just the ones that fall within the parameters you specify. So if you aren't a savvy searcher, you might miss the best deals (or the best destinations) even after hours of research.

Family travel Websites. It's a challenge to locate truly family-friendly sites among the hundreds available. For researching travel ideas and gathering travel tips, here are some of the best sites. Try our own website too—www.familyfun.com—it too has a lot of travel ideas.

♦ www.vacationtogether.com is a searchable database of family vacation ideas, reprinted from various publications (including *FamilyFun* magazine). You'll also find packing checklists and links to reservation sites here.

♦ www.travelwithkids.about.com is a terrific clearinghouse for family vacation ideas, package deals, current bargains, lists of accommodations, packing checklists, travel tips and games, downloadable maps, and more.

♦ www.thefamilytravelfiles.com is a well-organized family travel Website that showcases a range of trip ideas and offers a free travel e-zine.

♦ www.familytravelforum.com is a monthly on-line newsletter specializing in well-screened links to family-friendly accommodations, airfare deals, seasonal events, and more.

General travel sites. In addition to family-specific sites such as the ones listed above, there are literally thousands of useful Websites that can help you plan and book your vacation. They are too numerous to list here! We have included many of our favorites throughout this chapter; in addition to those, here are a few you may find useful.

♦ www.officialtravelinfo.com lists contacts for travel and tourism bureaus worldwide (you can search the United States by state).

♦ www.fodors.com, www.frommers.com, and www.nationalgeographic.com are sites related to travel magazines. Often, they'll post selections from current issues, as well as other travel-related articles.

♦ www.travel-library.com (a wide range of travel topics, travelogues, and destination information) and www.about.com (a general site with good travel links) are sites that can lead you to travel information that you may (or may not!) be looking for.

Book your own airline reservations. Using the same databases as travel agents use, the leading travel sites have made booking your own flight as simple as typing in when you'd like to leave, when you'd like to return, your origin and destination, and airline choice. They kick back a list of flights that most closely match

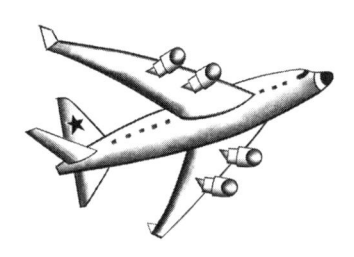

Broker a Hotel Deal

Great deals at major hotels usually turn up off-season or at the last minute, but here's another tactic families can try: work with a hotel consolidator (also called a hotel broker or discounter).

Consolidators work by securing blocks of hotel rooms at wholesale prices, then reselling them at rates that are—in theory, at least—lower than the published "rack" rate. Some consolidators will only reserve your room; you pay the hotel directly. Others require a prepaid voucher that you present to the hotel upon arrival. Many consolidators claim savings of 10 to 50 percent (some even more), but as with any bargain, it pays to know what you're getting into.

SOME TIPS:
- Ask about service charges. Is there a user fee for the consolidator?
- Are there financial penalties for trip cancellation or rescheduling?
- Compare rates. The consolidator may not beat a hotel's special offers.

With those caveats, try:
Quikbook: Good selection and easy to use, with hotels in 33 cities. Call 800-789-9887 or see www.quikbook.com
Central Reservation Service: Lists hotel deals in ten major cities. Call 800-555-7555 or visit www.roomconnection.com

Gumshoe Games

The detectives in your group will just love these tests of their sleuthing ability.

Secret highway messages: Pass out the pencils and paper, and keep your eyes peeled for official road signs. Each time you spot one, write down the first letter. When you've passed five to seven signs—and have five to seven letters—you're ready to crack the code. Here's how: each letter stands for a word. So the letters D, S, C, S, and A could stand for the secret message "Drive slowly, construction starts ahead." Of course, others in your family may interpret it as "Dad, stop, candy store ahead."

Two truths and one lie: The first person makes three statements about himself or herself. Two are true; the other is a lie. For example, you could say, "I had a dog named Puddles. My sister cut off my hair once when I was asleep. I won the school spelling bee when I was in third grade." Everybody then holds up one, two, or three fingers to show which statement they think is the lie. Reveal the answer and let the next person fib away.

your specifications and then let you choose the flights you want. After confirming your choices, you pay with a credit card, print your itinerary, and either receive your paper tickets in the mail or, more likely, pick up your tickets when you check in at the airport. **NOTE:** Some people prefer paper tickets because if a flight is missed or cancelled an e-ticket may not be exchangable at a different airline's counter.

Our favorite flight sites are Expedia (www.expedia.com), Travelocity (www.travelocity.com), and Trip.com (www.trip.com). Don't assume that all offer the same flights or the same prices; the important thing is to shop around, even among these sites.

Before you pay for your tickets, you should double-check with two other sources. First, look at your chosen airline's home site to see if they offer extra miles for booking flights on-line, or special, unadvertised Web deals. And call your travel agent, tell her the flight you're interested in, and see if she can beat the price. Lastly, be sure you're aware of the taxes, airport surcharges, and possible site use fees that may be added to your ticket price.

For more information about airlines, airports, and online reservations, go to www.iecc.com/airline/. Also, check out Ed Perkins' *Online Travel* (Microsoft Press, $19.95). To find out more about frequent flier mile programs, visit www.frequent flier.com

READY, SET, GO!

Book hotel and rental car reservations. In general, hotel and rental car reservations work the same way that airfare reservations do. The Web is an excellent source of hotel deals (especially for vacation packages, if you're a savvy shopper); rental car companies, on the other hand, generally offer little in the way of discounts above what you can get at the desk.

Sign up for e-mail newsletters. If you find a good travel Website that offers a free newsletter, it doesn't hurt to sign up—you may receive timely notice of travel deals that you otherwise would miss. Just be sure that you save any information on how to cancel the subscription in case you want to opt out.

Are Internet travel arrangements foolproof? No, unfortunately. The Internet is prime territory for scams, although you can guard against most of them with a few protective strategies. First, deal with major sites (like the ones listed in this book) or directly with brand-name company sites (like Avis or Holiday Inn) whenever possible. When you're transmitting your credit card information, make sure your connection is secure (your browser should tell you when one has been established). Also, you should double-check to see that the service provider's Website has a secure server. (Look for a locked padlock in the corner of your browser's window or "https"—the "s" stands for "secure"—in the URL.) If a site doesn't seem completely aboveboard, it may not be. Finally, when in doubt, back out. As long as you don't give a company your credit card number, they can't charge you anything.

FREE ATLAS
Best Western offers free road atlases with Best Western sites: call 800-528-1234.

FamilyFun READER'S TIP

A Colorful Road Game

This homemade road game is a big hit with my 4-year-old son, Tommy. I clip cards out of colored construction paper and print a different letter of the alphabet on each. During a car ride, each of us picks a card and searches for an object or a structure that matches the color and begins with the letter on our card. For example, a player with a *B* on a yellow card might spot a school bus. Since we began playing this game, my son tends to remember many more details about our travels. Instead of hearing, "Are we there yet?" we hear, "Oh no, I haven't found mine yet!"

Susan Robins, Cottage Grove, Oregon

✓ CHECKLIST
Happy Campers

If your family's idea of a vacation involves nightly campfires, sleeping bags, and potential wildlife sightings near (or in!) your living space, check out these great resources for tent and RV camping.

The Trailer Life Directory provides travelers with a list of several thousand campgrounds and RV parks throughout the United States and Canada. Each location is rated on a three-step scale that assesses the park's facilities, cleanliness, and overall appeal; ratings are updated on an annual basis. You can register at www.tldirectory.com to search the directory for free or order your own copy for the road online or at bookstores.

Woodall's campground directories also rate a large number of parks—more than 14,000 locations throughout the United States and Canada are scored on their facilities and recreation. You can purchase a directory which covers the entire area, or shorter versions of the guide are available for the western and eastern regions. Woodall's also publishes a directory exclusively for tent campers. Again, you can register to access campground listings for free at www.woodalls.com, but the online directory does not include Woodall's convenient rating system. The complete directories can be purchased at Woodall's Website or bookstores.

There's no centralized reservation system for every campsite within the **National Park system**, so your best bet is to contact each individual park. Campground reservations here usually must be made several months in advance since the sites are so popular, so don't count on finding a space unless you've planned ahead. Contact information for the National Parks can be found at their Website, www.nps.gov. Policies for state parks also vary from place to place, so you'll have to contact individual campgrounds for camping information.

Veteran car campers recognize **KOA Kampgrounds** by their familiar yellow, red, and black signs. KOAs allow your family to rough it while enjoying many of the amenities of home. Novice campers will be thrilled to have access to hot showers, flush toilets, laundry facilities, and convenience stores. All KOA locations have both tent and RV sites, and some even have cabins that your family can rent. If you plan to stay multiple nights at one or more KOA Kampgrounds, consider purchasing a Value Kard. You'll get a 10 percent discount on your registration fees and a free copy of the KOA directory (you'll still pay for shipping). You can also research KOA locations for free at www.koakampgrounds.com or purchase your own directory on-line or by calling 406-248-7444.

If you're looking for campgrounds where your family can pitch a tent in peace and quiet, check out *The Best in Tent Camping* series (published by Menasha Ridge Press). The books detail the best in scenic, tent-only sites without all of the bells and whistles.

One key to a great camping trip is remembering all of your supplies. If your family is RV or car camping, you can usually purchase any forgotten items on the road. However, if you're traveling far off the beaten path, you'll need to be careful to double-check your belongings.

Here's a checklist of supplies to make your camping experience go smoothly. If you're renting an RV, be aware that you may be able to rent your bedding and cooking supplies for an additional fee and save the trouble of bringing your own.

- Tent(s) and tent stakes
- Plastic ground cloth/tarp
- Sleeping bags (or bedding, for an RV)
- Sleeping pads
- Camp stove (with extra fuel)
- Pots, plastic dishes, mugs, and utensils
- Water bottle or canteen
- Lantern and/or candles
- Bottle and/or can openers
- Sharp knife (parents should hold on to this)
- Plethora of plastic/trash bags
- Dish soap (preferably biodegradable)
- Stocked coolers
- Water (or a portable filter or purifying tablets)
- Waterproof matches or lighter(s)
- Flashlights (and extra batteries)
- Bandanna (for use as a head covering, pot holder, and napkin)
- Trowel
- Folding saw
- First-aid kit, medications
- Sunscreen
- Insect repellent
- Toilet paper
- Day packs
- Child carriers (for little ones)
- Compass and area map
- Clothing (make sure to pack many layers)
- Two pairs of shoes (in case one gets wet)
- A hat
- Sunglasses
- Toiletries (try to take only necessary items)
- Camera
- Binoculars
- Kid supplies (toys, books, favorite stuffed animal)

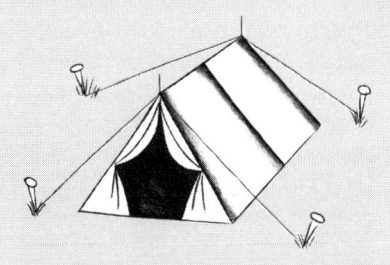

Florida

FEW PLACES CONJURE UP such playful vacation images for a child than do the attractions in the state of Florida—and no wonder. Consider near-perfect weather (shorts in January? *Awesome!*); more than 1,200 miles of soft, sandy beaches topped off with the greatest wave pool of all, the Atlantic Ocean; theme parks galore; and a host of historic treasures—and you'll see why kids think of Florida as the ultimate vacation.

Young surfers, shellers, anglers and sunbathers give Florida a big thumbs-up. More adventurous families can even get

Map labels:
- ★ Tallahassee and the Panhandle
- Northeast Florida
- ★ Orlando and the Space Coast, SeaWorld and Discovery Cove, Universal Orlando, and Walt Disney World Resort
- West Coast
- South Florida
- Southwest
- Florida Keys and the Everglades

to swim with dolphins!

But wait, there's more. From one end of the state to the other, historians, space buffs, and naturalists will be in their element as they savor such spectacular treasures as St. Augustine, Kennedy Space Center, and Everglades National Park.

Have we saved the best for last? We'll let you decide. Whether your vacation takes you to just one or maybe a couple of these mega-theme parks—Busch Gardens, SeaWorld, Universal Orlando, Walt Disney World—Florida promises, and delivers, a vacation that will linger in your child's memory long after you get home. It's a childhood (and grown-up) dream come true.

ATTRACTIONS
$	under $10
$$	$10 - $20
$$$	$20 - $30
$$$$	$30 +

HOTELS/MOTELS/CAMPGROUNDS
$	under $100
$$	$100 - $200
$$$	$200 - $300
$$$$	$300 +

RESTAURANTS
$	under $10
$$	$10 - $20
$$$	$20 - $30
$$$$	$30 +

***FAMILYFUN* RATED**
★	Fine
★★	Good
★★★	Very Good
★★★★	*FamilyFun* Recommended

Try to pull in a fish as large as your 3-year-old while deep-sea fishing with Critter Fleet.

INTRODUCTION

Northeast Florida

THE NATION'S oldest continuously occupied city, plus sun-sational beaches, and a big-city beat only begin to define the delightful blend that is Northeast Florida.

From Fernandina Beach in the north to Daytona Beach in the south, this region offers your family incredible diversity, reflecting the Florida of the past, present, and future.

With bustling Jacksonville as its beacon, the north end of the state's northeast plot is loaded with kid-friendly stops. You'll find fascinating museums (virtual reality is king at the MOSH in Jacksonville), amazing animal parks (don't miss the feeding at the Alligator Farm), and action-packed historical attractions (relive a Civil War battle at Fort Clinch) to keep young vacationers happy.

History rules in St. Augustine—the oldest city in the United States—with its really cool, centuries-worn fort and some not-to-miss historic landmarks. A walk down St. George Street in the heart of the city provides a snapshot of what life was like centuries ago—without Nintendo or Game Boy. If your kids are

THE FamilyFun LIST

Adventure Landing Daytona (page 46)

DAYTONA USA (page 47)

Fort Clinch State Park (page 47)

Jacksonville Zoo (page 48)

Main Beach (page 49)

Museum of Science & History (page 45)

St. Augustine Alligator Farm (page 49)

Sun Splash Park (page 50)

FamilyFun VACATION GUIDE

Map

- Georgia
- Fort Clinch State Park
- Fernandina Beach
- Amelia Island
- Jacksonville
- I-10
- Atlantic Ocean
- St. Augustine
- St. Augustine Beach
- I-95
- Ormond Beach
- Daytona Beach
- Daytona Beach Shores
- Port Orange
- Ponce Inlet

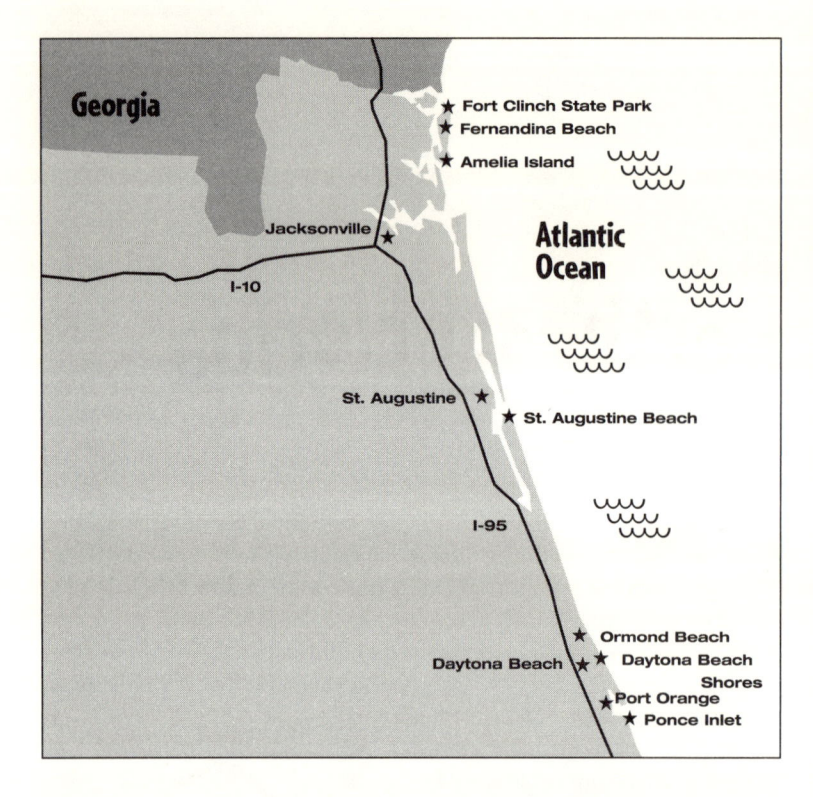

thinking "yawn time" here, they're in for a big surprise.

Children who are into racing know that Daytona has become synonymous with speed, a reputation that goes back to the turn of the century in nearby Ormond Beach, the official "Birthplace of Speed." It was here in 1903 that the first timed trials took place on the sand, creating a loyal following of die-hard race fans. Today, the speed craze lives on, thanks to such institutions as Daytona International Speedway.

History and speed notwithstanding, no visit to Daytona is complete without several fun-filled outings to the awesome Atlantic. Get ready for beautiful beaches, wonderful waves, and the perfect crystals for your 5-year-old's award-winning sand castle.

CULTURAL ADVENTURES

Colonial Spanish Quarter
★★/$

Give your children a close-up look at what St. Augustine was like in the

18th century by visiting this village in the pedestrian section of the historic district. The nine-building living museum is great for families who like plenty of variety (watch a blacksmith and woodworker demonstrate their trade, or visit with one of the village women as she prepares the day's meal over a charcoal fire), and the pace is as fast as you want it. If you have time, hang around for a tour of the de Mesa House. Kids get a kick out of seeing the primitive household appliances and kitchen utensils demonstrated during the 20-minute program. *53 St. George St., St. Augustine. (904) 825-6830.*

MUST-SEE FamilyFun Museum of Science & History
★★★/$

Virtual reality has taken up residence on the second floor of the Jacksonville Museum of Science & History (MOSH). If flying is your kids' passion, the MOSH simulated Explorer ride takes to the "skies," but only after you're securely belted in the seven-person spaceship. The shake-you-up experience lasts about five minutes and is not recommended for kids under 4 or those with superweak stomachs. Down a flight of stairs, children can get up close with snakes, baby alligators, and birds of prey in the museum's Living Room area. The not-to-be-missed Atlantic Tails exhibit creatively teaches loads of fun facts about the whales, dolphins, and manatees of Northeast Florida.

What's even cooler is that popular Jacksonville Jaguar football players do the accompanying narrations. A planetarium and the toy-filled Kidspace room are other museum highlights; there's a new dinosaur exhibit, too. Before hopping back in the car, let the kids release some of that built-up energy by running around the mammoth fountain at Friendship Park, adjacent to MOSH and overlooking the St. John's River. *1025 Museum Circle (south foot of the Main Street Bridge), Jacksonville. (904) 396-7062.*

Potter's Wax Museum
★★/$

From Princess Di and Michael Jordan to Pocahontas and Napoleon, this museum gives your kids a look at more than 170 startlingly real-looking figures dressed as they might have been in life. (The achievements of these life-size characters are described alongside the displays.) Skip the 15-minute movie and Chamber

---

FamilyFun SNACK

Good for You

Make some rocket fuel for your kids by mixing dried apples, pineapples, cranberries, mangoes, and cherries with banana chips and raisins. (One cup of this will fulfill 2 of the recommended 5 minimum daily servings of fruits and vegetables.)

of Horrors display, especially if traveling with toddlers. The *Star Wars* and gangster exhibits are sure to please. *17 King St., St. Augustine. (904) 829-9056.*

JUST FOR FUN

Adventure Landing Daytona ★★★/$$

This large entertainment center and seasonal water park just off Daytona Beach's main drag and across the street from the convention center offers oodles of fun. The dozen mild-to-wild thrill slides, wave pool, and relaxing drift river ride are kid pleasers. Castaway Bay delights all ages with its three-story tree house, six water slides, and 230 interactive squirt nozzles. The giant eight-foot-tall bucket dumps 1,000 gallons of water every few minutes—don't miss it! For those who've had enough water for the day, check out the park's lineup of other attractions, including a two-story go-cart track, three miniature-golf courses, and probably the largest arcade and prize center around, with more than 130 challenging games. If hunger strikes, choose from several snack bars. Multiple locations. *601 Earl St., Daytona Beach. (386) 258-0071.*

Castillo de San Marcos ★/$

Even if it's just a quick stop, make this fort part of your St. Augustine itinerary. Once inside the thick coquina walls, children's imaginations run wild as they conjure up images of defending the city and its people from intruders hundreds of years ago. Park rangers give four 20-minute tours each day. Pick up a copy of the helpful brochure and a fact sheet at the entrance. *1 S. Castillo Dr., St. Augustine. (904) 829-6506; www.nps.gov/casa/*

Critter Fleet ★★/$$$$

Deep-sea fishing can be fun, especially if you know where to go to catch "the big one." Thanks to fish-finding computers and an experienced crew, Coast Guard-approved Critter Fleet has been dropping anchor at some of the prime fishing spots in the area since 1972. Likely catches during a half-day outing (full-day outings are available, but may be too long for kids) include red snapper, grouper, and sea bass. Price includes rod, reel, and bait. You can buy food and drink inside the fully heated and air-conditioned cabin. The crew will even clean your catch (for an additional fee). *4950 S. Peninsula Dr., across from Ponce Inlet Lighthouse. (800) 338-0850; (386) 767-7676; www.critterfleet.com*

DAYTONA USA
FamilyFun ★★★★/$$

You don't have to be a motorhead to love Daytona USA, the popular interactive motorsports attraction at Daytona International Speedway. Kid-friendly activities include You Call the Race, where visitors "broadcast" a major race finish; E.A. Sports NASCAR Thunder, a stock car racing simulator; and Heroes of the Track, where you visit (via video) with your favorite NASCAR drivers. The Heritage of Daytona exhibit showcases the early days of racing, including some great shots of pre-speedway beach racing. Although you may want to skip the 15-minute pre-show, don't miss the *Daytona 500 Movie*—14 minutes of behind-the-wheel, in-your-face racing excitement; the sound effects are awesome! Take a few laps around the Speedway game center, 4th Turn Grill, and Pit Shop souvenir center before you wrap up the visit. You can tour the actual speedway for an additional fee. *1801 W. International Speedway Blvd., Daytona. (386) 947-6782*; www.daytonausa.com

Fort Clinch State Park
FamilyFun ★★★/$

Don't be surprised if you're greeted by a park ranger wearing a Union uniform when you pull up at this historic park at the north end of Amelia Island. During the Civil War, Fort Clinch reportedly was occupied by both Union and

TIDE POOL ROLL CALL

The pools of water that collect in rocky hollows along the seashore can be a great place for kids to enjoy a close-up view of ocean life–like the creatures listed below. If you're lucky enough to spot one, be sure to follow tide-pooling protocol: look but don't touch.

SEA CUCUMBERS: These knobby, oblong critters range in hue from gray to rose and tend to burrow under sand.

SEA URCHINS: Algae are the favorite food of these colorful porcupine creatures.

SAND DOLLARS: Adorned with star-shaped imprints, these disks can often be found lining the bottom of tide pools.

HERMIT CRABS: To protect their soft bellies, these crabs move into the shells of snails and other animals, sometimes pulling out the former resident first.

BARNACLES: These crusty creatures rely on their feathery feet to kick food particles through the valved openings of their bodies.

STARFISH: With their suction-cup-lined arms, starfish handily pry open the shells of the clams on which they feed.

SPONGES: One of the most primitive sea animals, a sponge sifts food from the water that flows through it.

Pet Savvy

It's easier than ever to bring your pet along on vacation. A number of hotels now accept pets, and some even offer exercise areas and pet room service. (A few go so far as to bring dog biscuits and bottled water to your room on a silver tray!)

Ready Buddy for travel by making sure his ID tags are complete and by taking him on short trips close to home (so he doesn't think getting in the car means going to the vet). Try calling these hotel and motel chains to find out their pet policies:
Best Western (800-528-1234);
Four Seasons (800-332-3442);
Holiday Inn (800-465-4329);
Loews (800-235-6397); and
Motel 6 (800-466-8356).

Confederate troops, and it also was an active site in the Spanish-American War. This place will give youngsters a fascinating look into military life during the War Between the States. Check out the monthly programs; featured activities include artillery demonstrations and marching drills. If that's not enough, Fort Clinch is great for picnicking (near the fort), fishing (Amelia River, Cumberland Sound, and Atlantic Ocean venues), hiking (30-minute Willow Pond trail), and swimming (wide Atlantic beachfront—great shelling, too). And another plus: comfortable campsites near the river and ocean let you sleep cheap. *2601 Atlantic Ave., Fernandina Beach. (904) 277-7274.*

Jacksonville Landing
★★/Free

For shops, eats, and treats—even an arcade with an old-time shooting gallery—all under one roof, check out Jacksonville Landing, a festive marketplace in the heart of downtown Jacksonville on the St. John's River. Kids love choosing, and the Landing's second-floor food court offers plenty of choices. After lunch, head to Ostrich Landing (next to the food court) where you can drop a few coins in the arcade and interactive video adventure (make sure your 5-and-unders visit the talking Bozo the Clown game). Speaking of clowns—and mimes and other showstoppers—the Landing really cooks on the weekend when entertainers set up center stage for some real razzle-dazzle. *2 Independent Dr., Jacksonville. (904) 353-1188;* www.jacksonvillelanding.com.

Jacksonville Zoo
FamilyFun ★★★★/$

A sure bet for fun, this zoo—filled with more than 800 rare and exotic creatures—is an animal lover's wonderland. The Main Camp and the Birds of the Rift Valley are a perfect way to begin your visit. You'll all feel like birds of a feather as you walk through Rift Valley because there are no nets, cages, or

NORTHEAST FLORIDA

glass between you and the birds. You can also catch the zoo's train, which encircles the property and gives you the lay of the land. Another highlight is the baby animal nursery; they're so cute, you'll want to take one home, or at least your kids will. And you can watch elephants swim and poisonous snakes do their slithering at the Overlook. It's the perfect place for kids and parents alike. Don't miss it. *8605 Zoo Pkwy., Jacksonville. (904) 757-4463; www.jaxzoo.com*

J&S Carousel ★/$

The 22-figure carousel in Davenport Park has been delighting children since 1927. The ride only costs a buck—about as close to free entertainment as you can get. Picnic tables and a small playground give the family a nice break from sight-seeing. *180 San Marco Ave., St. Augustine. (904) 823-3388.*

Main Beach
FamilyFun ★★★/Free

If your family wants a few hours of fun in the sun, head for Amelia Island's Main Beach, just a few minutes from the area's historic downtown. A wide sandy beach, kiddie playground, and lots of shaded picnic tables make this a popular spot, especially during the moderate and warm-weather months when the miniature-golf course and water slide (fees for both) are buzzing with activity. *Fletcher and Atlantic Aves., Fernandina Beach.*

Peterbrooke ★/$

Young (and older) chocoholics will be in seventh heaven when you tour this chocolatier's production facility in Jacksonville's San Marco district. Offered every weekday at 10 A.M. or by special appointment, the 60-minute visit costs a buck and includes touring the facility (where daily output is about 800 pounds of chocolate), checking out Peterbrooke's collection of antique candy molds, and sampling some of the most decadent indulgences around. Don't leave without trying the chocolate-covered popcorn. *1470 San Marco Blvd., Jacksonville. (904) 398-2489; www.peterbrooke.com*

St. Augustine Alligator Farm
FamilyFun MUST-SEE ★★★★/$$

Not only is St. Augustine the oldest city in the United States, it's also home to the world's original alligator farm. In business since 1893, the farm has been delighting families with a menagerie of wildlife, including Nile crocodiles, supersize tortoises, Burmese pythons, and, of course, alligators. It's the only place in the world where you can see the entire collection of crocodilian species—23 to be exact. Check out the Alligator Show—20 minutes of education and entertainment about one of Florida's most interesting (and feared) animals. The show runs three times daily in the nicely shaded Reptile Theater. Whatever you do,

49

don't miss the alligator swamp. From the elevated boardwalk, guests can safely feed what appear to be acres of alligators below—it's a mealtime you'll never forget! *999 Anastasia Blvd. (Route AIA South), St. Augustine. (904) 824-3337;* www.alligatorfarm.com

Sun Splash Park
★★★/Free

One of Daytona Beach's newest beachfront parks, this has a simple-but-fun playground and colorful, water-spouting dolphin statues, making it ideal for entertaining your kids when they need a break from the beach. Clean rest rooms, soda machines, free parking, and a lifeguard station on the beach make this a family favorite. *611 S. Atlantic Ave., Daytona Beach.*

BUNKING DOWN

Amelia Island Plantation
★★★★/$$-$$$

In addition to a wide variety of upscale but comfortable accommodation choices—from oceanfront to courtside—this luxury resort is tailor-made for families willing to splurge. The kid's program, called Kids Camp Amelia, thinks of everything—even the sunscreen—when you enroll your 3- to 10-year-olds in the half- or full-day recreation program. Your 11- and 12-year-olds are welcome to join too, but encouraged to link up with the teenage Amelia's Explorers Club. The Just For Kids evening program (all ages), where hayrides, bonfires, and pool parties are the norm, is wildly popular, too. (There are fees for all of the above.) It's pricey, but worth it. *6800 1st Coast Hwy., Amelia Island. (800) 874-6878;* www.aipfl.com

Anastasia State Recreation Area
★★/$

A popular spot for both tent and RV campers, Anastasia has nearly 140 campsites, most of which are only a short walk to the beach. The park store stocks camping supplies, ice, and firewood, and has bicycles, and beach- and water-related equipment for rent. Fishing, sunbathing, surfing, sailboarding, swimming, nature trails, and picnicking provide endless hours of family enjoyment. *1340-A A1A South, St. Augustine. (800) 326-3521; (904) 461-2033.*

Capri/Ocean Villa Motel/Sun Viking Lodge
★★★/$-$$

Affordable, comfortable accommodations await you at these three, longtime family-owned beachfront properties. The two-story Capri and Ocean Villa are next-door neighbors and share kid-favorite features like a 60-foot water slide, game room, and year-round recreation program. The Sun Viking, the largest of the three properties, is located in quiet Daytona Beach Shores and has pleasant guestrooms in either a low-rise unit or seven-story tower. Like its sister properties, its selling points are a 60-foot water slide, game room, and recreation program, and it also provides an on-site café, indoor pool, basketball court, and playground for kids. Capri/Ocean Villa: *828 N. Atlantic Ave., Daytona Beach. (800) 225-3691; (386) 252-4644.* Sun Viking: *2411 S. Atlantic Ave., Daytona Beach Shores. (800) 874-4469; (386) 252-6252.*

Embassy Suites Jacksonville-Baymeadows ★★/$

From the complimentary cooked-to-order breakfasts to the large indoor swimming pool, this member of the nationwide chain goes all out to make your family's stay a memorable one. *9300 Baymeadows Rd., Jacksonville. (800) 362-2779; (904) 731-3555;* www.embassysuites.com.

La Fiesta Oceanside Inn ★★★/$-$$

Located just a Frisbee throw away from the Atlantic Ocean and a 10-minute drive from the historic city center of St. Augustine, this inn is a perennial family favorite. With direct beach access, a large outdoor pool, and an 18-hole miniature-golf course, your kids will be more than content. *810 A1A Beach Blvd., St. Augustine Beach. (800) 852-6390; (904) 471-2220.*

Little Talbot Island State Park and Campground ★★/$

With only 40 campsites available, you can bet this 2,500-acre park fills up in a hurry. And, with more than five miles of white-sand beaches, a four-mile hiking trail, and nearly 200 species of birds calling Little Talbot home, you can see why it's a popular family hangout. Reserve early. *12157 Heckscher Dr., Jacksonville. (904) 251-2320.*

Monterey Inn ★★/$$

Kids get a kick out of the clippety-clop of the horse-drawn carriages that often grace the front of this longtime family-owned bayfront property in the heart of the historic district. The guest rooms are simple

FLAMINGOS ARE SOME of the best parents in the animal kingdom. Mother and father flamingos take turns sitting on the chalky-white egg (they only have one chick at a time). Parent flamingos are able to pick out their grayish chicks from a large flock.

but cozy, and the on-site ice-cream parlor serves up some of the best treats around. *16 Avenida Menendez, St. Augustine. (904) 824-4482.*

Perry's Ocean Edge Resort
★★★★/$

A year-round activities program, spacious rooms (all with sitting areas), three swimming pools, plus Perry's legendary homemade doughnuts served fresh each morning make this one of our simple yet favorite lodging choices. The 205-room beachfront property, in the quieter end of AIA, has been family-owned and -operated for more than 60 years, which is why it feels like home. *2209 S. Atlantic Ave., Daytona Beach. (800) 447-0002; (386) 255-0581.*

GOOD EATS

Dave & Busters ★★★/$$

If you're craving a juicy burger with a heaping helping of interactive games for dessert, this restaurant is just for you. The child's hamburger provides just the right amount of nourishment before your family heads to the restaurant's Million Dollar Midway, a huge entertainment center with nearly 200 awesome games. Don't expect to sit around while your kids play in the arcade: an adult must accompany underage guests at all times. Most of the games are suited for ages 8 and up. *7025 Salisbury Rd., Jacksonville. (904) 296-1525.*

Earl Street Café
★★/$

From homemade meat loaf to char-broiled hamburgers and hot dogs, this casual café, located a block or so from the beach and right next door to Adventure Landing Waterpark, has something on the menu to please everyone. Only problem is its size—it's supersmall and the bar seems to take up lots of room. Try for an outdoor table or takeout. *715 Earl St., Daytona Beach. (386) 239-8781.*

Florida House Inn
★★★★/$

Your kids are in for a real treat when they dine boarding-house style at this *really* old dining establishment—we're talking Ulysses S. Grant vintage. You'll feel right at home as heaping bowls and platters of fried chicken and mashed potatoes (heavenly) are passed around. It's an all-you-can-eat menu, so no one goes away hungry. *22 S. 3rd St., Amelia Island. (904) 261-3300.*

NORTHEAST FLORIDA

Harry's Seafood Bar & Grille ★★★/$$
This popular New Orleans-themed dining spot *loves* kids! From the Mardi Gras beads and souvenir cup to the ample portions of chicken tenders and fish bites off the kids' menu, this waterfront restaurant should be high on your list of eateries. Take along an amusement or two for the kids; because of its popularity, there's often a wait for a table. Multiple locations. *46 Avenida Menendez, St. Augustine. (904) 824-7765.*

Inlet Harbor ★★★/$$
Pop-in-the-mouth shrimp and tasty grouper fingers are gone before you know it at this casual riverfront restaurant near Ponce Lighthouse. A visit here not only guarantees great seafood but live entertainment, a riverwalk pier, and a fully loaded gift shop. *133 Inlet Harbor Rd., Ponce Inlet. (386) 767-5590;* www.inletharbor.com

Leverock's Seafood House ★★★★/$$
A 1926 Ford Model-T Huckster delivery truck outside welcomes hungry diners to this popular seafood restaurant on Deer Lake in southside Jacksonville. Weather permitting, try and grab a table outdoors on the deck overlooking the lake. See who's the first to spot a jumping fish or box turtle—even an alligator or two. No doubt your kids will think the boat that's "crashed" through the wall is way cool. There is also an interactive dinner theater with performances on Friday and Saturday evenings. It's one of the few restaurants around that allows you to call ahead and be put on a priority seating list—a blessing for families traveling with small (or not-so-small) children. Multiple locations. *9750 Deer Lake Ct., Jacksonville. (904) 997-1111.*

> **REEFS IN BRIEF**
> Coral is not a plant but a living animal. Reefs occur with the accumulation of sea creature skeletons over thousands of years.

Marina Restaurant ★★★★/$-$$
Quality ingredients, home-style cooking, and affordable prices keep families coming back year after year to this favorite eatery across the street from the port in downtown Fernandina Beach. Tasty fried shrimp, fries, and applesauce from the A'hoy Mateys menu are served quickly and with a smile. *101 Centre St., Fernandina Beach. (904) 261-5310.*

Mi Casa Café ★/$
Whether it's tacos, hot dogs (go for the supersize quarter-pounder), or Cuban sandwiches (delish!), there's something to please everyone's palate at this rustic and simple eatery just down the pedestrian street from the

FamilyFun **VACATION GUIDE**

FamilyFun READER'S TIP

Tic-Tac-Tine

While my sister Barb and I and our seven kids were waiting for dinner at a restaurant recently, my nephew Josh, age nine, surprised me with a game he invented using dinner utensils and sugar packets. He set up forks, spoons, and knives in the traditional tic-tac-toe grid and gave me the choice of being the *X's* (regular sugar packets) or *O's* (artificial sweetener packets).

Soon everyone at the table was pairing off to play, and it was a fun way for us to pass the time before our meal arrived.

Theresa Jung, Cincinnati, Ohio

Spanish Quarter. Dine outside and be entertained by the pigeons while waiting for your order. *69 St. George St., St. Augustine. (904) 824-9317.*

Pat's Riverfront Café ★★/$

A pancake the size of a dinner plate—complete with Mickey Mouse ears—seems to satisfy even the pickiest of eaters. No bells and whistles here, just wholesome, *very* affordable breakfast and lunch fare. Located a few miles south of Daytona at Seven Seas Marina, the café is small and popular, so be prepared to wait for a table. Fortunately, there are plenty of fish, birds, and other creatures around to help pass the time. *3300 S. Peninsula Dr., Port Orange. (386) 756-8070.*

Pizza Garden ★★★/$

This place is known for serving up New York-style pizza just the way your kids like it—oozing with cheese and all the trimmings. The friendly staff and outdoor garden setting will have you coming back for more. *21 Hypolita St., St. Augustine. (904) 825-4877.*

Saltwater Cowboys ★★★/$$

Tucked away in a watery marsh area of St. Augustine Beach is this casual eatery serving local dishes like alligator and oysters. Don't worry, kids aren't overlooked here, as the Cowboy Quickies menu features hearty portions of fish and clam strips, plus all the fixings. *299 Dondanville Rd., St. Augustine Beach. (904) 471-2332.*

Starlite Diner ★/$

Children get a bang out of this old-fashioned diner with its shiny rail-car design, black-and-white tiled floors, red booths, and lunch counter. You'll find lots of tasty dishes to choose from, plus shakes, malts, and sundaes. Multiple locations. *401 N. Atlantic Blvd., Daytona Beach. (904) 255-9555.*

SOUVENIR HUNTING

Charlotte Street Toy Shop
You'll find specialty toys, plus an extensive train, doll, and hobby section at this friendly shop. *46 Charlotte St., St. Augustine. (888) 869-8735; (904) 808-0449;* www.toytrek.com

Daytona Harley-Davidson
Get your motor running to this shiny showroom of used and never-before-seen custom-built motorcycles. Plenty of motorclothes and collectibles to choose from, too. *290 N. Beach St., Daytona. (386) 253-2453;* www.daytonahd.com

Joyce's Dolls
From Barbies to German antique bisque creations, you'll find the doll of your dreams at this cute shop. *1345 Cesery Terrace, Jacksonville. (904) 724-0749.*

The Kite Shop of St. Augustine
This teeny place will blow you away with its awesome wind socks, mini kites, megakites, stunt kites, and accessories. *97 St. George St., St. Augustine. (904) 829-0855.*

Pipeline Surf Shop
Long boards, short boards, fun shapes—you name it, they've got it at this cool surf shop just a block off the beach. *2022 First Ave., Fernandina Beach. (904) 277-3717.*

St. Augustine Toy Company
You're in store for nostalgic and innovative toys for kids of all ages. Lots of marbles and magic, too! *33 King St., St. Augustine. (904) 829-3266;* www.staugustinetoy.com

ZZToys
Your kids will want to spend hours looking, touching, and playing with the incredible array of specialty toys and kites in this colorful and friendly shop. *118 Centre St., Fernandina Beach. (904) 277-3319.*

More than 3,000 spacecraft have been launched from the Kennedy Space Center since 1950.

INTRODUCTION

Orlando and the Space Coast

What city starts with an O, ends with an O, and probably has more miles of jam-packed, once-in-a-lifetime stuff for vacationing families to do than any other destination on earth? Welcome to Orlando! Ever since Disney sprinkled its pixie dust over The City Beautiful in 1971, this destination has spiraled into the biggest, (hundreds of attractions to choose from), the brightest (shocking pink was invented here), and the best (year after year, *FamilyFun* readers rank Walt Disney World their favorite family destination) family tourist spot around.

Although your 6-year-old may find it hard to believe, Orlando's beloved Disney, Universal, and SeaWorld have not been here from day one—in fact, they're all relative newcomers to this city, whose historical landscape dates back to the mid-1800s. Never fear, we'll tell you all about the parks in the next chapter. One of the more intriguing accounts of how Orlando got its

THE FamilyFun LIST

Fun Spot Action Park (page 60)

Green Meadows Petting Farm (page 61)

Kennedy Space Center Visitor Complex (page 58)

Lori Wilson Park (page 62)

U.S. Astronaut Hall of Fame (page 59)

Water Mania (page 62)

WonderWorks (page 63)

FamilyFun **VACATION GUIDE**

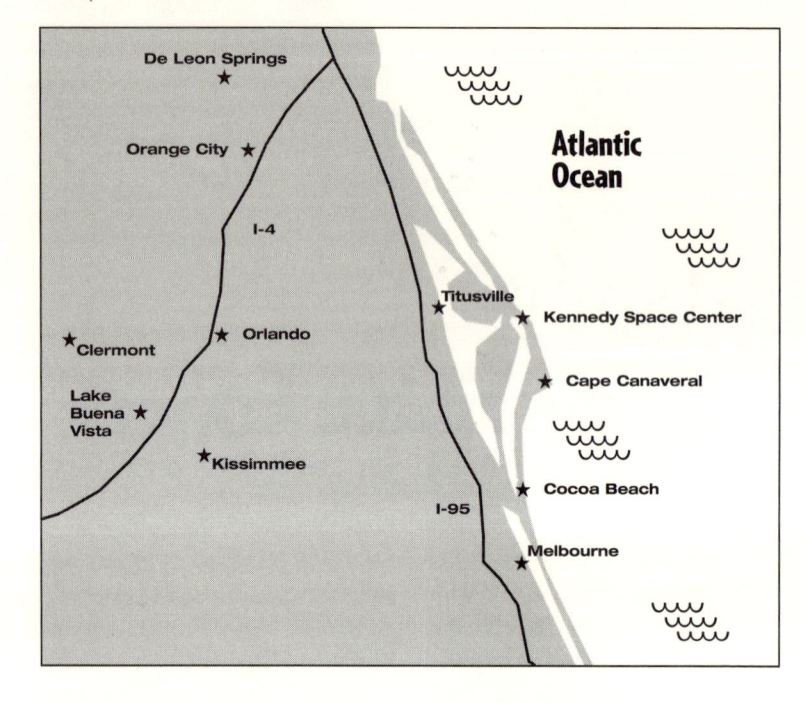

name involves a U.S. soldier during the Seminole War in 1835. While keeping watch at his post (what is now Lake Eola Park in downtown), Orlando Reeves noticed what appeared to be a log drifting in the lake. Once he realized it was an Indian sneaking up on the camp, he sounded the alarm and alerted the fort of the oncoming raid. Although Reeves was killed by an Indian's arrow, his bravery lives on in the city that bears his name.

While on vacation, don't overlook Orlando's neighbor to the east: the Space Coast. Cities like Titusville, Cocoa Beach, and Melbourne—with each area offering small-town, family-friendly charm year round.

Cultural Adventures

Kennedy Space Center Visitor Complex ★★★★/$$

"3, 2, 1—blast off!" takes on a whole new meaning after touring the Kennedy Space Center Visitor Complex, located on more than 140,000 acres of the Merritt Island National Wildlife Refuge. Imagine standing in the Apollo/Saturn V Center's Firing Room Theater—equipped with the actual launch consoles, countdown clocks, and status boards used during the first moon launch—where your young

ORLANDO AND THE SPACE COAST

astronauts will *hear* and *feel* the thunderous blast as Apollo 8 leaves the launch pad for the moon. For a bird's-eye view of space adventure, check out the LC 39 Observation Gantry, a 60-foot observation tower that gives you a clear view of the space shuttle launchpads. Although you probably won't want to spend as much time at the International Space Station Center, kids get a bang out of walking through the full-scale mock-ups of the modules—don't miss the upright "bed-in-a-bag" sleeping quarters and super-tiny bathroom. Other must-sees: the 3-D film L5: *The Space Station* at the IMAX theater, the cosmic adventures of Robot Scouts, Children's Play Dome, and the Astronaut Memorial Monument. In addition to plenty of refreshment carts throughout the complex, there's a space-load of dining options to choose from. An air-conditioned motor coach transports you to three of these exhibits. *S.R. 405 E. Kennedy Space Center. (321) 452-2121; www.kennedyspacecenter.com*

MUST-SEE FamilyFun U.S. Astronaut Hall of Fame ★★★★/$$

If you're vacationing with a crew of future space travelers, make sure this place—down the road from the Space Center—is on your route. From early science-fiction classics to an up-close-and-personal look at the *Mercury*, *Gemini*, and *Apollo* missions, your kids can trace the evolution of space flight through a historic collection of spacecraft and one-of-a-kind memorabilia. Zip through the first few sections, then climb aboard a full-scale shuttle for the 15-minute multimedia blastoff into the future of space. Back on earth, the show-stealing Astronaut Adventure Hall challenges young and old with hours of interactive fun and learning. Try your hand at launching and landing a shuttle, walking on the moon, or testing your reflexes in the *Mercury* capsule. Some of the simulator rides are *very* realistic and are not for those with weak tummies. Conclude your visit with a stop in the Hall of Fame, an inspiring tribute to the brave astronauts who journeyed into space. *6225 Vectorspace Blvd., Titusville. (321) 269-6100;* www.astronauts.org

Space Rocks

In 1969, Neil Armstrong and Buzz Aldrin launched the *Apollo 11* from the Kennedy Space Center in Brevard County, Florida—and landed on the moon! Florida celebrated this historic moment by declaring the moonstone the official Florida state gem, even though you can't find it in Florida. Or on the moon!

FamilyFun VACATION GUIDE

Just for Fun

Air Orlando Helicopter ★★/$$
For a super special splurge, try a tour of SeaWorld or Walt Disney World—by helicopter! Located in the heart of International Drive, Air Orlando Helicopter offers nine aerial tours of Central Florida hot spots. Rides aboard the air-conditioned chopper range from a five-minute tour of nearby SeaWorld ($20) to a 70-minute flight to Kennedy Space Center and area beaches ($295 children's rate). Kids love wearing the headsets for communicating with the friendly pilot who narrates the flight with colorful stories and local factoids. Cruising altitude is about 700 feet; it's just the right vantage point to see Shamu make her grand splash—without getting wet. *8990 International Dr., Orlando. (407) 354-1400.*

Brevard Zoo ★★/$
What sets this zoo apart is the Paws On animal study zone that's housed in a Godzilla-size wooden fort just inside the entrance to the right. Though this zoo features your typical alligators, crocodiles, monkeys, and the like, this section seems to be the epicenter for all ages. A petting zoo (deer, goats, roosters), a sandbox with a huge statue of a dinosaur in the center, a series of Do You Know? and What Do They See? mini learning exhibits, and a climb-up-hang-on-jump-around maze of swings, tires, and webs entertain—and educate—the kids for hours. *8225 N. Wickham Rd., Melbourne. (321) 254-9453;* www.brevardzoo.org

Fun Spot Action Park
MUST-SEE FamilyFun ★★★/$$
Prepare for the ride of your life (go-cart, that is) when you enter this multilevel amusement park. Although some of the go-cart rides require a parent to be behind the wheel, kids can expect megathrills on the Quad Helix (nearly a mile's worth of hills and curves on a four-story wooden track) and Conquest (with its three-level spi-

---

DAY-TRIP
White House South

Less than an hour northwest of Orlando is the small city of Clermont, home to the world-class National Presidents Hall of Fame ($; *123 N. Hwy. 27, Clermont; 352/394-2836*). Featuring a 60-foot miniature replica of the White House (*Guinness Book of World Records* calls it the world's largest dollhouse), this treasure displays mini versions of each Oval Office since the Lincoln administration—think tiny models of authentic hand-carved furniture, even crystal chandeliers and presidential portraits.

ral climb ending in a 26-foot ski-slope descent). For an awesome view of nearby I-Drive and attractions, check out the park's 102-foot Ferris wheel, especially at night. Your little ones will love Kid Spot, with five fun rides, including a cadet track for the mini go-cart racers in your family. A huge, two-story arcade will take care of your spare change—and then some! *5551 Del Verde Way, Orlando. (407) 363-3867;* www.funspot.com

Gatorland ★/$$

The entire family will get a kick out of this park's Alligator Wrestlin' show, where gator wranglers catch six- to eight-foot alligators by hand, climb on their backs, and then go a few rounds in the ring. The 15-minute show is just the right length to hold everyone's attention. *Gator Jumparoo* is another must-see show. Here, seven- to nine-foot alligators jump four or five feet out of the water to retrieve food—in some cases snatching savory snacks out of a trainer's hand. By the way, don't be fooled by the park's name: Gatorland also houses massive snakes, exotic birds, a 300-pound black bear (named Judy, Judy, Judy), and much more. Hungry? Visit Pearl's Smokehouse for some authentic smoked gator ribs or deep-fried gator nuggets, plus the typical burgers and dogs. *14501 S. Orange Blossom Trail, Orlando. (800) 393-5297; (407) 855-5496;* www.gatorland.com.

Green Meadows Petting Farm
★★★★/$$

If your kids are between the ages of 3 and 7, a trip to O-town is not complete without a visit to this petting farm, less than a 30-minute drive from Walt Disney World. Under the watchful eyes of friendly farmhands, youngsters can hold, touch, and carefully cuddle more than 300 tame animals. The hands-down favorite of the two-hour guided tour is the kids getting to milk the cow—an unforgettable encounter. Along the way, you can ride a pony and go on a hayride. Give Green Meadows a

---

The 42 wax presidential figures, collection of First Ladies' gowns, and a grand array of First Family china place settings make this a pleasant way to pass a morning or afternoon.

Before heading back to Orlando, travel airborne (via elevator) 226 feet up to the top of the **Citrus Tower** ($; next to Presidents Hall of Fame; 352/394-4061), Central Florida's tribute to the state's famed citrus industry. Once you've zipped to the highest point (equivalent to 22 stories), the observation deck affords a panoramic view of the area's lakes, rolling hills, even Walt Disney World on a clear day—remember the binoculars!

special place in your photo album. Multiple locations. *1368 Poinciana Blvd., Kissimmee. (407) 846-0770; www.greenmeadowsfarm.org*

Lori Wilson Park
FamilyFun ★★★/Free MUST-SEE

If you crave an escape from the theme parks—at least for a few hours—come to this park on the Atlantic Ocean about an hour from Orlando in Cocoa Beach. With a nature center, playground, and sand volleyball court, your kids will have no trouble keeping busy. The beach won't disappoint, either, with its wide stretches of sand, great surf, seasonal lifeguards, and nearby concessions make this a must-see. *1500 N. Atlantic Ave., Cocoa Beach.*

Vans Skate Park ★★★/$$$

Whether you're a beginning skater or an old pro, this skate park has the challenge to fit your personal abilities. Professional skaters (you know, those guys you see on ESPN) were called in as consultants to create a skating environment that would be thrilling as well as fun. Of course, because you're under your own power on the board, you have to use common sense. Note to parents: Your younger daredevils may want to challenge the biggest and baddest course—but be aware that spills and tumbles are part of the sport. The indoor, wood street course—is a good choice, as it has options for both beginner and advanced riders. Safety equipment is required (helmet, knee and elbow pads) and is available on-site for a minimal fee. *5220 International Dr., Orlando. (407) 351-3881.*

Water Mania
FamilyFun ★★★★/$$$ MUST-SEE

There's no better way for you and your family to beat the Florida heat than to cool down here at one of Central Florida's popular water parks. From the mini slides, pirate ship, and fountains of the Rain Forest pool for your younger fish, to the wild raft rides, twisting flumes, and speed slides (imagine a 72-foot drop!) for the real sharks in your family, Water Mania offers excitement for all ages. Your wannabe surfers will get a bang out of Wipe Out, a surfing simulator tank. Make sure you check out Cruisin' Creek, a leisurely float down an 850-foot tropical river, and the Whitecaps Wave Pool, 72,000 gallons of continuous wave and squeal action. Parents can rest easy, as certified lifeguards and slide attendants are on duty at all times. A three-acre wooded picnic area, complete with covered pavilions and picnic tables, is the perfect lunchtime respite. Seasonal. *6073 W. Irlo Bronson Memorial Hwy. (U.S. 192), Kissimmee. (800) 527-3092; (407) 239-8448;* www.watermania-florida.com

Wet 'n Wild ★★/$$$

It's the world's first water park, and it's serious about pleasing even your youngest tyke. For the 10-and-under crowd check out the Children's Playground, a humongous shallow pool area with mini versions of the popular adult rides. Whether it's a leisurely float down Children's Lazy River or a slide down the Children's Flumes, youngsters can spend countless hours under the careful watch of certified lifeguards. Child-size beach chairs, tables, and lounges—even a "sunken" mini food kiosk so that kids are at eye level with the food servers—are also in this area. Your experienced swimmers who want to go beyond the shallow water attractions are in for a thrill as they tackle such rides as the Fuji Flyer toboggan adventure, Surf Lagoon wave pool, and the Bubble Up, made just for kids to climb, bounce, and slide down into three feet of refreshing water. Refreshment stands and snack bars are plentiful, or opt for the picnic areas and pavilions, conveniently placed throughout the park. *6200 International Dr., Orlando. (800) 992-9453; (407) 351-1800;* www.wetnwild.com

WonderWorks
MUST-SEE FamilyFun ★★★★/$$

WonderWorks, part of Pointe* Orlando on International Drive, lives up to its tag line of "interactive science gone crazy." From the minute your kids see the place (the four-story building looks as though it has landed upside down atop a brick warehouse), they'll know they're in for some fun—and learning. From Bubblocity (billions of oversize bubbles) and Swim with the Sharks (your image is scanned into a shark tank where it's survival of the fittest) for the younger tykes to the WonderCoaster (design and ride your own spine-tingling virtual roller coaster) and LazerWorks (imagine more than 10,000 square feet of action and arcade fun) for the older crowd, families of all ages can choose from more than 85 hands-on, interactive exhibits. (There's an additional fee for LazerWorks games.) Your kids are bound to build up an appetite; check out the snack bar. And don't miss the gift shop's ColorWorks, an authentic M&M counter that features 21 different colored M&Ms (white, hot pink, and black are the most popular). It's one of only seven M&M displays in the world. *9067 International Dr., Orlando. (407) 351-8800;* www.wonderworksonline.com

DAY TRIP
No Theme, All Park

Don't let the one-hour drive from downtown Orlando discourage you. A trip to **De Leon Springs State Recreation Area** ($; West of S.R. 17, at corner of Ponce de Leon Blvd. and Burt Parks Rd., De Leon Springs; 386/985-4212) is well worth the occasional "Are we there yet?" from the crew in the backseat. Take some juice and fruit from your hotel's breakfast bar—just enough to curb your family's hunger for a spell—then load up the car and head north to De Leon Springs, a relaxing change of pace from the theme parks. The park got its name from *the* Ponce de Leon, who may have passed through the grounds in the early 1500s. The spring became a popular resort in the 1880s, with advertisements promising "a fountain of youth impregnated with a deliciously healthy combination of soda and sulphur." As long as the kids are armed with electronic gizmos or coloring books, they'll survive the drive in fine shape—and they'll be glad they did!

Once inside the 603-acre park, head to the **Old Spanish Sugar Mill and Griddle House Restaurant** ($; 904/985-5644), where diners of all ages cook up their own pancakes on griddles built right into the table. It's an all-you-can-eat extravaganza, and children 6 and under eat free when dining with an adult. Other breakfast dishes—including French toast and eggs, any style—are served, too, as is lunch (the ubiquitous grilled cheese).

There's lots to do here: DeLeon Springs offers canoeing and paddleboating through the lakes, creeks, and marshes of **Lake Woodruff National Wildlife Refuge**; with more than 18,000 acres to explore, you can bet your kids will see some pretty unusual animal and plant life. Stop by the concession stand for boat-rental information and a map to help chart your course. For hikers, there's a half-mile nature trail and five-mile loop trail. Before returning to your hotel, hop back in the car for a quick 20-minute drive south to **Blue Spring State Park** ($; 2100 W. French Ave., Orange City; 386/775-3663), where your kids can cool off in the spring's 72-degree waters. (DeLeon Springs has a similar "cool pool.") This spot is a must if your family is into manatees. The lovable mammals call Blue Spring home during the winter months, with larger groups between November and March.

> **MANATEES**
> Manatees spend the majority of their lives resting and eating. The gentle creatures snack 6 to 8 hours each day and snooze 2 to 12 hours.

BUNKING DOWN

All Star Movies
★★★★/$-$$

This, the newest of Disney's All Star properties, has some of the best theming around (expect to see lots of *Toy Story* and *101 Dalmatians*), but what really appeals to all your wanna-be starlets is the food court—it's bigger and brighter than its All Star counterparts. And the price is right, too. *1991 W. Buena Vista Dr., Lake Buena Vista. (407) 739-7000.*

All-Star Sports Resort
★★★★/$-$$

Sports fans will have a field day—and night—when they make this Disney sports-themed resort their vacation home. Whether you hang 10 at Surf's Up or slam-dunk at Hoops Hotel, any of the resort's five different sports themes will delight your kids—and your pocketbook. Surfboard Bay (main pool), Game Point Arcade, and End Zone Food Court also make this property a "triple double" with your entire team. The resort is just east of Disney's Animal Kingdom. *1701 W. Buena Vista Dr., Lake Buena Vista. (407) 939-5000; (407) 934-7639; http://disney.go.com/disneyworld/index.html*

Best Western
Space Shuttle Inn ★★/$

Not only will you get a bird's-eye view of the shuttle launch from here, every guest room television is equipped with special NASA programming that allows you to see and hear what's *really* happening at mission control. Outside, kids can romp in the mammoth recreation park, complete with playground, basketball court, and fishing pier. A pool, a small game room, and a steakhouse restaurant are on-site, too. *3455 Cheney Hwy., Titusville. (321) 269-9100; www.bestwestern.com*

Caribe Royale Resort Suites
★★★/$$

Good luck getting your kids out of this all-suite resort's gargantuan outdoor pool, complete with waterfalls and a 75-foot spiral water slide. There's also a nearby wading pool with interactive water toys for the little ones. Other family-friendly features include a full breakfast buffet (complimentary), spacious two-room suites, and a large video arcade. *8101 World Center Dr., Orlando. (800) 823-8300; (407) 238-8000; www.cariberoyal.com*

FamilyFun TIP

Do the Twist

Pipe cleaners and twist ties have saved many a parent's sanity on long car trips. Kids can quietly fashion these building tools into an endless array of designs — from stick figures to animals to houses with furniture.

FamilyFun **VACATION GUIDE**

Delta Orlando Resort ★/$
This gated, 800-room property, located at the main entrance of Universal Orlando affords a welcome respite for families. Thursday through Sunday feature a live DJ and activity coordinator for hours of fun at the main pool. A variety of guest room options are available; all rooms are stocked with Nintendo 64. *5715 Major Blvd., Orlando. (407) 351-3340;* www.orlandohotelsonline.com/ac-delta-or.htm

DoubleTree Guest Suites
★★★★/$$-$$$
Lots of pluses at this friendly high-rise, including chocolate-chip cookies and a kid's goody bag at check-in, extra-large suites (with three televisions), nightly Disney movies, and a poolside ice-cream parlor. Although a full-service restaurant is on site, take a quick walk down the street to Downtown Disney for still more tasty choices. *2305 Hotel Plaza Blvd., Lake Buena Vista. (800) 222-8733; (407) 934-1000;* www.galleriadoubletree.com

Embassy Suites Resort Lake Buena Vista
★★★★/$$
Your troops will feel like they're in a tropical paradise when they enter this six-story, atrium-style resort just minutes away from Walt Disney World. The spacious two-room suites have family-friendly amenities, along with the resort's large arcade, and indoor and outdoor pools. On-site dining options are plentiful, including complimentary cooked-to-order breakfast every morning. *8100 Lake Ave., Orlando. (800) 362-2779; (407) 239-1144;* www.embassysuites.com

Fort Wilderness Campground
★★★★/$
If you're looking to rough it for a few nights with the kids, but still want to be close to pixie dust, try this 784-site RV and tent campground that's just minutes away from Goofy and the gang. (About 70 log cabins are also available.) Not only are the grounds fully equipped with all the camping essentials, they've got tons of stuff to do: horseback riding, bicycling, fishing, swimming, a petting farm, video arcades, plus free outdoor showings of Disney movies and cartoons. One of our faves! *4510 N. Fort Wilderness Trail, Lake Buena Vista. (407) 824-2900;* http://disney.go.com/disneyworld/index.html

Hard Rock Hotel Orlando
★★★★/$$-$$$
Expect a big thumbs-up from the kids when you stay at this property, just steps away from Universal Studios and Islands of Adventure. Opened in 2001, the 645-room hotel includes loads of kid-favorites, including in-room CD players, and a swimming pool with a huge water slide and underwater audio system.

There's also a Kids Club, a Hard Rock retail shop, and a fitness center. Best of all, hotel guests go to the front of the line all day at nearly all of Universal's rides and attractions, plus enjoy early park admission on select days and times. No lines, no waits, no worries! *5800 Universal Blvd., Orlando.(800) 232-7827.*

Holiday Inn Cocoa Beach Resort ★★/$

Kids enjoy their own private space in many of the 500 guest rooms at the Cocoa Beach Resort, thanks to "Kidsuites"—private quarters complete with bunk beds, TV, Nintendo—all the must-haves. Add to all that a large outdoor pool, game room, playground, seasonal children's activity program (fee), plus the Atlantic Ocean right in your front yard—you can't beat it! *1300 N. Atlantic Ave., Cocoa Beach. (321) 783-2271.*

Holiday Inn SunSpree Resort ★★★★/$

This Lake Buena Vista resort—less than a mile from Walt Disney World—has family-friendly lodgings at bargain prices. More than half of the guest rooms come with specially themed "Kidsuites" *(see above)*. Free, on-site activities include a fully supervised program for children ages 3 to 12, a huge CyberArcade with the latest in high-tech games and fully loaded computers, a movie theater, and several swimming pools. Food court dining serves up something for everyone, and kids eat free for some meals. *13351 S.R. 535, Orlando. (407) 239-4500.*

Jetty Park ★/$

Double your family's pleasure at this park, where you can enjoy oceanfront camping and a great space-shuttle viewing site to boot. (Kennedy Space Center is just down the road.) Simple rustic tent and RV camping is permitted. Families can enjoy plenty of fishing, swimming, picnic tables and grills, plus the convenience of hot showers, a bait-and-tackle shop, a convenience store, and a snack bar. *400 E. Jetty Rd., Cape Canaveral. (321) 783-7111.*

Port Orleans Riverside ★★★★/$$$

Y'all don't need to be a southern aristocrat to stay here—but you'll sure feel like one. Many of the guest buildings at this resort, formerly known as Dixie Landings, were designed to look like historic mansions; even the food court has a

YOU NEVER KNOW WHERE you might run into Disney characters in the parks, but check your guide map—a pointing Mickey glove indicates a meet-and-greet area.

Southern feel to it. As for the kids, they enjoy dipping their hooks in the fishing hole (strictly catch-and-release) and splashing in the free-form pool on Ol' Man Island. *2201 Orleans Dr., Lake Buena Vista. (407) 934-5000.*

Yacht and Beach Club
★★★★/$$$$+

If your budget can accommodate it, this may be the most worthwhile splurge you'll make during your stay at Walt Disney World. In addition to a picturesque setting and top-notch service, these on-property sister resorts are all about location. For starters, you can walk to Epcot (and the Studios if you're feeling ambitious). You're also a stone's throw from the excitement of the bustling BoardWalk entertainment district—Mom and Dad will get to enjoy the relative peace of life on the quieter side of Crescent Lake. And the pool area's to die for. *1700 Epcot Resorts Blvd., Lake Buena Vista. (407) 934-7000.*

GOOD EATS

Beaches & Cream Soda Shop
★★★/$$-$$$

This restaurant, between the Yacht and Beach clubs, features oversize sundaes, cones, shakes, and sodas, as well as the Fenway Park Burger—which may be ordered as a single, double, triple, or home run. *10300., Lake Buena Vista. (407) 934-8000.*

Chef Mickey's ★★★★/$$-$$$

Chef Mickey and his pals host this buffet-style feast, with dramatic views of the monorail passing above. Colorful life-size illustrations of Disney characters decorate the room. The changing menu takes advantage of seasonal offerings; best of all, a sundae bar provides a sweet finish. *4600 N. World Dr., Lake Buena Vista. (407) 824-1000.*

Darryl's ★★★/$$

Don't be put off by this Kissimmee restaurant's saloon-style appearance. Once inside, your kids will be taken with its rustic-antique-y look, complete with a Ferris wheel booth reminiscent of your state fair days. Kids' meals start with a healthy helping of carrot and celery sticks and some of the best veggie dip around. In addition to the usual children's fare, Darryl's lineup for kids includes a roast beef sandwich (French dip)—a menu option added after frequent requests from the younger set.

Applesauce, fries, beverage, and a megascoop of homemade ice cream complete this scrumptious, affordably priced lunch or dinner. Multiple locations. *8282 International Dr., Orlando. (907) 351-1883.*

Dixie Crossroads ★★/$$

The kids' menu specials at this well-known seafood restaurant include popcorn-style rock shrimp that comes with fries and creamy pudding for dessert, and chicken nuggets and fries. It's a very popular place, so be prepared to wait for a table. Feeding the friendly fish helps the little ones pass the time. Multiple locations. *1475 Garden St., Titusville. (321) 268-5000;* www.nbbd.com/dixiecrossroads/

JungleJim's ★★★/$$

Pygmy burgers, gorillaed cheese sandwiches, and mutant macaroni 'n' cheese are among kids' favorites at this safari-themed restaurant; it's full of animals—the stuffed kind, that is, except for the sometimes noisy macaws. Order a round of the bar's famous nonalcoholic jungle drinks for a hyena of a good time. Don't pass up the monstrous mud pie for dessert—it's big enough for the whole table. *12501 S.R. 535, Lake Buena Vista. (407) 827-1257;* www.jungle jims.com

McDonald's ★★★★/$

What has 25,000 tubular feet of fun, more than 50 of the hottest arcade games around, pizza cooked in a brick oven, an old-fashioned ice-cream parlor, and a gift shop? Did somebody say McDonald's? Mickey D's, located in the heart of International Drive, is the largest McDonald's and PlayPlace in the world—it even has an elevator! After your kids chow down on the standard Happy Meal or atypical options like pizza, they'll want to head upstairs to where the *real* action is. The arcade requires tokens, so don't forget your wallet; careful, this could turn into an all-day event. This place is always superbusy, so don't expect speedy fast food here. *6875 Sand Lake Rd., Orlando. (407) 351-2185;* www.mcdonalds.com

> **FEMALE SEA TURTLES** lay eggs on the same beaches year after year, and there is strong evidence that they nest on the beaches where they themselves hatched.

Medieval Times Dinner Theater ★★★★/$$$$

Daring battles on horseback, thrilling jousting matches, brilliant period costumes, and lots of pomp and circumstance await your family at this popular and pricey-but-worth-it dinner theater. Once inside the 11th-century European-style castle, you'll be seated in the ceremonial arena where your kids—adults, too—will cheer their own knight on to victory as he competes in medieval tournaments, jousting matches, and sword fights. While watching the knights perform on beautiful Andalusian stallions, "serfs" and "wenches," dressed in period costume, serve a feast fit for a king—roast chicken, ribs, and all the trimmings. No kids' menu here, which is just fine for most children, especially when they hear they must eat with their hands in true medieval fashion (look, Mom, no silverware!). Skip the preshow hoopla and tour of the living museum with its dungeon and torture chamber—the latter may frighten young lords and ladies. Meal and show last about two hours. *4510 W. Irlo Bronson Memorial Hwy. (Highway 192), Kissimmee. (800) 229-8300; (407) 396-2900.*

NBA City
★★★★/$$

Your roundball fanatics will be in seventh heaven when you suggest lunch or dinner at NBA City, next to the Hard Rock Café at Universal Studios CityWalk. For the kids, order a Pistons Pizza or Bulls Burger from the Rookie menu, and you're guaranteed a slam dunk. For dessert you'll need a referee to oversee your family's last few bites of Cinnamon Berries, an NBA City original, featuring fresh strawberries battered, fried, sprinkled with cinnamon, and served in a to-die-for sauce along with a scoop of vanilla ice cream. Awesome! The first-floor dining area, modeled after an old gymnasium, features continuous footage of exhilarating moments in basketball history. A gift shop and playground where your preteens—not to mention, Mom or Dad—can test their hoop skills round out this memorable meal. *Universal Studios CityWalk, Orlando. (407) 363-5919; www.nba.com/nbacity/*

Old Port Royale
★★★★/$

The food court in Old Port Royale features a large dining area and something to satisfy almost any appetite. Have ice cream, croissants, or pastry at Cinnamon Bay Bakery, an Italian feast at the Kingston Pasta Shop, pizza at the Royale Pizza Shop, sandwiches at Montego's Deli, or burgers and chicken at the Port Royale Hamburger Shop. *In the Caribbean Beach Resort, 900 Cayman Way, Lake Buena Vista. (407) 934-3400.*

Race Rock ★★★★/$$

It's a toss-up as to what kids like best—the supercharged menu or the authentic racing memorabilia (from NASCARs and Indy cars to dragsters and motorcycles, it's all here). After the kids order from a quarter midget menu, complete with chicken dragsters (nuggets), and sticky track (peanut-butter-and-jelly sandwich), they're off to drop some change in the high-powered racing games situated throughout the restaurant. During the meal, monster-size screens flash scenes from racing's most famous finishes and hair-raising crashes, giving you the feeling of being at an actual race. *8986 International Dr., Orlando. (407) 248-9876;* www.racerock.com

Rainforest Café
★★★★/$$

A tropical wonderland, this member of the nationwide chain features cascading waterfalls, crescendos of thunder and lightning, whimsical butterflies, animated elephants and gorillas, and a volcano that erupts every 22 minutes. Adult portions are humongous (there's no sharing fee), and selections from the Rainforest Rascals menu are more than adequate in size. *Downtown Disney Marketplace. (407) 827-8500;* www.rainforestcafe.com

Sunset Café ★/$$

Enjoy a panoramic view of the Intracoastal while you dine on some of the tastiest fish around. Kids also go for the noodles marinara from their special menu. If you've got a picky eater in the bunch, just ask for buttered noodles instead of the red stuff. *500 Cocoa Beach Cswy., Cocoa Beach. (321) 783-8485.*

SOUVENIR HUNTING

The Endangered Species Store

Wild animal-print socks, fluorescent frog T-shirts, and expertly crafted wood carvings are just a few of the items found at this unique clothing and gift shop. *Universal Studios CityWalk, 6000 Universal Studios Plaza, Orlando. (407) 224-2310.*

FAO Schwarz

"Welcome to FAO Schwarz! Come in and play with our toys," commands the Toy Solider as you enter this world-famous wonderland. Even your kids will gladly snap to attention at this friendly request! Pointe* Orlando, *9101 International Dr., Orlando. (407) 352-9900;* www.fao.com

LEGO Imagination Center

Your Lego maniacs will go bonkers at this retail mecca and 3,000-square-foot hands-on playground filled with thousands of these interchangeable pieces. Multiple locations. *Downtown Disney Marketplace, Lake Buena Vista. (407) 828-0065;* http://disney.go.com/disneyworld/index.html

World of Disney

Leave it to your friends at Disney to create a store that nearly rivals its theme parks on the imagination and fun scale. With more than 50,000 square feet of clothes, collectibles, toys, and tasty treats to choose from, this one is the granddaddy of all Disney stores. *Downtown Disney Marketplace, Lake Buena Vista. (407) 828-1451;* http://disney.go.com/disneyworld/index.html

Orlando's Parks

FEEL YOUR stomach sink to your feet as you coast down, down, down on a roller coaster! Look up and watch a zillion fireworks light up the night sky! Smile when you shake hands with Mickey, have a towel handy when you get splashed by Shamu, and lots of wet wipes at the ready when you lick your way around what seems to be the tallest, creamiest ice-cream cone in the world. Sound like paradise? Ask your kids and you'll get a resounding "yes!" In fact, everyone who crosses into one of the parks in Orlando automatically reverts to the age of 8—nothing seems too silly, everything rates an "ooh" or an "aah," and, yes, we'd say that this could well be called Florida's version of paradise. In the chapters that follow this introduction—SeaWorld and Discovery Cove, Universal Orlando, and Walt Disney World Resort—we'll guide you through what's where, what's cool, what's too scary for little ones (and a thrill for older kids), where to get the best pizza, find a perfect souvenir, how to schedule a fun-filled (but not exhausting) vacation. It's all here—turn the pages and get ready to have the time of your life.

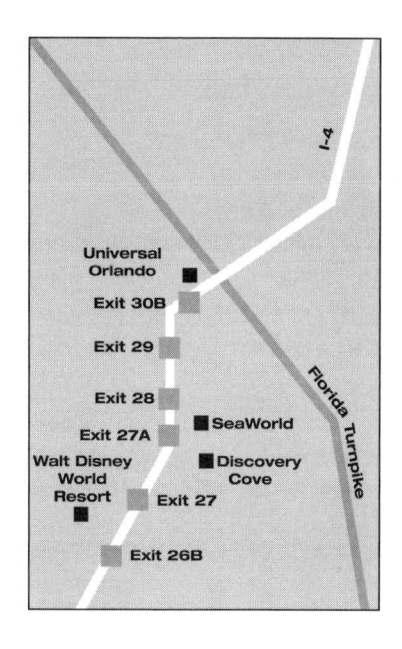

ATTRACTIONS
$	under $10
$$	$10 - $20
$$$	$20 - $30
$$$$	$30 +

HOTELS/MOTELS/CAMPGROUNDS
$	under $100
$$	$100 - $200
$$$	$200 - $300
$$$$	$300 +

RESTAURANTS
$	under $10
$$	$10 - $20
$$$	$20 - $30
$$$$	$30 +

***FAMILYFUN* RATED**
★	Fine
★★	Good
★★★	Very Good
★★★★	*FamilyFun* Recommended

Guests actually pet, even hug, the cetaceans during Discovery Cove's Dolphin Swim.

INTRODUCTION

SeaWorld and Discovery Cove

WHEN MOST kids go to theme parks, the main attraction is the rides: what goes fast, what gives you a good soaking, what makes Mom hide her eyes. Then there's the other stuff—shows, displays, movies, and such. SeaWorld Adventure Park in Orlando (www.seaworld.com) is basically made up of the other stuff. This is not really a "ride" theme park. Instead, SeaWorld gives your family unforgettable experiences, such as petting dolphins, feeding sharks, and seeing rare animals. Don't despair, thrill-meisters—SeaWorld has opened its own tummy tightening, gut-wrenching roller coaster, Kraken (see page 79).

The pace at SeaWorld seems just a little slower than at most theme parks—the perfect break after two or three frenzied days at the other parks. Here, you'll find a relaxed atmosphere mixed with a touch of laughter and wonder.

In fact, the underlying theme of SeaWorld is education. Very few shows or areas are intended solely as entertainment. Within each show, exhibit, or activity, SeaWorld weaves an educational message. *Manatees:*

THE FamilyFun LIST

Journey to Atlantis (page 78)
Kraken (page 79)
Pets Ahoy! (page 79)
Shamu Adventure Show (page 79)
Shamu's Happy Harbor (page 78)

FamilyFun **VACATION GUIDE**

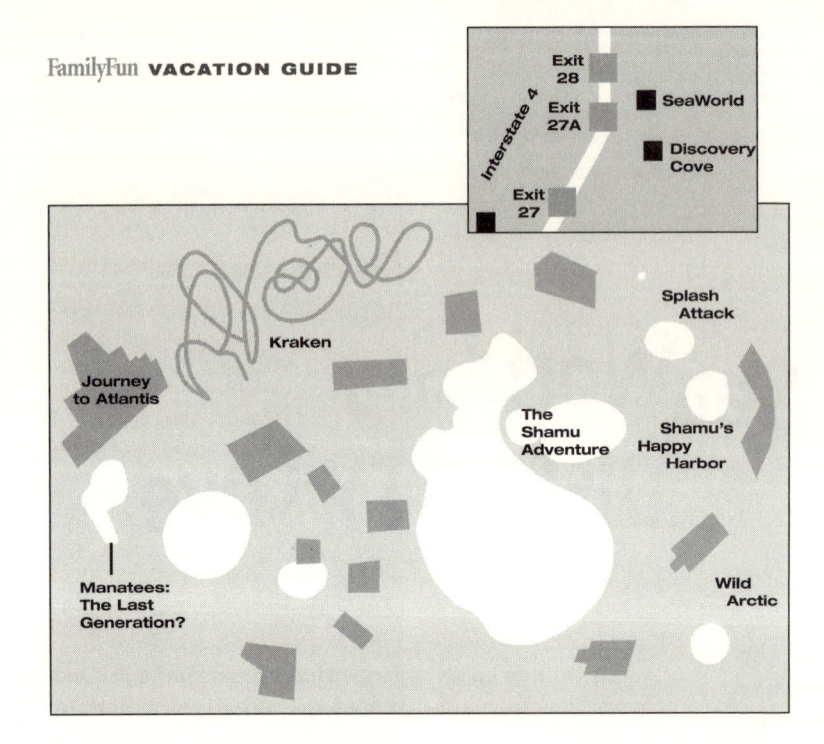

The Last Generation? teaches the importance of protecting endangered species. *The Shamu Adventure Show* educates guests about whales and their training. All the areas within SeaWorld teach respect for animals and their environments. If your kids aren't animal lovers before their visit to SeaWorld, they will be by the time you leave. And maybe they'll find out that education and fun aren't always mutually exclusive.

If ever there was a time to blow the family vacation budget, Discovery Cove is the place to do it. Although it's right next to SeaWorld Orlando, Discovery Cove (www.discoverycove.com) is a separate park, focusing on one-on-one animal encounters in a leisurely, tropical setting. Highlights include a dolphin-swim experience, scrumptious and oversize meal (adults devour the salmon; kids, the burger, dog, or fingers), full use of beach essentials, plus towels, lockers, and swim and snorkel gear. Along the way, such unexpected freebies as special sunscreen and a color photo are thrown in for good measure. But what really takes it over the edge is the seven-consecutive-day pass to SeaWorld Orlando. Talk about a bonus buy! (For those who don't want the dolphin swim, an $89 admission is available and includes all the features mentioned above.)

To swim with the dolphins, kids must be at least 6 years old. Although you don't need to be a super swimmer, you should be comfortable in the water. And, even though personal flotation vests are required (they're free), the ability to tread water really comes in handy during the dolphin swim. When you check in, you get a photo ID, which contains all the details you'll need for the swim. You can also swipe your credit card and put any amount onto your ID badge at check-in—so you don't have to carry money around.

Here's just enough hype to whet your appetite about what your family will encounter during this knock-your-socks-off, all-day experience at Discovery Cove. Best of all, SeaWorld and Discovery Cove are places that the entire family can enjoy together.

SEAWORLD ORLANDO
★★★★/$$$$

Key West at SeaWorld
Central to this Key West–themed area is the dolphin-feeding pool, where Flipper comes right up to you and eats fish from your hand. To get the most from your dolphin-feeding adventure, make sure you walk around the dolphin pool, *away* from the kiosk where you purchase the feeding fish. Most people congregate in front of the kiosk and jockey for position. Simply walk a little farther around the pool, and soon you'll have dolphins eating out of your hand. SeaWorld attendants are around to offer helpful suggestions and information about the dolphins. Hand-washing stations are nearby.

Manatees: The Last Generation?
You get a rare opportunity to observe up close an endangered creature few people have ever seen. A brief movie introduces the exhibit and explains the plight of the manatees, which are on the verge of extinction due primarily to human carelessness. Then you enter a viewing room, where you watch the manatees swim, float, and charm. Because they have been rescued from local waters, these manatees have visible scars from run-ins with boats, fishing lines, and other dangers. The younger set will especially enjoy getting close to the viewing window and watching as the large, lumbering mammals float back and forth before their eyes.

Wild Arctic
SeaWorld may not focus on screaming, hair-raising thrill rides, but it does offer a few that can make your heart skip a beat. Wild Arctic—a danger-dodging helicopter ride to an arctic base station—has something for everyone: the virtual helicopter ride will appeal to the adventurous at heart, which would include most older children; for families with young or easily frightened children, there's a stress-free walking version.

Both "modes of transportation" are the same, only the simulated chopper adds a little rattle and roll along the way. Once you arrive at Base Station Wild Arctic, you'll be greeted by resident creatures of the colder climates. You'll see Beluga whales, walruses, and even polar bears roaming in their refrigerated enclosures. Kids will find the base camp atmosphere *cool*, and, indeed, the chilly surroundings offer a great break from the Florida heat.

Shamu's Happy Harbor

This child-centered play area has one of the largest climbing, tunneling, and sliding setups you'll ever see—it must be at least four stories high! It also has water areas, so be sure to bring a swimsuit or a change of clothes, because the kids will get wet—big time. Kids under 42 inches tall have a special play area. Their playthings are just as cool, and you don't have to worry that they'll get run over by the larger kids.

Journey to Atlantis

In an effort to put its own spin on the word thrill, SeaWorld created its first true adventure ride: Journey to Atlantis. Here you board a fishing boat and enter a mythical world filled with twists, turns, and falls; it combines the adventure of a high-speed water ride with a brief but heart-pounding roller coaster. This is a great ride for those who love a good thrill (and don't mind getting drenched—you will, there's no way to avoid it).

NOTE: The ride is not appropriate for small children or those easily frightened; not only are there two breathtaking drops and some underwear-soaking dips, the lead-up to the adventure is dark and intense, possibly scaring younger kids. Those who don't ride should still check out the cool aquarium adjacent to Journey to Atlantis's gift shop. Unique sea creatures surround you—even under your feet and over your head. And a perfect "gotcha" for those who pass on Journey to

IDENTIFYING SEA TURTLES is a breeze because their names describe how they look. Loggerheads have long, loglike heads; hawkbills have beak-y noses. Leatherbacks don't have the typical hard shell most turtles have. Instead, they dress in stylish leather "jackets." You can tell an Australian flatback from its flat shell, and—if it strikes up a conversation—its accent.

Atlantis: there is a place to shoot water cannons at riders as they pass by. It's a great way for younger kids to get back at their older siblings.

★ Kraken
This monster, the newest of Orlando's roller coasters, claims to be the tallest, fastest, and longest coaster in Orlando. Its unique floorless design makes it seem as though you're dangling in space. The coaster climbs 15 stories, then plunges and twists you upside down and underground (three times!) at 65 mph. Just one look at these gyrations and you'll know which of your kids will have the stuff to ride it. Bravado aside, they must be at least 54 inches tall to climb aboard (for more information, see "Roller Coaster Roundup" on page 124).

Shows:

★ Shamu Adventure Show
Seeing Shamu, of course, is a requirement at SeaWorld. Trainers use both live action and video to create energized performances—like surfing on Shamu's back and Shamu and tankmates skyrocketing into the air—that will have you and your kids on the edge of your seats. Speaking of seats, yours may get wet, depending on where you are sitting. The first 14 rows are deemed "soak zones." And they are serious about that. If you're sitting in those rows, count on getting wet. If Shamu misses you, they have an even larger whale (about double Shamu's size), whose only goal is to splash water by the finfuls on all the guests.

Shamu: Close Up! If you don't get enough of Shamu during the show, discover more about these incredible creatures at *Shamu: Close Up!* Here, you can investigate killer-whale behavior from every possible angle and learn about SeaWorld's successful killer-whale breeding program in the marine mammal nursery.

Clyde and Seamore You can always count on Clyde and Seamore to be the water world's equivalent to Laurel and Hardy. A surefire laugh-getter, this show features the famous seals as well as otters, sea lions, and walruses in various vignettes, which usually involve a bad guy and some fish-loving heroes. It's sure to get your kids' *seal* of approval.

★ Pets Ahoy!
See Fido and Fluffy do things here that you could never get your pet to do at home. A "cast" of dogs, cats, birds, mice, and even pigs strut their stuff at this for-pet-lovers-only show. Most of these animals were rescued by local humane societies and have been trained to climb walls, jump through hoops, and, most amazingly, to get along with each other (something to remind your kids of on the long drive home).

FamilyFun VACATION GUIDE

Restaurants:
Almost all of the restaurants at SeaWorld are very reasonably priced, especially considering that this is a theme park. Expect to pay from about $6 to $8 for most adult meals and about $3 for kids' meals. All but one are casual, get-in-line-and-grab-a-plate kinds of places. There is one full-service restaurant, Bombay Café, where the menu is more formal and prices comparably higher. However, most kids would probably prefer to eat at a get-it-and-go restaurant and return quickly to the park.

Mama Stella's Italian Kitchen
When traveling with kids, you really can't go wrong with pizza and pasta. The serving sizes are substantial, and the bread sticks are yummy. Salads are also available.

Mango Joe's Café If you think your kids would enjoy making their own chicken or beef fajitas, this is the place. Expect ample servings.

Waterfront Sandwich Grill
This eatery has a selection of sandwiches, including hand-carved turkey and burgers. As its name implies, the restaurant overlooks the lake and provides good food and a pleasing atmosphere that kids can appreciate, too.

Shopping:
Shamu's Emporium Buying souvenirs throughout the park can quickly become time-consuming—and costly. Instead, you may want to wait and visit Shamu's Emporium, SeaWorld's main store, at the front of the park. Offering a selection of souvenirs from virtually every shop, this place has something to appeal to even your most discerning young shopper. *7007 SeaWorld Dr., Orlando. (888) 800-5447; (407) 351-3600.*

> **THE ORCA** or killer whale is the top ocean predator. It can hunt and eat any creature in the seas.

DISCOVERY COVE
★★★★/$$$$

Dolphin Swim:
The entire dolphin adventure lasts about 90 minutes, with about 30 minutes of it actually in the water with one of these superfriendly mammals. The session begins with a helpful orientation about dolphins and what makes them tick, kind of a Dolphin 101 primer. Once you're in the water with the trainer, your group downsizes to about eight people, allowing for plenty of supervised touching, kissing, and dancing with your funny new friend. And, just when your kids think it can't get any better, it does. The trainer takes two or three members of the group on an unforgettable dolphin ride.

NOTE: Dolphins love to make eye contact, so if possible, leave your glasses or shades on the shore. Also, the bottom of the dolphin pool is not supersmooth, making water socks or rubber pool shoes a blessing for tender feet.

Coral Reef:

If you want to come nearly face-to-face with a shark or a barracuda, exploring this saltwater pool's underwater shipwreck provides an exciting (but safe) view of the often-feared creatures. (A supersecure window keeps them at bay.) This pool is also home to coral reefs and thousands of bright tropical fish. You may first want to practice snorkeling in the shallower resort pool that's just a few steps away.

Ray Lagoon:

All your kids will love this small but fun saltwater wading pool full of stingrays. The tiny rays seem easier to touch, while the big guys (we're talking some as large as four feet) tend to be a bit more aloof. Of course, that independent manner could quickly change when the staff brings out the food. Or try lowering your hands in the water as though you're going to feed them—it's a safe technique, which may attract a ray or two your way.

Tropical River and Aviary:

A gentle river winds its way through most of freshwater Discovery Cove, allowing your family to swim or float through a variety of pretty settings. A hands-down favorite is the section near the Ray Lagoon that takes you through a waterfall and the aviary. Here you can take a water break and meet—even feed—some of the more than 300 tropical birds who live in this free-flight sanctuary. Trainers are on hand to answer questions and assist with feedings.

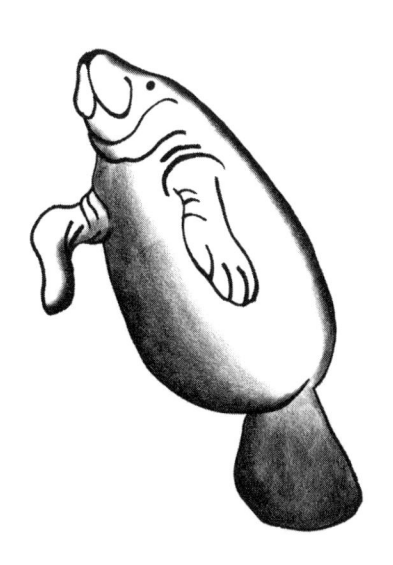

The Incredible Hulk Coaster launches riders to 40 miles per hour in just two seconds.

INTRODUCTION

Universal Orlando

ORLANDO HAS earned the coveted distinction as the granddaddy of all theme-park communities, thanks to the incredible experiences that mega-parks like Universal Orlando deliver day in, day out. From some of the best-in-the-world spine-tingling roller coasters to the warm-and-fuzzy character encounters and play areas, Universal is a wealth of not-to-miss vacation experiences whether you've got darling tykes in tow or those hard-to-please preteens who know it all.

Along with the awesome rides and adventures, plan on your kids going bonkers over touring Universal Orlando's Nickelodeon Studios—one of the largest production studios in the world dedicated to kids' programming. Depending on the day of your visit and the production schedule, you may be lucky enough to be part of a live studio audience for such

THE FamilyFun LIST

The Amazing Adventures of Spider-Man (page 91)

Back to the Future The Ride (page 87)

The Cat in the Hat (page 94)

E.T. Adventure (page 88)

Incredible Hulk Coaster (page 91)

Jurassic Park River Adventure (page 92)

Men In Black Alien Attack (page 87)

One Fish, Two Fish, Red Fish, Blue Fish (page 94)

83

FamilyFun **VACATION GUIDE**

Map labels:
- Jurassic Park River Adventure
- Turkey Lake Road
- Islands of Adventure
- Dudley Do-Right's Ripsaw Falls
- Dueling Dragons
- Earthquake—The Big One
- Adventure Way
- Kongfrontation
- The Amazing Adventures of Spider-Man
- Twister
- The Funtastic World of Hanna-Barbera
- Universal Studios
- Vineland Road
- Hollywood Way
- The Cat in the Hat
- E.T. Adventure
- Interstate 4
- Terminator 2:3-D
- Waterway
- Universal Boulevard
- Major Boulevard

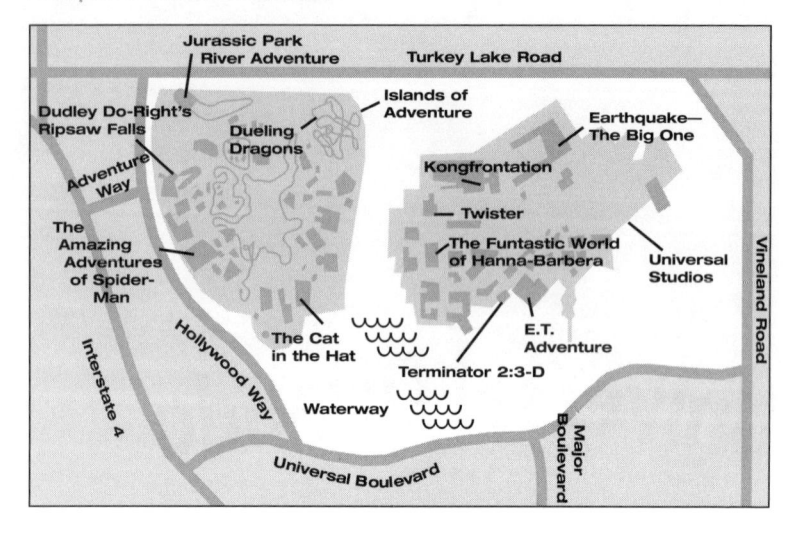

popular shows as All That, Gullah Gullah Island, and Family Double Dare. But more on Nick later.

Two parks make up this theme park's moniker (in Florida, that is): Universal Studios and Universal's Islands of Adventure. In this chapter, we've selected the two parks' very best in kid-friendly entertainment, dining, and shopping. Plan on spending at least one day at each park to experience every wow in the place. Also, during certain times of the year, guests holding multiday passes can enjoy early park admission (8 to 10 A.M., seven days a week) and no waiting at many of their favorite rides at Universal Studios and Universal's Islands ofAdventure. Get a head start on all the fun—and the crowds—with this free bonus! *1000 Universal Studios Plaza, Orlando. (407) 363-8000;* www.universalorlando.com

UNIVERSAL STUDIOS
★★★★/$$$$

Since the first film flickered across a screen, people have been fascinated by the movie industry. Universal Studios catered to this need with its original movie-theme park in Hollywood (in 1965) and brought its cinematic creation to Orlando in 1990, when it opened Universal Studios.

Here you find more than 400 acres of movie magic, where your kids can experience the world of television and film through exciting rides, shows, and attractions. The streets of Universal Studios are filled with what *appear* to be small shops, pubs, restaurants, and office buildings but are, *in reality*, merely facades, designed for use in film productions. Feel at home in New York?

UNIVERSAL ORLANDO

Then take a stroll around Gramercy Park. Want to enjoy a seaside village? Visit Universal's San Francisco/Amity area for a taste of both coasts. And of course, no trip to a movie studio would be complete without a walk down Hollywood Boulevard—it's here, too.

During your family's visit, you can all get behind-the-scenes looks at how movies and television shows are made. A lucky few may even get a chance to see the taping of an actual show. For the most current production schedule, call Universal's Guest Services office prior to your visit at (407) 224-6356. For information on Nickelodeon productions, call (407) 224-6425. If you're already on site, check the production schedules displayed at all the main entrance turnstiles or visit the Studio Audience Center (located at the Lost and Found department) to inquire about any production that may require an audience.

NOTE: Although our review of Universal Studios is laid out in a clockwise direction, some of the production backlots make navigating a bit tough at times. Don't be surprised or concerned if you find yourself backtracking once or twice.

Production Central

Nickelodeon Studios See where so much of the Nick magic is made with this behind-the-scenes look at new and upcoming movies and television shows. Here you'll have the chance to check out props, costumes, sets, special effects, and more. During your tour, you may get to watch a Nickelodeon show being taped as you walk through the glass viewing area overlooking the soundstages. You can also get in on the fun when you visit Game Lab, where your kids have the chance to play games based on popular Nickelodeon shows. And if they're lucky, they may even get slimed.

FamilyFun READER'S TIP

Taste Testers

While traveling cross-country on vacation a few years ago, my husband and I grew tired of our children's requests to visit the same old fast-food places for the latest kids'-meal prize. So we instituted the no-fast-food rule: when our family hits the road on vacation, we only stop at restaurants we can't visit back home. The idea is to find some regional flavor. The rule has an added benefit of taking us off the beaten path a bit. As it gets closer to meal time, we look for one-of-a-kind diners, rib joints, custard shops, and the like. Thanks to this rule, we have eaten Indian fry bread in the Badlands, great sloppy ribs in Tennessee, sensational seafood in South Carolina, and more.

Lisa Tepp, Milwaukee, Wisconsin

FamilyFun VACATION GUIDE

Funtastic World of Hanna-Barbera Rocket through the worlds of your favorite cartoon characters, including Scooby-Doo, the Jetsons, and the Flintstones. You and your kids have the choice of "riding along" with their cartoon friends or enjoying stationary seating. This is a fun ride for all ages—including cartoon-happy Moms and Dads.

Animal Planet Live Serious actors have an old adage that they live by. "Never do a scene with an animal or a baby." That's because animals and babies are naturals and the actor doesn't want to be outdone. Well, in this case, the animals *are* the actors. They're as unpredictable and outrageous as Robin Williams is—and at least as funny! This is a live stadium show, so you'll want to arrive early to get the best seats. Beware: this is an audience participation show, so if you don't want to be picked to go up onto the stage, better sit a little farther back. The show lasts about 45 minutes—go early, especially if you have toddlers in tow.

Jimmy Neutron Adventure You've seen the movie—Now ride the RIDE! Here's where you'll find all your kids' favorites, including the Rugrats and that wacky SpongeBob SquarePants. **NOTE:** This attraction was not open at press time, but if it includes a ride in Jimmy's rocket ship (as promised) and the rest of this familiar cast of characters, it sounds like it could be a real winner.

New York

Twister . . . Ride It Out If you've never experienced the terror of a tornado, here's your chance. Adapted from the movie *Twister*, this attraction takes you to the drive-in movie featured in the film. Electrical wires snap, lights pop, a cow flies by, and an "actual" tornado dances just feet away from your location. While there is really no ride involved (the storm moves the platform on which guests stand), there are loud noises and special effects that produce extreme winds and rain, making the performance realistically intense. **NOTE:** Universal rates this ride as a PG-13, but it should be fine for kids ages 11 and up.

And We Hear...

Universal plans to open a Shrek attraction based on the monster animated hit *Shrek*. Although few details were available at press time, this is what we've been able to find out: At the heart of the show is a 10-minute 3-D film. The adventure will include moving simulators, as well as other special effects all based on the movie. If the popularity of the attraction is anywhere near the popularity of the film, be prepared for long lines.

Kongfrontation You're taking a leisurely tram ride through the streets of New York, when suddenly a giant gorilla attacks the tram. It's King Kong, only this time it's you, not airplanes, he's swatting. Overall, this adventure should be fine for most children ages 6 and older. However, since King Kong attacks the sides of the tram, you should seat younger children toward the middle of the seat. Children under 48 inches tall must be accompanied by an adult and must be able to sit upright to enjoy the ride.

San Francisco/Amity

Earthquake—The Big One Where's the best place to be when "the big one" hits? Underground in a subway, of course. This attraction shows you the fright and fury of an earthquake in a jarring—and realistic—ride; use your discretion with children ages 6 and under. Children under four feet tall must be accompanied by an adult and able to sit upright to enjoy the ride.

Jaws Anyone who has seen *Jaws* or its two sequels knows that a ferocious—and determined—great white shark can eat through almost anything. This time, that "anything" is you. Just the scream this ride generates is enough to scare a little one—Mom and Dad, too: it's best left to those over the age of 6. An adult must accompany children under four feet tall.

World Expo

Back to the Future The Ride Join Doc Brown as you chase a hijacked time machine through—what else? — time. You'll blast from the future to the dawn of the dinosaurs in an eight-passenger time machine that climbs, dives, and turns. Save this ride for Mom and Dad and children over 6 who are at least 40 inches tall. For those with children who don't want to or can't ride, there's a "child swap" area within the attraction. Child swapping ensures Mom and Dad get to ride what they want without one parent having to wait in a long line twice or miss out altogether. For example, Mom can ride a scary ride first while Dad watches the kids, then when Mom gets off the ride, Dad can get on—without having to get back in line. While most parks offer child-swapping areas on size-restricted rides, Universal is the only one to offer a formal waiting room for families. When one parent gets off, attendants will help ensure that the baby-sitting parent gets a no-waiting place on the ride.

Men in Black Alien Attack Head back to the World's Fair to protect the earth from an alien attack. Armed with your personal ray gun (mounted on the ride vehicles), you can try to zap the more than 120 Audio-Animatronics aliens you encounter along the way. This interactive experience allows for many different ride endings and thousands of ride experiences. Can you score more points than the vehicle next to you? **NOTE:** This ride isn't nearly as scary as the hype would lead you to believe and the aliens aren't that creepy, but the seat size of the vehicles limits this attraction to children over 6.

Woody Woodpecker's Kidzone

Curious George Goes to Town Be prepared with another set of clothes; your kids won't have a dry inch left on them when they leave this place, where they can squirt, dump, and shoot water and have a wet and wonderful time. **NOTE:** Listen for the ringing of the bell; that's when gallons of water are dumped from high above onto the kids below.

Woody Woodpecker's Nuthouse Coaster This mini coaster is brief but fun. It's a good start for a young coaster novice. Kids who are veteran coaster riders may find it too tame.

Fievel's Playland If dry fun is more to your liking, then let the kids loose in Fievel's Playland. The area comes complete with a two-story-tall talking cat and oversized household items that turn into mazes, slides, seesaws—and hours of fun!

A Day in the Park with Barney See Barney, Baby Bop, and BJ at this live sing-along show featuring all of Barney's favorite tunes. After the performance, your kids can meet Barney and then explore his backyard. Great for kids under 6, but probably scorned by the older crowd.

E.T. Adventure While airborne on a flying bicycle your family gets to help everyone's favorite alien, E.T., get away from the bad guys and return home safely. This charming ride can be a tad adventurous, but still is suitable for all ages. However, children under 4 feet tall must be accompanied by an adult; parents with kids less than 40 inches tall should check with an attendant for assistance with riding the bicycle.

Hollywood

Terminator 2: 3-D Battle Across Time This megablast of a show picks up where the movie left off. Watching a show that combines live actors with film and special effects, you go to the future to once again save the human race from destruction. It's by far one of the best stage shows around. Expect lots of loud gunfire, really big weapons, and some bumping and jumping of your seat. Families with children under the age of 6 or children who are easily frightened may want to skip this one. If you do decide to see it, try sitting in the back half of the auditorium, so you can get a full view of all the action.

The Gory, Gruesome, and Grotesque Horror Make-up Show If you've got kids who love icky, repugnant stuff, this show about special effects and movie monsters is for you. (We recommend not watching this right after lunch!) Universal suggests parental discretion for children under 13, although, if you're easily grossed out, age doesn't matter, does it?

Restaurants

Universal Studios' Classic Monsters Café A meal here is sure to make your whole family shriek with delight. Enjoy favorites such as pizza, pasta, chicken, and salads surrounded by Universal's own cool-looking memorabilia from such classic movie monsters as Dracula, Frankenstein, and the Wolfman. It's a real scream for the whole family.

Louie's Italian Restaurant This place serves everything kids love: pizza, lasagna, ravioli, spaghetti, and other Italian favorites. For a sweet treat, order up a cannoli.

Boardwalk Snacks You can almost hear the ocean roar and smell the sea air as you enjoy corn dogs, chicken fingers, frozen yogurt, and more at this quick snack shop. Stop here if you're trying to make fast work of lunch and leave more time for experiencing the park.

Richter's Burger Co. Don't miss out on the chance to build your own masterpiece burger at this colossal fixings bar. But if you're not in the mood for a burger, Richter's also serves grilled chicken sandwiches and hot dogs, all with a heaping order of fries.

International Food and Film Festival This food bazaar offers a little bit of something for everyone; featured here are a variety of traditional dishes from around the world, including pasta and pizza from Italy; bratwurst, goulash, and apple strudel from Germany; fajitas, nachos, and tacos from Mexico; and egg rolls, sweet-and-sour chicken, and stir-fried beef from China. There's even some good ol' American fare for your traditionalists.

Animal Crackers With all the action-packed fun your kids are having in this area, they'll need some nourishment. Animal Crackers' menu includes such kid favorites as hot dogs, chili dogs, grilled-chicken sandwiches, chicken fingers, and soft-serve yogurt.

Schwab's Pharmacy Grab a bite in this famous eatery while you wait to be discovered by a Hollywood talent scout. Enjoy tasty turkey or ham sandwiches or classic milk shakes and ice-cream floats.

Cafe La Bamba This eatery offers Texas-style favorites such as barbecue ribs, rotisserie chicken, barbecue sandwiches, and burgers. Parents can also enjoy a little fiesta with some frosty alcoholic indulgences from the adjoining cantina.

Mel's Drive-In Step back to the 1950s at this happenin' drive-in restaurant, situated at the heart of Universal Studios. Kids will love the tasty burgers, fries, onion rings, and frosty shakes served here.

Shopping

Jurassic Park Visitor's Center and T-Rex Attack In addition to dinosaur toys and souvenirs, you'll find some ferocious photo opportunities.

Universal Studios Store This is where you can find a little bit of everything Universal. **NOTE:** Stop here on your way *out* of the park; it will save you from having to carry a lot of souvenirs around with you all day.

Aftermath This store is a virtual bovine bonanza (FYI: A flying cow is the mascot of the Twister attraction). In fact, this Twister-related emporium has some of the cutest cow critters and other cow goodies around. Even if you're not buying, it's worth walking through here just for laughs.

Safari Outfitters Limited Don't miss the chance to get a photo of you and your family in the clutches of King Kong—it's the highlight of the store.

Second Hand Rose This shop, which is adjacent to Safari Outfitters, stocks a variety of discounted items such as T-shirts, action figures, and souvenirs for the whole family.

ISLANDS OF ADVENTURE

Where Universal Studios is focused on movies, Islands of Adventure is pure excitement and fun. And though many of the rides have movie or television themes, this is first and foremost a theme park—and a great one at that—where adventure is the theme! There are no soundstages here, just action-packed rides—most of which are stomach wrenching or clothes drenching.

Many of the rides here are designed for thrill seekers. But although Islands of Adventure does offer a larger percentage of white-knuckle rides, it hasn't overlooked the needs of your young set. Every thrill ride has a comfortable, well-designed child-swap area (see Back to the Future, page 87). Unlike most parks, which at best let parents stand off to the side amid crowds of bustling riders, Islands of Adventure has designated waiting rooms where parents can allow their kids to walk around in a safe and confined setting.

Be aware, too, that the numerous water rides here don't get you just a little damp—they drench you to the skin. Fortunately, nearly all the water rides are confined to Toon Lagoon and its neighbor, Jurassic Park. Bring a set of clothes for the kids to change into after their last water ride. Better yet, bring a change for the whole family and stash the damp duds in a locker until you're ready to leave.

The excitement of Islands of Adventure is contagious. The park is easy to navigate and the bright colors and festive music add to the fun. Also, many of the characters used throughout the park, such as Dudley Do-Right and Woody Woodpecker, make regular appearances at selected locations. After a few minutes at the Port of Entry, it's off you go in a clockwise direction with Marvel Super Hero Island leading the way!

Port of Entry
Marvel Super Hero Island

Incredible Hulk Coaster Probably unlike any coaster ride you've ever experienced, this one lets you forget slowly climbing up the first big hill—instead, you're launched full force out of the gates. Veteran thrill seekers will love it, with its smooth ride and numerous rolls, corkscrews, and dives. However, it is not appropriate for most children under 10. Children must be at least 54 inches tall to ride this coaster.

The Amazing Adventures of Spider-Man This 3-D simulator adventure is a cutting-edge high-tech thrill ride. You are recruited to get the scoop on a legion of bad guys who have stolen the Statue of Liberty. Amazing 3-D action takes place all around you as you're propelled into the battle. The ride is jarring and the effects—villains and all—are *very* realistic. This ride is best suited for kids 8 and up. To ride Spider-Man, children must be at least 40 inches tall.

I SPY

Someone says, "I spy with my little eye something green." Whoever guesses the item correctly goes next. You could limit the items to what's in the area. Or you could get tricky and play I Spied, selecting items that you've already passed.

Dr. Doom's Fearfall Just one look at this ride and you'll know it's not for the faint of heart. Here you're rocketed 150 feet into the air only to plunge back down to earth. A bit like gut-wrenching bungee jumping—Universal style. Not recommended for children under 10, and they must be at least 52 inches tall to ride.

Storm Force Accelatron This ride provides a whirling alternative for anyone not tall enough for, or not wishing to face, the G-forces of the hugely popular Incredible Hulk Coaster. Special effects create a thunderstorm of swirling sound and light, while guests spin beneath Storm Force Accelatron's circular dome. The Accelatron spins 360 degrees every two seconds, making this a questionable ride for the queasy. Barring that, Storm Force Accelatron should be fine for those over 7.

Toon Lagoon

Popeye and Bluto's Bilge-Rat Barges If you make it out of Toon Lagoon dry, then you're doing something wrong. One of the many underwear-soaking rides at Islands of Adventure, Popeye and Bluto's Bilge-Rat Barges is an adventure on the high seas that takes you through a twisting, churning, hair-raising, white-knuckle raft ride. Olive Oyl will probably sit this one out. This ride is waves of fun for children 7 and older, and who are at least 4 feet tall.

Me Ship, the Olive Kids of all ages will have a soaking good time exploring Popeye's fun ship. This interactive children's play place, with whistles, bells, and organs that play at the touch, features areas for both younger and older kids. Your preteens will have a blast drenching unsuspecting Bilge-Rat Barge riders with water cannons.

Dudley Do-Right's Ripsaw Falls Dudley Do-Right is out to rescue a damsel in distress, and you're along for the ride—a very wet one. This flume ride goes through myriad turns, dips, and falls, eventually plummeting you 15 feet *below* the water. According to Universal, the final flume fall is the largest in the world—no argument from our crew! In fact, you will probably come out of your seat. The ride itself is lighthearted and fun, so kids who meet the height requirement of at least 44 inches will have a drenchingly good time.

Jurassic Park

Jurassic Park River Adventure Just when you thought it was safe to go back to the dinosaur lab.... On this river-raft adventure you'll flee from ravenous raptors and other deadly dinos. But that's not the worst of it: a raging T-rex is after your family and the only thing that will save you is an 85-foot plunge into total darkness. This ride is dark, scary, and extremely wet. It is not recommended for children under 8, and children must be at least 42 inches tall to ride.

Triceratops Encounter Come face-to-face with a moving, breathing dinosaur. You'll be amazed as the ancient creatures react to you with snorts, blinks, and flinches. This is a wonderful attraction for the whole family.

Jurassic Park Discovery Center Explore this hands-on, interactive exhibit with numerous dinosaur displays. You and your kids will enjoy studying fossils, watching raptors hatch from their eggs, and learning about prehistoric life. Birds and bees, anyone?

Pteranodon Flyers Flying high above Jurassic Park, the Pteranodon Flyers glide effortlessly over the treetops of a prehistoric jungle in this gentle but brief ride. It's fine for all ages, except for those who may be afraid of heights. Riders must be between 36 and 56 inches tall.

FamilyFun GAME

Race to 20

Two players take turns counting to twenty. On each turn, a player can say one or two numbers. (If the first says "One," the second might say "Two, three.") Try to force your opponent to reach twenty first.

Camp Jurassic This prehistoric play area—complete with rumbling volcanoes and cascading waterfalls — serves up big-time family fun. Kids can explore secret caves, crawl through huge nets, and play on a variety of slides, suspension bridges, and more. There is only one entrance here, so parents can take a breather at the benches while the kids run wild.

The Lost Continent:
Dueling Dragons Your roller coaster aficionados will be in seventh heaven as they soar up to 125 feet in the air at speeds of 55 mph on one of this inverted roller coaster's two different tracks. Even the veteran coaster rider will flinch as he or she is hurled perilously close to the opposing coaster. Once your thrill seekers ride one coaster, either Fire or Ice, make sure they ride the other—if they're true-blue roller coaster lovers, they shouldn't miss either track. For younger children or roller coaster novices, Dueling Dragons is intense and probably not recommended. Also, if you suffer from motion sickness, you'll want to sit in one of the front cars, which are a bit more stable. Children must be at least 54 inches tall to ride.

Poseidon's Fury: Escape From the Lost City Witness the ancient gods Zeus and Poseidon battle for control of the Lost City of Atlantis. You'll be amazed at some of the never-before-

FamilyFun VACATION GUIDE

seen effects, like a 42-foot, swirling vortex of water, which you walk through. The explosions, fire, and darkness may frighten younger children, but most will find this attraction incredibly fascinating.

Flying Unicorn While most of the rides at Islands of Adventure are best suited for older kids, the Flying Unicorn was designed to appeal to younger children (it's exciting enough to interest their big brothers or sisters, too). Riders enter a wizard's workshop, complete with alchemist's tools, potions, and even an elf or two, then climb aboard the unicorn's back and head skyward on a fun yet gentle ride. This beginner's roller coaster is fine for young children—as well as those who can't stomach the monster coasters.

Seuss Landing:

The Cat in the Hat Everyone's favorite mischiefmaker takes you on a fun and silly ride through this famous children's tale. Don't let the comical theme fool you—Mom and Dad will enjoy this one every bit as much as the kids. The Cat in the Hat is the hands-down, thumbs-up favorite.

Caro-Seuss-el One look at the Caro-Seuss-el, and you'll soon realize that this is the most unusual merry-go-round you've ever encountered. But Caro-Seuss-el is more than a ride; it's a performance. Riders can make their ride characters turn their heads, wiggle their ears, or blink their eyes. Don't miss it!

One Fish, Two Fish, Red Fish, Blue Fish A high-flying fish tale, it takes riders on an obstacle course of fountains that squirt water on riders. You can try to stay dry by listening to the song's instructions, but figure on getting damp anyway. Great for all ages.

If I Ran the Zoo This interactive play land houses a "zoo" of strange and unusual animals. Children will find such oddball offerings as flying snakes of water, which are likely to soak unsuspecting guests, and Toe Tickle stations, where children can tickle the toes of a Seuss character. Have an extra shirt or towel handy.

Restaurants

Arctic Express A great stop for snacks, including fruit-topped funnel cakes, Belgian waffles, and waffle-cone sundaes.

Confisco Grill This full-service restaurant offers character lunches every Monday through Friday from noon until 2 P.M. Spiderman, Woody Woodpecker, and many more are on hand to sign autographs and liven the lunch hour for young diners. Menu selections include individual pizzas, pasta, seafood, and specialty burgers. A bit pricey, but a lot of fun.

Blondie's: Home of the Dagwood Who could pass up a chance to have the sandwich made famous in the funny papers—a three-foot Dagwood sandwich? For those with a less hearty appetite, Blondie's features chicken-noodle soup, turkey sandwiches, veggie sandwiches, and kids' meals.

Comic Strip Café No matter what your kids like to eat, you're sure to find it here. This café features individual American, Mexican, Italian, and Chinese fast-food lineups.

The Burger Digs Your family will really dig lunch here! This restaurant offers traditional fast-food family favorites, including burgers, chicken sandwiches, and kids' meals.

Pizza Predattorria After chasing dinosaurs, your family is probably ready for a hearty meal. Pizzas, subs, and Italian sausage sandwiches are featured at this popular Jurassic Park restaurant.

Green Eggs and Ham Café Who could pass up the opportunity to try some green eggs and ham? And you won't have to eat it in a boat or with a goat, in a box or with a fox. After chowing down here, you will be so excited that you'll exclaim, "I like green eggs and ham so much. I'm so very glad we came."

Circus McGurkus Cafe Stoo-pendous This eatery's circus-fun setting is almost an attraction itself. Everyone in your family is sure to find something here to enjoy: fried chicken, pasta, pizzas, kid's meals, a dessert bar.

Shopping

Universal Studios Islands of Adventure Trading Company This emporium features products from each of the islands: apparel, accessories, gifts, toys, and collectibles.

Mulberry Street Store If you want something Seuss, this is where to find it—videos, apparel, gifts, and goodies. The shop even has an infant Baby Seuss assortment that is too cute for words.

Stormalong Bay, the three-acre pool at the Yacht and Beach Club, includes a lifesize shipwreck, a sandy swim area, and pools with tides and currents.

INTRODUCTION

Walt Disney World Resort

DISNEY. FEW WORDS in the English language conjure up such delightful visions of family fun and excitement as this maker of merriment and magic. Near Orlando, you'll find more than 40 square miles of dazzling Disney at Walt Disney World—a vacation wonderland about the size of San Francisco (fewer hills, more thrills at WDW).

Whether your troops are pint-size or preteen, white-knuckled thrill-seekers or gentle giants, kids (and their parents) will find supercharged excitement around every corner at Walt Disney World. Been here, done that? Think again, as even veteran Disney dudes will find new adventures time and time again. (Speaking of visits, low season—meaning fewer crowds—is generally September to the Christmas holidays and from

THE FamilyFun LIST

Buzz Lightyear's Space Ranger Spin (page 103)

Cirque du Soleil (page 122)

Cranium Command (page 112)

DisneyQuest (page 122)

Festival of the Lion King (page 118)

Kilimanjaro Safaris (page 119)

Pirates of the Caribbean (page 100)

Rock 'n' Roller Coaster Starring Aerosmith (Page 107)

Space Mountain (page 102)

Test Track (page 112)

The Twilight Zone Tower of Terror (page 107)

FamilyFun **VACATION GUIDE**

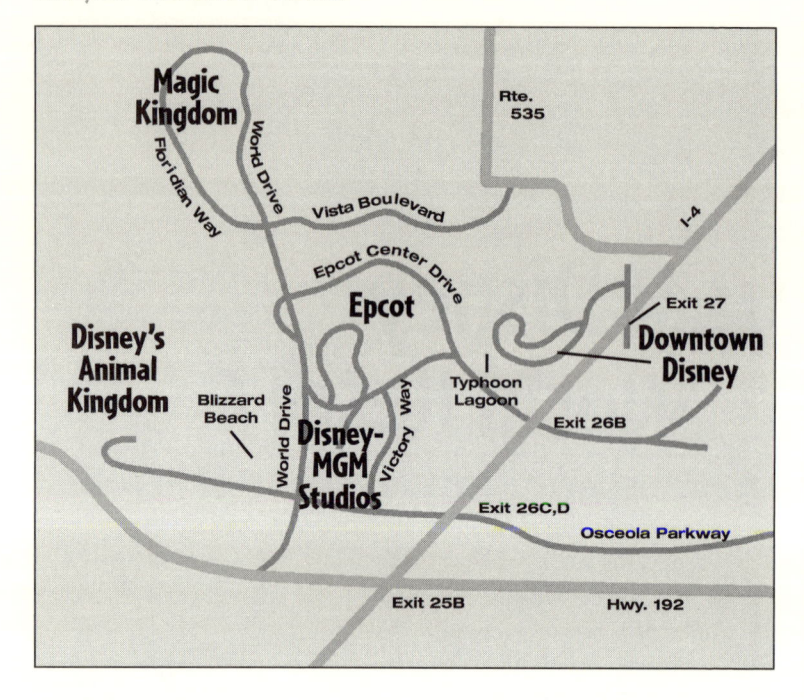

Map showing Walt Disney World area with Magic Kingdom, Epcot, Disney's Animal Kingdom, Disney-MGM Studios, Blizzard Beach, Typhoon Lagoon, and Downtown Disney. Roads labeled include Floridian Way, World Drive, Vista Boulevard, Epcot Center Drive, Victory Way, Rte. 535, I-4, Osceola Parkway, and Hwy. 192. Exits marked: Exit 25B, Exit 26C,D, Exit 26B, and Exit 27.

New Year's to mid-February.)

Thanks to the FASTPASS system, families will spend less time waiting in line at more than a dozen of Walt Disney World's most popular attractions. Just pick up your designated ride time at the FASTPASS attraction, and then head off to enjoy another amusement or two. When your ride time rolls around, return to the attraction's FASTPASS entrance and enter with little or no wait. It's a breeze—and it's free!

Walt Disney World is composed of four separate theme parks— Disney's Animal Kingdom, Disney-MGM Studios, Epcot, and Magic Kingdom—each offering its own version of knock-your-socks-off entertainment, excitement, and education. This chapter mostly takes a look at each park based on the order in which you would see the attractions when you're traveling through the park in a clockwise direction. (That's not to say you can't go counterclockwise. The choice is yours.) Within each major area of the park, we've described the best of the best—the best rides, dining, and snack spots, and shops that make this place sizzle as a family favorite. As a bonus, we're including a few other not-to-miss Disney highlights to fire up your kids' imagination and curiosity. *(407) 824-4321;* http//disney.co.com/disneyworld/index.html

98

MAGIC KINGDOM
★★★★/$$$$

When most people think of Walt Disney World, what they're thinking of is the Magic Kingdom. It's no wonder, since the Magic Kingdom *was* Walt Disney World until 1982. Now, it's one of four Walt Disney World Resort theme parks, yet it is still the one that most hold dear, and the one that must be seen above all others on a family vacation. It's the place that's made just for kids—and that can easily make *you* feel like a kid again. With so many sights to see and tastes to discover, try to allow more than one day here. From the shows to the rides to the parades, you really can't afford to miss out on all that the Magic Kingdom has to offer. If you're visiting more than one theme park, you may want to save Magic Kingdom until last. With all the fairy-tale excitement, kaleidoscope colors, and child-centered fun, kids may find the more educationally focused parks less exciting

FamilyFun TIP

Quiet Zones

October tends to be the least busy time at Walt Disney World, say reservation agents. The two weeks before Thanksgiving and the last three weeks of January are also relatively quiet times.

by comparison. A quick stroll through Main Street, U.S.A., delivers you onto the grounds in front of Cinderella Castle. The lands of the Magic Kingdom fan out like a wheel from the Castle. The first stop (after Main Street, U.S.A.) on our clockwise quest for the best of Magic Kingdom fun is Adventureland.

Transportation
Ferry vs. monorail It's really a personal preference. Your youngsters may enjoy hitting the open seas aboard the majestic ferry, while your preteens simply want to get there, so they may opt for the monorail. Truth is, although the monorail *seems* faster, the actual time to get to the park is about the same however you travel. If your crew goes for the monorail, ask if you can sit up front with the driver.

Main Street, U.S.A.
Walt Disney World Railroad The best introduction to the Magic Kingdom, the 1-mile, 20-minute journey on this rail line is as much a must for the first-time visitor as it is for railroad buffs. It offers an excellent orientation as it passes by most of the park's major lands—Frontierland, Mickey's Toontown Fair, and Main Street, U.S.A. Trains arrive in each station every 4 to 10 minutes. The line is usually shortest in Toontown, but there's rarely a long wait at any of the stations. The train is also the most efficient way to reach

the exit when parades take over Main Street. **NOTE:** Trains do not run during fireworks presentations. **SHOPPING NOTE:** As the central shopping strip, Main Street has lots of small shops to catch your fancy—and pocketbook. Whatever type of souvenir you're looking for, you're bound to find it here. If your kids are up for some shopping along Main Street, try to plan it for midday, then leave your packages in a locker and retrieve them on your way out.

Emporium If Disney makes it, it's probably here. Beware, though, it gets quite crowded toward closing time. You may want to visit here and then grab a bite to eat before you exit the park.

Disney Clothiers You'll find more than just your average Mickey Mouse T-shirt here. Don't forget, grown-ups need souvenirs, too.

Harmony Barber Shop Need a haircut? No problem, because at Magic Kingdom men and kids can get a haircut from an old-time barber, right off Main Street. It may not be as much fun as Space Mountain, but certainly a "wow" getter!

Adventureland

Pirates of the Caribbean Although it's one of the oldest rides at the Magic Kingdom, Pirates is still one of the best family-friendly excursions around. Sail through a burning village while pirates pillage and steal. The realism and detail of the characters is amazing; from dirty feet to hairy legs, these pirates look real. Expect one small water drop and a few loud cannons, but nothing else truly scary.

Jungle Cruise Sail on the river through the misty jungle filled with animals, plants, and wisecracking guides. See exotic animals and ancient ruins. And expect a few surprises along the way. FASTPASS attraction.

Magic Carpets of Aladdin This high-flying adventure is one of the latest (and greatest!) additions to the Magic Kingdom. Younger kids will love taking their Magic Carpet on a little spin. The giant, mystical genie at the center of this journey powers your carpet onward and upward—seemingly through the sky. But be careful: you better know how to fly a carpet or you might find yourself the target of a water-spewing camel. **NOTE:** This ride is best for those who prefer a more gentle ride, not for kids looking for roller-coaster speed and centrifugal force.

Frontierland

Splash Mountain This boat ride through Brer Rabbit's briar patch has one of the best shows for a water ride. Of course, you'll get wet as you "zip-a-dee-doo-daaaaah" down the five-story drop. Kids must be at least 40 inches tall. FASTPASS attraction.

Big Thunder Mountain Railroad Great for all ages, this runaway train ride isn't too wild for the young or timid, but it's still a lot of fun. You'll travel into caves, under falling boulders, and through a flooded mining town.

Tom Sawyer Island You can play a leisurely game of checkers while the kids explore Injun Joe's Caves, travel along dirt trails, and balance on barrel bridges. **NOTE:** Consider making this a midday rest stop so the kids can wind down and you can relax. It's only accessible by raft, so the kids can't wander too far.

Country Bear Jamboree A foot-stomping great time, featuring singing bears with some country and western musical flair. A big hit, especially for the 8-and-under crowd (plus Mom and Dad.)

Liberty Square
The Haunted Mansion One of the best haunted houses your family will ever visit. You'll be amazed at the realism of the ghosts. Great for kids of any age because there is no blood or guts. It's kind of haunted with a sense of humor. And don't forget to watch out for hitchhiking ghosts!

The Hall of Presidents Though it is really geared more toward adults,

My Sweet
Here's an easy activity while you wait for restaurant food to arrive. Grab the sugar packets on the table and try these sweet games:
   Arrange 12, 16, 20, or 24 packets on the table in straight lines of four. Now have two players take turns removing one, two, or three packets at a time. The player who picks up the last packet loses. Or, hide an even number of pennies, nickels, dimes, and quarters under the packets and take turns trying to find matching pairs.

children 7 and up will enjoy many of the little touches presented in this presidential tribute. Watch the other presidents whisper to one another while the speeches are given.

Fantasyland
The Many Adventures of Winnie the Pooh Your Pooh lovers won't want to miss this lighthearted visit through the Hundred Acre Wood. You'll ride a honeypot through Pooh's blustery day, followed by a bouncy romp with Tigger and other Pooh storybook adventures. To exit you must walk through a Pooh-themed store, so hold tight to your wallet! FASTPASS attraction.

Dumbo the Flying Elephant Fly high with the lovable, big-eared elephant.

Little ones will love it. Older kids will want to move on. Long lines are a way of life at this ride.

Cinderella's Golden Carrousel
Although the carousel is Walt Disney World's oldest attraction—built in 1917—it certainly doesn't show its age. A ride will make anyone feel like a kid again. Great for all ages.

It's a Small World Sorry, parents, this song will rattle around in your head the rest of the day—and longer. Younger kids will especially enjoy the tune and the different nations on display. Plus, there's a hidden Mickey in one of the African flowers. Can your troops spot it?

Mad Tea Party Ride a giant teacup as you spin your way around the Mad Hatter's Tea Party. Great for kids of all ages.

Mickey's Toontown Fair
The Barnstormer (at Goofy's Wiseacre Farm) The perfect first-time roller coaster for your younger crowd, it's brief but not boring—and great for the mild at heart.

Donald's Boat This is a boatload of fun for younger children. There's an interactive fountain and lots of hidden surprises.

Mickey's Country House Walk through Mickey's humble abode with its giant garden, garage, Pluto's doghouse, and other Disney dandies. Follow it out for a chance to see Mickey in the Judge's Tent. Minnie has a country house, too, but don't expect to see Minnie at the end. She can be found in the Toontown Hall of Fame. Your tots in tow will enjoy seeing all the things that pop and make noise. Beware of long lines for these attractions.

Toontown Hall of Fame This is the premier place to meet Minnie, Goofy, Pooh, and other well-loved Disney characters. Don't forget your autograph book and camera. **NOTE:** be advised that if your kids want to meet *all* the characters, you'll have to enter three separate lines. If your child wants to meet a specific character, make sure to ask a cast member if that character is appearing during your visit.

Tomorrowland
Space Mountain Magic Kingdom's only real roller coaster (and Disney World's, until the recent addition of MGM's Rock 'n' Roller Coaster). As thrill rides go, this one's pretty good, especially since the darkness of the attraction adds extra excitement. Most kids ages 8 and up will give it a thumbs-up. The minimum height requirement is 44 inches, which is fine because small children may not want to sit by themselves, and the coaster is designed for individual seating. FASTPASS attraction.

WALT DISNEY WORLD RESORT

The ExtraTERRORestrial Alien Encounter "Terror" is highlighted in the name of this attraction for a reason. It's scary. Big-time scary. **NOTE:** Don't say we didn't warn you. Avoid taking most youngsters—or anyone who may not enjoy having the pixie dust scared out of them—to this encounter. The guide map states that this attraction may be too intense for younger children. Believe it. For the fearless, however, the special effects and realism of this ride are not to be missed.

MUST-SEE FamilyFun MUST-SEE Buzz Lightyear's Space Ranger Spin This is a great ride for families. Your mission is to help Buzz Lightyear save the universe from the Evil Emperor Zurg by zapping his henchmen. You can move your car in any direction and zap the bad guys with your own laser gun. You also score points when you hit the targets, making this a delightful competition among the kids—and Mom and Dad, too.

Restaurants

Tony's Town Square A great Italian restaurant with table service, the menu here lists all the things kids—and parents—like, including pizza, pasta, and sandwiches. Tony's makes a great dinner stop before the fireworks.

El Pirata Y el Perico This restaurant is easy to overlook, which means it often is not as crowded as other dining areas. Stop in for some tasty Mexican treats, including tacos, nachos, taco salads—even hot dogs.

Aunt Polly's Dockside Inn Enjoy a lunch that takes you back to the good old days. Lemonade, cold fried chicken, peanut butter and jelly sandwiches, and apple pie make lunch feel like a picnic.

Pecos Bill Café One of the most popular eateries in the Magic Kingdom, this is *the* place for hamburgers, hot dogs, wrap sandwiches, and salads.

Columbia Harbour House The menu here includes chicken strips, fried fish, vegetarian chili, sandwiches, and New England clam chowder. Reasonable prices for some stick-to-your-ribs fare.

Pinocchio Village Haus This restaurant features cheeseburgers, turkey hot dogs, and salads, plus a lovely view of It's a Small World.

Plaza Pavilion This covered outdoor eatery features pizza, deli sandwiches, salads, and fried chicken strips—good ol' family favorites. Good news is that crowds here may be smaller since the place is often overlooked. Plus, it provides a quick shortcut from Main Street to Tomorrowland.

Cosmic Ray's Starlight Café A counter-service restaurant that is really three restaurants in one. While it offers something for everyone in your family—rotisserie chicken, cheeseburgers, veggie burgers, sandwiches, soups, and salads—you may have to stand in three different lines, because each specialty has its own kitchen.

Snacks

Main Street Bake Shop and **Plaza Ice Cream Parlor** These side-by-side emporia are hosted by Nestlé; it may be tough to decide between them. Enjoy the best of both worlds with an ice-cream cookie sandwich. Be warned, it's huge—enough for *at least* two to share.

Aloha Isle On a hot day don't miss out on the frosty, fruity Dole Whips featured here.

Frontierland Kiosk Just a few steps from Pecos Bill Café, this kiosk is a favorite for kids—it features nothing but *real* McDonald's French fries and drinks.

Sleepy Hollow Treats galore here—from caramel corn made in huge kettles to cobblers and ice cream. Just like Mom would make—if she weren't on vacation!

Mrs. Potts' Cupboard Here's the place for some cool treats, including soft-serve ice cream, floats, and sundaes.

Toontown Market This stop offers a break from junk food with fresh fruit snacks.

Shopping

Traders of Timbuktu This market-like complex features an eclectic collection of trinkets and treasures with an African theme. This is not your ordinary souvenir stand.

The Yankee Trader Get some Disney souvenirs at this kitchen accessory store. What better way to keep your great vacation memories alive than by serving dinner prepared with Disney utensils?

FLORIDA BLACK BEARS don't have dainty appetites. If you wanted to eat as much as they do, you'd have to eat 50 hamburgers and 12 large orders of French fries every day.

County Bounty Here your kids will find all the character stuff they could ever want. Don't forget to pick up something for the characters to sign. Instead of an autograph book, let them sign a Disney hat or T-shirt. Wearable memories!

Disney-MGM Studios
★★★/$$$$

The magic of Disney began long before the first Disney theme park ever broke ground. It started with a little black-and-white mouse whistling away on a tugboat. Since those early steps into movie making—and on to television, videos, and theatrical productions, Disney has become an undisputed leader in the entertainment field—especially family entertainment. Unlike the other three parks at Walt Disney World, Disney-MGM Studios is more than just a theme park. It is a full-time, working movie-and-television studio; the many apparently empty streets that you see were actually designed for use as backdrops for television or movie productions.

Of course, this is still Disney, so you can expect to find ample doses of fun and fantasy sprinkled throughout. Because of the working nature of the park, you encounter fewer rides and shows than at other Disney parks, which means your family can see the park in a day or less. Although this park may not be as easy to navigate as its siblings, it still follows the basic circular design. *FamilyFun*'s review of Disney-MGM Studios' coolest of the cool attractions, restaurants, and shops begins at Hollywood Boulevard and continues clockwise around the park. Lights... camera... action!

Hollywood Boulevard

Indiana Jones Epic Stunt Spectacular Get ready to gasp at the amazing feats and incredible special effects. Sit toward the front and show a lot of enthusiasm, and you just may get selected as an extra. This show produces some loud noises, but overall it's a good choice for all ages.

Star Tours Climb aboard this *Star Wars* simulator ride and sail at light speed to adventure. Your guide on this journey is a droid piloting his first trip—and of course, mayhem ensues. The simulation itself isn't

---

FamilyFun SNACK

Bag o' Bugs
Place a few graham crackers in a plastic bag, seal it shut, and crush the crackers into a fine sand using a large spoon. Add a few raisins and let your kids dig for bugs in the sand. Experiment with other tasty critters: dried cranberry ladybugs, chocolate or carob-chip ants, even gummy worms.

scary, but the ride is quite jarring. In fact, sometimes it's difficult to stay in your seat. However, children meeting the height requirement of 40 inches should enjoy the adventure. FASTPASS attraction.

The Great Movie Ride Located in a reproduction of the famous Mann's Chinese Theatre, The Great Movie Ride takes you through the history of the movies—from classics such as Busby Berkeley films and *Singin' in the Rain* to modern movies like *Alien* and *Raiders of the Lost Ark*. There is some loud gunfire and a tame-looking alien but little else that could frighten. The Great Movie Ride is appropriate for all ages.

Playhouse Disney—Live on Stage! Kids 3 to 10 will enjoy seeing Bear, his Big Blue House, and all his friends. Don't be surprised if you find yourself dancing along with your kids. The fun is contagious.

Sounds Dangerous Starring Drew Carey Older kids and their parents will find this sneak peek at movie sound effects fascinating. Younger kids may find it a snooze.

New York Street
***Honey, I Shrunk the Kids* Movie Set Adventure** If your kids didn't feel small before, they will after crawling, climbing, and sliding around this area of 20-foot-tall grass blades, giant sprinklers, and more.

Jim Henson's Muppet* Vision 3-D 4-D No, it's not a mistake. Disney crossed out the "3-D" and replaced it with "4-D" for a reason. The effects of this far-out film are so real you can feel them! Everyone from toddlers to grandparents will enjoy seeing Kermit, Miss Piggy, and the gang in this hilarious production. FASTPASS attraction.

Mickey Avenue
Disney-MGM Studios Backlot Tour Get a sneak peek at how special effects are created—as well as a look at Disney's backlot. This adventure includes a shuttle ride through Catastrophe Canyon, which simulates an earthquake, fire, and flash flood. The "catastrophe" only lasts a moment, making this ride a good bet for all ages.

Animation Courtyard
Voyage of the Little Mermaid Join Ariel, Sebastian, and all their friends and foes in this fabulous performance. Combining animation, live performers, puppetry, lasers, and more, this stage show takes you under the sea, because down where it's wetter, everything's better! This voyage is one not to be missed by any age. FASTPASS attraction.

Sunset Boulevard
Beauty and the Beast Join Belle, the Beast, and all the gang at this show-stopping musical stage production.

This adaptation of the popular movie is probably best appreciated by children ages 3 to 8.

★MUST-SEE FamilyFun ★MUST-SEE★ The Twilight Zone Tower of Terror Picture this: an elevator making its way up to the 13th floor of the ill-fated Hollywood Tower Hotel. Then snap, before you know it, you're descending faster and faster down 13 stories. But that's not all, because you're whooshed back up the elevator shaft just to fall again. This intense thrill ride is certainly a rush, but perhaps too much for young tykes—or those with weak stomachs. An enjoyable and shriek-filled ride for kids 5 and up. Children must be at least 40 inches tall to ride. FASTPASS attraction.

★MUST-SEE FamilyFun ★MUST-SEE★ Rock 'n' Roller Coaster Starring Aerosmith This is one great coaster! You climb aboard a stretch limo and rocket from 0 to 60 in less than three seconds through twists, turns, loops, and dips, all accompanied by Aerosmith music (gives a whole new meaning to the word loud). The indoor track is completely dark, except for a few glow-in-the-dark signs. As much fun as it is, the darkness and speed make it unsuitable for most children under 8. This ride also has a higher height restriction than most, of 48 inches. FASTPASS attraction.

Fantasmic! The fight between good and evil takes on entertaining proportions with Fantasmic! Starring Mickey Mouse as the Sorcerer's Apprentice from *Fantasia*, this action-packed show features lasers, lights, pyrotechnics, and dancing waters, all set to Disney music. Located in the Hollywood Hills Amphitheater, this awesome show is not to be missed.
NOTE: During the holidays and peak season, take advantage of the second showing of Fantasmic! It's typically easier to get a seat.

Restaurants

50's Prime Time Café It may not be the most affordable place to eat at Disney-MGM, but it sure is fun! Here you get to eat in a kitchen straight from the 1950s while watching nostalgic TV clips. Thanks to the wacky waitstaff, parents are treated like kids and vice versa. Don't be surprised if Dad is ordered to the

TALL TALE

The Twilight Zone Tower of Terror is the tallest attraction at any Disney theme park. If the tower were any taller than its 199 feet, it would need to post a red flashing light to warn low-flying aircraft.

THEME PARK FUN 101

Planning the perfect family vacation, you get to go somewhere new, somewhere fun, a place where you want to do everything. You want your kids to come home with hundreds of lifelong memories all from a single afternoon, and you want to walk away knowing you have provided your family a picture-perfect vacation.

Then reality hits. Your kids get cranky, you get frazzled, and your camera goes kaput. It's enough to make you want to go home and never try to have "fun" again. Perhaps we can provide a few suggestions to make your theme-park outing as peaceful as possible.

- Eat and drink frequently, in fact, more frequently than you do at home. Avoid, as much as possible at least, too many sugary treats and soft drinks. Virtually all parks offer healthful snacks such as fruit, and bottled water is everywhere.

- Take a break about midday. If you are staying on park property, you may want to venture back to the room for a brief siesta. If you can't do that, try finding a quiet place in the park to sit and wind down. Tom Sawyer Island in Disney's Magic Kingdom is an excellent retreat. It may seem impossible to do, but everyone will be happier at the end of the day if you take time to relax.

- To help keep track of smaller children, dress them in the same bright color. They'll be easier to spot in a crowd. Plus, put your name, hotel address, and, if you have one with you, cellular phone number in their pockets in case they do get lost. As a family, come up with a game plan of what to do if you get separated.

- If your children are old enough to venture out on their own, set up a meeting place and time. Also, make sure they have the hotel name and number with them just in case. You may also want to invest in the new small-size walkie-talkie-type electronic devices. They are becoming quite affordable and usually have a range of up to two miles, just right for inside a theme park.

- Leave the purse at the hotel. It gets in the way and can be lost or stolen. Fanny packs are much more theme-park friendly, and they leave your arms free so you can hug your favorite character.

corner for not finishing his veggies. It's a riot—for the kids. The menu offers dishes your Mom used to make—and you're sure to find something the kids will like, too.

Hollywood & Vine Serving breakfast and lunch, Hollywood and Vine offers an all-you-can-eat buffet. Chicken and rice, barbecue, and other satisfying dishes are served in the Art Deco cafeteria. A large lunch here may carry you through the day.

ABC Commissary Humongous helpings make this counter-service restaurant a good bet. Your family can enjoy lots of kid favorites such as hamburgers, chicken nuggets, and sandwiches.

Sci-Fi Dine-In Theater This 250-seat eatery re-creates a 1950s drive-in theater. The tables are actually flashy, 1950s-era cars, complete with fins and whitewalls. Fiber-optic stars twinkle overhead in the "night sky," and real drive-in theater speakers are mounted beside each car. All the tables face a large screen, where a 45-minute compilation of the best (and worst) of science-fiction trailers and cartoons plays in a continuous loop. Aside from the standard hamburger and barbecue ribs fare, there's a list of yummy desserts, including milk shakes and the Sci-Fi Sundae (a colossal sundae made with vanilla ice cream and an assortment of toppings).

Toy Story **Pizza Planet** This pizza parlor is a re-creation of the one in *Toy Story*. In addition to cheese-y pies, it also offers your children the opportunity to try their hand at some of the latest video games. Pizza, video games—say no more. This is our pick for your child's favorite place to eat at Disney-MGM.

Rosie's All-American Café This open-air, market-style restaurant features family favorites such as cheeseburgers, sandwiches, soup, and salads. However, if you don't want to lose your lunch, you may want to save this for after you ride the Twilight Zone Tower of Terror.

Sunset Ranch Market Located adjacent to Rosie's, this is a place where families on the run can grab a quick hot dog, smoked turkey leg, pretzel, or beverage.

Shopping

Celebrity 5 & 10 This store specializes in personalized gifts and embroidered items, plus gifts depicting hard-to-find characters.

Mickey's of Hollywood Right at the entrance to Disney-MGM, this shop—where you can find a little bit of everything—is perfect for picking up something on your way out of the park.

Sid Cahuenga's One-of-a-Kind Even if you don't want to buy anything, this

FamilyFun VACATION GUIDE

store filled with movie memorabilia is a lot of fun. You can't miss it when you walk in the front gate.

Stage 1 Company Store Here's the one place in all of Walt Disney World that you can find Sesame Street merchandise. Little ones love it!

The Writer's Stop This amusing shop offers books, gifts, and snacks. Keep your eyes open: there are celebrity book signings here on selected days.

EPCOT
★★★/$$$$

Walt Disney envisioned a park of the future where people from countries around the world would work and live in harmony—a community where visitors could learn about different cultures and varying ways of life. It is still a place where your family can learn about other countries and take a look at some of the innovations that may shape our future. Visiting Epcot is like visiting an ongoing world's fair: it offers countries from around the world a chance to showcase their culture, cuisine, and community. Although Epcot's offerings always held a wide appeal for adults, in recent years more child-friendly elements have been added to its attractions. Nearly all of the rides, exhibits, shows, and interactive areas are designed to educate and enlighten. **FUN FACT:** the name Epcot stands for Experimental Prototype Community of Tomorrow. This concept is reflected in the two areas of Epcot: Future World and World Showcase. And, while the two areas seem distinctly different, both represent two sides of Walt Disney's dream: a look at the technology of the future and a world community that would encompass elements of all countries.

In this section we've set out to capture those attractions, shops, and dining spots at Epcot that educate, entertain, and engage your chil-

FamilyFun READER'S TIP

Institute a Good Deed Bank

A chance to see Mickey Mouse inspired the Mohan family to start a Good Deed Bank. We knew that after paying for the trip, we would have little money left for extras at the park, so I had my kids decorate a coffee-can bank to look like Mickey Mouse. In the weeks leading up to the trip, whenever Hannah, age 9, or Dylan, 6, got caught doing something helpful, we dropped a coin in the bank. The kids' good deeds earned them money to spend on vacation. And, we had the bonus of a more considerate household.

Marci Mohan, Eden Prairie, Minnesota

dren—big time. Since this park is designed like a figure eight, it's a breeze to navigate. First on our list is Future World, with World Showcase only a circle away!

Future World

When it comes to kid appeal at Epcot, Future World is the hands-down winner. Throughout this land of tomorrow, you and your children can explore state-of-the-art technologies that touch every area of our lives, plus discover what future innovations will shape our tomorrows. Since Future World is the first area you enter when you visit Epcot, it is usually very crowded early in the day. Be aware that World Showcase usually opens about two hours later than Future World.

Mission: SPACE

(This attraction is scheduled for public opening Summer 2003.) This is definitely out of this world! But better to be warned first: not for the faint of heart, the ride has some restrictions: You must be at least 44 inches tall and free of back or heart problems, motion sickness, or other physical limitations. Still game? Great! Blast off!!! The sustained G-force during this ride is supposed to be quite intense. You and your crew will feel something truly unearthly—weightlessness! Throughout the ride, you and your team (the car has seating for four and you are assigned positions: captain, engineer, navigator, and pilot) will work toward a common goal . . . a successful completion of your mission.

Spaceship Earth

Epcot's landmark, this colossal, 180-foot-tall sphere displays scenes of the evolution of communication and how communication technology is making our world a global community. **NOTE:** the lines for Spaceship Earth are often nonexistent just before closing, so you may want to view this attraction on your way out of the park.

Innoventions

While it looks unassuming from the outside, Innoventions can probably be the place in Epcot where you'll spend the most time. The two Innoventions pavilions—east and west—are both filled with interactive fun. You'll discover the latest products and technology in industries such as medicine, agriculture, and, of course, computers. There's something for everyone to discover here— from preschoolers to adults. Be sure to plan plenty of time to wander around and play.

Universe of Energy
Ellen's Energy Adventure

Ellen DeGeneres and Bill Nye the Science Guy are your guides as you travel back when dinosaurs roamed the earth. You move around in an audience-size vehicle to the prehistoric era, complete with smells, sights, and sounds. The ride gets a little dark and the dinosaurs—although friendly—are realistic, so easily frightened children may need reassurance.

Wonders of Life

Fitness Fairgrounds A variety of exhibits, including the AnaComical Players, and Goofy About Health, as well as fun with a focus on health are what you'll find at numerous interactive areas throughout the pavilion. Plan on fun for all ages here.

Cranium Command
MUST-SEE FamilyFun Cranium Command takes you into the brain of a 12-year-old boy, where you can see what his heart and stomach are put through on a typical day. (You know the routine—kid oversleeps, skips breakfast, stuff like that.) Well-known comedians add their comic touch along the way. This attraction is great for kids of all ages—not only 12-year-olds.

The Making of Me This film, featuring comedian Martin Short, provides a sensitive look at how life begins. A sweet film for families with parents who are not afraid to answer questions afterward. Younger kids may not get it; older kids may already know it.

Body Wars This joyride through the body takes you on a rescue mission through the heart, lungs, and brain. A simulator ride, it gets very bumpy, kids. But it's really not as scary as some other simulator experiences, so those who meet the height requirement—40 inches or over—are likely to enjoy it.

Test Track
MUST-SEE FamilyFun It may not *sound* thrilling, but this thrill ride gives you an opportunity to become a crash-test dummy for a day. You'll zoom through a variety of test situations, including taking curves at more than 60 mph. While you wait in line, you can see some fascinating ways in which vehicles are tested for safety. Although the ride is not very scary, it is fast and is limited to those 40 inches or taller. Most children old enough to meet the height requirement are old enough to share in the fun. **NOTE:** If your family is willing to split up on the ride, join

HOW HOT IS THE SUNSHINE STATE?

It depends on which area you're basking in. Here are the average temps for major cities: Fort Lauderdale area: 70. Jacksonville: 75. Miami: 76. Orlando: 72. Tampa: 73. Key West: 77.

the line to the left of the regular Test Track line for single riders. It generally moves a lot more quickly. FASTPASS attraction.

Imagination!
Journey Into Imagination with Figment This journey takes you into the Imagination Institute, where you can test your imagination and creativity. There are a few loud scenes that may startle young children, but most will find this simply fun.

Image Works: Kodak "What If" Labs After Journey Into Your Imagination, you can stretch your creativity further in this interactive playground. You can even e-mail a photo of yourself to friends and family. What a fun way to say, "Wish you were here!"

Honey, I Shrunk the Audience This time it's you, not only the kids, who gets shrunk. This is not your ordinary 3-D movie; it also includes a lot of special effects to add to the realism. However, the effects are so real, this adventure may likely frighten children under 8. FASTPASS attraction.

The Land
Living with the Land Your kids may complain that a tour of agricultural technology sounds boring, but the boat ride actually provides a fascinating look at how our food is grown and shows Epcot's own prototype greenhouse and the cutting-edge technology being used here. Even young ones will have fun seeing the growing food, such as cucumbers, lettuce, and tomatoes, which is served in restaurants throughout Walt Disney World. You never know—learning about these high-tech farming methods may be a great way to get kids to eat their veggies!

The Circle of Life Simba, Pumbaa, and Timon from Disney's *The Lion King* star in this lighthearted film about how we all affect the environment, for good and bad. The antics of the jungle friends make it fun, while the message makes it important.

Food Rocks! You've heard of singing for your supper; well here, your supper sings for you. This musical tribute to nutrition is food fun for everyone.

The Living Seas
After the movie, travel far under the oceans to Sea Base Alpha, where you can view tropical fish, sharks, and manatees. The Living Seas is great for kids and animal lovers of all ages. Don't rush through the exhibits at the end—they're the true attraction.

World Showcase

World Showcase gives you a taste of an international holiday amid your Disney vacation. Whereas Future

FamilyFun VACATION GUIDE

World provides more hands-on activities, at World Showcase, the visual dominates. Each country that wraps around the World Showcase Lagoon offers a sampling of its cuisine, architecture, and commerce. However, there are few rides, something kids may find disappointing. To pique kids' interests, Epcot has created the Epcot passport program: children can get a passport stamp in each country they visit. You can purchase a passport in Mouse Gear or any World Showcase store. You may also bring your own notebook, which will come in handy as an autograph book for character signatures. Epcot, in conjunction with *FamilyFun* magazine, has also introduced Kidcot Fun Stops throughout World Showcase. Each country has a Fun Stop—an area with art supplies and an ambassador from that country to help your kids make creations like masks from the respective countries. They can also get their passports stamped while they're there.

Most children, especially older ones, will find the chance to sample culturally different foods throughout World Showcase. Expect lots more live performances than at Future World; many of the shows feature young children. **SHOPPING NOTE:** Unlike most Disney areas, there isn't one store that offers an overall selection of the goods available throughout World Showcase—each store is representative of the country it's in. And while many include Disney items, most do not. Expect to find—and possibly purchase—some unique items within these shops.

Mexico

EL RIO DEL TIEMPO: THE RIVER OF TIME *Hola!* Take a scenic boat ride through ancient Mexico and discover the mysteries and beauty of our southern neighbor.

Norway

MAELSTROM Norway's famous trolls turn this cruise aboard a Viking boat into a fearsome trek into the North Sea. Although an interesting and entertaining look at Norway, this ride may not be for small children. The overall ride is dark and stormy, and there is a flume drop at the end. Maelstrom is the only ride-oriented adventure in World Showcase.

VIKING BOAT Kids can explore this Viking boat, which looks as though it grounded itself many centuries ago. Great for all ages.

China
PU YANG ACROBATS Chinese acrobats perform amazing acts in the China courtyard.

Germany
TRAIN GARDEN Little ones may want to take a peek at the authentic German train garden.

United States
THE AMERICAN ADVENTURE This moving account of America's history, complete with its struggles and successes, is not to be missed. The Audio-Animatronics figures will capture the attention of the younger ones, while the older kids will learn a valuable lesson about our nation's history. Be prepared to get a patriotic lump in your throat.

Japan
MIYUKI Watch Japanese candy artists create delicate sculptures out of sugary sweetness. The tiny treasures are almost too beautiful to eat.

Canada
O CANADA! This Circle-Vision 360 film showcases the beauty of our neighbor to the north. Younger children will probably get restless; save this one for the older kids.

Illuminations: Reflections of Earth
This symphony of lasers, music, and fireworks lights up the sky above the World Showcase Lagoon. It's a spectacular show, and people line up early—sometimes almost two hours beforehand. **NOTE:** If you don't want to spend your last hours in Epcot camped out at a rail, there are a few spots you may want to try about 30 minutes before the festivities. Germany and Italy are often less crowded because they are farther from the entrance than most other good viewing spots. Keep in mind that most of the activity is in the sky, so wherever you park your family, make sure nothing is blocking your view overhead.

Restaurants
Pasta Piazza Ristorante This is a must-stop for your pizza-loving kids, especially if they see the Mickey Mouse-shaped personal pizzas. Also offered here are lots of pasta, eggplant parmigiana, and salads. *Future World*

Fountain View Espresso and Bakery This is the perfect place to pick up a pastry, espresso, or coffee and watch the fireworks at the end of the evening. Of course, it's also a refreshing daytime sweets stop. *Future World*

Ice Station Cool Enter the ice cave and sample some popular beverages from around the world. Some are tasty; others are, well, an acquired taste—sweet, bitter, and fruity. This is a fun, refreshing, and free break! *Future World*

Pure and Simple This café offers healthful and tasty meal choices, from salads and sandwiches to waffles and sundaes. Need a quick snack? Try one of the rich chocolate milk shakes. *Future World*

Sunshine Season Food Fair This food court features eight distinctive restaurants, so you'll find something to please everyone. Menu selections include pasta, breads and pastries, barbecue, ice-cream cones, soups, salads, and specialty sandwiches. Probably the best place to have a meal while in Future World. *World Showcase*

Cantina de San Angel Sit lagoonside and sample tasty tacos, burritos, guacamole, and churros. Mom and Dad can even enjoy a margarita. Careful—the outdoor cantina is a favorite spot for hungry birds. *World Showcase*

Kringla Bakeri og Kafé The café offers diners a wonderful selection of pastries, sweet pretzels, and cinnamon rolls, as well as turkey, roast beef, and smoked-salmon sandwiches. *World Showcase*

Liberty Inn To many visitors from other countries, American food means burgers, hot dogs, and fries, and these are the staples at the Liberty Inn, located near the entrance to The American Adventure show on the far side of the World Showcase lagoon. Salads, grilled chicken sandwiches, ice cream, apple pastries, and chocolate-chip cookies round out the selection.

Lotus Blossom Café You'll find most of your Chinese favorites here. Featuring indoor and open-air dining, the Lotus Blossom serves up excellent egg rolls as well as fried rice and stir-fried chicken with vegetables. *World Showcase*

Sommerfest If German food is what your family craves, Sommerfest serves bratwurst, sandwiches, pastries—and for Mom and Dad—genuine German beer. *World Showcase*

L'Originale Alfredo di Roma Ristorante Unless you live in New York or Rome, this is the only place you can get fettuccine Alfredo from the restaurant that created it. The strolling musicians are another highlight. Besides, what kid doesn't love spaghetti, even if it's pricey? *World Showcase*

Yakitori House If your kids love to eat with their hands (what child doesn't?), then try one of Yakitori's chicken, beef, or shrimp kebabs. *World Showcase*

Teppanyaki Dining Room White-hatted chefs chop and stir-fry vegetables, meats, chicken, and fish prepared at lightning speed right before your eyes. *World Showcase*

Boulangerie Patisserie A great place to get some tasty French pastries and coffee amid some lovely French boutiques. *World Showcase*

Shopping

Camera Center You may want to purchase your film before you get to Epcot, but this camera store offers unique—and sometimes invaluable—services such as video battery recharging. *Future World*

Mouse Gear Here you'll find the best selection of Disney stuff in Epcot. Keep your eyes open; you may find a clearance sale you can't resist. Disney characters may also be hanging out next door in their "creative studio." *Future World*

Disney's Animal Kingdom
★★★★/$$$$

This newest member of the Walt Disney World family offers more of an educational focus than you'll find in some of the other parks. (Don't worry—they disguise it well as fun.) In other words, don't expect any loud fireworks, as the resident animals may not appreciate all the hoopla. Also, because the animals are morning creatures, Animal Kingdom opens and closes earlier than the other parks. The earlier you get there, the better your opportunities for viewing the animals. Its intimate setting—similar in feel to that of Disney-MGM Studios—makes it a place your family can see in a day. Take advantage of the cast members; they'll offer suggestions (such as which show to see next) that will allow your family to make the best use of your time. Animal Kingdom is laid out in a hub-and-spoke pattern, so that's how we've set it up here, reviewing the Oasis and Discovery Island or front and center areas, then moving around the park in a clockwise motion. The park has something for everyone: adventurous kids can try the action rides while the less daring (or younger) stick with the easygoing walks. And an easygoing walk is how your adventure begins . . .

The Oasis

You'll think at first that the Oasis is nothing more than an extended path into Animal Kingdom. Look again: it's a lush, tropical area filled with wildlife, including miniature deer, macaws, anteaters, and tree kangaroos. The animals aren't immediately visible because the park tries to maintain a natural setting as opposed to merely putting the animals on display. This natural approach requires that you look carefully and patiently to locate the animals. Your kids may be too excited to stop and look on their way into the park, but it's a great way to wind down your visit as you exit.

FamilyFun **VACATION GUIDE**

Discovery Island

It's Tough to be a Bug! This attraction in the center of Animal Kingdom is based on the Disney/Pixar film *A Bug's Life*. It's hosted by Flik, who shows us the wonderful world of bugs, up close and personal. Although it's hard to imagine everyone's favorite ant being scary, this 3-D special-effects movie is just that. When the evil Hopper arrives on the scene, things turn nasty. The theater becomes very dark, and bugs start to make their presence truly known. **NOTE:** This attraction is not suitable for small children. For older children—we suggest bug lovers 7 and older—it's a great show, with 3-D as only Disney can do. You won't soon forget this one.

The Tree of Life While you're waiting in line for It's Tough to be a Bug, look at the more than 325 animals intricately carved into this park's centerpiece. How many animals can your kids find?

Camp Minnie-Mickey

Festival of the Lion King *(MUST-SEE FamilyFun)* If there's one must-see show, it's this one. No matter what your age, you'll find yourself swept up into this energetic musical feast. The audience is seated in one of four sections: elephant, giraffe, warthog, or lion. Timon, Pumbaa, and Simba from *The Lion King* host the show with a selection of monkeys, birds, and other jungle creatures. This extravaganza features songs from *The Lion King*, as well as dancers, acrobats, fire dancers, and more. Smaller children may even have the chance to make some music of their own during a mini parade. Hakuna matata—it's perfect for all ages.

Pocahontas and Her Forest Friends This show is on a much smaller scale than Festival of the Lion King, but your youngsters will find it just as delightful. The main message here is on the consequences of deforestation, with Pocahontas and Grandmother Willow explaining the importance the forest and trees play in the circle of life (oops, wrong movie). Live animals, including birds and raccoons, accent the show. Children are encouraged to sit up front without their parents, and will delight in catching the "leaves" that blow from the stage.

FOUNDING DINOS

During the days of the dinosaurs, Florida was completely underwater. Fossil records show that some early inhabitants were the giant sloth, the saber-toothed tiger, and *Nannippus*, a horse similar in stature to a medium-sized dog.

Character Greeting Trails Travel down these wooded trails to visit your favorite Disney characters. Signs at the start of each trail indicate which characters can be found at the end. Because of the secluded setting, you may get away without visiting all three character trails—smaller kids may not realize there's more than one choice. Staff will take kids' photos with the characters, which you may purchase if you want to.

Africa

Kilimanjaro Safaris This ride takes you through a fascinating African savanna where your family helps wardens fend off poachers who have stolen a beloved baby elephant. Riding in a sport-utility-type vehicle, you'll see hippos, lions, elephants, giraffes, and dozens of exotic creatures. Another cool feature: You won't see any fences, and there are no visible barriers. Children—and parents—of all ages will have a blast. **NOTE:** Make sure your kids stay seated during the entire trip; they will likely want to stand to see some of the animals, but there are no seat belts, and your young passengers can easily get bounced a bit aboard this bumpy ride. FASTPASS attraction.

Rafiki's Planet Watch To get to Conservation Station at Rafiki's Planet Watch, your troops must board a train that takes you "backstage" past the animal-holding areas. Once there, you can visit the inside exhibitions and learn about animal protection and care. Afterward, venture outside to the Affection Section, a live-animal area similar to a petting zoo (younger children will probably find this area more entertaining than preteens).

Asia

Kali River Rapids Know this: you *will* get wet. While this looks similar to other rafting rides, Disney adds its special magic to give it a big-time splash. But wet is about as bad as it gets—the rapids aren't too scary, and your kids will be busier laughing at your getting drenched than worrying about the next drop. Don't be surprised if they want to hit this one again. FASTPASS attraction.

Maharajah Jungle Trek See Bengal tigers, Komodo Monitor dragons, gibbons, bats, and other native Asian animals closer than you've ever seen them before. This trek takes you through "ruins" where these exotic creatures seem to be only a few feet away. Sure to be worthy of a "cool" from your older kids.

DinoLand U.S.A.

Dinosaur This action-packed ride begins in a laboratory designed to send riders back in time to see "real" dinosaurs. However, on your voyage, a sneaky lab assistant who's set on catching the rare dinosaur sends you back just as a dino-endangering meteor is about to hit. The ride is

FamilyFun VACATION GUIDE

dark, loud, and fast moving. Older children will enjoy the action, but kids under 8 will likely get scared. FASTPASS attraction.

The Boneyard Here's a playground that your kids will really dig! There are the usual slides, nets, and tunnels, and a few unique touches—such as dinosaur footprints that make sounds when you step on them, Jeeps to climb, and waterfalls to play in that don't actually require a change of clothes. Another plus: there's only one way in and out, so parents can relax while the kids run wild.

Restaurants

Pizzafari Pizza, need we say more? And good pizza to boot! Salads and sandwiches, plus special kids' meals, are also offered, as they are at all Disney restaurants.

Flame Tree Barbecue Here you'll find delicious, ample portions of barbecue chicken, ribs, and sandwiches. The barbecue includes a choice of two sauces so everyone can pick a favorite.

Tusker House Restaurant If you're tired of fast food, this is the place to dine. Highlights here include rotisserie chicken complete with garlic mashed potatoes, as well as sandwiches, salads, and more. The dining area is so authentic-looking that you feel as if you've stepped into an African building that's seen better days—a dusty, worn-looking, bleached white clay structure with handwritten signs, bus schedules, and such.

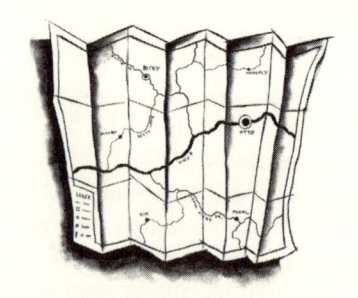

Mr. Kamal's Burger Grill Disney guide maps list this among the Quick Bites, but the beefy burgers are quite a meal. Great for families who don't want to waste time sitting down to eat.

Restaurantosarus This restaurant, presented by McDonald's, just screams "kids." It offers typical McDonald's favorites like McNuggets and Happy Meals, as well as hot dogs and sandwiches. If you're not in the mood for a meal, just pick up some McDonald's fries at the nearby DinoLand Snacks.

Snacks

Chip 'n' Dale's Cookie Cabin A quaint little cabin in the woods offers up some tasty cookies and ice-cream sandwiches. The treats may help pass the time while you're waiting to visit Mickey.

Harambe Fruit Market Keep your kids' nutrition on track with a stop at this healthful snack shop featuring a welcome selection of apples, bananas, and other fresh fruit.

Anandapur Ice Cream What could be better after a refreshing rapids ride than ice cream? The dusty, broken-down "bus" that houses this snack stop looks as though it drove every mile from India to Orlando.

Shopping

Island Mercantile You can find a little bit of everything from the various lands here. This is not your typical souvenir stand.

Disney Outfitters If you want something more than just your usual take-home trinkets, check out Animal Outfitters, featuring fine apparel and gifts. This is also where you can pick up any character photos that the Animal Kingdom photographers may have taken during the day.

Creature Comforts A hands-down favorite for your little ones, featuring stuffed animals, character gifts, and T-shirts aplenty.

Out of the Wild If your family prefers to buy environmentally friendly products, this is your stop. From soap to T-shirts, you'll find things that will do no harm to nature.

Chester and Hester's Dinosaur Treasures This is the place to get weird and funny dino souvenirs.

Mombasa Marketplace and Ziwani Traders An African marketplace and trading company, these connected shops feature animal toys, safari clothing, T-shirts, books, and Africa-themed gifts such as pottery, masks, and musical instruments.

AND DON'T FORGET

Parades

Disney parades are musical and dancing spectaculars. No matter what your age, you'll find yourself singing (or at least humming) along to many of Disney's favorite songs. Of course, everyone else wants to see the parades too, which means prime viewing space is at a premium. The Magic Kingdom parade route runs from Main Street, U.S.A. through Liberty Square and out through Frontierland. Main Street, U.S.A. fills up early, so you may want to watch the parade from Liberty Square or Frontierland, especially if you have young children who would find it difficult to see over other folks' heads. Check your guide map for parade times in all parks. And if you're not parade watchers, now's the time to get on some rides that normally have excessively long lines.

Fireworks

Fantasy in the Sky fireworks add that last touch of sparkle to a full day of Magic Kingdom fun. One thing to keep in mind: The fireworks are high overhead, which means you can see them even if you're not in the middle of the park. One less crowded vantage point is the terrace of the Plaza Pavilion restaurant between Main Street, U.S.A., and Tomorrowland. If you want to make a quick getaway, try capturing a spot on the upper platform of the Walt Disney World Railroad Station at Town Square. *Check maps for fireworks in other parks.*

DisneyQuest
★★★★/$$$

This Downtown Disney amusement must own the patent on the phrase "virtual reality." Whether you're paddling the rapids (Virtual Jungle Cruise, floor 1), whooshing around on a magic carpet (Aladdin's Magic Carpet, floor 2), or surviving a 13-loop roller coaster ride (CyberSpace Mountain, floor 2), the magicians at Disney have done it again by creating a five-story, totally interactive dream come true, especially for kids 7 and up. Regardless of their age, if your kids are prone to motion sickness, this place is not for them.

Disney Quest is divided into four zones—Score, Explore, Replay, and Create. CyberSpace Mountain, where you design and ride your own roller coaster, is the hands-down favorite attraction among thrill seekers who don't mind waiting in line for one minute's worth of shriekdom. (It's comforting to know that the 360-degree ride simulator has an emergency button that will stop the action immediately, no questions asked.) Other mega-thrillers include Ride the Comix (floor 4) and Invasion! An Alien Encounter (floor 5). A tad lower on the thrill scale is the very popular Buzz Lightyear AstroBlaster (floor 3)—a battle of bumper cars and soft cannonballs. The Create Zone's Animation Academy, Sid's Create-a-Toy, Magic Mirror, and Living Easels (floor 3) will also provide loads of time for your pulse to return to normal, as will the family-friendly arcade and video games on floors 3, 4, and 5. Children 9 and under must be accompanied by an adult. *Downtown Disney West Side, Lake Buena Vista. (407) 828-4600.*

Cirque du Soleil
★★★★/$$$$

Maybe it's the death-defying somersaults performed high above on a half-inch steel wire. Or, perhaps it's the BMX wizard whose twists, turns, and boomerangs make your head spin. Then again, it may be the grace, poise, and strength of the aerial artists who seem to fly through the air on red silk ribbons. What we have here is a little bit circus, a little bit drama, a bit bizarre (the tasteful kind), and a barrel of fun. Welcome to Cirque du Soleil's *La Nouba* at Downtown Disney West Side in Walt Disney World Resort.

WALT DISNEY WORLD RESORT

La Nouba is the time to throw fiscal responsibility to the wind, especially if your troops are older than 6. A few minutes into this show and you'll know it's money well spent. Instead of words (none are spoken), the more than 70 international performers mesmerize young theatergoers by the music, costumes, lighting, dancing, and what seems to be their superhuman athletic ability. Imagine balancing on top of eight chairs, atop a table, 25 feet in the air while carrying a spinning cake lit with candles or flying feetfirst through a third-story window and living to tell about it? Cirque performers do it with a vengeance at the 6 P.M. and 9 P.M. shows Thursday through Monday. The early performance is the best bet for families. *Downtown Disney West Side. Lake Buena Vista. (407) 939-7600.*

Blizzard Beach
★★★/$$$

A snowstorm, in Florida of all places? You'll find it at Blizzard Beach, the largest of Disney's supercharged water parks. Blizzard is made to look like an abandoned Alpine ski village, chairlifts and all—in which all the snow is melting into puddles and rivers. What distinguishes this water park from its siblings is the collection of heart-wrenching plunges, twists, and turns that seem to be around every corner. Its signature slope, Summit Plummet, is thought to be the tallest speed slide on the planet. While your thrill-meisters will adore the ride's 65 mph plunge, your gentle giants will find hours of fun at Ski Patrol Training Camp—cool slides and drops—or Tike's Peak for your 3- and 4-year-olds. Blizzard Beach is a good bet, especially if everyone in your party is 10 and older. *(407) 560-3400.*

Typhoon Lagoon
★★★★/$$$

Typhoon Lagoon gives a whole new meaning to the phrase "surf's up," thanks to its almost three-million-gallon wave pool that erupts every 90 seconds. Here you can try your hand at snorkeling with a shark or two (the harmless variety, of course) at Typhoon's popular Shark Reef. Direct your 8- to 10-year-olds to Humunga Kowabunga, a 30 mph body slide, for just the rush they're looking for. Little ones love Ketchakiddee Creek with all its mini slides and rides. Raft rides like Gangplank Falls and Keelhaul Falls add to family fun and excitement. *(407) 560-4141.*

Cool!
Did you know that air-conditioning is a Florida invention? About 150 years ago, a doctor named John Gorrie developed an ice machine to help lower the body temperatures of people with yellow fever.

ROLLER COASTER ROUNDUP

For those who love heart-pumping, adrenaline-surging, roller-coaster action, Orlando has long been, well, a disappointment. Disney's popular Space Mountain at the Magic Kingdom was Orlando's only entry in the "you're not getting me anywhere near that thing" ride category.

How times have changed! Since 1998, four new roller coasters have debuted in the Orlando area, making this area a destination for thrill seekers of all ages. So make sure your safety restraint is fastened; here's our hair-raising rating of Orlando's best screamers.

Our Scream Factor Scale runs from 1 to 5, with 5 producing the whitest knuckles.

The Original:
Space Mountain

Orlando's first roller coaster is still the favorite of many. While the ride itself is tame, compared to many of its twist-and-turn neighbors, the completely indoor coaster has darkness on its side to add to the scariness rating. Located in Tomorrowland, Space Mountain also offers riders the choice of two mirror-image tracks, although there is debate as to which of the sides is fastest. (Trust us, it's the right-side track.) **NOTE:** This ride takes advantage of Disney's fabulous FASTPASS, which reduces waiting time at the most popular Disney attractions (for more information, see page 98). Since Space Mountain isn't overly frightening, kids older than 7 will enjoy it. However, be aware that the coaster is designed for individual seating, so some children may not want to ride by themselves. There is a minimum height requirement of 44 inches.
Scream factor: 3

Pre-teen Favorite:
Rock 'n' Roller Coaster Starring Aerosmith

Disney's latest addition to the coaster wars is a great one. If you like Space Mountain, you'll love this baby. Like Space Mountain, Rock 'n' Roller Coaster Starring Aerosmith is indoors, ensuring that the ride is completely dark, except for a few glow-in-the-dark street signs. With two-person seating aboard a super-stretch limo, you are "rocketed" from 0 to 60 mph in less than three seconds, then whipped through corkscrew twists, hairpin turns, and head-over-heels loops, all accompanied by earsplittingly loud Aerosmith music. **NOTE:** Like Space Mountain, this roller coaster also offers FASTPASS. It is located at Disney-MGM Studios and is best suited for those older than 7 and kids must be four feet tall to ride.
Scream factor: 4

Split Personality: Dueling Dragons

When Universal Studios' Islands of Adventure opened in 1999, it took the thrill factor in Orlando to new heights. One example—or should we say, two examples—of that is Dueling Dragons, located in the Lost Continent. These roller coaster tracks are inverted, which means the tracks are *above* you, and you hang *from* them; you don't sit *on* them. Each track sends you up to 125 feet in the air at speeds of 55 mph. The kicker on this coaster is that the tracks, called Fire and Ice, are intertwined. Plus, they are timed so that as you roll over one turn on your coaster, your feet seem to come perilously close to hitting the other coaster as it sails by.

NOTE: These coasters are not for novices, nor should children under age 10 ride. Children must be at least 54 inches tall to ride.

Scream factor: 5

Best of Show: Incredible Hulk Coaster

True to its name, the Incredible Hulk Coaster is, in fact, incredible! No slow climb up the first big hill. Instead, you are launched at mind-numbing speed into the wildest arrangement of loops, turns, corkscrews, and drops you'll find just about anywhere. And some drops actually propel you underground and underwater. If you truly love coasters, get in line for the first car; it's worth the wait.

Located in Marvel Super Hero Island, the Incredible Hulk Coaster is appropriate for coaster lovers age 10 and over and who are at least 54 inches tall.

Scream factor: 5

The New Kid on the Block: Kraken

The newest monster coaster to take a bite out of Orlando is SeaWorld's Kraken, located near Journey to Atlantis. Based on the story of a massive, mythological underwater beast kept caged by Poseidon, this coaster is one of the highest, fastest, longest—and wildest—roller coasters around. Even the seats on Kraken are unique: They're open-sided and on a pedestal, high above the track—and there's nothing in front of you or beneath your feet. Kraken hurls you into weightlessness amid loops and turns, and that's not all—the coaster plunges you *underground* three times! Kraken is not for the timid—best suited for coaster riders ages 9 and older. Riders must be at least 54 inches tall.

Scream factor: 5

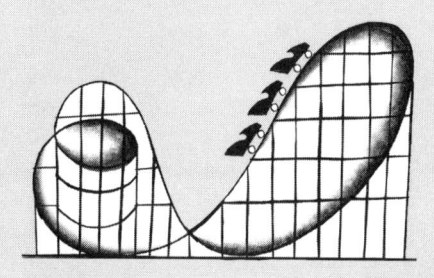

Families flock to the wildlife viewing spots along the shores of John D. MacArthur Beach State Park.

INTRODUCTION

South Florida

For decades, South Florida was really only a place where the rich and richer spent the winter—in a multitude of luxurious resorts. Today, however, much of the area has shed its ritzy image and been transformed into a much more diverse and interesting vacation destination.

Although you'll often hear Miami mentioned in the same "big city" sentence with New York, Los Angeles, and Chicago, it is truly in a class by itself. Yes, you get all the urban charms of other metropolises, but Miami gives your family something that those others can't: a visit to a city that has as much of an exciting Latin feel as you'll get without actually heading south of the Rio Grande. This, coupled with Florida sun and sand, and an abundance of kid-oriented activities and events, makes Miami a vacation spot everyone will remember. But families planning a visit here should know that while Miami is getting the big-city accolades, its neighbors to the north—

THE FamilyFun LIST (MUST-SEE)

Crandon Park (page 132)

IGFA Fishing Hall of Fame and Museum (page 128)

John D. MacArthur Beach State Park (page 133)

Lion Country Safari (page 134)

Miami Seaquarium (page 135)

Museum of Discovery and Science (page 130)

FamilyFun **VACATION GUIDE**

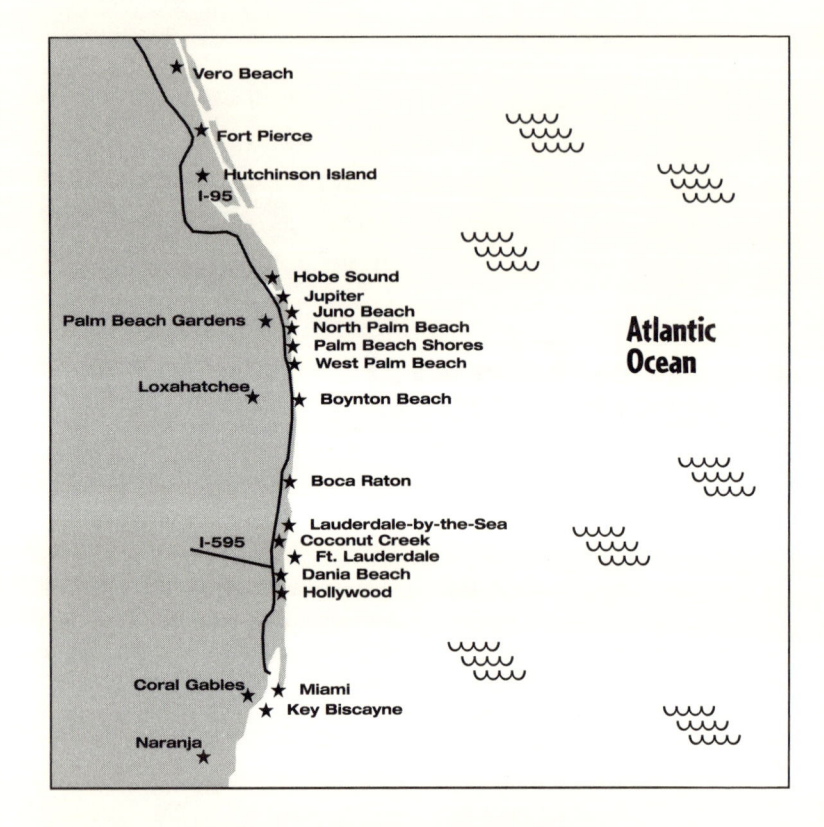

Map locations:
- Vero Beach
- Fort Pierce
- Hutchinson Island
- I-95
- Hobe Sound
- Jupiter
- Juno Beach
- Palm Beach Gardens
- North Palm Beach
- Palm Beach Shores
- West Palm Beach
- Loxahatchee
- Boynton Beach
- Boca Raton
- Lauderdale-by-the-Sea
- I-595
- Coconut Creek
- Ft. Lauderdale
- Dania Beach
- Hollywood
- Coral Gables
- Miami
- Key Biscayne
- Naranja

Atlantic Ocean

Fort Lauderdale and the Palm Beaches—are also great places for families to visit, rich with must-sees. Whether your kids are pint-size or preteen, they'll get a kick out of the area's parks, beaches, and, of all places, museums

Fort Lauderdale is known as the Venice of the Americas, and a short spin on one of the popular and convenient water taxis gives your kids a view of the area's 300 miles of waterways. In the Palm Beaches, they get a good sampling of science, nature, and creatures large and small.

CULTURAL ADVENTURES

IGFA Fishing Hall of Fame and Museum
★★★★/$

Don't pass up this whale of a museum because you figure it's just for the experienced angler. It is definitely a place that kids will enjoy. Start your visit by watching the awe-inspiring, 15-minute film *Journeys*—even your 6- and 7-year-olds will be spellbound. The Catch Gallery is the hands-down favorite among kids (and adults). Here, five anglers at a time try to catch the big one, thanks to fish-fighting simulators, video screens, and heaps of personal determination and cheers from the crowd. Very *reel-istic*! Other not-to-miss stops are the Fish Gallery (taste the difference between fresh, salt, and brackish water), Tackle Gallery (look up for an incredible array of rods and reels suspended from the ceiling), and the Marina (board the boats, don't be shy!). Children ages 2 to 7 have their very own fishing pond—plus fish puppets and lots of coloring—in a special place called the Discovery Room. *300 Gulf Stream Way, Dania Beach; (954) 922-4212;* www.igfa.org

International Museum of Cartoon Art ★/$

This museum with a sense of humor is a strip joint in the most family-friendly way: it's solely devoted to cartoon art. Through 160,000 comic strips, comic books, and editorial and advertising cartoons from around the world, your family will get a chuckle or two (some of the 'toons will have you laughing out loud). For youngsters, the highlight of the museum is the Create-a-Toon Center, where budding cartoonists can test their skills at one of the computer animation stations or do it the old-fashioned way (by hand), where they experiment with the likes

Sculpt a Dune Buggy

A well-built sand castle is a joy to behold, but here's a beach craft your kids will really get into. This two-seater dune buggy has all the options: sand dollar headlights, a Frisbee steering wheel, a driftwood windshield, and a pebble license plate.

Get your assembly line rolling by helping your kids pile up a big mound of sand and pack it down firm. Now, start sculpting the body. Keep in mind the old artist's trick: working from the top down, carve away anything that doesn't look like a dune buggy.

For our model, we rounded the car's hood and trunk, carved fat tires into the sides, and dug out a seat, a slanted dashboard, and a hole where the driver's and passenger's feet fit comfortably.

Once the basic shape is in place, your kids can add the trim: tire treads, driftwood windshield and bumpers, a shell hood ornament, a beach grass antenna, a towel seat cover, or whatever else they dream up.

As a last step, they can fill 'er up with shell gasoline, smooth out a highway, and hit the open road.

of Garfield the Cat and other characters. Non-artists can curl up in a beanbag chair with a good comic book. *201 Plaza Real (Mizner Park), Boca Raton. (561) 391-2200;* http://cartoon.org

Miami Museum of Science and Space Transit Planetarium ★★★/$

The traveling exhibits at this well-loved Miami museum (its mantra is "making science fun") are of national stature—past showings included such must-see collections as Richard Scarry's BUSYTOWN and High Wire Acts and Feats of Balance. Another all-time favorite exhibit is The Sports Challenge: Your Body at Play, where kids can play virtual reality basketball, test their pitching speed, and scale a rock-climbing wall (don't worry—this one goes sideways, not up). A recent affiliation with the Smithsonian takes the museum to even greater heights with the incredible exhibit Exploring Latin America & the Caribbean. If your kids are thinking *boring!* tell them to give it a chance; they'll be amazed at all the cool stuff—from a mini interactive dig to a dark and gloomy tomb housing a giant sarcophagus. Before they know it, they're immersed in the jungle and discoveries of ancient cultures. Stargazers in the group will be on cloud nine at the Space Transit Planetarium, located in the left wing of the museum. *3280 S. Miami Ave., Miami. (305) 646-4200;* www.miamisci.org

MUST-SEE FamilyFun Museum of Discovery and Science ★★★★/$

You'll get the most out of your visit to this very popular Ft. Lauderdale museum by arriving early, starting on the second floor, and working your way down. (The second level houses most of the hands-on activities that may require some muscle or mental power—best to do it when the kids are fresh.) Gizmo City is a good place to begin since it's right next to the escalator and offers a gazillion gizmos and machines. Check out the "innards" of a house at the nearby No Place Like Home, and learn what organs go where by meeting lovable Fred in Choose Health. Before heading downstairs, blast off in Space Base's Vista Voyager

Cool it With Cocoa

Wake up and smell the cocoa—butter, that is. In 1944, Benjamin Green, a pharmacist in Miami Beach, invented tanning cream in his own kitchen. He cooked up some cocoa butter in a coffeepot on his wife's stove to create suntan lotion. The inventor must have believed in his product—Green tested each early batch on his own balding head.

six-minute virtual ride to the moon; it's a jolting good time, best for kids ages 4 and up. Back on the ground floor, wander through Florida's EcoScapes full of sharks, bats, sea turtles, and the largest living captive Atlantic coral reef in the world. Speaking of sea life, your little urchins have their own space to climb, splash, explore, and learn in the Discovery Center—great for kids under age 6. The five-story IMAX 3-D theater shows several movies throughout the day and evening—all of them kid-friendly. The combined museum/IMAX admission package provides the best bang for the buck. *401 S.W. Second St., Ft. Lauderdale. (954) 467-6637.*

South Florida Science Museum
★★★/$

It's not a fancy megaplex, but what you will find here is one of the area's best hands-on collections of cool activities, especially for kids ages 5 to 12. Don't pass up the cloud ring or tornado tunnel near the entrance—youngsters will get a bang out of creating their own smoke signals and windstorms. Outside offerings feature loads of young fun like the sea turtle game (a Candy Land clone), fossil dig, and the largest pair of whisper dishes (you know, those satellite dishes that carry even the faintest sound) this side of Texas! For a little more money, the 40-minute laser light show at the Buzz Aldrin Planetarium is the perfect place to rest your feet (but certainly not your mind) in the afternoon—as lasers, videos, stars, and special effects are set to rock, country, classical, and kids' tunes in awesome surround sound. Be selective—your youngest may get sensory overload from the laser show. *4801 Dreher Trail North, West Palm Beach. (561) 832-1988;* www.sfm.com

Sports Immortals Museum and Memorabilia Mart
★/$

Sports fans are in their element when touring this spectacular collection of more than one million sports mementos. Little Leaguers will want to check out the "ballroom" containing more than 6,000 autographed baseballs dating back to 1865. Another must-see: the largest autographed bat in the world (says *Guinness*), weighing in at 57 pounds and signed by 60 Hall of Fame greats. For the hoopsters in the group, it's Michael Jordan mania, with lots of signed jerseys, shoes, even a pair of signed Baby Air Jordan shoes. Other sports aren't left out: The museum also commemorates some of the greatest moments and stars in boxing, soccer, golf, drag racing, hockey, and tennis. The Memorabilia Mart, located on the first floor, stocks more than 10,000 items for sale, ranging from trading cards to an autographed Bulls uniform worn by MJ. Asking price? A hefty $20,000. Skip the intro video. *6830 N. Federal Hwy. (U.S. 1), Boca Raton. (561) 997-2575;* www.sports immortals.com

JUST FOR FUN

Bill Baggs Cape Florida State Recreation Area ★★/$

Your young swimmers will take great delight in the wide sandy beaches and relatively shallow waters, while the family anglers can dangle from eight fishing platforms along Biscayne Bay—some of the best shoreline fishing around. If you want some real exercise, stop at the bike station near the Lighthouse and rent a bike, tandem, tricycle, or even quadracycle limo (it holds eight) for a workout through the park's numerous bike paths. The two restaurants—the Lighthouse Café and Boater's Café (in No Name Harbor)—offer the same menu and mission: good food at reasonable prices. From hot dogs to salmon, you can't go wrong. *1200 S. Crandon Blvd., Key Biscayne. (305) 361-5811.*

Boomers Dania Beach ★★★/$-$$

Imagine an amusement park that stays open nearly 24 hours a day, featuring a jam-packed arcade, a gut-wrenching roller coaster, and batting cages galore. It's your 10-year-old kid's dream come true! For the younger set there are bumper boats and cars, a soft playground, plus five miniature-golf courses (check out the castle and old woman in the shoe) to entertain your golf enthusiasts. Boomers has tons of racecar driving options for all ages and abilities. Height, weight, and age restrictions may apply and vary, depending on the activity. Multiple locations. *1801 N.W. First St., Dania Beach. (954) 921-1411.*

Butterfly World ★★★/$$

Surefire, relaxing relief from the inevitable vacation overload awaits at Butterfly World, 10 miles north of Ft. Lauderdale in Tradewinds Park. You'll marvel at the brilliant blues, shocking yellows, and exotic fragrances that your family will encounter in the five aviaries. Although the Tropical Rainforest is the epicenter of activity (home to more than 5,000 butterflies), don't miss the emergence displays where real butterflies come out of their cocoons right under your kids' fascinated gaze. *3600 W. Sample Rd., Coconut Creek. (954) 977-4400;* www.butterflyworld.com

Crandon Park
FamilyFun ★★★/$

This Key Biscayne park features one of the widest beaches around, which is a good thing since the place is wildly popular among locals and tourists. Park your car in the south beach lot, don your flip-flops, and make your way around the sea of shaded picnic tables until you reach the real reason you came here: the ocean. The water here is calm enough for both older and younger kids, and lifeguards are on duty year round. Youngsters can take a break with a romp in the playground or ride the carousel (seasonal), both located at the southernmost end of the park. A snack bar is conveniently located near the play area. *4000 Crandon Blvd., Key Biscayne. (305) 361-5421.*

Island Queen Cruises
★/$$

For your starstruck crew, check out Millionaires Row, a 90-minute peek into the lifestyles of Miami's rich and famous, aboard one of the Island Queen's Coast Guard-certified cabin cruisers. Sail past mega-mansions belonging to such sizzling stars as Gloria Estefan and Oprah Winfrey while satisfying hunger pangs at the onboard snack bar: ice cream, chips, and soda. Sightseeing excursions depart from Bayside Marketplace in Downtown Miami every hour beginning at 11 A.M. Remember to pack the sunscreen and a sweater, depending on time of day and year. *401 Biscayne Blvd., Miami. (305) 379-5119.*

John D. MacArthur Beach State Park
★★★★/Free

Whether you're looking to swim, fish, picnic, or even snorkel along the

A Few Hours with Mother Nature

The Palm Beach area plays host to a number of outdoor venues where families get a really close look at the wonders of Mother Nature. For instance, the Marinelife Center (Free; 14200 U.S. Hwy. 1, Loggerhead Park, Juno Beach; 561/627-8289), on the ocean in Juno Beach is a nonprofit education and conservation center that houses a variety of exhibits, mostly related to sea turtles and other coastal creatures. Guided turtle walks happen nightly on the beach in June and July. Although the one-hour turtle walks are free, advanced registration (as in May) is a must due to their popularity.

Another not-to-miss outdoor experience is a leisurely canoe trip with Canoe Outfitters of Florida ($$; 8900 W. Indiantown Rd., 1 mile west of the Turnpike and I-95, Jupiter; 888/272-1257; 561/746-7053) on the Loxahatchee, the state's only federally designated Wild and Scenic River. Although you can choose from among several full-day and guided tours, the most memorable for families is to rent the canoe for a couple of hours and meander through the river's twists, turns, and tree-lined banks. If it's not too chilly (these animals are more prevalent and active in warm weather and it can get cool in Florida), plan on seeing a few turtles, snakes, and maybe a gator or two along the way.

nearby offshore reefs, this place gets a thumbs-up from nature lovers and sun worshipers. The beach is a prime nesting spot for sea turtles from May to August. Turtle walks, led by in-the-know park rangers, are a cool nighttime activity in June and July—education disguised as fun. *10900 S.R. 703 (AIA), North Palm Beach. (561) 624-6950.*

Lion Country Safari
MUST-SEE FamilyFun ★★★★/$$

Rhinos have the right-of-way at this 500-acre wildlife preserve 15 miles west of West Palm Beach. Recognized as the nation's first drive-through cageless zoo, Lion Country is home to more than 1,000 animals from around the world. Just imagine, an Australian emu staring right through your car window—a good reason to abide by the "keep your windows closed" rule while meandering through the park's seven distinct regions. Count on a roaring good time, especially while in the Gorongosa Reserve, home to a pride of frisky African lions, and the Wankie National Park, full of giraffes, zebras, chimps, and rhinos. An informative cassette tape, available on loan at the front gate, offers interesting tidbits about these residents. Best viewing times: 9:30 A.M. and 4 P.M., during feedings. Park admission also includes guided boat tours, a carousel, miniature golf, a petting zoo, and a reptile park at Safari World Amusement Park, adjacent to the wildlife preserve. *2003 Lion Country Safari Rd., Loxahatchee. (561) 793-1084.; www.lioncountrysafari.com*

Miami Metrozoo
★★★/$

Make sure you've got your sturdy, comfortable walking shoes on when you head to this expansive zoo, just west of the Florida Turnpike in south Miami. With its huge collection of animals spread out over a total of 750 acres, you can count on doing some serious trekking here. If your strategy is to see it all, catch the monorail at station 1 (near the gibbons) and get off at station 4, where the fun and excitement begin as you take in all the sights. Along the way, the giraffes, elephants, and camels are sure to delight, as are the chimps—especially at feeding time. The two o'clock feeding is a hoot (literally!)—watch as the chimps line up along the moat just waiting for a snack to be thrown their way. Another favorite kids' stop is the Australian exhibit, complete with the koala (usually rather stolid in appearance), wallabies (adorable miniature roos), and the star of the show—the warthog (one of the oddest-looking creatures this side of the Mississippi). This place gets an A-plus for its super-friendly and knowledgeable staff. *12400 S.W. 152 St., Miami. (305) 251-0400;* www.metro_dade.com/parks.metrozoo.htm

Miami Seaquarium
MUST-SEE / FamilyFun / MUST-SEE
★★★★/$$$

Whether your pleasure is watching a trio of disco-dancing dolphins or having a game of catch with the frolicking dolphins, you're sure to satisfy it at this popular Miami institution on Key Biscayne. Although Lolita, the show-stopping killer whale, may be the centerpiece here (a look at true bonding between animal and trainer), don't miss the Top Deck Dolphin Show. The show's smaller tank and mini stadium allow your kids to see these frisky mammals up close—some of them appear to be straight out of a disco era when their favorite high-energy song of the moment is blasted through the pavilion's sound system. **NOTE:** The Top Deck Dolphin extravaganza is a standing show (sorry, no cushy seats), and you can almost count on getting wet. Go for it—you won't be disappointed! Another must-see is the Flipper Dolphin Show, in the actual lagoon where the 1960s television show *Flipper* was filmed. It's a great audience participation event; performers frequently call for a few youngsters to join the trainers on stage. Your wanna-be animal trainers may want to volunteer—try sitting front row, far right, for a crack at celebrity status. *4400 Rickenbacker Cswy., Miami. (305) 361-5705.*

Palm Beach Zoo at Dreher Park
★★★/$

Small and intimate, this zoo at Dreher Park is in the middle of a multimillion-dollar expansion. But don't let the construction keep you away from this kid-friendly spot. Many of the new exhibits—such as Tiger Falls and the otter display—are open. And, although your old favorites are still here, they may have shifted a bit during the expansion. Your kids won't want to miss the animal contact area, which is a traditional petting section with goats, sheep, rabbits, miniature horses, and more. For an added weekend bonus, zoo docents host animal encounters, allowing visitors to see and even touch some intriguing creatures. Another exciting area is the Florida exhibit, which includes a timeline from the early 1900s to the present that reveals how Florida's growth and development has affected the state's ecosystem. *1301 Summit Blvd., West Palm Beach. (561) 533-0887;* www.palmbeachzoo.org

FamilyFun GAME

Crazy Menu

On a paper restaurant menu, take turns crossing out key words. Then have your kids read aloud the new and often grotesque combinations they've created. Anyone for Pepperoni Cake with Strawberry Lettuce?

Parrot Jungle
★★★/$$

This place is for the birds . . . and monkeys, and alligators, and flamingos and more. True to the jungle's name, birds are the main attraction here. Whether it's red fronted, white fish, or slender billed, you're sure to find it among the park's more than 1,200 winged residents. Check out the Trained Parrot and Creatures in the Night shows: your kids won't believe their eyes—or ears—at the sight of creepy tarantulas and the sound of opera-singing parrots. The Primate Encounter show is also fun and educational, thanks to the friendly trainers who share their knowledge in language that everyone can understand. Next to the monkey area is a great playground (especially for kids under 6), plus a petting zoo and snack bar. Don't leave before you've seen the Dragon and Monsters show, featuring the rare albino alligator—one of only a handful in the United States. **NOTE:** Use caution when allowing your kids to feed the birds (in rare instances the birds have been known to take a nip out of their feeders—not their feeders' food). *11000 S.W. 57th Ave., Miami. (305) 666-7834; www.parrotjungle.com*

Rapids Water Park
★★★/$$$

From the mild to the wild, kids of all ages will go bonkers over the oceans of fun at this 12-acre water park in Palm Beach County. Your preteens will head straight for the Tubin' Tornadoes, which feature 1,000-foot tunnels of dark twists and turns on a single or double tube. (The double tube is great for those wanna-be daredevils who still need a safety blanket—aka Mom or Dad—every once in a while.) Body Blasters, another fave among the more accomplished water park aficionados, offers dips, curves, and twists much like the Tubin' Tornadoes, but this time there's no tube or partner to depend on. Yikes! Moderate thrill seekers will spend hours at the Water Flumes area—four rides that serve up a blast around every turn and loop of the 1,600-foot course. Your young fish will be in their element at Splish Splash Lagoon (slides, forts, cannons, floating swamp animals), Lazy River (a quarter-mile of waterfalls, fountains, just plain easy floating), and the always-popular Big Surf (a megapool with six-foot waves). The park has done a nice job infusing the tropical landscaping with the megatubes and tunnels. Open March through September. *6566 N. Military Trail, West Palm Beach. (561) 848-6277;* www.rapids waterpark.com

Topeekeegee Yugnee (T.Y.) Park
★★/$

Your kids will have a tough time deciding what they like best at this neighborhood park in Broward County. Whether you're up for meandering around the 40-acre lake in paddleboats (let your 12-year-old do the steering) or whizzing down one of the super slides at Castaway Island water playground (lots of lounge chairs for Mom and Dad if you arrive early), this park offers supercharged fun for the entire family. Whispering Pines, the on-site campground, has 60 RV and tent sites for a cheap, comfy sleep. *3300 N. Park Rd., Hollywood. (954) 985-1980.* www,co.broward.fl.us/pri02200.htm

Tropical Fun Center
★/$$

On your way down to the Keys, give your kids a treat and stop at this small but fun family-oriented outdoor amusement center on U.S. 1, just north of Homestead. The soft playground amuses kids 5 and under while the rest of the gang goes for the go-cart track, 18-hole miniature-golf course (challenging even for mini duffers), and an innovative paintball field for the nearly teens and older. If you don't have much time, skip the indoor arcade. *27201 S. Dixie Hwy., Naranja. (305) 246-3731.* www.tropicalfuncenter.com

Venetian Pool ★★/$

Formed from a coral rock quarry in 1923, Venetian's 820,000-gallon pool is fed with cool spring water (74-76 degrees) daily, making it the perfect spot to chill out for a couple of hours with the family. If your kids are ho-hum, expecting to find a run-of-the-mill public pool, they're in for a pleasant surprise. Venetian has waterfalls, coral caves, and grottoes set amid breathtaking flora and architecture. *2701 DeSoto Blvd., Coral Gables. (305) 460-5356.*

BUNKING DOWN

Boca Raton Resort & Club
★★★★/$$-$$$

Expect your kids to be pampered and treated like royalty at this 356-acre waterfront property in ritzy Boca Raton. (Speaking of pampered, this resort even offers a special Boca Baby menu for tots 3 and under.) Its Camp Boca program (fee) offers an action-packed lineup of wild and crazy activities. For your 3- to 5-year-olds, there's Boca Tots, which has them doing pudding painting, going on butterfly hunts, and taking part in other novel activities. Art (the edible kind), scavenger hunts, and manners seminars are just a few of the items that take center stage for children ages 6 to 11. The resort is big on family activities—witness its jam-packed array of get-togethers like Old Fashioned Family Ice-Cream Sundays and Sun-Fun catamaran cruises—many of which are free. The resort offers various choices for comfy lodging based on your lifestyle—and your budget. *501 E. Camino Real, Boca Raton. (800) 327-0101; (561) 447-3000;* www.bocaresort.com

Doral Golf Resort and Spa
★★★★/$$-$$$$

If your idea of the perfect vacation is a luxury resort, then this prestigious place is for you. Doral gives you the usual golf, tennis, aquatics, and spa facilities that all posh resorts have; what sets it apart is the special summer children's program that makes it an excellent family destination. At Camp Doral (fee), your kids will have fun from sunrise to sunset. They'll play sports (basketball, golf, and tennis), and go on scavenger hunts, compete in putting and sand castle contests, play poolside bingo, and team with other kids in tug-of-war and boat-building contests (yep, boat building). The Blue Mountain Waterslide is sure to please everybody. *4400 N.W. 87th Ave., Miami. (800) 713-6725;* www.doralgolf.com

Hampton Inn ★/$$

You won't find a super kids' program or warm, sandy beach at this property. Instead you'll enjoy a great location (one block off U.S. 1 at the

---

DAY TRIP
Charge In, Sail Out

Less than an hour's drive north of the Palm Beaches takes your family to a power plant worth plugging into. Florida Power and Light does a first-rate job of weaving entertainment into education at its hands-on energy center at the St. Lucie Nuclear Power Plant (free; *6501 South Ocean Dr. on Hutchinson Island, AIA. near Ft. Pierce; 877/375-4386; 561/ 468-4111*). Best suited for kids ages 8 and up, Energy Encounter has more than 30 interactive displays on the 3-E's—energy, electricity, and the environment, not to mention nuclear power. Through touch-screen computer games and other activities, including a treasure hunt and a nature trail, the entire family will definitely get a charge out of this experience. Open 10 A.M. to 4 P.M. every day but Saturday.

Fun and learning continue another 14 miles north at the Harbor Branch Oceanographic Institution (*5600 U.S. 1 N., Ft. Pierce; 561/465-2400, ext. 688*), one of the world's leading oceanographic

entrance to happening Coconut Grove and centrally situated for your South Miami stops), substantial savings (affordable hotel rates and dining discounts at some of the coolest restaurants in the Grove), and a pool and kid-friendly continental breakfast. *2800 S.W. Terrace, Coconut Grove. (800) 426-7866; (305) 448-2800*; www.hamptoninn.com

Jonathan Dickinson State Park ★★★★/$

Whether your fancy is camping, hiking, fishing, birding, horseback riding, or just plain "chilling," this humongous park is the place to be. Your kids will get a kick out of the ranger-guided tour of Trapper Nelson's 1930s pioneer homesite and a boat tour of the Loxahatchee River, the state's only Wild and Scenic River. You can choose from among 135 tent and RV campsites—45 near the river, another 90 in heavily shaded Pine Grove. Many of the sites offer essentials like water, electrical hookup, grill, and picnic table; showers and bathrooms are nearby. If you're looking for a tad more comfort, try the park's basic yet comfy cabins with kitchenettes. Sorry, kids—cabins lack TV, radio, and phone. A concessionaire sells camping supplies, food, and soft drinks. *16450 S.E. Federal Hwy., Hobe Sound. (561) 546-2771.*

Lion Country Safari KOA Campground ★★/$

Although it may take a little longer to get the kids to sleep (expect to hear lions roar, cranes call, and gibbons

research organizations. Although its primary focus is the exploration of the earth's oceans, estuaries, and coastal regions, it also offers tours of its facility (by bus) and local wildlife (by boat). The 90-minute cruise around the Indian River Lagoon is a favorite among families. While aboard the covered pontoon cruiser, see who's first to spot a dolphin or a pelican, or maybe even a stingray or bald eagle. Don't forget sunscreen and a light jacket (depending on the time of the year). Boat tours depart at 1 and 3 P.M. Tuesday through Sunday. Among the popular and most intriguing stops on the bus tour is exploring one of the submersibles. Very cool!

How about dinner at Disney—it's less than 20 miles north of Harbor Branch at Disney's Vero Beach Resort ($$; *9250 Island Grove Terrace, Vero Beach; 561/234-2000*). Enjoy a tasty pizza or loaded grilled cheese from Shutters Restaurant, a casual eatery just perfect for families. From many of the tables you get a great view of Disney's magical chefs preparing their culinary masterpieces. What an absolutely perfect way to end a day.

FamilyFun **VACATION GUIDE**

whoop), the unique experience is well worth it when your family overnights at this KOA campground adjacent to Lion Country Safari. Tents and RVs are welcome, or you can rent one of the four log cabins (shared bathroom facilities). Swimming pool, recreation facilities, and a general store are all on site. *2003 Lion Country Safari Rd., Loxahatchee. (561) 793-9797.*

Radisson Palm Beach Shores Resort
★★★/$$

An awesome beach, cool pool, and action-packed kid's program (fee) are the highlights of this all-suite resort on Singer Island. From building sand castles to face painting, the Beach Buddies Club serves up a bucket-full of hands-on activities for kids 3 to 12. *181 Ocean Ave., Palm Beach Shores. (561) 863-4000;* www.radisson.com

Sheraton Yankee Trader/ Sheraton Yankee Clipper
★★★/$-$$

These sister hotels are a hit with families—they've thought of everything, even enclosed skywalks linking them to the beach so that you don't have to worry about little ones crossing busy A1A traffic. The supervised kids' programs are creative and hands-on, and many of the activities are free. The Clipper offers some guest rooms directly on the beach. Trader: *321 N. Atlantic Blvd. (A1A), Ft. Lauderdale. (800) 958-5551; (954) 467-1111*; Clipper: *1140 Seabreeze Blvd. (A1A), Ft. Lauderdale. (800) 958-5551; (954) 524-5551;* www.sheraton.com

Sonesta Beach Resort
★★★★/$$-$$$

Once you check in, it's a sure thing your kids (not to mention parents) won't want to leave this lovely resort on one of the best beaches around. Rooms are decorated in rich tones of purple, emerald, and ruby—a perfect fit for your royal princes and princesses. In-room video games (such as PlayStation) challenge your supercreative crew. Granted, rates can be pricey, but you know you're getting your money's worth with special treats like the Just Us Kids program (crafts, visits to the Sea Aquarium, movies, most of them free—except for meals and off-site excursions). All that and more should put this on top of your luxury-lodging list. *350 Ocean Dr., Key Biscayne. (305) 361-2021;* www.sonesta.com

Villas By The Sea ★★★/$-$$

This oceanfront resort is perfect for families looking for just the right amount of action without being in the thick of traffic and crowds. You can choose from among five kinds of lodgings—from clean and comfortable rooms with refrigerators to spacious apartments with full kitchens. There are five heated swimming pools, a kids' playground, beach volleyball, and shuffleboard. A picture-perfect beach and stretch of friendly Atlantic waters will keep your family happy all day long. *4456 El Mar Dr., Lauderdale-By-The-Sea. (800) 247-8963; (954) 772-3550.*

Good Eats

Angelo's Corner Restaurant & Pizzeria
★★★/$

From the super French toast at breakfast to the tasty pizza and pasta for lunch and dinner, Angelo's has been pleasing throngs of beach-going families for years. Along with great food, the setting is perfect for kids: beachfront plus a playground and paddleball courts just a pizza toss away. *200 Garfield St., Hollywood. (954) 923-0679.*

Bubba Gump Shrimp Co.
★★★★/$$

Even if you're in the minority—those who have not seen *Forrest Gump*—you'll still feel at home at this kid-friendly restaurant at Bayside Marketplace in Downtown Miami. Youngsters love the Hubba Bubba fried shrimp, fries, and Jell-O with an Oreo Magic smoothie to wash it all down. Order one helping of the Alabama mud pie—it's enough to feed your whole troop! *401 Biscayne Blvd., Miami. (305) 379-8866;* www.bubbagump.com

Café Tu Tu Tango
★★★/$$

With about 90 percent of the items on the menu designed to be shared and eaten with your fingers, you can bet your kids give a thumbs-up to this artsy, friendly place in Coconut Grove's CocoWalk. Bypass the kid's menu (though it's so distinctive you should ask to see one anyway) and urge your youngsters to share a round of the Cajun chicken egg rolls, beef tenderloin brochettes, or the five-cheese pizza. The tapas-size portions are just right for pint-size appetites. Multiple locations. *3015 Grand Ave., #250, in the Coconut Grove part of Miami. (305) 529-2222.*

La Carreta
★/$

Large portions, quality ingredients, and inexpensive prices have made this chain of Cuban restaurants a Dade County tradition for more than 20 years. Kids go for the Spanish chicken and rice or the Elena Ruz sandwich (cream cheese, roast turkey, and strawberry marmalade). Order any of the custard desserts for an awesome finish. Multiple locations. *12 Crandon Blvd., Key Biscayne. (305) 365-1177.*

Mai-Kai
★★★/$$$

If you want to splurge, this is the perfect place. Not only is the food worlds beyond good (kids devour the sweet—and messy—Captain Cook's ribs), the 45-minute Polynesian Islanders Revue is a real showstopper. Shows are performed twice each night and are free for kids 12 and under. Sunday in the summer the show features a not-to-miss kids' version, complete with Mai-Kai dancers ages 3 to 14. *3599 N. Federal Hwy., Ft. Lauderdale. (954) 563-3272.*

Whoosh!

Hold a shell to your ear and listen to the waves. There's no ocean inside the shell, so what is really making the sound? A popular myth has people thinking that they're listening to their own blood circulating, but that's not it. You're actually listening to the noises occurring around you, but they sound different in the shell. You can hear the same sounds by cupping your hand over your ear. Go ahead—try it!

Miami's Best Pizza
★★★★/$

Just when you thought all pizzas tasted alike, you come across a superior pie like those served at Miami's Best Pizza, near the University of Miami. The pizza (and any topping) is great, and kids get just as much pleasure standing at the window to watch their pizza be kneaded, tossed, dressed, and baked. The place is not easy to spot: Look for it on the east side of U.S. 1, a few blocks north of Shops at Sunset Place. *1514 S. Dixie Hwy., Coral Gables. (305) 666-5931.*

Pete Rose Ballpark Café
★★★/$

Families who love sports: stop here. This family-friendly restaurant just west of the Florida Turnpike, adjacent to the Holiday Inn, is in a league of its own with great food (tasty chicken littles and fries), huge portions, a giant video arcade, and more than 50 television sets carrying primarily sports and lots of them. Some of the booths have individual televisions—avoid them if your kids are fussy eaters. Multiple locations. *1601 N. Congress Ave., Boynton Beach. (561) 732-3333.*

R.J. Gator's
★★/$

It's tough to keep the kids away from this popular eating spot that's located about 15 minutes west of the beach in Jupiter. Although the chicken nuggets are among the favorites, the kids' menu even offers a pint-size salad—and a selection of free baby food. Birthday time? At R.J.'s, make it extraspecial by requesting a pie in the face—it's the in thing. Multiple locations. *6390 Indiantown Rd., Jupiter. (561) 746-9660;* www.rjgators.com

Sailfish Restaurant
★★/$$
If you don't mind waiting for a table, this Intracoastal Waterway eatery is a perfect fit for families. The breakfast, lunch, and dinner menus feature tasty dishes to satisfy every craving. Kid-pleasing entrées include coconut chicken strips, grilled dolphin sandwiches, and basic burgers. Afterward, check out the adjacent marina, home to some megayachts, and the seawall aquarium, which attracts myriad fish native to the South Florida coast. Kids love to feed them. The artsy Sunset Celebration, held every Thursday at the marina, really packs 'em in. *98 Lake Dr., Palm Beach Shores. (561) 842-8449.*

Shula's On the Beach
★★/$$$
This upscale restaurant, located across the beach in the Sheraton Yankee Trader Hotel, is perfect for a special night out with the kids. Although on the expensive side, it's worth every penny. Order the kids the five-ounce filet from their own menu and watch it disappear!

Indoor and patio seating are available. Multiple locations. *321 N. Atlantic Ave., Ft. Lauderdale. (954) 355-4000.*

SOUVENIR HUNTING

Bayside T-Shirts Co.
Looking for a classy souvenir shirt to show off back home? You'll find it at this shop in Downtown Miami's Bayside Marketplace. *401 Biscayne Blvd., Miami. (305) 375-0226.*

Build-a-Bear Workshop
Welcome to teddy bear central where you can stuff, stitch, fluff, and dress your very own bear (or another warm and fuzzy creature) to take with you. Multiple locations. *Gardens Mall, 3101 PGA Blvd., Palm Beach Gardens. (561) 630-7734.*

PLAYMOBIL FunPark
One of the few places on earth where kids are encouraged to test out the toys in the megaplayroom before buying them. Multiple locations. *8031 N. Military Trail, Palm Beach Gardens. (800) 351-8697.*

Sawgrass Mills
With more than 300 retailers to choose from, your troops will find a bargain or two at Sawgrass—the. *12801 W. Sunrise Blvd., in the Sunrise section of Miami. (954) 846-2350.*

The American alligator is known as the king of Everglades National Park.

INTRODUCTION

Florida Keys and the Everglades

FORGET THE BUSTLING CITY of Miami and the magical thrills of Orlando—at least for the moment—and think quiet; think untouched; think laid-back. Welcome to the Florida Keys and Everglades, two of the most unforgettable vacation spots that showcase Mother Nature's finest.

Although Florida's outdoors can be enjoyed by youngsters of all ages, the region is truly appreciated by children ages 8 and older, who have started studying wildlife, ecosystems, marine life, and diverse cultures in school.

If your family vacations in the Florida Keys, you will be rewarded with more than 100 miles of fishing, camping, and snorkeling, plus a few sight-seeing stops along the way. At day's end, order up some fresh seafood and legendary Key lime pie,

THE FamilyFun LIST

Ah-Tah-Thi-Ki Museum and Billy Swamp Safari (page 146)

Bahia Honda State Park (page 148)

Everglades National Park (page 149)

John Pennekamp Coral Reef State Park (page 151)

Key West's Shipwreck Historeum (page 148)

Robbie's (page 151)

Sunset Celebrations (page 152)

Theater of the Sea (page 153)

FamilyFun **VACATION GUIDE**

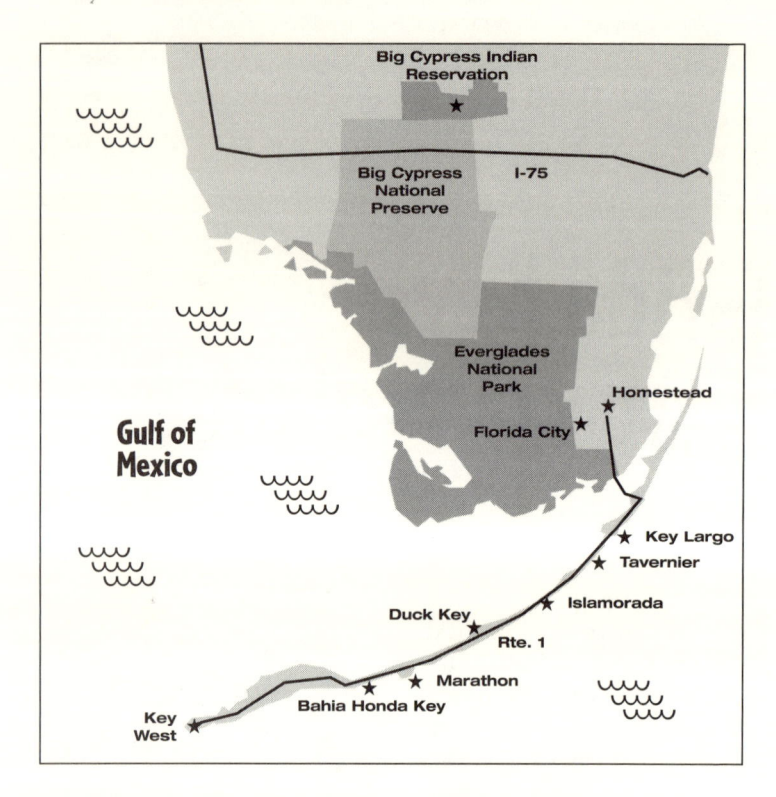

then enjoy some of the most spectacular sunsets this side of paradise.

Backtracking a bit north is Florida's star natural attraction: the Everglades. The 1.5-million-acre Everglades National Park (with Florida City as the southeast entrance and Everglades City as the northwest gateway) comprises most of this vast, unspoiled area, appropriately called River of Grass, whose best-known feature is the long, sharp-bladed sawgrass. Your kids will view the Everglades as an outdoor classroom where another living lesson lies around every corner.

CULTURAL ADVENTURES

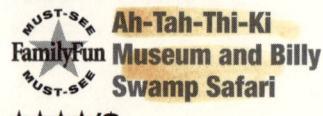

Ah-Tah-Thi-Ki Museum and Billy Swamp Safari
★★★★/$

About halfway between Naples and Ft. Lauderdale, right in the heart of the Big Cypress Reservation, this museum gives families a fascinating look into the life and culture of the Seminole Indians. The museum's curators have taken great care to

146

portray Seminole life accurately in the Florida Everglades and Big Cypress Swamp as it was in the 1800s. Several galleries depict the essence of daily life—religion, agriculture, and transportation, to name a few. Don't miss the 17-minute orientation film, *We Seminoles*, which chronicles the tribe from its early decades to the present. Looking at the five-screen format will leave your kids with a lasting impression. Outside, check out the Living Village, halfway along the 1.5-mile boardwalk. You'll meet some friendly Seminoles eager to show off the lost arts of basket weaving, beading, wood-carving, and canoe-making this a perfect destination for kids ages 8 and up.

After a visit to the Ah-Tah-Thi-Ki Museum, head to Billy Swamp Safari, just three miles down the road from the museum. (Don't worry—everything here is well marked.) If you want to experience all the beauty of the Everglades but don't want to expend lots of energy doing it, try taking the family on a swamp buggy ride aboard one of Billy Swamp Safari's motorized vehicles. It's the perfect way for kids to get a bird's-eye view of panthers, water buffalo, and cypress heads. The ride lasts about an hour and is our "vehicle of choice"—the other choice being sight-seeing on an airboat. (The buggy offers youngsters more to see and less chance of getting cold and wet; the airboat poses a potential danger to wildlife and the environment.) The safari site presents an alligator and snake show every afternoon, but you may want to pass and put your money toward a truly unique sleeping experience: an overnight in a traditional Seminole Indian chickee. The thatch-roofed, dormlike chickees sleep 8 or 12 and come with electricity, but no bathroom (never fear—one is only a few steps away). Two-person chickees are also available—sorry, no electricity with the smaller version. Those families overnighting at Billy Swamp Safari are in for a special treat—Swamp Owl, a local guide, weaves Seminole legend into bedtime stories. If these overnight arrangements sound a bit too primitive for your crew, check out nearby Big Cypress Campground, where you have several

Youth or Truth

In 1513, Spanish explorer Juan Ponce de León was on a quest for the mystical Fountain of Youth. In early April, his boat landed in a lush tropical land. Though he found nothing to prevent gray hairs, Ponce de León was thrilled by his discovery, and named the land after the Spanish Easter holiday, "Feast of Flowers," or "Pascua Florida."

choices for accommodations. The Ah-Tah-Thi-Ki Museum and Billy Swamp Safari are about 90 minutes from Naples and 60 minutes from Ft. Lauderdale. Take I-75 to exit 14. Head north on County Road 833 for 16 miles. The museum is at the intersection of County Rd. 833 and West Boundary Rd. Safari is 3 miles west. *Ah-Tah-Thi-Ki Museum: (863) 902-1113; Billy Swamp Safari: (800) 949-6101; Campground: (800) 437-4102*; www.seminoletribe.com/museum

Key West's Shipwreck Historeum ★★★/$

In the mid-1800s, Key West was known as the richest city in the U.S.A., mainly because of the many treasure-filled ships that sank in and around its harbor. This one-of-a-kind attraction combines actors in period costume, with films, and actual artifacts—all designed to amuse and educate kids of all ages about the real meaning of the infamous phrase "wreck ashore." Children warm up to cranky old Asa Tift, a local wrecker who invites the audience to join his crew about to salvage another unlucky vessel that hit a reef and went down, booty and all. After the show, check out some of the artifacts on display and climb the 100-or-so steps to the top of Key West's only remaining observatory—it's the best view around. *1 Whitehead St., Key West. (305) 292-8990;* www.maxpages.com/floridakeys/shipwreck_historeum

Mel Fisher Maritime Heritage Society Museum ★★/$

Welcome to the world of sunken treasure—a fascinating collection of this famous diver's undersea adventures. Whether you're looking at the shiny gold wedding chain (one day's catch brought in 15 chains) or the awesome gold-and-emerald crucifix (at first thought to be a sardine can; closer scrutiny revealed the cross, chain, and a ring), your family can relive the glory days of Fisher's "Motherlode." If time permits, watch the 20-minute video *Pieces of the Past*, chronicling Fisher's life and the Spanish galleons that so influenced him. Most fun for the 10-and-up crowd. *200 Greene St., Key West. (305) 294-2633;* www.melfisher.org

JUST FOR FUN

Bahia Honda State Park ★★★★/$

Unlike most spots in the Keys, this park has several wide sandy beach areas that are perfect for swimming. Walking the easy-to-follow Silver Palm Nature Trail is a great way for youngsters to burn off some of that stored-up energy. Its half-mile loop takes you through a mangrove, over a dune, and along the beach. The Old Bahia Honda Bridge (left over from Henry Flagler's railroad days), at the southernmost point of the park, is another kid favorite. From the bridge, you get an awesome view of the island, ocean, and bay. The park's concession services offer water-sport activities, including snorkeling, boat tours, and equipment rentals. Reserve well in advance: the park's 80 campsites and six fully furnished cabins are wildly popular. *36850 Overseas Hwy. (U.S. 1). Mile Marker 37, Bahia Honda Key. (800) 326-3521).*

> **EVERGLADES NATIONAL PARK** represents the largest subtropical wilderness in the country. It's also the second-largest national park in the U.S.

Conch Tour Train
★/$$

There's no better way to get an overview of the heritage and funkiness of Key West than on this popular train ride that departs every 30 minutes from Mallory Square. On the 90-minute journey, you'll chug past the city's most legendary—and colorful—sites, including Hemingway House and the "Southernmost Point" (a giant buoy marks this, the most southern point in the continental U.S.)—it's a great photo op. During a summer scorcher, the train's covered seating is a welcome relief. *Mallory Sq., Key West. (800) 868-7482; (305) 294-5161; www.conchtourtrain.com*

Everglades Alligator Farm
★★/$$

A fast and furious airboat ride through the Everglades, live alligator and snake shows, and the chance to even kiss a baby gator (if you so choose) await your family at this working reptile farm that's eight miles from the main entrance of Everglades National Park. Every hour on the hour, professional trainers delight adults and children alike with demonstrations of how early settlers had to wrestle and fight to capture the big gators—a feat definitely not to be tried at home (if you happen to have an alligator in residence). You'll also learn some pretty amazing factoids about these creatures—like baby gators can grow as much as three feet a year! *40351 SW 192 Ave., Homestead. (305) 247-2628; www.everglades.com*

MUST-SEE FamilyFun Everglades National Park
★★★★/$$

Mother Nature's showplace, this park—an ideal introduction to the 8-and-over set—is a real Who's Who

FamilyFun **VACATION GUIDE**

FamilyFun READER'S TIP

Counting the Miles

Last summer, we set out on our first big road trip. To get us through the first long day of driving (500 miles), I strung a long string with a marble-size bead for every 25 miles we would travel. Every fourth bead was a white bead. As we completed each 25 miles, the children moved a bead to the other end of the string. Our children could visualize how far we had to go by how many beads were left. After 100 miles, the white bead was moved, signaling a treat from Mom's Bag. Every day, our kids stayed occupied counting the beads, comparing how far we had come to how far we had to go. Our first-grader added the 25's and informed us often of our progress.

Jane Rice, Maple Grove, Minnesota

of the outdoor world: birds (more than 400 species), mammals (25 species), amphibians and reptiles (60 species), fish (125 species from 45 families), and trees (more than 120 species). Begin your Everglades exploration at the park's main meeting place: the Ernest F. Coe Visitor Center (about 10 miles west of Florida City), where you'll get an excellent overview of the park's ecosystem and its residents. If time permits, check out the 15-minute orientation film and numerous touch-screen encounters. Staff members are superfriendly and eager to advise, distribute literature, and assist with boat tours and overnight accommodations. Depending on your family's interests and enthusiasms, you can spend anywhere from a few hours to a few days exploring the park. Some of the must-see, kid-friendly highlights include: Anhinga Trail, a half-mile elevated boardwalk that passes alligators, turtles, colorful birds, and of course the trail's namesake, the wide-winged anhinga; Long Pine Key Trail, a perfect picnic paradise (biking and camping, too) amid myriad friendly creatures and plants; and Flamingo, located on Florida Bay, about 40 miles south on the main road but well worth the drive for a host of super-charged activities like the two-hour Back Country boat ride. Though airboat rides are not offered anywhere in the park (because of potential danger to wildlife and the environment), you'll find many "cruises" to choose from throughout the vast Everglades area. Two other park entrances offer nature lovers several additional not-to-miss options. Shark Valley (U.S. 41 West, Tamiami Trail) features a 15-mile bike or tram ride culminating in a 60-foot spiral ramp and observation tower. Water—and lots

FLORIDA KEYS AND THE EVERGLADES

of it—is the main kid-friendly ingredient of the park's Gulf Coast area (located a few miles off U.S. 41 at 815 S. Copeland in Everglades City, about 40 miles east of Naples on U.S. 41), where folks on boat tours have been known to spot dolphins, manatees, and other marine life. Throughout the park, expect crowds (although they are generally manageable ones) November through April or May. We can't say this often enough: regardless of the season, insect repellent, bottled water, and sunscreen are essential. Main entrance: *40001 S.R. 9336, Florida City. (305) 242-7700; www.nps.gov/ever/*

Florida Keys Wild Bird Center ★/Free

A quick stop at this bayside rehab center is sure to enrich your family's understanding, appreciation, and compassion for these winged residents, many of whom have been injured by the carelessness of both tourists and residents. A brochure, available at the trailer-type office, guides you through the boardwalk that passes by owls, falcons, hawks, egrets, and ospreys. Be careful when you approach busy pelican row: many of them are perched above and like to leave their mark on just about anything… including visitors! *93600 Overseas Hwy. (U.S. 1), Mile Marker 93.6, Tavernier. (305) 852-4486; www.florida_keys.fl.us/flkeyswildbird.htm.*

MUST-SEE FamilyFun John Pennekamp Coral Reef State Park ★★★★/$

Welcome to the first undersea park in the United States. Sure, there's lots to discover and enjoy while on the mainland—young explorers are in their element on the Mangrove Trail and swimmers take great delight on Cannon Beach—but the park's real treasures lie several miles from shore in the awesome coral reef formations and neighboring marine life. Whether you tour the park by glass-bottom boat, snorkeling, or scuba diving, your kids are in for the time of their lives when they encounter such awesome sites as the Christ of Abyss statue and the wildly colorful fish that live in the Molasses and French Reefs. To arrange boating, scuba, snorkeling, or fishing excursions, visit the park's marina or main concession area, or link up with one of the many experienced outfitters in Key Largo. Make sure you stop at the visitor center, stocked full of fish and plant life; there's also a friendly, knowledgeable staff. Call six months ahead for reservations if you want to stay at one of the park's few campsites (fee). *Mile Marker 102.5, Key Largo. (305) 451-1202; www.pennekamppark.com*

MUST-SEE FamilyFun Robbie's ★★★/$

Sometimes you don't have to break the budget to have a blast. For one of the cheapest and most

FOOTPRINTS IN THE SAND

On beach vacations, sand seems to end up everywhere, especially between the toes. The simple plaster-casting project lets your child capture that sandy barefoot feeling – and a record of his feet.

MATERIALS
- Plaster of paris
- Small bucket
- Freshwater
- 4-inch lengths of string or wire (for hangers, if desired)

Choose a site to cast your molds – the moist, hard-packed sand near (but not too near!) the water's edge works best. Have your child firmly press both feet into the sand. The prints should be about 1 1/2 to 2 inches deep. If your child can't press down that hard, he can use his finger to dig down into the print, following its shape. Mix up the plaster, according to the directions on the package, so that it has a thick, creamy consistency. Pour the wet plaster gently into the footprints.

If you want to make hangers, tie a knot about a half inch from each end of your pieces of string or wire. As the plaster begins to harden, push the knotted ends into the plaster and let dry. After 20 to 25 minutes, gently dig the footprints out of the molds and brush away any excess sand. Set sole-side up in the sun (away from the rising tide) for about an hour to let harden.

bizarre thrills of your vacation, visit this small, full-service marina where pet tarpons rule the waters—guaranteed, you've never seen anything like it. Armed with your bucket of fish food, head out to the dock where nearly 100 of the largest tarpon await your bait, and watch as these monster fish vie for your attention. It's a barrel of laughs as long as the pesky pelicans keep their distance. After your family takes in the feeding frenzy, Robbie's can set you up with all kinds of boat rentals and ecotours through the mangroves and hammock islands of the Florida Bay. *Mile Marker 77.5, Islamorada. (877) 664-8498; (305) 664-9814.* **NOTE:** A second location at *Mile Marker 84.5 (305/664-8070)* arranges fishing charters and party boat fishing for large groups.

Sunset Celebrations
★★★/FREE

Don't miss this, one of the zaniest (and free) street parties on earth. Key West is famous for its sunset celebrations, happening each night at Mallory Square and behind the Hilton Resort. From flame-tossing jugglers and balancing acts to funny felines and crazy street vendors, it's an experience you've got to see to believe. Arrive at least 30 minutes before sundown to take it all in. *Mallory Square (overlooking the harbor) and Hilton Resort (245 Front St.), Key West.*

Theater of the Sea
FamilyFun ★★★/$$

There's no more natural setting than this theater's saltwater lagoon, home to Atlantic bottle-nosed dolphins, California sea lions, sharks, stingrays, and other marine life. Kids love the 30-minute dolphin show—belly buttons, blowholes, and all. The covered stadium offers plenty of shade and dry seating, except for a few splashes to the front-row crew. The trainers always are looking for volunteers to lend a helping hand: The closer you sit to the ship, the more likely your chances of being chosen. Check out the sea lion show for a humorous glimpse into the habits of these adorable mammals. For those families lucky enough to have a few hours—and bucks ($55 for adults, $33 for children 2 to 12)—to spare, the theater's four-hour dolphin adventure snorkel cruise is the perfect venue to see the real beauty of the Florida Keys, both from the boat and while snorkeling a coral reef. You'll need advance reservations and can rent snorkeling gear. Don't forget your sunscreen—and binoculars! *Mile Marker 84.5, Islamorada. (305) 664-2431;* www.theaterofthesea.com

BUNKING DOWN

Coconut Cove Resort ★/$
Kids delight in having their own small private beach, oceanfront volleyball court, and free use of kayaks while calling this small (11-room) mom-and-pop property home for a couple of days. Rooms are simple and clean and have kitchenettes. *84801 Overseas Hwy. (U.S. 1). Mile Marker 85, Islamorada. (305) 664-0123.*

Flamingo Lodge ★★/$
The Everglades National Park's only hotel-like accommodations, this wildly popular lodge is located on picture-perfect Florida Bay. Although furnishings are modest, all rooms have TVs, and you can rent VCRs and movies. Outside is where it's really happening—kids can boat, bike, swim, and fish. The best time of year to enjoy the surroundings is between December and March, when mosquito levels are at their lowest. Campsites are also available—sorry, no electricity, water, or sewer hookups. *1 Flamingo Lodge Hwy. (at the end of main road; 38 miles from park main entrance), Everglades National Park. (800) 600-3813; (941) 695-3101;* www.flamingolodge.com

FamilyFun TIP

Essentials

The Magellan's catalog (800-962-4943) has inflatable pillows (saving graces on long trips) and a variety of light, durable travel essentials, such as hair dryers, luggage straps, alarms, adapter plugs, and clothing organizers.

FamilyFun VACATION GUIDE

Hawk's Cay Resort
★★★★/$$-$$$

This is one of the few places on earth where it's okay for kids ages 3 to 5 to "make a mess"—it's one of the daily themes of the resort's action-packed Little Pirates activity program. The 6- to 12-year-old crowd will not be disappointed as they indulge in World of Science Day, part of the spectacular lineup of Island Adventure Club activities (there's a charge for both programs) offered by this premier resort located just north of Marathon. Room rates, although on the high end, do offer several options for price-conscious families. Added benefits include a friendly staff, a pirate ship pool for your young mateys, and three types of dolphin interaction programs. *61 Hawk's Cay Blvd., Duck Key. (800) 432-2242; (305) 743-7000;* www.hawkscay.com

Hilton Key West Resort & Marina
★★★/$$-$$$

Although the price tag may be a bit high, this luxury bayfront property is ideally located in the heart of Old Town Key West. The tropical furnishings in the guestrooms add to the friendly, Key West feel. And when you and the kids want to get away from it all, you can do just that on Sunset Key, the Hilton's secluded tropical island, 500 yards across the harbor from the main resort. It's the perfect place for your sun worshipers to catch a few rays—on their own private beach or pool; a super-cool getaway, it's free for kids, with a nominal charge for Mom and Dad. At the end of the day, Sunset Celebrations make this place sizzle. *245 Front St., Key West. (800) 621-2193; (305) 294-4000;* www.hilton.com

Southernmost Motel in the USA
★★/$-$$

Kids can't wait to get back home and tell their friends that they stayed at the end of the earth—well almost. Across the street from the beach, this friendly property has comfortable rooms, two pools, and rental bikes for a leisurely ride down to Mallory Square. *1319 Duval St., Key West. (800) 354-4455; (305) 296-6577;* www.oldtownresorts.com/southernmost1.htm

Westin Beach Resort
★★★/$$

Two pools with cascading waterfalls, a private bayside beach, and a jam-packed Fun Factory daytime and weekend evening kids' program (there's a charge) will more than fill the bill at this Key Largo resort. Inside, the spacious guestrooms feature Nintendo; outdoors, the Westin's unbeatable selection of water sports will keep your youngsters busy for hours. *97000 S. Overseas Hwy. (U.S. 1), Mile Marker 97, Key Largo. (800) 539-5274; (305) 852-5553; www.westin.com*

Good Eats

Blue Heaven ★★★/$$
A few blocks down from the often crowded Mallory Square and nearby environs is a little slice of heaven—Blue Heaven, that is. A handful of friendly roaming roosters and a big 'ol rope with plenty of room to swing make this funky eatery a favorite among families. Order the oversize grilled cheese sandwich on healthful, multigrain bread for lunch. The breakfast menu is also family-friendly: yummy banana bread and a big fruit cup, for example. **NOTE:** Plan to make this a daytime stop; the menu turns pretty eclectic for dinner—unless your youngsters fancy such delicacies as Caribbean barbecue shrimp or Jamaican jerk chicken. *729 Thomas St., Key West. (305) 296-8666.*

Café Tropical of Key West ★★/$
After exploring the gold mine of treasures at Mel Fisher's, stop next door for a delightful lunch at this casual outdoor restaurant right in the heart of Old Town. There's no kids' menu, but the restaurant serves such favorites as grilled cheese, chicken salad sandwiches, and quiche. Mom and Dad can order one of the Caribbean-inspired dishes (tasty mangoes, kiwis, coconuts) or the overstuffed grilled ham and cheese. *218 Whitehead St. #1, Key West. (305) 294-7622.*

Fish House ★★/$$
You know you're in a special place when you open the kids' menu here and find lobster as one of the children's dinner selections. For the not so daring, order up the southern

---

WHAT IS AUTHENTIC "FLORIDA CUISINE"?

Florida cooks draw inspiration from their Cuban, Caribbean, and South American neighbors, as well as from the Greek communities in Florida. But any dish can have a Floridian flavor when you sauté chicken or vegetables with orange slices, or if you add orange juice to a marinade.

fried chicken or barbecued ribs for a delectable meal. *102401 Overseas Hwy. (U.S. 1). Mile Marker 102.4, Key Largo. (305) 451-4665; www.fishhouse.com*

Flamingo Restaurant & Buttonwood Café
★★★/$-$$

These casual eateries have the distinction of being the only two restaurants on-site at Everglades National Park. Both are at the park's southernmost point, on the grounds of Flamingo Lodge, with awesome views of Florida Bay. The food's good, too, with the Buttonwood serving pizza and sandwiches and the Flamingo a more extensive menu three meals a day. *1 Flamingo Lodge Hwy., Everglades National Park. (941) 695-3101.*

The Key to Limes

What's the difference between a regular lime and a Key lime? Key limes, formally known as *Citrus aurantifolia Swingle*, are smaller than their regular—or Persian—counterparts. The Ping Pong- to golf-ball-sized fruits also have smoother peels that are lighter in color. The strong aroma and flavor of the Key lime makes it popular for cooking, especially for making the famous local pies.

Islamorada Fish Company
★★★★/$$

Come hungry to this fun eatery: the portions are huge; even the kids may have trouble finishing their tasty fish fingers, fries, and applesauce. An outdoor table right on the bay provides the perfect setting for youngsters to read and complete their fun—and educational—kids' menu. Multiple locations. *81532 Overseas Hwy. (U.S. 1), Islamorada. (305) 664-9271.*

Leigh Anne's Coffee House
★★★★/$-$$

Your family is made to feel right at home at this casual eatery, thanks to the friendly staff and freshly prepared goodies like the homemade bagels and cinnamon rolls—a perfect way to start the day. Don't be confused by its breakfast-y name: This place doesn't close up when the sun goes down. Dinners are great here, too—especially the kid-friendly specials, like spaghetti, lasagna, and focaccia (Italian flat bread) with your choice of toppings. *7537 Overseas Hwy. (U.S. 1). Mile Marker 51, Marathon. (305) 743-2001.*

Sundowner's
★★★★/$$

A gorgeous spot to take in the sunset, the place offers some of the best casual waterfront dining around. Your kids can literally dangle their feet in the bay while waiting for an order of yummy fried fish, steak, or pasta. Okay, there's grilled cheese and chicken fingers, too! *Mile Marker 103.9, Key Largo. (305) 451-4502.*

Souvenir Hunting

The Blue Cat
Animal lovers—especially cat and dog owners—will get a kick out of this pet-inspired gift shop located in the Clinton Square Market. *291 Front St., Key West. (305) 293-9339.*

Caribbean Adventures
Plenty of cool toys, including compact travel games for the trip home, will keep your kids busy for days. *408 Greene St., Key West. (305) 296-5666.*

Key West Kite Co.
From stunt kites to flying toys, this shop is "kite central" for the beginner as well as the seasoned kite-meister. *409 Greene St., Key West. (305) 296-2535;* www.shopfloridakeys.com/kites

The Shell Man
Whether your kids are searching for a special shell like the Mexican Lion's Paw or are content with a bag of shells to search through, you'll find what they want here. Multiple locations. *Mile Marker 106, Key Largo. (305) 451-0767;* www.theshellman.com

Conches and whelks and scallops.
Oh, my! See how many you can find at Bowmans Beach.

INTRODUCTION

Southwest Florida

SOUTHWEST FLORIDA, consisting of Ft. Myers, Sanibel/Captiva, and Naples, plus a few treasures in between, is the smallest vacation area—based on miles covered—in this guidebook's Florida section. Packed within, though, are some unforgettable family destinations waiting to be explored—and given its compact size (less than 50 miles separate the most southern and northern stops)—it's a destination your family can enjoy within a day's drive.

In addition to visiting the popular winter homes of Thomas Edison and Henry Ford, Fort Myers also offers family-friendly beach life on its laid-back stretch of some 15 miles of powdery sand and surf. History records that the explorer Ponce de León passed through this area in the early 1500s.

Families return year after year for the lazy life of Sanibel and Captiva islands. Alert your kids that they won't find roller coasters or an

THE FamilyFun LIST
MUST-SEE

Bowmans Beach (page 161)

Caribbean Gardens (page 162)

Edison-Ford Winter Estates (page 161)

J.N. "Ding" Darling National Wildlife Refuge (page 163)

King Richard's Medieval Family Fun Park (page 163)

Teddy Bear Museum of Naples (page 161)

FamilyFun VACATION GUIDE

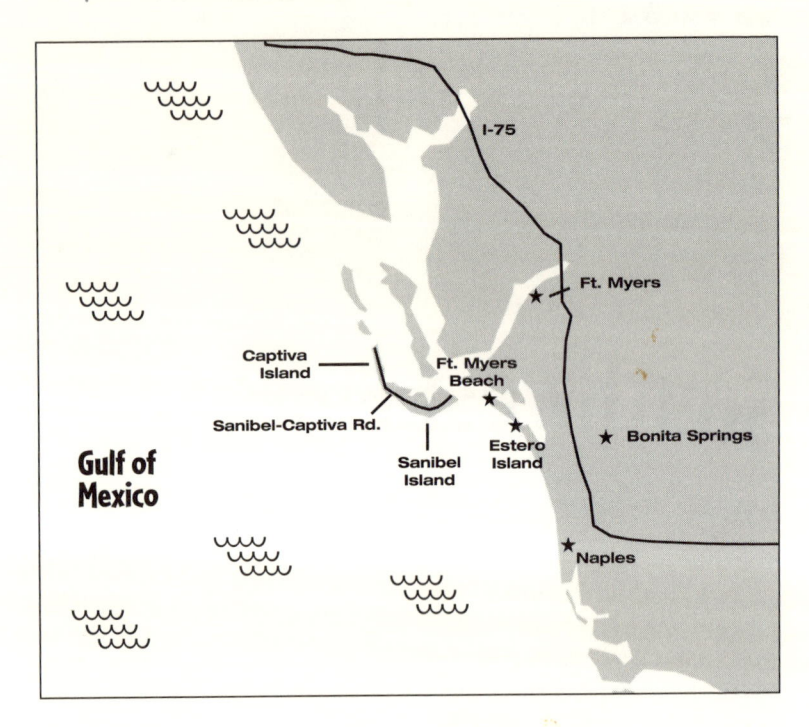

overload of fast-food restaurants on these sister islands. Instead, get them psyched for some spectacular shelling, wildlife watching, and funtastic fishing. Some families also report that several of the resorts' children's programs have produced strong friendships that live far beyond the last good-bye hug.

In upscale Naples, you'll find gorgeous homes, sophisticated shopping, and a museum that honors the world's third-most-collectible item: teddy bears. Even if your family's not into golfing (Naples has been dubbed the Golf Capital of America), you'll find plenty of other things to do for a few days of good times.

CULTURAL ADVENTURES

Bailey-Matthews Shell Museum ★★/$

Some reports put the beaches of Captiva and Sanibel as among the best shelling beaches around; that said, a stop at this museum is a must during your island visit. The half-hour educational program (offered four times a day) is a good introduction to conchology, and presented so that kids 6 and up will understand. Make sure you check out the learning center area, which

SOUTHWEST FLORIDA

is designed just for kids and houses many live shells. More than likely your children won't go away empty-handed, as small prizes are awarded for correctly identifying certain shells. *3075 Sanibel-Captiva Rd., Sanibel Island. (941) 395-2233;* www.westwindinn.com/bm_shell.htm

Edison-Ford Winter Estates ★★★★/$$

The hour-and-a-half guided tour of these homes focuses less on the awesome accomplishments of these two geniuses (that comes after the tour) and more on how they lived as Florida snowbirds. You'll tour the gorgeous gardens (don't miss the sausage tree), Edison's office, swimming pool, main house and guest quarters, then pass Ford's garage housing three Model T's and one Model A, and on to Ford's seasonal home. Along the way, friendly tour guides offer humorous insights into these two families. The last stop is Edison's laboratory, where he spent endless hours researching the properties of goldenrod as a source for natural rubber. Kids love this last stop because the lab is so real—beakers, bulbs, and all. Don't leave until you've explored the adjoining museum that's filled with Edison artifacts. Curious kids ages 8 to 12 will be fascinated. *2350 McGregor Blvd., Ft. Myers. (941) 334-3614.*

Teddy Bear Museum of Naples ★★★★/$

A special stop for that special little girl in your family, this treasure of a place displays more than 4,000 cuddly animals set in delightful vignettes. There's even a "li-beary" where your kids can spend some quiet time with their favorite bear books while Mom explores the extensive collection of antique figures. It's not easy to find (the museum is tucked behind some large retail stores), but persevere—it's well worth it. *2511 Pine Ridge Rd., Naples. (941) 598-2711.*

JUST FOR FUN

Bowmans Beach ★★★★/Free

Don't expect lots of restaurants, live music, and concessionaires at this beach. Just an extra-wide expanse of soft, sugary-fine sand, a perfect spot for your kids to run around—that is, in the rare moments when they're not swimming in the

Popcorn-banana Munch Mix

Measure 6 cups cheddar popcorn; 1 to 2 cups banana chips, broken into small pieces; 2 cups dry-roasted peanuts; 1 to 2 cups sweetened, dried cranberries into a big bowl. Stir well, then dig in. Serves about 4 to 6 kids.

Who Lives There?

Travel exposes your family to new places and different styles of living. As you pass a lime-green house with a yard full of plastic pink flamingos and a working waterwheel, it's hard not to wonder what type of family lives there. Why not run with that? Suggest that your kids speculate on who lives inside the houses you pass and what they might be doing at that moment. Perhaps the people in the green house invented mint chocolate chip ice cream. Perhaps they have seven children and three pets— a Lhasa apso, an iguana, and a Persian cat wearing a pink leather collar. If it's dinnertime, perhaps they're gathered around the kitchen table enjoying tuna casserole topped with potato chips that will be followed by a dessert of cherries flambé. They'll be playing a game of Pictionary after dinner and, well, you get the idea.

---

warm gulf waters. Bowmans is also a good shelling spot, so don't forget your bucket. There are on-site grills, picnic tables, showers, and rest rooms; metered parking only. *North end of Sanibel-Captiva Rd.*

MUST-SEE FamilyFun ★★★★/$$ Caribbean Gardens

MUST-SEE It's hard to tell who's the star at this legendary Naples attraction—is it the hundreds of towering trees and bushes (tons of oaks, bamboos, palms, ferns, and a larger-than-life fig, among others) that seem to be everywhere or the rare animals that live here? Decide for yourself when you bring the family. Several must-sees during your visit include Safari Canyon, a half-hour multimedia experience where live animals team up with some of the most incredible video footage to teach guests about the world's diverse animal kingdom; Primate Expedition Cruise, a 15-minute ride aboard a covered catamaran to view lemurs, monkeys, and apes; and Scales and Tails Show, 30 minutes of nonstop laughs, featuring some amazing creatures (including the humorous host). Expect lots of audience interaction during this program, including a chance to win a lion whisker or porcupine hair. Sit in the front row for a chance to pet the animals as they're paraded before the audience. *1590 Goodlette-Frank Rd., Naples; (941) 262-5409;* www.caribbeangardens.com

SOUTHWEST FLORIDA

Everglades Wonder Gardens
★★/$

Texas isn't the only place where they grow 'em big in the United States. Check out Everglades Wonder Gardens in Bonita Springs (sandwiched between Ft. Myers and Naples), home to Big Joe, the world's largest crocodile, who weighs in at a trim 1,000-plus pounds. Although this place looks a little worn around the edges—you would too if you'd been hosting visitors since 1936—it's still a great place for families to get a glimpse of more than 2,000 species of native wildlife and plants, even a Mexican bald eagle—bad toupee and all! Friendly tour guides who really know their stuff offer continuous tours throughout the day. Kids can even pet a gator at no extra charge. Skip the natural history museum adjacent to the gift shop. *27180 Old U.S. 41, Bonita Springs; (941) 992-2591.*

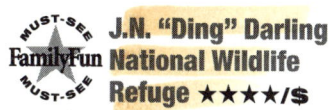

MUST-SEE FamilyFun J.N. "Ding" Darling National Wildlife Refuge ★★★★/$

Your kids will probably describe these more than 6,300 acres of diverse wildlife as awesome—and they'll be right. Named after the Pulitzer Prize–winning political cartoonist whose lifelong passion was environmental conservation, the refuge is located halfway between the two ends of Sanibel Island. Start your exploration at the visitor information center, chock-full of interesting stuff and interactive displays that whet your family's appetite for what's ahead on the five-mile main trail. (Don't miss the lifelike alligator and crocodile display—it's one of the best around for depicting the differences between these reptiles.) Although you can drive, bike, or walk some (or all) of the trail, families also opt for the two-hour tram tour (daily at 10:30 A.M. and 1:30 P.M.) through this wildlife wonderland. The knowledgeable guides answer questions and identify more than 230 species of birds, not to mention mudflats, mangroves, and mammals. Reservations are suggested *(941)472-8900). 1 Wildlife Dr., Sanibel; (941) 472-1100.*

MUST-SEE FamilyFun King Richard's Medieval Family Fun Park ★★★★/$$

Expect your 7-and-unders to tell their friends this place was amazing. Although there's a batting cage, go-carts, and full-blown arcade for the preteens, King Richard's really caters to the younger set with rides like the Flying Dragon mini roller coaster, bumper boats, and free-fall (a super-tame bungee ride that even your 5-year-old will enjoy). Rounding out the fun are junior go-carts, an antique Ferris wheel, and a super-charged water playground. Remember a change of clothes and lots of sunscreen. If you plan on spending more than an hour or two here, the

FamilyFun VACATION GUIDE

daily pass is the best value. *6780 N. Airport-Pulling Rd., Naples. (941) 598-2042.*

Lovers Key State Recreation Area
★★★/$

Take a day and really relax at this four-islands-in-one, now a gigantic family-friendly park between Ft. Myers Beach and Bonita Beach. If you're looking to swim and sun, hop on the free tram and head for the south beach. Although it's narrow, there's plenty of room to sun, swim, and explore. Don't forget your binoculars so the kids can watch for dolphins and manatees. The nearby hammock and waterways offer your bird-meisters some of the best viewing around. Trout, sea bass, and sheepshead are just a sampling of some of the fish you'll find in the park's canals and lagoons. Rent your gear from the supercongenial folks at the Kayak Shack at the north parking area. *8700 Estero Blvd., Ft. Myers Beach. (941) 463-4588;* www.absolutelyflorida.com/parks/loverskey/loverskey.htm

BUNKING DOWN

Best Western Pink Shell Beach Resort
★★★★/$$-$$$

This slice of paradise—with sleeping quarters—is at the northernmost end of Ft. Myers Beach's main drag. Accommodations range from standard hotel rooms to homey beachfront cottages. Your kids will love the property's recreation program (fee), which offers weekday fun-filled water games, environmental activities, and of course, some great beach adventures on its 1,500-foot stretch of sugary sand. *275 Estero Blvd., Estero Island. (800) 237-5786; (941) 463-6181.* www.bestwestern.com

Park Shore Resort
★★★/$-$$$

This resort offers affordable apartment-style lodging, plus 13 acres of lush landscaping, boardwalks, waterfall and pool, and fun kids' activities (lots of cool stuff like Mardi Gras bracelets, wacky water balloon fights, popcorn art, and scavenger hunts—and most are free). It's a surefire family favorite. *600 Neopolitan Way, Naples. (800) 548-2077; (941) 263-2222.*

The Registry Resort
★★★★/$$-$$$

From its striking street appeal (expect "wows" from the backseat gang) to its fun and fanciful Camp Registry kids' program (fee), this luxurious property is pricey, but if you *can* splurge, you'll find it's well worth it. In the north end of Naples on 23 acres that front the Gulf of Mexico, the resort has three cool pools, and tennis, plus sailing, windsurfing, canoeing, and kayaking (fees). Your kids will get a kick out of the short tram ride to the beach (free rides offered throughout the day) or enjoy the 15-minute walk along the boardwalk to some of the softest sand around. *475 Seagate Dr., Naples; (941) 597-3232.*

Shalimar Motel
★★/$$-$$$

Take old Florida charm, mix it with down-to-earth rates, kitchen facilities in each unit, a prime gulf-front address, and you have a great place for families to call their home away from home. Don't expect a huge complex with hundreds of rooms—the Shalimar property only has 33 cottages and efficiencies, a good size for 10-year-olds to explore on their own, knowing the rest of the family is nearby. *2823 W. Gulf Dr., Sanibel Island; (800) 995-1242; (941) 472-1353; www.shalimar.com*

South Seas Resort
★★★★/$$-$$$

A family vacation doesn't get much better than the knock-your-socks-off experience you'll have at this resort at the northernmost tip of Captiva Island. From cottages and beach homes to deluxe hotel rooms and suites, you'll find a place to stay that suits your taste—and your budget. If you want to be in the ideal location for your kids, request accommodations in the north end of the property near the main pool, game room, ice-cream emporium, and the Fun Factory Kid's Club (fee). The program's trademark—"because you can never have enough fun"—is proof positive that South Seas loves kids. *5400 Plantation Rd., Captiva Island. (800) 227-8482; (941) 472-5111; www.southseasplantation.com*

Sundial Beach Resort
★★★★/$$-$$$$

A 450-gallon touch tank, charming bedtime stories, a pen pal club, plus the Fun Factory recreation program (fee) will no doubt put the Sundial at the top of your Sanibel lodging list. To top it off, all units offer fully equipped kitchens, dining and living areas, plus sleeping quarters—lots of running-around room for your tireless troops. Five heated pools and a mile of shell-laden beach offer a sea of splash options. *1451 Middle Gulf Dr., Sanibel Island; (800) 237-4184; (941) 472-4151; www.sundialresort.com*

Good Eats

Bubble Room ★★★★/$$-$$$
Hollywood, Christmas, and an eclectic art gallery join forces on Captiva for one of the most high-energy dining options on the island. From movie stills and windups to trains and Tonka toys, this place is weird, wacky, wonderful—and delicious. Expect portions so large that you're bound to ask for a doggie bag. The kids' menu is more extensive than most, with pizza, ravioli, and even a pint-size prime rib to please young diners. *15001 Captiva Dr., Captiva Island. (941) 472-5558.*

Cheeburger Cheeburger ★★★/$
In the heart of Old Naples's upscale shopping district, this casual hamburger haven dishes out mouthwatering burgers in about any size imaginable. (Its motto is "big is better," so look out!) Top it off with fries and a shake—Oreo and peanut butter cup get our votes. Multiple locations. *505 Fifth Ave., South. Naples; (941) 435-9796; www.cheeburger.com*

Hungry Heron ★★★★/$$
Few restaurants can hold a candle to this local island favorite with more than 275 items on its main menu, nightly all-you-can-eat specials, plus a kids' lineup of nearly 40 mouthwatering dishes, including polka-dot macaroni 'n' cheese (with hot dogs), pizza, and hammy heron (incredible ham-and-cheese melt). With two large-screen TVs tuned in to Disney Channel or Nickelodeon and a treasure chest of trinkets for kids to choose from on the way out, you'll find yourself coming back regularly. Multiple locations. *2330 Palm Ridge Rd., Sanibel. (941) 395-2300; www.hungryheron.com*

Iguana Mia ★★/$$
Hard to miss, the lime-green building is a colorful beacon that beckons hungry families to come inside and sample some tasty dishes from south of the border. The kids' menu offers tacos, enchiladas, and burritos, along with standard fare like grilled cheese, chicken tenders, and peanut butter and jelly. The more adventurous may want to try a build-your-own Mexican pizza or nachos. *28051 S. Tamiami Trail, Bonita Springs. (941) 949-1999.*

Juicy Lucy's ★/$
For a hearty lunch sandwich, swing by Juicy Lucy's and order up a fried chicken or pork-loin sandwich with delicious seasoned fries. Since everything here is takeout, load up and head over to the nearby grounds of the Edison-Ford Winter Estates for a memorable picnic under some of the oldest and most awesome trees around. Early risers may want to

SOUTHWEST FLORIDA

pick up breakfast and eat before touring the estates. Multiple locations. *2725 Cleveland Ave., Ft. Myers. (941) 337-1988.*

Mucky Duck
★★/$$
Boasting prime beachfront property on Captiva Island, this well-established English eatery is the place for a round of traditional fish 'n' chips; your kids will love the chicken fingers or the Mucky Duck super frankfurter or hamburger. More adventurous youngsters may want to try the Scottish-style meat pie. The beach is a great playground for the kids while parents enjoy their dessert. *11546 Andy Rosse La., Captiva Island; (941) 472-3434.*

Riverwalk Fish and Ale House ★★/$$
Peanut butter and jelly never tasted better than it does at this eatery. Located at funky-looking Tin City, a popular waterfront-shopping stop in Old Naples, the menu lists lots of good eats (kids will snarf down the grouper, fried shrimp, or pasta)—with nearly all seats offering a view of the water. If the kids finish before Mom and Dad, they'll enjoy checking out the fish along the restaurant's boardwalk. *Goodlette Rd. and U.S. 41, Naples. (941) 263-2734.*

Strawberrie Corner ★/$
About halfway along the main drag of Ft. Myers Beach is this cute little eatery and ice-cream parlor decorated in a cheery berry motif. It's perfect for a midafternoon cooldown with a cone, cup, shake, or sundae. Or order up a few sandwiches to go (Reubens for grown-ups, PB&J for the kids) and then head a block or so east to the beach. *7205 Estero Blvd., Ft. Myers Beach. (941) 463-1155.*

Souvenir Hunting

MacIntosh Books
Before you go shelling, hiking, or canoeing, stop in this friendly bookstore and pick up a title or two about the wonders you're about to experience. Kids will love the large selection of junior nature books. *2365 Periwinkle Way, Sanibel Island; (941) 472-1447.*

Teddy Bear Museum Gift Shop
From T-shirts and jewelry to purses and postcards, this adorable museum shop has all the bearaphernalia you've ever imagined—maybe more. *2511 Pine Ridge Rd., Naples. (941) 598-2711. www.teddymuseum.com*

FamilyFun TIP

Pit Stops
Six top games to beat the fidgets: leapfrog, four square, spud, tag, Frisbee, wheelbarrow races.

Take a break from the waterskiing shows at the Big Lagoon at Cypress Gardens.

INTRODUCTION

Florida's West Coast

KIDS MAY NOT realize it, but there's more to Florida than Orlando. The west coast of Florida, which includes Tampa Bay, St. Petersburg, Clearwater, and Sarasota, has quickly grown into a favorite vacation spot for many families who are seeking the same fun factor as The City Beautiful (aka Orlando) but without the crowds.

The region offers a wide array of tastes and cultures to experience. You'll notice the Latin influence throughout this coastal area, especially the Cuban culture of Tampa's Ybor City. Just north of Clearwater, your family can step into another land in Tarpon Springs, a small Greek fishing village that seems as though it was picked up in Greece and plunked down in Florida.

This is a beach community, and its wealth of white-sand beaches showcase spectacular sunsets over the Gulf of Mexico. Water is the main element of many of the attractions around here, most of which

THE FamilyFun LIST *MUST-SEE*

Busch Gardens Tampa Bay (page 171)

Captain Memo's Pirate Cruise (page 171)

Cypress Gardens (page 172)

Florida Aquarium (page 173)

Great Explorations (page 170)

Kid City (page 170)

Mote Marine Aquarium (page 174)

Siesta Beach (page 175)

FamilyFun **VACATION GUIDE**

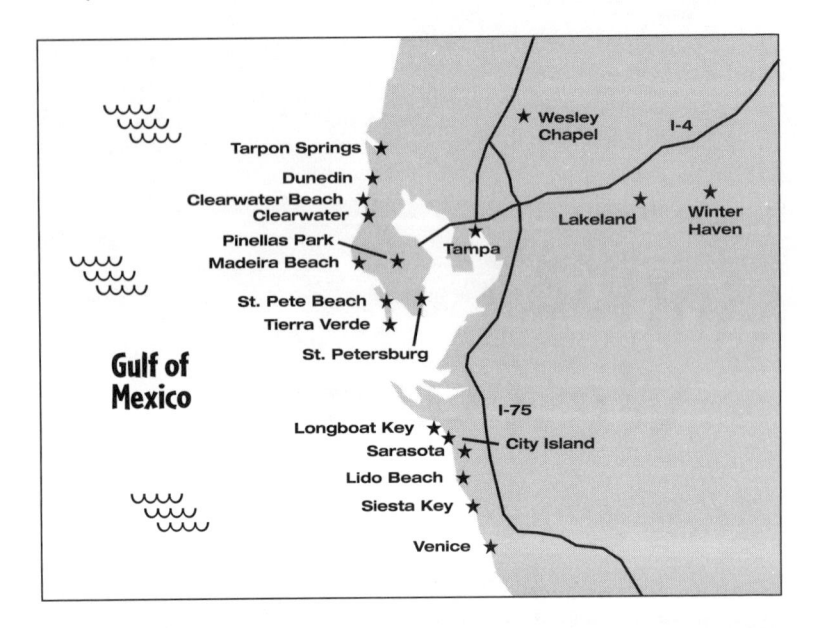

Map showing Florida's West Coast with labeled locations: Tarpon Springs, Dunedin, Clearwater Beach, Clearwater, Pinellas Park, Madeira Beach, St. Pete Beach, Tierra Verde, St. Petersburg, Longboat Key, Sarasota, Lido Beach, Siesta Key, Venice, Wesley Chapel, Tampa, Lakeland, Winter Haven, City Island. Also showing Gulf of Mexico, I-4, I-75.

feature some type of sea life to view, study, and enjoy.

Cultural institutions abound on Florida's West Coast—from theaters and art museums to more family-oriented adventures such as zoos, parks, and children's museums. The region also has its share of theme-park fun at the ever-popular Busch Gardens Tampa Bay.

CULTURAL ADVENTURES

Great Explorations
FamilyFun ★★★★/$$$

This children's museum on the third floor of the touristy St. Pete Pier takes fun and learning to new heights. Kids over 7 will get a bang out of the Touch Tunnel—more than 100 feet of touching, twisting, and turning in total darkness to experience life without eyesight. In the strobelike Dance Prance, kids (preteen girls love this one) can strut their stuff as their movements are colorfully projected for all to see. Kids 6 and under aren't left out—they have their own space in Explore Galore, an enclosed area complete with a fire truck and a safety speed drill to test their emergency readiness. *800 Second Ave. N.E., St. Petersburg; (727) 821-8992.*

Kid City ★★★★/$
FamilyFun Wanna-be doctors, firemen, and librarians will have a ball at Tampa's recently ren-

170

FLORIDA'S WEST COAST

ovated Children's Museum, located right next to the Lowry Park Zoo (see page 174). The perfect spot for your 7-and-under crowd, this hands-on exhibit whets youngsters' appetites about the working world through a dozen venues down miniature Main Street and connecting avenues. Unsure of your future? Kid City even has a career placement center for those looking to find their professional niche. Great place for a picnic, too. *7550 North Blvd., Tampa; (813) 935-8441.*

Museum of Science & Industry ★★★★/$$

A skeleton riding a bicycle and a simulated hurricane ride are just two of the treasures awaiting you at MOSI, the largest science center in the Southeast. Whether your kids are looking to better understand Florida's *weird* climate and weather conditions (don't miss ZAP on the second floor and the hurricane room on the third floor), or exactly how and why the body works (check out the third floor's Amazing You), it's all happening at MOSI. The science center also boasts the state's first IMAX Dome Theater, and is only one of a handful in the world to display two huge articulated dinosaur skeletons—*awesome*! **NOTE:** Because of MOSI's immense size, the layout is a tad confusing. Stick together. On cool days, don't forget a jacket: Some of the exhibits and walkways are outdoors. *4801 E. Fowler Ave., Tampa; (813) 987-6300; www.mosi.org*

JUST FOR FUN

Busch Gardens Tampa Bay ★★★★/$$$$

The place to go when visiting Florida's West Coast. In fact, there's so much to see here that we've devoted an entire section to it! You'll find it on page 180. *3000 E. Busch Blvd., Tampa; (888) 800-5447; (813) 987-5465; www.buschgardens.com*

Captain Memo's Pirate Cruise ★★★★/$$$

Time flies when you're having fun, especially when cruising the Gulf of Mexico aboard Captain Memo's *Pirate's Ransom.* After the ship has

The Real Skinny on SpongeBob

If natural sponges are animals, do they have skeletons? Yes, but their skeletons are softer than a human's and are surrounded by a jelly-like substance. Sponges, like coral, live in colonies in the warm ocean waters. Florida's sponge-harvesting industry in concentrated in the Gulf of Mexico coast and the Keys. For more on sponges, see "It's Greek to Me," page 172.

set sail, kids gather as a group for two hours of treasure hunting and other cool swashbuckling adventures; dancing the limbo and the Macarena for the young and young-at-heart is also part of the entertainment. Frequent dolphin sightings add to the excitement, as do the pirate coins, beads, and souvenir certificates that youngsters get at the end of the cruise. Complimentary free-flowing soft drinks (beer and wine for the adults) are also included. Captain Memo's runs several cruises daily with champagne served on the sunset excursion. Although the bubbly tends to attract an older crowd, the children's program is still a key ingredient. *Clearwater Beach Marina, Clearwater Beach; (727) 446-2587; www.pirateflorida.com*

Caspersen Beach
★★/Free

Known as the Shark's Tooth Capital of the World, Venice is home to Caspersen Beach (about 20 miles south of Sarasota) where you're likely to find some unusual shells and a few petrified treasures that have washed ashore. Before you head to the beach, stop at the local hardware store and pick up a "Florida snow shovel" (about $15 at press time), which makes it a lot easier to sift out the riffraff from the real thing. Let everyone have a turn at lightly raking the shell line for the dark, triangle-shaped teeth that measure about an inch in size. Sorry, sleepyheads, this activity calls for an early start: like 7 A.M. *4100 Harbor Dr. South, Venice.*

Cypress Gardens
★★★★/$$$

We'll whet your appetite for this water-skiing wonderland on page 177.

Dolphin Encounter ★★★/$$

Flipper fans should be sure to take the Dolphin Encounter and Bird Feeding cruise aboard the 125-pas-

---

DAY TRIP
It's Greek to Me

Imagine traveling to Greece without the hassle of a marathon flight, customs, and passports. In fact, if your family is coming from the Clearwater/St. Pete area, you can reach Tarpon Springs, a Mediterranean-like village, in less than 30 minutes. Is it fantasy? Not really. Tarpon Springs is a historic, friendly community surrounded by lakes, bayous, and the Gulf of Mexico. And since the early 1900s, the Greek influence has shaped this area's economy and culture through the rise and fall—and rise again—of the sponge industry. If your kids are thinking "boring," they will quickly change their minds after a half-hour cruise aboard one of St.

FLORIDA'S WEST COAST

senger *Clearwater Express* tour boat. During the 90-minute ride into the Gulf of Mexico, you're bound to see at least one of these popular mammals or your next trip is free, thanks to this operator's high regard for customer satisfaction. Speaking of free, even the bird feed is complimentary! Check out the other crusies the company runs, too. *West end of Clearwater Beach Marina (next to Captain Memo's Pirate Ship), Clearwater Beach; (727) 442-7433.*

Florida Aquarium
MUST-SEE FamilyFun ★★★★/$$

It's nearly impossible for your children to pick a favorite among the sea of possibilities at this aquarium, which is located next to the Port of Tampa. Could it be the free-flying spoonbills and other wildlife that swoop, dip, and navigate the airways? Maybe it's the offshore gallery where moon jellyfish, sharks, stingrays, and barracudas test kids' and parents' knowledge of and skill on the open waters—expect lots of cool hands-on stuff in this area. Add to these treasures the open-tank environment where kids as young as 5 literally come face-to-face with aquarium residents, plus the Frights of the Forest where they'll meet tarantulas, cockroaches, and electric eels. You're sure to get a thumbs-up for this choice. *701 Channelside Dr., Tampa; (813) 273-4000.*

Fort De Soto Park ★★/$

Whether you're looking to swim, hike, bike, or explore, this island park (at the entrance to Tampa Bay) has it all: five different nature trails, two great swimming holes, a fishing pier, an artillery of guns and cannons, and more than 230 fully equipped camp sites. During World War II, the island was used for bombing practice by the pilot who dropped the atomic bomb on Hiroshima. *3500 Pinellas Bayway South, Tierra Verde; (727) 582-2267; http://fortdesoto.com*

Nicholas Boat Line's charters (*693 Dodecanese Blvd.; 727/ 942-6425*), where they can see how hard-hat divers "fish" for sponges. Back on land, visit the **Konger Coral Sea Aquarium** (*850 Dodecanese Blvd.; 727/938-5378*) for an up-close look at some of the Gulf of Mexico's most popular residents. For sustenance, there's no better place to sample authentic Greek cuisine than at **Louis Pappas' Riverside Restaurant** (*10 W. Dodecanese Blvd., 727/ 937-5101*), a local—and probably national—dining legend that's been in the same family since 1925. Before heading back to your hotel, pick up a few souvenirs and gifts at the **Sponge Exchange** (*735 Dodecanese Blvd.; 727/934-9262*), a shopping village with Greek flair, about two blocks west of Pappas'.

Lowry Park Zoo
★★/$

A morning or afternoon at this Tampa attraction, ranked as one of the nation's best midsized zoos, is guaranteed to bring lots of smiles to kids of all ages. On your list of must-sees should be the Asian Domain of the park, where you'll meet sloth bears (as in the hanging-upside-down type), Sumatran tigers, Persian leopards, and a rare Indian rhinoceros. Other must-see attractions include the Florida Manatee and Aquatic Center (huge tanks, humongous residents), Harrell Discovery Center (lots of hands-on stuff here), and the Jungle Carousel Ride (maybe your only chance to ride a giraffe or gorilla). The carousel is great fun for the little ones—and only two bucks per spin. *7530 North Blvd., Tampa; (813) 935-8552; www.lowryparkzoo.com*

Mote Marine Aquarium
FamilyFun MUST-SEE ★★★★/$$

Mote gets an A-plus for training its volunteers to be extra outgoing, especially with the younger set who may not always know what questions to ask when exploring this fascinating aquarium and laboratory. Contact Cove, the hands-on area, holds a series of the most extensive touch tanks around, stocked with horseshoe crabs, a horse conch, and several types of rays. The tanks are designed so that visitors of all heights can reach the creatures. Before calling it a day, check out the marine mammal center in a nearby building that houses most of the research facilities. The massive loggerhead turtles and lovable manatees, Hugh and Buffett, live there, too. If this has piqued your family's interest in sea creatures, take the two-hour cruise of Sarasota and Roberts Bay offered by Sea Life Excursions (941/388-4200). You're sure to get a close-up look at pelicans, herons, egrets, and maybe even a dolphin or manatee, and you'll be surprised to see what the captain may bring up and share with your crew after a few minutes of trolling. Located directly behind the main aquarium. *1600 Ken Thompson Pkwy., City Island/Sarasota; (941) 388-4441; www.mote.org*

Myakka River State Park ★/$

Less than half an hour west of Sarasota is Myakka, one of the largest and most diverse natural areas in Florida. It's all here, whether your kids are up for hiking (more than 40 miles of trails), fishing (plenty of bass and catfish to go around), or discovering (boat rides provide a close-up view of gators, herons, cranes, and other local inhabitants). Stop by the visitors' center so the kids can try some of the great interactive displays. *13207 S.R. 72., Sarasota; (941) 361-6511;* http://myakka.sarasota.fl.us

Siesta Beach
FamilyFun ★★★/Free

Are your kids begging for a day just to hang out at the beach? You can't go wrong at the Siesta Public Beach on Siesta Key near Sarasota. With scores of shaded picnic facilities, several snack stops, equipment rentals, not to mention some of the most powdery soft white sand your pinkies have ever encountered, you'll want to stay for days. *948 Beach Rd., Siesta Key; (941) 346-9916.*

BUNKING DOWN

Colony Beach and Tennis Resort
★★★★/$$$-$$$$

Sure it's pricey, but nearly everything is included in the rate at this all-suite tennis and beach resort on swanky Longboat Key: beach stuff, tennis court time, and family fun like Sundae Socials for your ice-cream fanatics. The awesome (and complimentary) kids' program will have you coming back for more. As for the accommodations, children love the extra playroom in the oversize guest quarters, while parents appreciate the fully equipped kitchenettes—not to mention their own bedroom! *1620 Gulf of Mexico Dr., Longboat Key; (800) 426-5669; (941) 383-6464;* www.colonybeachresort.com

Helmsley Sandcastle Hotel
★★/$$

Two pools, volleyball, sailing lessons, and the Gulf of Mexico await your family at this property on Lido Beach. Comfy guest rooms with refrigerators and complimentary children's activities (weekends) are family pleasers. You're only a short walk to St. Armands Circle, where the cheerful carousel in the park has been delighting youngsters for years. *1540 Ben Franklin Dr., Lido Beach. (800) 225-2181; (941) 388-2181;* www.helmsleyhotels.com

---

SEA SICK?

Dolphins take care of their own. When a dolphin is too sick to swim up to the water's surface to breathe, his fellow dolphins will swim beneath him, and lift him up for every breath.

FamilyFun **VACATION GUIDE**

Holiday Inn Tampa
★/$

Conveniently close to Busch Gardens Tampa Bay is this recently refurbished hotel where many of the rooms have the popular room-within-a-room Kidsuites (partitioned-off play and sleep quarters). After a day of beaches, museums, or whatever, kids have a blast cooling off in the pirate ship pool area, complete with mini slides and cannons. *2701 E. Fowler Ave., Tampa. (813) 971-4710;* www.holidayinncity centre-com

Hilton Clearwater Beach Resort ★★★/$$

Located directly on one of the best sandy white beaches around, this resort has a great lineup of kids' activities through its popular Fun Factory educational enrichment program (fee). The family-friendly resort is ideally situated within walking distance of restaurants, shops, and play stops. *400 Mandalay Ave., Clearwater Beach. (727) 461-3222;* www.hilton.com

Myakka River State Park ★★/$

In addition to tent and RV camping, Myakka rents five fully furnished log cabins. Built in the 1930s, they've been updated and have modern conveniences: heating/air-conditioning, kitchens with stove, refrigerator, and microwave, and a bathroom. A fireplace, back porch, and deck with picnic table and charcoal grill round out the amenities. Linens and kitchen utensils are furnished. Sorry, kids, no television or phone. **NOTE:** These cabins are *extremely* popular, with weekends and holidays booked months in advance. *13207 S.R. 72, Sarasota. (941) 361-6511;* http://my akka. sarasota.fl.us

FamilyFun **READER'S TIP**

Travel Trivia

My husband and I wanted our family trip to be both educational and fun for our 9 and 11 year old boys. To engage their interest, we devised a game to play while sightseeing. Every morning I would give my sons three questions pertaining to the places we would visit that day. If they answered all three they could order the dessert of their choice at dinner. They could use any resource, including a plaque at the site, a tour guide, brochures, and the like. They thought it was great fun to win a dessert off Mom and Dad, and they were so successful that we bought a round every night. Websites and guidebooks were our sources for the questions. With that little bit of preparation, our kids ended up not only having a great time but learning a lot, too.

Kathy Davis, Charlotte, North Carolina

Saddlebrook Resort
★★★/$$$-$$$$

Families on working vacations will go for this place. When Mom and Dad are tied up in meetings all day, there's no better place for kids to hang their hats than at the S'kids Club (fee), part of this resort's many family-friendly programs. Although it's primarily a conference center (it's located about 10 miles north of Tampa), lots of families return to Saddlebrook every year just for vacation. Rates include breakfast and dinner for parents; kids under 13 bunking with their parents stay free, though their meals carry an extra charge. *5700 Saddlebrook Way, Wesley Chapel. (800) 729-8383; (813) 973-1111.*

Sandpiper Beach Resort
★★★★/$$

Most of this beachfront resort's guest rooms are suites complete with kitchens, perfect for vacationing families. The Sandpiper is part of the nearby TradeWinds Resort (a quick five-minute walk), which has one of the greatest kids' activities programs around. Whether you opt for the supervised KONK (kids only, no kidding) program (fee) or ongoing family-focused festivities, most of which are complimentary, the Sandpiper goes out of its way to cater to kids of all ages and interests. *6000 Gulf Blvd., St. Pete Beach. (800) 344-5999; (727) 360-5551.*

The Art of Water Skiing– Cypress Gardens Style

Cypress Gardens (*S.R. 540 West, Winter Haven; 800/282-2123; 877/595-0509*), located about 50 miles west of Tampa, is the uncontested capital of waterskiing. Ramp jumping, swivel skiing, human pyramids, daredevil hang gliding, and highly executed water ballet artistry will keep your kids on the edge of their seats during the Rock Around the Dock show, performed several times daily. Your water-skier wanna-bes can have their day at the park thanks to the Extreme Experience program (fee) that pairs students ages 6 and older with certified instructors for behind-the-scenes tours and skiing adventures. Not to be outdone, the attraction's Junior Belle Program (fee) offers girls ages 3 and older the chance to become the park's signature character, a Southern belle—bonnet and all—for a two-hour chance of a lifetime; a great photo op. And be sure that you don't leave before seeing the Make 'Em Laugh Variété Internationale show, the electric boat ride through 16 acres of original gardens, and Carousel Cove, which has some of the best kiddie rides around.

Good Eats

Broken Egg ★★★/$
Hungry diners young and old will find "egg-septional" breakfasts and lunches at this popular eatery; it's located just off the main drag in Siesta Key Village. The menu is known for its mammoth-size buttermilk pancakes (to die for!); the kids' menu has a smaller but ample version. *210 Avenida Madera, Siesta Key. (941) 346-2750.*

Columbia Restaurant
★★★/$$
The oldest eatery in Florida, this legendary restaurant has been satisfying hungry appetites since 1905. Order a round of Cuban sandwiches (a wonderful combination of sliced ham, pork, salami, Swiss cheese, and pickle on scrumptious bread) or the traditional *arroz con pollo* (chicken and yellow rice)—both are guaranteed winners. The 45-minute Spanish flamenco dance performance (fee) is a big hit, especially with preteen girls. Multiple locations. *2117 E. 7th Ave., Tampa. (813) 248-4961.*

Frenchy's
Salt Water Café
★★★★/$
Just a stone's throw from Clearwater Beach's main drag is this funky little eatery that goes out of its way to please kids. Although a standard kids' menu is available (BLTs and fried shrimp get good reviews from junior restaurant critics), youngsters love the tasty fried grouper nuggets from the grown-ups' menu. The well-trained staff offers finicky eaters a toy now and then to keep everyone happy. Laid-back from the get-go (outdoor deck-type seating is ideal), this place is casual with a capital C. Multiple locations. *419 Poinsettia, Clearwater Beach. (727) 461-6295.*

Friendly Fisherman
★/$$
Located in Madeira Beach's popular John's Pass Village and Boardwalk, this place serves super-fresh seafood in a casual atmosphere. Seafaring youngsters will snarf up the popcorn shrimp while their landlubber friends chow down on tasty BLTs from the children's menu. *150 John's Pass Boardwalk, Madeira Beach. (727) 397-8764; (727) 391-6025.*

Jim Strickland's
Old Meeting House ★★★/$
Whether you're in the market for breakfast or lunch with the family, this diner-style eatery in Tampa's SOHO District fills the bill. Kids with hearty appetites go for the gorilla-size cheeseburger and fries, while the lighter eaters may opt for the grilled cheese. For dessert, young ice-cream aficionados favor Oreo or chocolate chip, which they can get in servings that range from marble-

to basketball-size helpings; The diner charges by weight, not scoop. *901 S. Howard Ave., Tampa. (813) 251-1754.*

Monkey Room
★★★★/$$
Whether it's the tasty grilled cheese for lunch or spaghetti with meatballs for dinner, you can't go wrong when dining with kids at the Monkey Room, part of the Colony Beach and Tennis Resort. Thanks to the friendly staff, kids are made to feel just as important as those footing the bill. *1620 Gulf of Mexico Dr., Longboat Key. (800) 426-5669; (941) 383-6464.*

Old Salty Dog ★★/$
If you think hot dogs are hot dogs, try this ultra-laid-back eatery on Siesta Key, where the signature dish is a lightly battered and deep-fried hot dog. Called Dog Bites, it's cut up in chunks and served on a bed of tasty fries. Multiple locations. *5053 Ocean Blvd., Siesta Key. (941) 349-0158.*

Sharky's ★★/$$
The scrumptious popcorn shrimp and fries and the casual and friendly atmosphere of the adjacent Venice fishing pier make Sharky's a winner with the younger set. At the shack at the entrance to the pier, you can rent all the fishing equipment and bait you'll ever need to reel in the big one! *1600 South Harbor Dr., Venice. (941) 488-1456.*

SOUVENIR HUNTING

H&R Trains
From the hands-on children's area and weekly running of the outdoor choo-choo to the themed kids' clothes and vintage merchandise, you can easily spend a few hours at this friendly station. *6901 U.S. Hwy. 19 North, Pinellas Park. (727) 526-4682;* www.hrtrains.com

Kid's Corner
Colorful clothing is what's in store at this upscale specialty shop for kids 8 and under. Although you won't find any denim here, you'll love the selection of funky brands like Chicken Noodle (lots of colorful prints) and Sweet Potatoes (cool cargo shorts). The store also carries lots of interactive toys, games, and puzzles. *346 Main St., Dunedin. (727) 738-0260.*

FAMOUS FLORIDIAN

Zora Neale Hurston, African-American writer and folklorist, was born in 1891. Hurston is best known for *Their Eyes Were Watching God*, a novel about a strong woman and her quest for love in rural Florida.

BUSCH GARDENS—
A Visit to Africa... in Tampa Bay

A THEME PARK with an African flavor, Busch Gardens Tampa Bay caters to hard-core roller coaster enthusiasts, animal lovers, and good, old-fashioned boardwalk carnival aficionados. For kids ages 3 to 7, there's a special mini park called **Land of the Dragons** with kiddy rides and other activities guaranteed to keep them busy for hours. For the older crew, there are some rides in addition to the roller coasters, but not a lot; you might want to make sure your older kids understand beforehand that the focus of Busch Gardens is roller coasters and wild animals. A plus for the whole family: this place isn't as crowded as some other theme parks, which means less time waiting in lines. Make sure to keep your park map handy though, as signs are somewhat confusing.

For those families headed over from Orlando just for the day (about 80 miles), round-trip bus transportation is available; buses depart daily from SeaWorld at 9 A.M. and return at 6 P.M. Cost (at press time) is $5 per person. For reservations, call *(800) 511-2450 or (800) 221-1339*.

Note that the park's five roller coasters vary in the scare factor department for kids. Height restrictions notwithstanding, what's too scary for one 12-year-old may be just the right challenge for another. You'll probably notice a lot of 7- to 12-year-olds standing around debating whether or not to ride a particular coaster.

If you're not up to the roller coaster experience, there are a few rides that the entire family can enjoy. The **Congo River Rapids** is a white-water raft trip that's just wild enough to produce screams as you're hurled down the rapids. **WARNING:** You may get soaked, so bring a change of clothes. **TIP:** Watch out above you: for 25 cents, the more spirited in the crowd can use the Congo Waterblasters to bombard you with powerful shots of water as you pass underneath them.

What many people may not realize is that Busch Gardens Tampa Bay is also home to one of the largest zoos in North America. It houses nearly 300 species, some of which are endangered. The park's **Edge of Africa**, a self-guided safari, provides everybody with a close-up view of animals they may have seen only in pictures. The unique sounds of wild animals, including lions, hyenas, hippopotamuses, baboons, and many more, fill the air along with children's voices asking such questions as, "Do hyenas really laugh?"

Roller Coasters
Busch Gardens is a paradise for roller coaster enthusiasts. There are five—

or six, if you count Gwazi, which is a double wooden roller coaster, as two—and each has its own distinctive features.

Gwazi "Your stomach doesn't even have time to fall." "A lot of flybys." These comments by 11-year-olds sporting big grins, and the fact that there is a lot of hair literally standing on end, attest to the thrill of Gwazi, one of the largest double wooden roller coasters in the United States. Its lower height restriction and lack of inverted loops allow most members of the family to experience it—but many younger kids may not be able to convince Mom or Dad to take the plunge. Gwazi's dueling coasters, the Lion and the Tiger, hold 24 riders each and reach speeds of 50 mph with six thrilling flyby encounters. Brave hearts will try them both!

Kumba This coaster is all about speed. It takes riders on a 60-mph journey that includes a "diving loop," a "camelback" with a 360-degree spiral, and a 108-foot vertical loop. You'll dry off from the water rides quickly on this one.

Montu "One minute you're at the top; the next minute you're at the bottom." If you want to kick up the thrills a notch, try Montu, named after a hawk-headed Egyptian warrior god. This humongous and lightning-fast inverted steel coaster drops riders 13 stories and hurls them through one of the world's largest inverted vertical loops before plunging them into a steep dive. Montu provides more loops and more speed; you provide the extra nerve.

Python Roller coaster novices might do well to start with Python. The six-story drop, and twirls through a double-spiraling corkscrew maneuver at speeds exceeding 40 mph, may be too tame for some, but for the beginner, this one will do just fine, thank you.

Scorpion Approaching 50 mph, the sting of the Scorpion may be less intense than some of the other coasters, but there are still plenty of maneuvers to keep your heart pumping, including a 360-degree vertical loop.

Other Rides

Congo River Rapids Prepare for bumps, grinds, and good-natured screams as you take a raft trip down the rapids. No matter where you're sitting in the raft, you'll probably get soaked, so a change of clothes is recommended. For kids under 5 and those who don't like getting drenched, the Stanleyville Falls Log Flume (see next page) is a bit tamer.

FAST LEARNERS
Baby hippos are born under water and start to swim as soon as they are born.

Skyride This is a great and relaxing way to see what's in the park. The monorail-type cars each accommodate four people. Your kids may find it a cool way to check out the roller coasters and other rides. You can enter or depart the Skyride at Crown Colony and Stanleyville. You can also get around the park on the **Trans-Veldt Railroad/Stanleyville Station.**

Stanleyville Falls Log Flume While older brothers and sisters are riding the coasters, parents can take the younger kids on this relatively tame flume ride. You won't get soaked, and it's a nice respite from the more frantic ups and downs of the coaster scene.

Tanganyika Tidal Wave This is another thrilling fast-water adventure that will dampen your body but not your spirits. If you still haven't gotten your fill of water rides, visit Adventure Island, adjacent to Busch Gardens.

More Cool Stuff
Congo Waterblasters Here's your chance to get revenge on those who bombarded you with massive shots of water from above as you rafted past them on the Congo River Rapids. For a quarter, you can get ready, aim, and fire the water from up above. And the best news is, *you* don't get wet at all.

Edge of Africa There's something really nifty about experiencing free-roaming herds of animals—giraffe, zebra, antelope, to name a few—alongside action-packed thrill rides. The roars of lions can be heard along with the roars of roller coasters and leave you all wondering which is more majestic. (Maybe a topic for discussion with the kids.) The 65-acre Serengeti Plain holds hundreds of animals and dozens of species, including hippopotamuses (ask your child to spell it), lions, baboons, crocodiles, hyenas (many kids are listening for the laugh), and lots more.

For the birds Bird-watchers will find plenty of opportunities in different areas of the park. Lory Landing, a lush aviary, features tropical birds from around the world, from beautiful pink flamingos to iridescent peacocks. A walk-through aviary may remind parents of a famous Hitchcock movie as birds dive amazingly close to your head. The air is filled with loud chirping, and the excited chatter of children as they look upward. Cups of liquid feed are available for $2 each. **NOTE:** Though children will enjoy feeding the birds, the feathered creatures *will* perch on your arms and shoulders, which may be a little scary for younger kids. Also, consider wearing a cap if you plan on staying in the aviary very long. The longer you stay, the greater the odds are that a bird may give you a gift you hadn't planned on.

Skill games You'll find a variety of skill games throughout the park. Try your luck at Water Wars, where you try to shoot a water balloon at your opponent with a giant slingshot. One bucket of water balloons costs $3; two buckets cost $5.

Where to Shop

The many shops throughout the park sell clothing, leather goods, and toys either handmade in the park or imported from Africa. You might find some unusual native gift items from Egypt, Kenya, or Timbuktu. Then there's the traditional souvenir fare such as "I Survived Montu" T-shirts. For something different, visit the Busch Gardens Wildlife Art Gallery, which showcases a collection of wildlife art and photography, artist demonstrations, and ostrich-egg painting. The kids probably won't want to stay long, though.

Entertainment

Several theaters have live entertainment throughout the day. Featured shows include *Hollywood Live on Ice* and *International Show*. Pick up an entertainment schedule when you enter the park.

Where to Eat

You'll find a variety of get-it-and-go restaurants throughout the park. **Vivi Storehouse Restaurant** ($) makes a pretty good chicken fajita sandwich and a child's hot dog and fries. There are also several snack places and one restaurant with table service: **Crown Colony House Restaurant** ($$). This might be a good choice if you want to enjoy a more leisurely meal. Of course, even if you can get the kids to slow down long enough to sit and eat, you'll pay more for the R&R. The **Anheuser Busch Hospitality House** ($$) offers pizza and sandwiches as well as complimentary samples of beer to adults over 21 years of age. For your sweet tooth, check out **Sultan's Sweets Bakery** ($).

Busch Gardens Tampa Bay, 3000 E. Busch Blvd., Tampa. (888) 800-5447; (813) 987-5465.

The waters of Destin are reputed to hold some of the most bountiful fishing spots.

INTRODUCTION

Tallahassee and the Florida Panhandle

SITUATED BETWEEN the Gulf of Mexico and the Deep South, Florida's Panhandle resembles its neighboring states more than the rest of Florida. Often called the other Florida, the Panhandle is where southern hospitality reigns amid the magnolia and oak trees. The area has also been referred to as the Emerald Coast, reflecting the richness of the majestic green waters, swamps, and lush foliage—all in sharp contrast to the stark white-sand beaches.

The Panhandle is home to Florida's state capital, Tallahassee. This community is truly a city with two faces: a serious legislative focal point and a fiercely loyal college town. At the same time, it has a variety of activities and interests to make most families feel welcome.

Outdoor adventure lovers seek out this area of Florida because it is

THE FamilyFun LIST

Gulf World (page 189)

National Museum of Naval Aviation (page 187)

Okaloosa Pier (page 190)

St. Andrews State Recreation Area and Campground (page 190)

Seaside (page 190)

Shipwreck Island WaterPark (page 190)

Tallahassee Antique Car Museum (page 188)

FamilyFun VACATION GUIDE

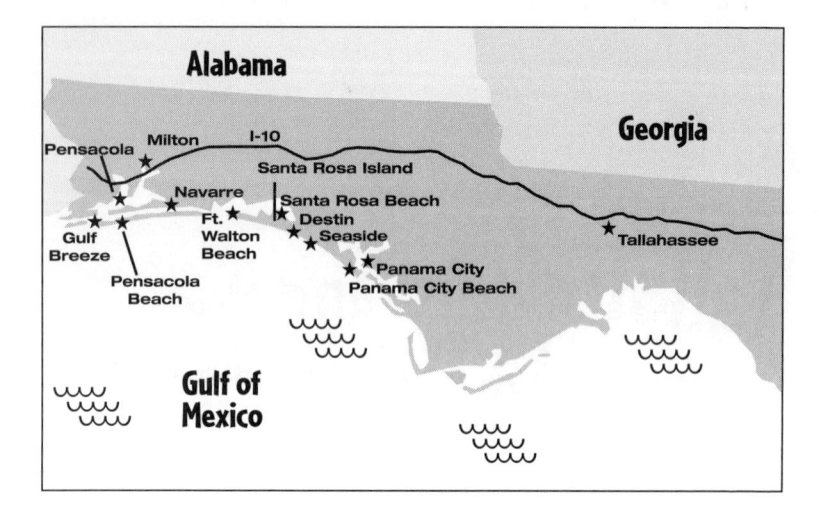

[Map showing Alabama, Georgia, and the Florida panhandle with locations: Pensacola, Milton, I-10, Santa Rosa Island, Santa Rosa Beach, Navarre, Ft. Walton Beach, Destin, Seaside, Gulf Breeze, Pensacola Beach, Panama City, Panama City Beach, Tallahassee, Gulf of Mexico]

truly another world, filled with opportunities for canoeing, biking, hiking, and just plain relaxing. And, of course, since it is a coastal community, water sports—surfing, scuba diving, and fishing—are also a way of life. Don't be surprised to find a water ride, aquarium, or amusement park thrown in for good measure and lasting vacation memories.

Cultural Adventures

Junior Museum of Bay County
★★/Free

Want to launch a hot-air balloon? No problem at this friendly—and free—museum where science, history, and culture come alive before your eyes. In addition to the 12-foot balloon ascension, your kids will get a kick out of Mr. Bones, a full-size bike-riding skeleton, and the nature corner, full of touchy-feely stuff like fossils, animal skulls, and skins. *Creepy!* Outside, take a self-guided tour of an authentic pioneer village and nature trail. *1731 Jenks Ave., Panama City. (850) 769-6128;* www.panamacity.com/recreation/jrmuseum

Mary Brogar Art and Science Center ★★/$

Kids can't get enough of this hands-on science center that's right across the street from the state capitol. Level one features a traveling science exhibition—usually of national acclaim like Dinosaurs or K'nex—plus a fully stocked museum-type gift shop. Level two houses the center's permanent collection, with interactive experiments like a whisper dish, Bernoulli Ball, and a television encounter where kids get to see themselves reporting the local weather. When your troops need a breather, rest a spell in the break room complete with miniature tables, chairs, and games for the kids and benches for the older folk. Unless you have a budding Matisse under your wings, you can skip the Museum of Art on the third level. *350 S. Duval St., Tallahassee. (850) 513-0700.*

Museum of Florida History
★/Free

Replicas of a giant armadillo, saber-toothed cat, and North American bison are members of the greeting committee for this intriguing—and free—walk through Florida's past. Skip most of the prehistoric displays near the entrance and go straight to the cool collection of dugout canoes used in navigating, hunting, and basic survival skills thousands of years ago. Your shopping mall mavens will get a chuckle out of the Crossroads Exhibit that reconstructs the days of the "you name it, we've got it" general store. A citrus-packing house from the 1920s and 1930s offers a behind-the-scenes glimpse of one of Florida's key industries. Don't miss the near-ballroom size exhibit on Florida and the movies. Kids (adults, too) will be surprised to learn that before World War I, Jacksonville, Florida, rivaled Hollywood, with more than 30 movie studios. *500 S. Bronough St., Tallahassee. (850) 488-1673.*

National Museum of Naval Aviation
★★★★/Free

Another of Florida's no-charge treats, this showplace prides itself on being the most visited museum in the state—and for good reason. With more than 130 beautifully restored aircraft and related pieces of equipment, it captures the spirit of nearly 90 years of U.S. Navy, Marine, and Coast Guard Aviation. Don't-miss exhibits include the Pensacola-Blue Angel Atrium, a collection of Blue Angel A-4 *Skyhawks* hanging suspended in the familiar diamond formation; Homefront, an authentic and entertaining look at life in the United States in 1943; and Flight Simulator, a 15-passenger full-motion "flight" similar to those flown during Operation Desert Storm. The museum's IMAX theater offers two action-packed, 40-minute movies—*The Magic of Flight* and *The Living Sea*. There's a nominal

FamilyFun VACATION GUIDE

charge for the Flight Simulator and IMAX movies. *1750 Radford Blvd., Pensacola. (800) 327-5002; (850) 452-3604;* www.naval-air.org

MUST-SEE FamilyFun Tallahassee Antique Car Museum ★★★/$

The entire family will get a charge out of this impressive showroom of award-winning automobiles. Youngsters will love the two Batmobiles used in *Batman Forever* and *Batman Returns,* and other popular memorabilia, including the Bat Jet and Bat Cycle from the hit television series. Attention-getters for Mom and Dad (and older kids) also include the 1860 hearse used for Abraham Lincoln's funeral (check out the trapdoor, which may have been used by the Underground Railroad during the Civil War), a 1909 electric carriage, and 1969 Plymouth Road Runner (of Warner Bros. cartoon fame). The younger set will get a kick out of the museum's collection of more than 100 colorful pedal cars. *3550 Mahan Dr., Tallahassee. (850) 942-0137.*

JUST FOR FUN

Big Kahuna's Lost Paradise
★★★/$$$

With more than 50 water attractions—from the near-heart-stopping Jumanji slide to the carefree lazy river tubing—you'd think Big Kahuna's was just a seasonal water park. But wait—don't forget the go-carts and miniature golf, or the video arcade. With a host of fun-filled activities to please the entire family, it's one-stop entertainment. *1007 Hwy. 98, Destin. (850) 837-4061.*

Florida's Gulfarium
★★/$$

Since 1955 this legendary attraction has been delighting locals and visitors alike with entertaining shows, adorable animals (the penguins are *sooo* cute!), and interactive encounters for audiences of all ages. Four 20-minute live marine shows are offered four times a day, usually once every two hours. Don't miss the *Sea Lion* and *Multi-Species* performances.

DAY TRIP
What Floats Your Boat?

Santa Rosa County, 25 miles from Pensacola and 40 miles from Ft. Walton Beach, has earned the reputation of the Canoe Capital of Florida thanks to its collection of first-rate waterways. Whether you've got two hours or two days to spare, **Adventures Unlimited Outdoor Center** ($-$$; *Rt. 6, Tomahawk Landing Rd., north of Milton; 850/623-6197*) can fix you up with some kind of fun water trip. Although canoes and kayaks are available, most families opt for tubing on the four-mile Fun Float

The latter combines the near impossible: bottle-nosed dolphins and a California sea lion performing *together* in the same show! For those really into the dolphin scene, check out the Spotted Dolphin Experience, Florida Gulfarium's up-close-and-personal "hand-to-flipper" 40-minute encounter with dolphins named Kiwi and Daphne (there's an extra charge for this). *1010 Miracle Strip Pkwy., S.E. Hwy. 98, Ft. Walton Beach. (850) 244-5169; www.gulfarium.com*

Gulf World
FamilyFun ★★★★/$$

This popular marine park on the main drag in Panama City Beach boasts a megaseat dolphin stadium, a humongous tropical garden, and a one-of-a-kind laser light show called *SplashMagic*. Kids delight in this high-energy extravaganza complete with aerial laser beams, synchronized fountains, and low-level fireworks. New exhibits focus on the American alligator, South American iguana, otter, and a large tropical bird theater with colorful (and noisy!) macaws, toucans, and cockatoos. Check out the park's full schedule of entertaining and educational shows, plus the dolphin and stingray petting pools. *15412 Front Beach Rd., Panama City Beach. (850) 234-5271.*

Miracle Strip Park
★★★/$$

Spending an evening at this family-friendly seasonal amusement park has been a Panama City Beach tradition for nearly 40 years. Thrill seekers have a ball with rides like the Starliner Roller Coaster and Sea Dragon, while Hilda's Hotel of Horrors and the Haunted Castle Ride entertain a tamer crowd. The 5-and-under bunch love rides like Kiddie Bi-plane, Tea Cup Ride, and Route 63. Check out the Midway Theater, home each night of live stage shows featuring comedy, magic, and musicals for guests of all ages. You can also stop by the arcade and food stands. *12000 Front Beach Rd., Panama City Beach; (850) 234-3333.*

---

down Coldwater Creek. Even your preteens will enjoy the not-too-fast, not-too-slow pace of these shallow wandering waters. The frequent sandbars along the way are great for sunning and picnicking. Lunch and other goodies can be stored in an extra tube that can be bungee-corded to yours. Picnicking is welcomed, but glass bottles and litter aren't. For the Fun Float, plan on about three hours without stops. If you're too pooped to return to your hotel, campsites, cabins, and a bed-and-breakfast housed in a historic schoolhouse are affordable options on Adventures Unlimited's 88 wooded acres.

Okaloosa Pier
MUST-SEE FamilyFun ★★★/$

The town of Destin has earned the reputation as the World's Luckiest Fishing Village, and, with supposedly four times more catches in the Florida Gulf than most other fishing spots, it's no wonder. One of the easiest—and cheapest—places for your kids to try their angler skills is at the Okaloosa Pier, located next to Gulfarium on Highway 98 on Okaloosa Island. With 1,200 feet of boardwalk to dangle from, there's a good chance they won't go away empty-handed. Well lighted, it's also a fun spot to try for a "night bite." Rental equipment and snacks are available on-site. No fishing license required. *1030 Miracle Strip Pkwy. E., Ft. Walton Beach. (850) 244-1023.*

Pensacola Bay Fishing Bridge ★★★/$

Of the many terrific fishing opportunities around, one of the greatest for families (free for kids 13 and under—life jackets included) is the 1.5-mile-long fishing bridge between Gulf Breeze and Pensacola (Pensacola side). Among the many catches families can expect to reel in are white and speckled trout, king and Spanish mackerel, crabs, and bluefish. No equipment? No problem: the Bridge Store carries rental equipment, bait and tackle, sodas, snacks, and sunscreen. The on-bridge parking and well-lighted areas for nighttime fishing make this a superconvenient spot. No fishing license required. You may also want to check out the bridge fishing on the Gulf Breeze side. *1750 Bayfront Pkwy., Pensacola. (850) 444-9811.*

Seaside
MUST-SEE FamilyFun ★★★★/Free-$$$

Seaside is more—much more than just another pretty beach. See what we mean on page 194.

Shipwreck Island WaterPark
MUST-SEE FamilyFun ★★★/$$

This seasonal water park was one of the first of its kind in the United States, and it is continually upgraded to offer waves of fun for everyone. The 600-foot-long White Knuckle River attractions contain several hair-raising turns and switchbacks for the brave at heart. Tadpole Hole, Zoom Flume, and Pirates Plunge Racing Slide, plus the Lazy River and Rapid River give kids hours of refreshing excitement. Not much shade here, so bring lots of sunscreen. *12000 Front Beach Rd., Panama City Beach. (850) 234-3333.*

St. Andrews State Recreation Area and Campground
MUST-SEE FamilyFun ★★★★/$

Located at the easternmost tip of Panama City Beach, this park offers you an unspoiled view of both the Bay and Gulf waters. Your younger fish will enjoy swimming and splashing in the shallow, protected pool behind the jetty, while your older sharks may want to snorkel in nearby open waters. Two fishing piers provide the perfect venue for catching Spanish mackerel, redfish, flounder, sea trout, and dolphin. The park's nature trail showcases a number of different plant families, including pine flatwoods and sand pine scrub. Along the way, see who can spot the first alligator or wading bird. During spring and summer, shuttles run to Shell Island, an undeveloped, 700-acre barrier island located just across the channel from St. Andrews. If you've got a few explorers along, this may be just the place for them to look for hidden treasure. The park has 176 campsites with electricity, water, picnic tables, and grills. Shower facilities, rest rooms, playgrounds, concession area, and picnic shelters are also available. *4607 State Park La., Panama City Beach. (850) 233-5140.*

The Zoo Gulf Breeze ★★/$

Lions and tigers and bears, oh my! Experience more than 700 animals, many in their natural habitats, when you visit this zoo between Ft. Walton Beach and Pensacola. Kids can hand-feed a giraffe, discover free-roaming rhinos, and ride the Safari Line train through 30 acres of wildlife preserve (full of wildebeests, hippos, and gators), plus three islands populated by chimps, gorillas, and monkeys. It's a hoot! Throughout the day, the zoo's friendly staff entertains and educates guests with stories about their encounters with bears, orangutan, and reptiles. *5701 Gulf Breeze Pkwy. (Hwy. 98), Gulf Breeze. (850) 932-2229; www.the-zoo.com*

Name Games

Why is Tallahassee Florida's capital? From the late 1700s to the early 1800s, Florida was split into two states with separate capitals: St. Augustine and Pensacola. When the United States regained control of the land in 1821, the country reunited the two Floridas and Tallahassee was chosen for its central location between the two former capitals.

Bunking Down

DoubleTree Hotel Tallahassee ★/$-$$

Kids can unwind in the large outdoor swimming pool and sundeck. Ideally located, the 243-room, high-rise property is just a stone's throw from the state capitol, family-friendly museums, Florida State University, and Florida A&M University. The warm, homemade chocolate-chip cookies—DoubleTree's signature amenity—are a tasty bedtime snack. *101 S. Adams St., Tallahassee; (850) 224-5000.*

Four Points Hotel by Sheraton
★★★/$-$$

Take one of, if not *the* best, beaches in the south, add to it a property that goes out of its way for families—as in complimentary seasonal kids' programs, summertime parents' night out, in-room Nintendo—and you've got a grand slam home run when you call this Okaloosa Island hotel home for a few nights. *1325 Miracle Strip Pkwy., Ft. Walton Beach. (800) 874-8104; (850) 243-8116;* www.fourpoints.com

Ft. Pickens National Park
★★★/$

Whether you pitch a tent, hook up your RV, or just tour the fort, there's lots to choose from at this humongous park. Most of the 200 campsites are superclose to the beach, which means instant entertainment for the entire family. Showers, a picnic area, and a camp store round out this cheap sleep. Ft. Pickens, a Civil War fortress and prison for the Indian chief Geronimo, is worth a quick stop before moving on to one of the park's nature or bike trails or the fishing pier. *Ft. Pickens Rd., West end of Santa Rosa Island. (800) 365-2267; (850) 934-2622.*

Grayton Beach State Recreation Area ★★/$

Call superearly to reserve one of the 37 campsites at this popular beach and nature retreat. Each site has a picnic table, grill, water, and electricity. During the day, explore more than 2,000 acres of migrating dunes, salt marshes, and pine flatwoods, and then swim or fish along the park's one-mile shoreline. *357 Main Park Rd., Santa Rosa Beach. (850) 231-4210;* www.graytonbeach.com

Hampton Inn ★★/$-$$

Affordable accommodations, two beachside pools, and a fun-filled seasonal activity program and parents' night out make this Pensacola Beach hotel a favorite among families; they'll also appreciate one of the most extensive complimentary continental breakfasts around. Great beach, too! *2 Via De Luna, Pensacola Beach. (800) 320-8108; (850) 932-6800;* www.hamptoninn.com

Hilton Sandestin Beach & Golf Resort Spa ★★★★/$-$$$

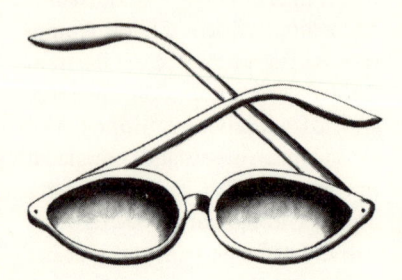

Expect an extra hug from your kids tonight after they experience the appeal of this premier resort on the beach midway between Panama City and Pensacola. Your young athletes will go for the great lineup of sports options, including tennis, golf, boating, and swimming. From the oversize guest rooms and the bunk beds in the junior suites to the morning Kid's Krew program and the Kid's Night activities nearly every evening (fees for both), kids give this place a thumbs-up! *4000 Sandestin Blvd., South. Destin. (850) 267-9500;* www.hilton.com

Holiday Inn SunSpree Resort ★★★★/$-$$

Don't be surprised if your kids are content to stay at this oceanfront resort all day. Between the cool pool, neat beach, and *awesome* kid's program (fee), can you blame them? Your tots in tow will also get a bang out of Splash (the resort's dolphin mascot), while kids young and old will be in awe each night at sunset during the Polynesian Torch-lighting Ceremony. All 340 spacious guest rooms have oceanfront views and private balconies. *11127 Front Beach Rd., Panama City Beach. (850) 234-1111.*

Sandestin Resort ★★★★/$-$$

This upscale beach and bayfront vacation haven is almost a city unto itself. Located on nearly 2,400 acres, the resort boasts its own nature park, kids' sailing academy, children's recreation and environmental science programs (fees), tram system, shops, restaurants—even a Swiss Family Robinson–type tree house. Pick from a variety of lodging types included in the resort's 700 rental accommodations. (A supersize— $400-million—expansion project is underway at the resort, including an aquatic recreation complex.) *9300 Hwy 98 West, Destin. (800) 277-0800; (850) 267-8150;* www.sandestin.com

GOOD EATS

The Back Porch ★★★/$$

This popular seafood and oyster house serves lunch and dinner in a laid-back atmosphere. While Mom and Dad discuss the day's events, kids can romp on the beachfront playground until the dinner bell rings. For kids tired of seafood, the children's menu offers a crowd-pleasing pizza. *1740 Old Hwy. 98 East, Destin. (850) 837-2022.*

Billy's Oyster Bar ★/$

Nothing fancy or gourmet here—just fresh steamed seafood at affordable prices. Order a few rounds of the fresh, steamed shrimp and garlic bread and you'll have a family of happy campers. Ask the kitchen to go easy on the special sauce for the kids' shrimp—it may be too spicy for young tummies. *3000 Thomas Dr., Panama City Beach. (850) 235-2349.*

Cowboys ★★/$$

If your kids are craving something besides seafood, check out this place, located on the water next to the Navarre Bridge. The Kit Carson Sirloin or Billy the Kid Burger are sure to satisfy. *8673 Navarre Pkwy., Hwy. 98, Navarre. (850) 939-0502.*

EATZ ★★★/$

This cafeteria-style restaurant is in the lower level of the state capitol building. Kids can choose from subs, burgers and fries, or Florida home-style cooking. Order the meals to go and then head to the 22nd floor observation level where your family can enjoy their breakfast, lunch, or snack "picnicking" high above the city. *400 S. Monroe, Tallahassee. (850) 224-3353.*

Flounder's Chowder & Ale House ★★★/$$

An authentic shrimp boat welcomes diners large and small to this popular waterfront restaurant. Children's specials include macaroni and cheese, chicken 'n' chips, and popcorn shrimp. Ask for a table around the playground on the beach. *800 Quietwater Beach Rd., Pensacola Beach. (850) 932-2003.*

McGuire's Irish Pub ★★★★/$$

Kids can be kids at this lively Pensacola eatery that's housed in the city's original firehouse. Before dining on such concoctions as PB&J, fries, and a fudge brownie, pint-size eaters are kept busy with a place mat full of coloring and games like McTic Tac Toe. A favorite among locals and visitors alike, even families of non-Irish descent can be declared official Irishmen here; it only costs a buck. *600 E. Gregory St., Pensacola. (850) 433-6789; www.mcguiresirishgifts.com*

Morgan's ★/$

Downstairs, Morgan's offers tasty eats in a food-court setting. Burgers, pasta, chicken, sandwiches, and an on-site bakery for dessert are sure to please all types of appetites. The upper level is jam-packed with more than 170 futuristic games—3-D, virtual sports, and motion simulation rides, among others. A play maze entertains the younger crowd. *Silver Sands Factory Stores, Hwy. 98 West, Destin. (850) 654-3320.*

Pompano Joe's Seafood House ★★★★/$$

With the beach just a few steps away, your kids will work up a hearty appetite while waiting for their meal at this friendly waterfront eatery. The well-stocked fish tank, ocean

---

DAY TRIP

Life's a Beach

Tucked between Panama City and Pensacola on scenic County Road 30-A is **Seaside**, one of the most charming, funky, and family-friendly places around. Plan on spending at least half a day exploring all that this popular beach town has to offer, including bike riding, boogie-boarding, or shopping. There's a half- or full-day (best value) **Camp Seaside program** *(850/231-2246)* that's

paraphernalia plastered on the walls, and a friendly waitstaff put this restaurant near the top of the food chain. Kids will quickly snarf up the heaping helpings of popcorn shrimp or chicken fingers. *2237 Old Hwy. 98 East, Pensacola Beach. (850) 837-2224.*

Schooners Last Local Beach Club
★★★★/$$

Really fresh seafood and classic beach-style ambience make this a not-to-miss meal stop in Panama City Beach. Kids love the popcorn shrimp, not to mention a frolic on the beach while they're waiting for their meal to arrive. Plan to dine early, as this place really "cooks" with nightly and weekend entertainment. *5121 Gulf Dr., Panama City Beach. (850) 235-3555*; www.schooners.com/last-local.htm

SOUVENIR HUNTING

Get in the Wind

Before heading out to enjoy one of the area's sun-sational beaches, make a quick stop at this whimsical, friendly shop to pick up a colorful kite or two. *109-A Hwy. 98 East Destin. (888) 854-9463; (850) 654-9463.*

Go Fish T-shirt and Sole Co.

This is more than your run-of-the-mill shirt shop. Unique T-shirts, many featuring funky fish and funny phrases, and cool and comfy sandals are Go-Fish's signature products. *400 Quietwater Boardwalk, Pensacola Beach. (850) 934-0274.*

Museum Shop of Tallahassee

Puzzles, stuffed animals, interactive games, and a load of "to do" kits await your crew at this friendly shop in Betton Place, about 15 minutes north of the capital. *1950 Thomasville Rd., Tallahassee. (850) 681-8565.*

Silver Sands Designer Outlet Center

From Barbie to Batman, Bugle Boy to Big Dog, your kids are bound to find it at Silver Sands, the largest designer factory store center in the nation. *Hwy. 98 East, Destin; (800) 510-6255; (850) 864-9780.*

---

packed with supercool activities, especially for the 5- to 10-year-old set. If your kids are a tad older, let them hang at the beach while you stroll through more than 50 retail shops and art galleries. Reconnect for lunch or dinner at the casual 83 **Central Square** ($-$$; 850/231-1950), located across from the amphitheater. Chow down on a tasty corn dog or plain buttered noodles from the kids' menu. A toy-stocked kids' corner is a great reward for those in the clean plate club!

Georgia

GEORGIA, the largest state east of the Mississippi and largest of the southern United States, stretches 315 miles from north to south, acres of room for family fun.

Whether your dream vacation is active or laid-back, or maybe a little of each, you'll find it here, where down-home hospitality and friendliness come to life around every corner. Whether you're panning for gold in Dahlonega or rocking out at the Georgia Music Hall of Fame in Macon, you'll quickly realize that Georgians know how to make visitors feel welcome. Speaking of down-

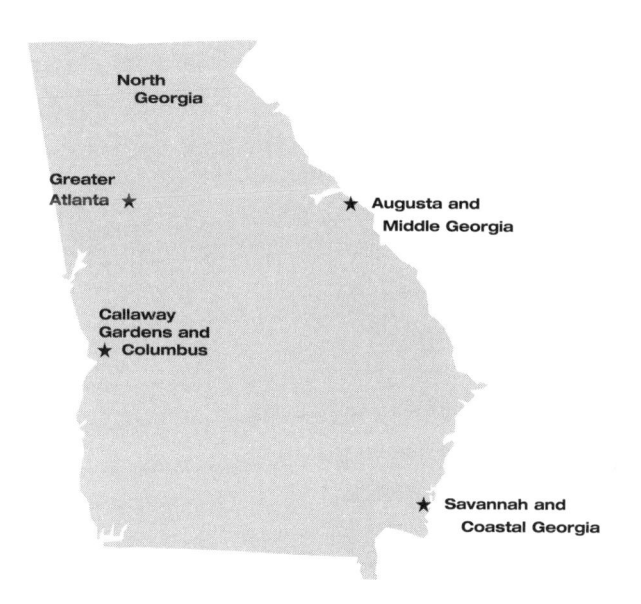

Map labels:
- North Georgia
- Greater Atlanta ★
- ★ Augusta and Middle Georgia
- Callaway Gardens and ★ Columbus
- ★ Savannah and Coastal Georgia

home, there's also no better place to experience Southern-style cooking than in Georgia. Encourage your kids to try a heaping helping of grits—but know that peanut-butter-and-jelly is only a request away.

On the thrill-a-minute meter, kids *love* greater Atlanta. And with such amusements and pastimes as Six Flags, American Adventure, White Water Park, and Stone Mountain, who can blame them?

But Georgia's kid-friendly fun doesn't stop there. From gorgeous—and action-packed—Callaway Gardens to historic Savannah and its southern neighbor, the resort-rich area of Brunswick and the Golden Isles, the Peach State is a sweet treat for all ages.

ATTRACTIONS
$	under $10
$$	$10 - $20
$$$	$20 - $30
$$$$	$30 +

HOTELS/MOTELS/CAMPGROUNDS
$	under $100
$$	$100 - $200
$$$	$200 - $300
$$$$	$300 +

RESTAURANTS
$	under $10
$$	$10 - $20
$$$	$20 - $30
$$$$	$30 +

***FAMILYFUN* RATED**
★	Fine
★★	Good
★★★	Very Good
★★★★	*FamilyFun* Recommended

Play a game of hoops or practice your play-by-play at the Georgia Sports Hall of Fame.

INTRODUCTION

Augusta and Middle Georgia

UNLIKE MOST other regions in the state, Augusta and Middle Georgia relies less on nature and more on human achievements to delight vacationing families. Sure, Augusta's azaleas are awesome during the Masters, and Macon's Cherry Blossom Festival is an annual good time, but what *really* rocks this region—from a kid-friendly perspective, that is—are the museums and other centers that give kids a glimpse of the area's history and what its residents have accomplished.

Although museums and the like get top billing here, you can preempt those oh-so-familiar groans from your youngsters by taking them to Augusta's Fort Discovery's National Science Center, the Georgia Sports Hall of Fame in Macon, or even the Georgia Agrirama in Tifton. We guarantee they'll change their tune.

Culture aside, Middle Georgia does offer some knock-your-socks-

THE FamilyFun LIST

Flint River Outdoor Center (see page 204)

Fort Discovery's National Science Center (see page 201)

Georgia Agrirama (see page 202)

Georgia Sports Hall of Fame (see page 203)

Museum of Arts and Sciences (see page 204)

Wild Adventures (see page 207)

FamilyFun **VACATION GUIDE**

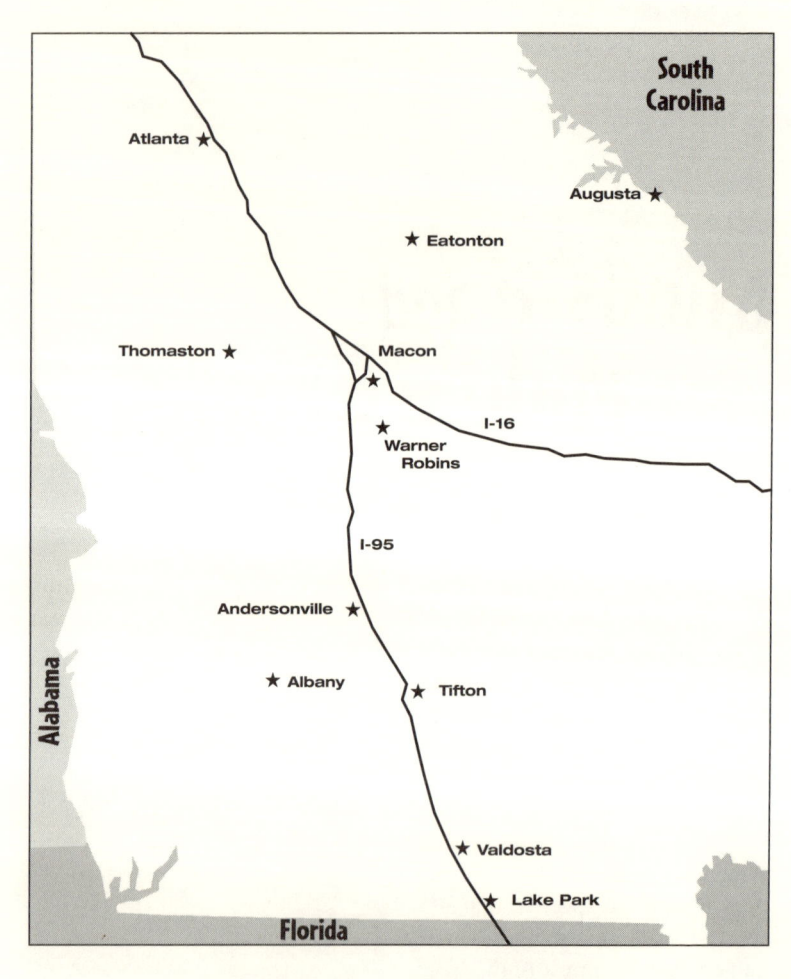

off amusement-parklike fun at Wild Adventures, just north of the Georgia-Florida border near Valdosta. And before you start thinking about standing in endless lines, keep in mind that you'll have an average wait there of about 10 minutes or less during peak season. This wildly popular attraction is a blast for kids of all ages.

Cultural Adventures

Andersonville National Historic Site ★★/FREE

A sobering and memorable experience best describes a visit to this site for kids 10 and up. During the

Civil War, the Confederates imprisoned more than 45,000 Union soldiers here. Stop first at the visitors' center, which uses pictures, video, and artifacts to accurately depict the prison's horrendous conditions during the War Between the States. The center is also home to the National Prisoner of War Museum for all military conflicts through the Persian Gulf. Young history buffs will appreciate the 27-minute orientation film, which includes interviews with POW survivors from WWI to Desert Storm. Once outdoors, drive slowly around the prison grounds, stopping to explore the Stockade, the Deadline, and other landmarks before moving on to the adjacent Andersonville National Cemetery, where more than 18,000 veterans are buried. Skip the audiotape for the outdoor driving tour, and depend on the brochure, your knowledge, and the curiosity and imagination of your own children. *State Rd. 49, Andersonville. (229) 924-0343;* www.nps.gov/ande

Augusta Museum of History
★★/$

Just down the Riverwalk is this deceptively large museum chock-full of (what else?) history—the collection's artifacts mirror 12,000 years of local happenings, from prehistoric Native Americans to astronaut Susan Still, who grew up in Augusta. The museum's Children's Discovery Gallery is aimed at the 5- to 10-year-old set and named after Still, a member of the Space Shuttle team in the late 1990s. Designed as fun, hands-on history lessons, the exhibits give kids a chance to do everything from packing a canoe fashioned from a hollowed-out pine tree to sitting at the helm of mission control during a shuttle launch. Other play-and-learn areas, especially for the younger crowd, include Children Through History, where exhibits showcase the Colonial period as well as the 1920s and the 1950s—kids can dress up and play with period clothing and toys. Separate from this gallery is the expansive Augusta Story, which chronicles the history of this river city. A 56-foot-long Petersburg boat copied from the 1700s, a passenger train from the not-too-distant past, and some neato artifacts will keep your preteens interested. *560 Reynolds St., Augusta. (706) 722-8454;* www.augustamuseum.org

Fort Discovery's National Science Center ★★★★/$

Whether you're traveling with an antsy 3-year-old or the most sophisticated 12-year-old, plan to spend a good three hours or more at this

fabulous attraction—it's a must-see, must-touch, and must-try for all. With more than 270 interactive exhibits, the museum is a public-private partnership with the United States Army designed to stimulate kids' interest in math, science, and technology. The experience begins outdoors, where your kids try to propel the giant gyrocycle (motorcycle). Move inside to see if you can activate huge fountains by way of laser beam, then wander through the six areas: robotics; math, motion, and momentum; everyday technologies; space technology; communication; and imaging. Especially fun for the pre-K through second grade bunch is an entire room called Kidscape, where they can indulge in pint-size interactive exercises. The older crowd—those under 110 pounds and over 44 inches tall—can (and do, in droves) take a walk on the Moonwalk in the Space Technologies Gallery. Also cool is the compact disc exhibit in the Communications Gallery, where kids can record their pictures on a computer game and take the CD home to play on their computers (there's a fee). If your energy—or theirs—flags, take a breather at the hands-on demonstrations at the Power Station Theater and a movie at the Paul S. Simon Discovery Theater. Still, there's really so much to see and do that three hours might not be enough. *1 Seventh St., Augusta. (800) 325-5445; (706) 821-0600; www.nscdiscovery.org*

Georgia Agrirama
★★★★/$

There's no better way to teach your kids about the good old days than to have them actually see, touch, and taste bits of the past. That's what they can do at this outdoor living-history museum, where they get a bird's-eye view of what life was like in the late 19th century—barnyard animals, one-room schoolhouse, steam-powered locomotive, and all. With more than 30 restored buildings to explore, your family—especially grade-schoolers and older—will enjoy watching friendly costumed guides go about their daily chores and answer the myriad "what's that?" inquiries bound to come up from the peanut gallery.

Postcards to Me

You want your child to write; she wants mail when she gets home; and a travel journal of your trip would be something you'd both enjoy. Make it all happen by having your child record what she's done on a different postcard each day and then mail it to herself. At home, she can turn her stack of mail into a record book by punching holes in the edges of the cards and stringing them together.

Top off your visit with a cool beverage or ice cream from the drugstore soda fountain. *I-75 and Eighth St., Tifton. (229) 386-3344; www.ganet.org/agrirama/*

Georgia Sports Hall of Fame
★★★★/$

From hoops and links to bats and gridirons, the Georgia Sports Hall of Fame proudly honors the state's greatest sports heroes with the largest museum of its kind in the United States. The many interactive areas will keep your players busy for a morning or afternoon of fun. One of their hands-down favorites is sure to be the "on-air" media desk on the second floor, where your wannabe broadcasters call the play-by-play and then hear a replay of their colorful commentary. Other not-to-be-missed spots are the Hall of Fame's basketball court and football field, where kids can get tips on such basics as shooting and passing, and are also great venues to work up an appetite—or work off a meal. Skip or make a swift pass through the displays immortalizing the achievements of high school, collegiate, and even professional athletes (few are household names, even to a preteen, unless you're from Georgia)—your kids' eyes may glaze over. Still, this place is a slam dunk for the entire family. *301 Cherry St., Macon. (478) 752-1585; www.gshf.org*

High-Flying Games

Games that use a pen or pencil are perfect to play on airplanes, since you can lean on the tray top. The following ideas are especially enjoyed by players who are sitting in a row. Unlike backseat games, which can get fairly boisterous, these plane pastimes are a bit quieter, so you won't make enemies of your fellow fliers.

CRAZY CREATURES
Create strange-looking people, beasts, or any combination of both by folding a piece of paper into three equal sections. One person draws the face in the top section, then folds down the paper so the next person can't see it. That person then draws the midsection of the body, folds down the paper, and passes it to the third person, who sketches the legs in the bottom section. Finally, unfold the paper and name your creature.

TOUCHY TELEPHONE
This is a good game for people sitting in a row. Player 1, on one end, thinks of a word. Player 2, next to 1, closes his or her eyes and holds out an arm. Using a finger, Player 1 "writes" the word on Player 2's arm. The word gets passed down the row – and maybe across the aisle – until it reaches the last person in your party. That person says the word he thinks was written on his arm out loud, and Player 1 says the original word. Let Player 2 start the next round, and so on.

FamilyFun **VACATION GUIDE**

Lights on Macon... Historic Intown
★★★/Free

The same designer who created Disney's Electric Light Parade dreamed up this unique tour of Macon's spectacular historic homes. The self-guided evening walking tour illuminates the most prominent architectural features of 31 to-die-for homes; a perfect end to a day of sightseeing, especially if you've got some 10-and-older wanna-be architects along. Pick up a detailed guide at the Convention & Visitors Bureau at Terminal Station. *200 Cherry St., Macon. (800) 768-3401; (478) 743-3401.*

Morris Museum of Art
★/$

At one end of Augusta's Riverwalk is this delightfully accessible collection of southern art that represents artists of the last 200 years. Far from the stuffy galleries in larger cities, this one invites a leisurely stroll. Kids, especially the preteen crowd and older, get a glimpse of some works that explore the cultures of the Old South and the New South, including slavery and the Reconstruction era. This might be just the place to introduce your youngsters to the art of museum-going. On Sunday, the museum hosts a great—and also free—family outing called Artrageous Sundays, full of hands-on workshops for kids, including puppetry, quilting bees, and African rhythms. (You also get free admission to the museum on Sundays.) *1 Tenth St., Augusta. (706) 724-7501;* www.traoi.com/nmus8.htm

MUST-SEE FamilyFun Museum of Arts and Sciences
★★★★/$

Musical stairs, a dream room, and a virtual artist's palette are just three of the many showstoppers vying for your kids' attention at this popular Macon museum. Sure, there's lots of art, but it's mostly grown-up stuff. What will really capture the family's imagination is the three-story Dis-

---

DAY-TRIP
Georgia's Kid-Friendly Rapids

Whatever floats your boat, you'll find it at **Flint River Outdoor Center**, about an hour west of Macon. The friendly owners have been in business for more than 20 years and know the Flint River like the backs of their hands. The more seasoned crew may go for the half-day excursion in a two-person canoe—a voyage that will challenge your navigation skills as you encounter class I, II, and III rapids. This high-energy excursion is most

covery House: The first floor looks like a scientist's workshop—filled with microscopes, mazes, even a fossil find for budding archaeologists. The second floor (which is actually the main entrance level) focuses on the humanities, with maps and globes, a poet's corner, and some quirky collections, like children's shoes from around the world. Check out the Back Yard, a group of mini habitats designed around a humongous banyan tree, with monkeys, tropical birds, and other creatures. Let your imagination run wild on the top floor, where you'll find engaging activities like the dream room (a cozy, semidark area where sound images and light sequences let your imagination run wild), air paint encounter, a live beehive, even a loom for your craft-meisters. Ziggy—a 40-million-year-old whale fossil found in 1973 only 20 miles from the museum—hangs from the ceiling of the Discovery House atrium and greets your family from all three levels. The museum's planetarium offers an array of shows for your young stargazers. *4182 Forsyth Rd., Macon. (478) 477-3232;* www.masmacon.com

Museum of Aviation
★/Free

Your eager-to-be pilots will be on cloud nine when they set foot into the nation's fourth-largest aviation museum, less than 30 minutes from Macon in Warner Robins. The 30-minute Smithsonian movie *To Fly* is a good way to begin your visit, as you watch the history of aviation unfold, from balloons to the space age (fee). If you need a break from the educational, a second movie—*Flyers*—is pure entertainment, with some fancy flying and daredevil acrobatics (fee). The museum's collection of more than 90 aircraft is spread throughout four cavernous buildings and includes such record-breaking notables as the U-2 (climbed to nearly 74,000 feet in about 12 minutes) and the SR-71 (set world speed record of 2,193 mph—it *cruises* at

certainly a thrill, but may be a bit much for most families with kids 10 and under. A fun and relaxing alternative—and one that still gives you classes I and II rapids—is the one-mile tube ride. This is perfect for the novice tuber, allowing you to meander at your own pace for an hour or two before you arrive back at the center. Rent a floating cooler for your lunch and you've made a day of it! The canoe trips are seasonal; tubing is year-round fun. Overnight accommodations (camping and bed-and-breakfast-type facilities) are also available here. *4429 Woodland Rd., Thomaston. (706) 647-2633.*

FamilyFun TIP

The Masters

Visiting an art museum? Pick up the kids' book series *Getting to Know the World's Greatest Artists* by Mike Venezia to set the mood.

speeds in excess of three times the speed of sound!). You can skip or take a quick look at the We The People (in Century of Flight Hangar) and Windows to a Distant Past (in Heritage Building) displays, especially if your kids are under 10—the exhibits seem somewhat out of place in an aviation museum. *SR 247 and Russell Pkwy., Warner Robins. (912) 926-6870;* www.navalair.org

Uncle Remus Museum and Park
★★/$

Most kids have heard about Br'er Rabbit (he's the good guy) and Br'er Fox (he's the bad guy) even if they haven't read the stories. Here's your chance to let them get up close and personal with these legendary characters. Situated about 40 miles northeast of Macon, in Eatonton's Turner Park, the log cabin museum was once two slave cabins. The memorabilia and carvings are eye-catching and kid-pleasing, and, if you're lucky and are there when the curator is, she may even tell you an Uncle Remus story or two. (Joel Chandler Harris wrote 185 stories in all.) After a visit to the museum, tour the flower and bog gardens and then have a picnic lunch in the park. *Hwy. 441 South, Eatonton. (706) 485-6856.*

JUST FOR FUN

Flint River Outdoor Center
★★★★/$$

Awesome outdoor fun awaits at this spectacular vacation spot. Want to know more? See page 204.

Georgia Music Hall of Fame
★★★/$

Whether your family listens to rock and roll, country, or classical music, they're bound to find a little bit of melodic paradise at this downtown Macon tribute to the state's rich musical heritage. Kids take great delight in wandering down the Tune Town streetscape to check out the glittery costumes, electrifying guitars, and the 45's and 33's of a bygone era. Maintain your musical mood with a visit to Tune Town's Gretsch Theatre, where an applause meter measures your group's favorite vocalist (you've got to whoop it up really loud for it to register). Your cheers are rewarded as your "fave" (the artist who gets the loudest applause) then appears on stage (via video) to perform one of his or her most popular tunes. Before you leave, visit the Music Factory, a special children's wing filled with a great collection of hands-on educational activities. Check out "Twinkle, Twinkle, Little Star" arranged with a salsa beat. It's way cool. *200 Martin Luther King Blvd., Macon. (888) 427-6257; (478) 750-8555;* www.gamusichall.com

The Parks at Chehaw
★★★/$

If you're looking for an afternoon of affordable family fun that will satisfy all ages and interests, check out this group of five diverse parks-within-a-park in Albany. Young naturalists will have a heyday exploring miles of scenic trails that run along the Muckalee Creek. Animal lovers will delight in the zebras, monkeys, elephants, and other furry and not-so-furry friends—some of which may be a bit hard to spot in the Wild Animal Park's natural settings (there's an extra fee). If you brought bikes (no rentals here), check the miles of bike trails, plus a challenging course for serious BMXers. Chehaw's play park has got to be one of the largest jungle fortress playscapes on the planet, jam-packed with turrets, rockets, ships, motorcycles, slides, swings, and much more. And if you're loath to leave, you can stay in Chehaw's RV Park, which has basic camping facilities for motor homes and tents (fee). *105 Chehaw Park Rd., Albany. (229) 430-5275;* www.parksatchehaw.org

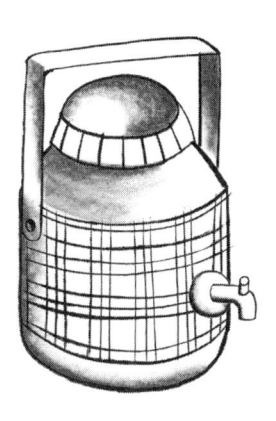

Wild Adventures
MUST-SEE FamilyFun ★★★★/$$$

Halfway between Atlanta and Orlando, there's a must-stop for thrill-seeking families. Take Exit I-75 in Valdosta and head to Wild Adventures Theme Park, one of the fastest-growing attractions in the region. Creatures great and small are the park's major draw (don't miss the *Snakes of the World* and *Amazing Cats* shows, plus hundreds of exotic animals), but it's the heart-pumping, handle-gripping, smile-inducing rides that provide the requisite scream factor. Wild Adventures sports six roller coasters, ranging from the fast-but-not-furious Ant Farm Express and Gold Rush to the hair-raising, multi-inversion Hangman, which is guaranteed to scare the bejeebees out of even your bravest of warriors. Want to cool off? You're at the right place, especially if your clan includes preteens who may opt for the Blackfoot Falls water ride that plunges 50 feet into the splash pool. Expect to get drenched—in fact, nearly all of the park's water rides call for a change of clothes. Don't overlook the park's great mix of little-tyke rides, including the Froghopper, Bongo's Bumper Boats, Windjammer, Super Trucks, and one of the most creative soft playground areas around. *3766 Old Clyattville Rd., Valdosta. (229) 559-1330;* www.wild_adventure.com

Bunking Down

Arrowhead Park/ Claystone/Sandy Beach ★★★/$

Fans of the outdoors will love spending a few nights under the stars at this picturesque camping and fishing park that's part of Tobesofkee Recreation Area, just 20 minutes from downtown Macon. Although nearly all of the tent and RV sites have lake views, call ahead to reserve one directly on the water. After a day of fishing (bass and catfish galore), let the older kids test their scouting skills by building a real campfire for your fish fry. Nonanglers can wile away the day swimming or sunning at the beach or biking along the park's well-paved roads. Sorry—fishing and cycling equipment are not provided. *6600 Mosley Dixon Rd., Macon. (478) 474-8770.*

Comfort Suites Merry Acres ★★★/$

Although this property is part of the Choice Hotels chain, it's been run with personal and loving care by the same family for more than two generations. From the lush grounds and spacious suites (actually, one room divided with a bedroom/living area and a small kitchen) to the outdoor pool and friendly service, this place lives up to its cheery name. Count on the same southern hospitality at the Quality Inn (on the same grounds), or across the street at Sleep Inn—they're all managed by the same family. *1400 Dawson Rd., Albany. (229) 888-3939;* www.merryacres.com/hmtl/comfort_suites.html

Days Inn ★/$

Families looking for a comfortable, convenient, and cheap sleep will find it all when staying at this member of the nationwide chain directly off I-75 near Valdosta. An outdoor swimming pool, free continental breakfast (or Cracker Barrel and McDonald's within walking distance), plus nearby outlet malls and Wild Adventures Theme Park make this property a winner. *4913 Timber Dr., Lake Park. (229) 559-0229;* www.daysinn.com

Homewood Suites Hotel ★★★/$

If space—and lots of it—is a priority for your family, that's exactly what this apartment-style hotel offers in all of its guest rooms. The convenient kitchen, outdoor swimming pool and spa, and sports court make this a family-friendly place, not to mention the free breakfast featuring kid-popular waffles and pastries. A five-minute drive from the Riverwalk, this is a good value if you want convenience and comfort at an affordable price. *1049 Stevens Creek Rd., Augusta. (706) 650-5858; www.homewood_suites.com*

Partridge Inn ★★★★/$-$$

Definitely top of the line, this historic hotel (100-plus years old) will give your kids an authentic taste and feel of the Old South. Some of the 156 rooms are suites or studios—just right for families needing extra space and the convenience of complete kitchens; there also are many connecting rooms. An outdoor pool and video games complete the family-friendly experience. *2110 Walton Way, Augusta. (706) 737-8888; www.partridgeinn.com*

Queen Anne Inn
★★/$

This friendly inn is somewhat of a newcomer on the Augusta lodging scene. You can choose among various rooms, but make sure you check out the property's family suite: it has a kitchen area and its own kid-themed playroom. (Expect lots of "way cools.") Parents will appreciate the antiques and stained-glass windows. Even if the family suite is booked, there's a fully equipped (yes, even tomato soup and cereals in the pantry) common kitchen. *406 Greene St., Augusta. (706) 723-0045.*

GOOD EATS

Andersonville Restaurant
★/$

After a visit to the Andersonville National Historical Site, head for this haven of southern hospitality and good eats. Lunchtime features

---

FamilyFun READER'S TIP

Window Box Organizer

In the past on family road trips, I've found that keeping books and games organized and within reach (instead of under the seats) was a challenge for my boys, Joshua, 6, and Brooks, 4. I finally figured out the perfect solution: I purchased a plastic window planter and cut two parallel slits through the bottom of one end. I threaded the middle seat belt through the slits, so the box stays safely attached to the backseat. I even attached battery-operated lights (the kind you clip to books) on both sides of the box so the boys each have a lamp for reading. Best of all, the box keeps them on their own sides of the car, reducing the fight factor tremendously.

Angela Ruder, San Antonio, Texas

a buffet laden with hearty country-fried steak, fried catfish, meat loaf, fried chicken, and all the fixin's. Entrée specials change daily, but if your kids can't find anything they like on the buffet, the staff will prepare some chicken nuggets for them. Call for weekend and evening hours. *213 Church St., Andersonville. (229) 928-8480.*

Nu-Way Wieners
★★★★/$

Though it sounds like a place that serves futuristic hot dogs, this eatery has been in business in Macon since 1916, making it one of two of the oldest hot dog stands in the nation (the other being Brooklyn, New York's Nathan's Famous). Kids of all ages love the specially made dogs (a combination of beef and pork) that are fried on a grill for extra flavor. Pair up the great-tasting dog and the beanless chili, and you've got a surefire winning kid-friendly combination. But Nu-Way is more than just wieners. Other treats include thick-cut fries, superthick chocolate malts, and yummy breakfast sandwiches. Multiple locations. *430 Cotton Ave., Macon. (478) 743-1368; www.nu_wayweiners.com*

Quickie Restaurant
★★★/$

In spite of its name, this diner-style restaurant is not a fast-food joint, but a stick-to-the-basics dining institution that's been around since 1954. Although omelettes are their claim to fame, the sausage-and-egg breakfast sandwich also gets rave reviews. Quickie's is one of the best values around: Even the dinner entrées are priced well under $10. *1906 N. Slappey Blvd., Albany. (229) 432-1906.*

Villa Gargano
★★★★/$$

Whether you're hungry for pasta, pizza, or pannini (Italian for sandwich), you'll find it at this Albany mainstay. Start off by sharing a crispy Italian onion flower (mild enough for kids) and then let everyone choose their own favorites; individual pizzas, baked macaroni, and fettucine Alfredo get top billing. *1604 N. Slappey Blvd., Albany. (229) 436-7265.*

FamilyFun GAME

Color Safari

This all-ages game is easily adaptable to your kids' attention spans and the amount of time you have to play. All you do is agree on a basic color—such as red, blue, green, or yellow—and challenge your kids to find 100 items that are this color. Younger kids can play a shortened version—counting items to 10 or even 25; older kids will be challenged if you set a time limit and make them race against one another. You can also give each player a different color to search for.

Zaxby's ★/$

If your kids like chicken, then head for this do-it-yourself fast-food restaurant, complete with TVs and video games. The chicken fingers (served with fries, coleslaw, and Texas toast) are some of the best in the South; and the kids can get their own smaller version (with fries) for only a couple of bucks. The wings are yummy, too. Mild or spicy, it's all good. Multiple locations. *2629 Peach Orchard Rd., Augusta. (706) 798-3000.*

Souvenir Hunting

Bobs Candies Outlet Store

Everybody loves candy canes and Bobs makes more of them than anyone on the planet. Choose from the sugary sweet canes and mints in a handful of assorted flavors. *900 S. Westover Blvd., Albany. (229) 430-8383;* www.bobscandies.com

Father Goose's International Toys

This friendly shop carries loads of entertaining and educational toys and games of all shapes and sizes. Looking for something really unusual? Ask about the horse swing made out of recycled tires! *4524 Forsyth Landing, Macon. (478) 477-8538.*

Sorensen's Doll Houses

Not far from the Georgia Agrirama in Tifton, this haven for the serious and not-so-serious doll aficionado stocks dolls, dollhouses, miniatures, and even hard-to-find lighting and electrical kits. *2075 Whiddon Rd., Tifton. (229) 382-2888.*

Search for shells, feathers, and claws along the shores of Tybee Island.

INTRODUCTION

Savannah and Coastal Georgia

IF YOU ARE LOOKING for just the right place to spend a laid-back holiday with the kids, a getaway where the family van may take a backseat to the bicycle or trolley car, or even a horse-drawn carriage, welcome to Savannah and more than 100 miles of Coastal Georgia—a stretch of friendly seashore where you and your kids will find a host of vacation treasures.

Perhaps you'll unpack your bags in Savannah; with its wealth of kid-friendly history—note that the pirate Blackbeard and Girl Scout Founder Juliette Gordon Lowe's stomping grounds were within blocks of each other here. You can expect a big thumbs-up from the peanut gallery. A day—or maybe several—at nearby Tybee Island with a dip in the awesome Atlantic will be a refreshing change of pace.

Down the road from Savannah (about 80 miles south) begins the popular vacation haven known as Brunswick and the Golden Isles.

THE FamilyFun LIST

Fort Pulaski (page 215)

Okefenokee Swamp Park (page 219)

St. Simons Trolley Tour (page 220)

Summer Waves (page 220)

Tybee Island (page 220)

Victoria's Carriages and Trail Rides (page 220)

FamilyFun **VACATION GUIDE**

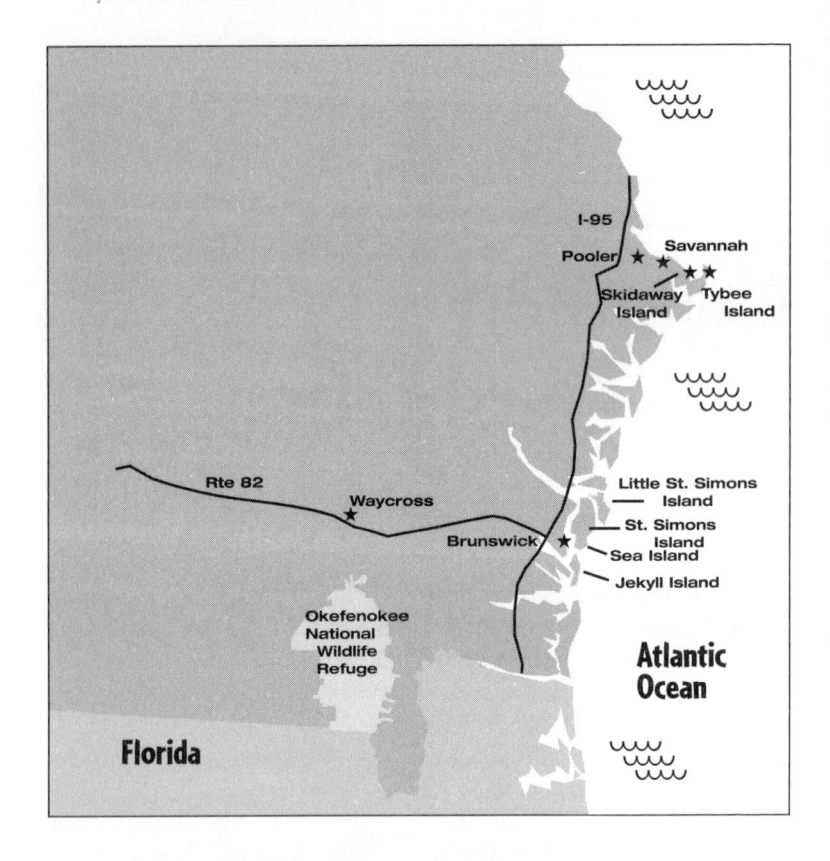

More than 400 years ago, Spanish explorers came here searching for gold. Instead, they found glorious weather, pristine nature, and unmatched radiance—a trio of treasures that later became known as The Golden Isles. Made up of the mainland city of Brunswick and islands called St. Simons, Sea, Little St. Simons, and Jekyll, this area is a favorite among families who return year after year for its sand and surf, memorable meals, and awesome activities.

Cultural Adventures

Fort Frederica National Monument ★★/Free

If your crew is good at using their imaginations, make sure that you stop at this former military town in St. Simons. At first, Fort Frederica may look like nothing more than a huge park with lots of trees. But, with a heaping helping of imagination and a stop at the visitors' center, your family will see that Fort Frederica is so much more. Check out the cool artifacts and interactive kiosk—the latter offers a look at what kept kids busy in the 1740s (sure to make your own youngsters' chores seem like a breeze). The 20-minute orientation film is helpful for kids ages 7 or older. Once outside, you'll have to hold them back from running up and down Broad Street, originally this town's main thoroughfare. Although the only ruins still standing (sort of) are the fort, barracks, and bastion; with a few reenactments on your part, this town of yesteryear comes alive. *6500 Frederica Rd., St. Simons Island. (912) 638-3639;* www.nps.gov/fofr/

Fort Pulaski
FamilyFun ★★★★/$$

About 10 miles from Savannah, on the way to Tybee Island, you'll run into Fort Pulaski—a must-see for the entire family. It's one of the few forts around that remains intact—at least the cool parts like the moat, drawbridges, and bunkers. It's also one of the few Civil War structures that you can truly experience up close—you can touch the bricks, run through the tunnels, and climb to the top where the cannons once defended the approach to Savannah. Also on display are several models of the officers' living quarters. A short nature trail and road lead to a well-shaded picnic area. If you're hiking to the picnic area, stay on the well-marked path—snakes and alligators sometimes like to hang out nearby. Remember bug spray and sunscreen. *SR 80 East, Cockspur Island, Savannah. (912) 786-5787;* www.nps.gov/fopu

Juliette Gordon Low Birthplace ★★/$

You don't have to be a Girl Scout to enjoy a tour of this historic home in Savannah. In fact, the ornately decorated home is not so much a shrine to the scouting movement as it is a tribute to its founder, Juliette Gordon Low. On the 30-minute tour, your kids will chuckle at the amusing anecdotes told by some of the best tour guides around. (Listen for the one about Juliette's mother sliding down the stair rail.) Juliette, or Daisy (to family and friends), was quite an artist, and examples of her work are displayed throughout the mansion. Save time for a visit to the gift shop on the garden level—it's stocked with Scout memorabilia and items related to 19th-century life in Savannah. *142 Bull St., Savannah. (912) 233-4501.*

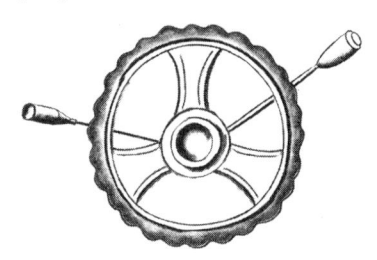

FamilyFun VACATION GUIDE

Marine Education Center and Aquarium ★★/$

A 10-minute drive from Skidaway Island State Park is this small but kid-friendly learning center that's operated by the University of Georgia. Although it doesn't offer all the bells and whistles of a big-time aquarium, you'll still find a bunch of cool stuff to see and do. For instance, your toddlers will squeal with delight when creatures like the octopus and spiny lobster come out to say hello (behind glass, of course). The preteen crowd will get a kick out of the fossils of prehistoric animals that used to hang out near the Skidaway River. Also sure to get a "wow!" is the center's collection of teeth—from beavers and sloth to rhinos and camels. Outside you'll find several nature trails, a playground (kids love the boat!), and an ideal picnic spot overlooking the Skidaway River. Rumor has it that dolphins are often spotted from the banks, so look closely. *30 Ocean Science Circle, Skidaway Island. (912) 598-2496.*

Mighty Eighth Air Force Heritage Museum ★/$

Although visitors of all ages are welcome here, reserve this stop for your nearly teens who may be studying about the U.S. Armed Forces or World War II in school. Located about 15 minutes northwest of Savannah's historic district, the museum is a tribute to the men and women who have served in the Eighth Air Force from World War II to the present. Key exhibits for your

DAY-TRIP
Getting Swamped

Just a hop, skip, and a jump (that's less than an hour) from Jekyll Island is Waycross, one of three major gateways to the eerie, mysterious, and kid-friendly **Okefenokee Swamp Park** *(eight miles south of Waycross off U.S. 1; 912/283-0583).*

Headwaters of the Suwannee and St. Mary's Rivers, Okefenokee is a National Wildlife Refuge that has within it a ton of activities to delight even the hard-to-please child. A good place to start (you've got nearly a half million acres to choose from) is the 30-minute boat tour along the Seminole Indian Waterways. There's also a one-hour train ride, which takes you through the wetlands. If time is limited, opt for the boat ride. A quick walk from the boat dock is the Living Swamp and Deer Observatory. Here, make sure your kids check out the Land of the Trembling Earth (the Swamp's nickname) display and Old Roy, an artificial yet convincing-looking 650-pound model alligator, just perfect for a photo op or two. The 20-minute Eye On Nature show is both funny and educational—a look at some of the Swamp's most popular

12-year-olds include Prelude to War (a look at Hitler's dark power over the masses, including German youth willing to give up their lives for their "savior"), Mission Experience (a three-part exhibit on the briefing, preparation, and actual mission), Gunner Exhibit (a simulated fuselage section depicting conditions and weapons of an Eighth Air Force bomber gunner), and Prisoner of War (a recreation of a Stalag Luft prison camp in World War II). Many of the museum guides are World War II veterans and love to share their colorful military stories. Encourage your children to visit with the guides to learn of their personal experiences. *175 Bourne Ave., Pooler. (912) 748-8888;* www.mighty8th museum.com

Ships of the Sea Maritime Museum ★★/$

Don't let the elegant and often quiet setting deter your crew from touring this wonderful museum. All ages are welcome to explore the nearly two dozen ship models and the boatload of maritime artifacts. As you enter the museum, make sure you pick up a gallery search sheet for each child. The simple questions go a long way toward making sure your family gets the most out of the visit. (Who knows—there may be a prize at the end of the sailing.) There's a replica of the *Titanic* for those who haven't gotten their fill of the famous ship and movie hoopla. Don't miss the large scrimshaw display on the second floor. *41 M. L. King Blvd., Savannah. (912) 232-1511.*

swift and slimy residents. The Nature Center and Bear Observatory houses a not-to-miss display called What am I?—lots of fuzzy feels to choose from. Families should plan on at least a half-day to enjoy the key sites at Okefenokee Swamp. Other entrances to the Okefenokee are located southwest of Folkston and east of Fargo.

Before heading back to the Golden Isles, if time permits, visit **Obediah's Okefenok** *(5115 Obediah Trail, Waycross; 912/287-0090)*, a tribute to Obediah Barber and others who chose to live on the edge of the Okefenokee Swamp. A colorful character, Obediah had 20 children and was said to have killed a large black bear almost with his bare hands. The homestead consists of buildings and exhibits representative of life in the mid-1800s to early 1900s. More than 75 different critters also call Obediah's home, including some extremely talkative parrots.

If your family is too tired to drive back to the coast, Waycross has affordable hotels, including a friendly Holiday Inn *($; 1725 Memorial Dr.; 800/465-4329; 912/283-4490)*, where kids will head immediately for the putting green or pool.

Tree Spirits

A tree is a tree is a tree, right? Not on St. Simons Island, home to five mysteriously real-looking tree spirits. Their detailed, weathered faces have been carved by skilled artisans into centuries-old oak trees to immortalize the countless sailors who lost their lives at sea on the sailing ships made from St. Simons' oak. Their sad expressions reflect the grieving appearance of the tree itself with its drooping branches and moss. Guaranteed to rate a "way cool" from the younger set. Look for the tree spirits at the following locations:

- Demere Road at Skylane Drive
- Demere Road at the Coastal Center for the Arts
- On Mallery Street next to Murphy's Tavern in the village
- In front of the Wine and Cheese Cellar in Redfern Village (off Frederica Road)
- 305 Frederica Road

St. Simons Island Lighthouse ★/$

Sure, it's 129 steps to the very top. But once you've reached the pinnacle and take in the incredible view of the Golden Isles, you quickly forget your tired muscles. Located in the village, the lighthouse is one of only five surviving light towers in Georgia and remains a beacon for traffic entering St. Simons Sound. A two-story museum, formerly the lighthouse keeper's dwelling, contains exhibits on the history of the lighthouse and what life was like at the turn of the century for the lighthouse keeper and family. Some even say the place is haunted. Hmmm. *101 12th St., St. Simons Island. (912) 638-4666;* www.schoonerman.com/stsim.htm

JUST FOR FUN

Dolphin Tours ★★/$$$

It's more than possible that a 75-minute boat ride through the coastal marshlands and inland waters will be just enough to turn your kids into dolphin fanatics. Dolphins love shallow water, so shortly after launch, you can count on seeing several frolicking near shore. Most dolphins come up for air every 90 seconds or so; make sure your family joins the crew in constantly looking out for these gentle creatures. When the voyage hits a dry spell the captain does a fine job entertaining and educating you with fascinating factoids. The pontoon boat's canopy offers adequate shade, but bring the sunscreen along, just to be safe. There are rest room facilities and life jackets on board. *1 Pier Rd., Jekyll Wharf Marina, Jekyll Island. (912) 635-3152.*

Earth Day Nature Trail
★/Free

Although you'll have a tough time finding this self-guided trail, the effort is worth it, especially if your family has some nature lovers. This is a time for total silence so that your family can hear the *who-ah, whoo, whoo* of the mourning doves or the rustling of the grasses that will tell the kids where to spot a marsh rabbit or two. Take the north loop to the observation tower, which overlooks the marshes. Large, stationary binoculars (free) at the observation tower provide miles of uninterrupted views of some of the most extensive and productive marshlands in the world. It is vistas like this one that inspired the Georgia poet Sidney Lanier to write *The Marshes of Glynn*. To reach the Earth Day Nature Trail from Jekyll, take U.S. 17 over the Sidney Lanier Bridge. At the foot of the bridge on the Brunswick side, look for the Department of Natural Resources sign. Turn right at the sign and continue a short distance to the parking lot of the DNR's coastal regional headquarters. The trail is to the left. *Brunswick. (912) 264-7218.*

GHOST TALK/GHOST WALK
★/$$

Rumor has it that Savannah is one of the most haunted cities in the U.S. What better way to find out than to take this 90-minute after-dark guided walk of the historic district, where you'll learn of some mysterious "happenings"—or at least, legends—that didn't make the official history books. Bizarre tales of unidentified footsteps, missing clothes, flickering lights, and rearranged furniture will intrigue even the most skeptical youngster. Although the stories are not scary, the one-mile walk at night may be a bit much for kids ages 8 and under. Tours depart from *Reynolds Square in the historic district. (800) 563-3896; (912) 233-3896;* www.savannahgeorgia.com/ghostwalk

Okefenokee Swamp Park ★★★★/$$

Think the name sounds yucky? Think again. This place provides family fun in countless varieties. For more, see page 216.

Old Savannah Tours
★★★/$$-$$$

For a colorful overview of this intriguing city, try a 90-minute narrated ride aboard one of Old Savannah Tours' white trolleys. Not only will you learn about the city's early days, your kids will get a bang out of some of the lesser-known points of interest—including the dueling ground, the "residents" of Colonial Park Cemetery, and the fancy fish downspouts. **NOTE:** It's worth the few extra dollars to take advantage of the unlimited on/off boarding privileges at 13 convenient trolley stops in the historic district. This option also includes free admission to one of four popular museums and attractions. Tours depart from the downtown visitors center. *250 M.L. King Blvd., Savannah. (800) 517-9007; (912) 234-8128;* www.oldsavtour.com

St. Simons Trolley Tour
★★★★/$$

What better way to get your bearings for a visit to St. Simons than on this entertaining 90-minute tour around this island? You'll hear about the early days of this funky town, and here's a plus: your friendly guide knows some of the more colorful stories not always found in guidebooks. At Christ Church, you'll walk among the tombstones or go inside for a quick peek at this landmark. Along the way, listen for tips on where to eat, sleep, and, perhaps, shop. *Departs from the pier on Mallery Street in the village. St. Simons Island. (912) 638-8954.*

Summer Waves
★★★★/$$

With over a million gallons of splashtacular fun, everybody will find something to enjoy at this seasonal attraction. Your daring preteens will want to check out Pirates Passage, while toddlers will have a heyday in the twister and otter slide. In between are oceans of fun on more thrilling flumes, a big-time wave pool, and a meandering floating river. And when hunger pangs hit, take your kids to any of the park's three Larry's Giant Subs stands. Pack lots of sunscreen and hats since shade is a tad scarce here. **NOTE:** Children under 10 must be accompanied by an adult. *210 S. Riverview Dr., Jekyll Island. (912) 635-2074.*

Tybee Island
★★★★/Free

Island adventures galore await your whole family at this sensational seasonal spot. For more information, see page 222.

Victoria's Carriages and Trail Rides
★★★★/$$$$

Your kids will be chomping at the bit to tell their friends where they went horseback riding on vacation—the beach! That's just a part of what's in store with this friendly operator, that is, as long as everyone is older than 8 and weighs less than 230 pounds. Guides do a great job with instructions and matching up your troop's riding experience with the right horses. The one-hour ride on Driftwood Beach and through the Maritime Forest is the perfect length for families. **NOTE:** Make sure you inquire about the tide schedule when you make your reservation: Low tide offers the most beach time. Bring insect repellent. Also, doing a dozen or so deep-knee bends—several times before and after the ride—goes a long way toward reducing the sore and aching muscles that usually follow. *You buy tickets at the visitors' center on Stable Road. Rides leave from Clam Creek picnic area at the northernmost point of Jekyll Island. (912) 635-9500.*

Bunking Down

Blythe Island Regional Park and Campground ★★/$
Just six miles from downtown Brunswick, this 1,100-acre public park offers loads of family-friendly things to do, plus a comfortable place to rest your head at night. From primitive tent sites in the backwoods to really snazzy digs (complete with water and electricity), all come with picnic tables and fire rings. During the day, choose from fresh and saltwater fishing, boating, swimming, and hiking; even horseshoes and field archery bring out the outdoorsman in all of us. *6616 Blythe Island Hwy., Brunswick. (800) 343-7855; (912) 261-3805.*

The Cloister
★★★★/$$$$
If you're looking for just the right place to splurge, to throw budgets to the winds and indulge in action-packed fun for the kids and a pampered, relaxing retreat for parents, this resort is just what you're looking for. With a wide range of accommodations and rates, The Cloister offers a wildly popular—and free (well, included in the rates)—seasonal childrens' program, plus complimentary afternoon tennis and golf on select courses for your kids.

FamilyFun READER'S TIP

Foil Boredom

This one is so simple you won't believe it. Just buy a roll of aluminum foil (make sure to remove the saw on the box), and toss it into the backseat. Although foil is hardly a traditional sculpture material, it works. In the hands of your kids, aluminum foil can be turned into snakes, crowns, masks, and more. (You might need to switch activities when it turns into a bat and balls.)

Angela de la Rocha, Sterling, Virginia

FamilyFun **VACATION GUIDE**

The Cloister's all-inclusive American Plan gets you accommodations, all meals, beach club facilities, lawn sports, entertainment, and dancing. Children under 19 sharing accommodations with parents pay only for their meals. *Sea Island. (800) 732-4752; (912) 638-3611.*

Jekyll Inn ★★★/$
It's the largest resort on the island, but the the friendly staff is still aiming to please *all* guests—pint-size and older. You can choose among various types of lodging at the oceanfront property, including roomy one- and two-bedroom villas. Seasonal Fun Factory children's activity programs (fee), game room, and in-room Nintendo are just a few of the kid-friendly features. *975 N. Beachview Dr., Jekyll Island. (800) 736-1046; (912) 635-2531; www.jekyllinn.com*

Jekyll Island Club Hotel
★★★/$$
Far from stuffy, this historic landmark—once the winter home of the rich and famous—offers charming historic ambience with just the right level of modern convenience. A children's program (it's seasonal and there's a fee) and Family Festival series (fee) offer fun for everyone. Celebrate that special occasion by dining at the hotel's Grand Dining Room. *371 Riverview Dr., Jekyll Island. (800) 535-9547; (912) 635-2600.*

King and Prince Beach and Golf Resort
★★★/$-$$
Your kids can choose from not one, two, or even three, but *five* cool pools, plus the Grand Daddy of 'em all—the Atlantic Ocean—when you stay at this popular St. Simons resort.

DAY-TRIP
Fantastic Island

If you're looking for endless strands of sand with lots of lifeguards, you'll find them less than 20 miles due east of Savannah on **Tybee Island**. And there's so much more. Begin your coastal visit with a spectacular view of the island and ocean from the top of the **Tybee Island Lighthouse** *(off U.S. 80 at Fort Screven; 912/786-5801),* some 178 steps nearly straight up. Although you can stop at the periodic landings to catch your breath, forget the climb if your kids are under 7.

Across the street from the lighthouse is the **Tybee Island Museum** *(off U.S. 80 at Fort Screven; 912/786-5801),* a mishmash of local memorabilia. Kids love the working periscope just inside the museum, the antique doll collection, and the amusement park exhibit.

Hop back in the car and head for the **Tybee Island Marine Science Center** *(at the south end of the 14th*

Choose from a range of lodgings, including two- and three-bedroom villas with fully equipped kitchens and awesome ocean views. For a fun morning, rent a couple of banana bikes and ride along the beach, or for the more adventurous, kayaks and sailboats make for great family outings. There's also a children's program (fee). *201 Arnold Rd., St. Simons Island. (800) 342-0212; (912) 638-3631;* www.kingandprince.com

La Quinta Inn Midtown ★/$

This friendly chain property is on one of Savannah's main thoroughfares. If you head east, it's a straight shot to the action-packed historic district or to the west, a quick five minutes to the mall. In-room Nintendo and a refreshing outdoor pool are kid-pleasers. *6805 Abercorn St., Savannah. (800) 531-5900; (912) 355-3004.*

Mulberry Inn ★★★/$$

Although you'll find more B&Bs than motels in Savannah's Historic District, places like the Mulberry Inn (affiliated with Holiday Inn) are here for vacationing families. Kids like the outdoor heated pool and a chance to show off their social skills during the complimentary high tea (served daily between 4 and 6 P.M.). An in-the-know concierge service can recommend loads of kids' activities during your stay. *601 E. Bay St., Savannah. (912) 238-1200.*

Skidaway Island State Park ★★/$

If you're in the mood for roughing it—but not too rough—try camping at Skidaway. The park has 88 sites complete with water and electrical hookups, elevated tent pads, a grill, and picnic tables. Before calling it a day, make sure you check out the

---

Street Beach Parking Lot; 912-786-5917). Depending on the season and time of day, you may arrive in time for a one-hour guided beach walk. Inside the center, there's a very small aquarium, touch tank, shell collection, and a telling lesson on what litter does to our beaches and oceans. It isn't SeaWorld, but it does give kids a glimpse into local marine life. (If the Marine Center piqued your family's interest, you may want to check out the 90-minute **Dolphin Cruise** offered by Bull River Yacht Club Marina, *8005 Old Tybee Rd.; 912/897-7300.*)

If hunger strikes, check out family-friendly spots like **The Grill** *($-$$; 404 Butler Ave.; 912/786-4745)* and **Macelwee's Seafood Restaurant** *($-$$; Hwy. 80; 912/786-4259).* **The Beachside Colony** *($-$$; 404 Butler Ave.; 800/424-4777; 912/786-4535)* and **River's End RV Resort** *($; 915 Polk St.; 800/786-1016; 912/786-5518)* offer comfortable and fun accommodations—both are sure to please the whole family.

FamilyFun VACATION GUIDE

Mr. Mom
Warning: this activity is decidedly addictive. Bring along a Polaroid camera and, while eating at a rest stop, take each person's picture in the exact same sitting or standing position (and from the exact same vantage point).

Once you are back in the car, use safety scissors to cut the pictures in half horizontally. You can then shuffle your family's faces and torsos (if the pictures were taken from a distance) or the top and bottom halves of their faces (if you took close-ups). If you're feeling particularly creative, you can paste each picture onto a piece of paper, cut the paper along the same horizontal lines, and secure it in a loose-leaf binder to form your own Family Mix and Match book. Any way you slice it, this activity is worth the effort.

---

marked nature trails (choose from the one-mile or three-mile) that will guide you through some of "hey, what's this?" lessons disguised as fun. From Memorial Day to Labor Day, cool off in the Junior Olympic swimming pool (fee). *52 Diamond Causeway, Savannah. (912) 598-2300.*

GOOD EATS

Barbara Jean's ★★★★/$-$$
If your family eats only one meal in St. Simons—or the entire Golden Isles for that matter—this should be the place. Although you may have to wait for a table, this haven for southern dining is worth it—even the fries are awesome! Kids get a bang out of ordering—and then devouring—such side dishes as "dirty rice" and out-of-this-world desserts like "chocolate stuff." For Mom and Dad (and your more adventurous youngsters): don't pass up the restaurant's signature crab cakes or the creamy she-crab soup. Once you're seated, service is swift, efficient, and friendly. *214 Mallery St., St. Simons Island. (912) 634-6500.*

The Lady & Sons ★★★★/$-$$
If your family is in the mood for good ole' southern cooking, you're sure to find it at this popular restaurant located in downtown Savannah's City Market District. Although the lunch and dinner entrées are more adult-oriented, you can't go wrong with the yummy buffet, offered at both meals. Your kids will have a tough time choosing from the buffet's crispy fried chicken or macaroni and cheese. Both are crowd pleasers among the young set. *311 Congress St., Savannah. (912) 233-2600.*

Mrs. Wilkes Boarding House ★★★★/$-$$
Tucked away in a small nook in Savannah's historic district, this

legendary restaurant serves up some of the best southern cooking this side of... well, nearly anywhere! It's family-style seating and serving, meaning you'll end up easily chatting with your tablemates within minutes. Don't expect to order an individual serving from the menu—in fact, menus don't really exist at Mrs. Wilkes. For breakfast, it's usually fresh fruit, homemade biscuits, gravy, grits, eggs, and meats. Enjoy heaping bowls of local specialties—dishes like fried chicken, meat loaf, macaroni and cheese, and all the traditional sides for lunch. It's the only restaurant we know of where everyone helps clear the table—and nobody argues! Open for breakfast and lunch only (closed Saturdays and Sundays). *107 W. Jones St., Savannah. (912) 232-5997.*

Pirates' House
★★★/$$

Families can choose from 15 different dining rooms—many of them boasting intriguing and colorful histories that go as far back as the mid-1700s. In fact, when you tell your kids that some of the action from Robert Louis Stevenson's classic *Treasure Island* reportedly was set in the Pirates' House, you can expect everyone to be on their best behavior! Youngsters will love the First Mate's Menu, which also doubles as a one-eyed pirate's mask. Suggest to your kids that the pirates also might have gone for the Tough Captain Flint entrée—fried chicken and two side dishes—or the Long John Silver—hamburger or cheeseburger and fries. *20 E. Broad St., Savannah. (912) 233-5757.*

Sand Castle Café & Grille
★★/$

Experts say that breakfast is probably the most important meal of the day—and nonexperts can tell you it is often the tastiest. So get off on the right foot by indulging at this place, which serves one of the best breakfast buffets around. Among the favorites: biscuits, grits, and eggs cooked to order. It's also a popular lunch stop. *117 Mallery St., St. Simons Island. (912) 638-8883.*

SeaJays
★/$$

Location, location, location—with tasty food to boot. That's the winning recipe here at marshside, in the Jekyll Harbor Marina. Kids won't

---

FamilyFun TIP

Cool It

Whether you use a cooler, an insulated bag or box, or Tupperware, here's how to keep snacks cool without messy, melting ice: Add frozen juice boxes; make sandwiches on frozen bread; pack some frozen grapes; include a smoothie frozen in a tightly sealed container; use sealed ice packs.

mind the wait for a table when they've got some supercool boats to check out just a few steps away. Make sure you request an outdoor table for the incredible view of the Golden Isles' setting sun, not to mention some extra leg and running room for the kids. The chicken tenders from the childrens' menu hit the spot, or for a real culinary adventure, try the Shrimp Bowl Buffet—a mildly spicy combo of shrimp, sausage, corn, and potatoes. *1 Harbor Rd., Jekyll Island. (912) 635-3200;* www.seajays.com

Spanky's Marshside
★★★★/$-$$

If you can overlook the hint of its saloon-type appearance, you'll find yourself quickly won over by the outgoing staff, humongous wooden booths complete with built-in aquariums (great amusement while waiting for your meal), and tasty and oversized helpings (expect a doggie bag with these hearty servings). Multiple locations. *1200 Glynn Ave., Brunswick. (912) 267-6100.*

Willie's Wee-Nee Wagon
★★★/$

You might have a hard time imagining anyone going seriously gaga over a hot dog, but there's no denying that kids young and old line up at Willie's counter for some of the top dogs and best boneless pork-chop sandwiches around. (So confident is Willie that the place offers $2,000 in cash if a better boneless pork-chop sandwich can be found in the county.) Outdoor picnic tables make up most of the seating. *3599 Altama Ave., Brunswick. (912) 264-1146.*

Zachry's
★★/$-$$

There's nothing fancy about this place—just wonderful food at reasonable prices. It's a winning combination that keeps visitors and locals coming back for more. Your youngsters are sure to scarf down the shrimp or fish from their own special menu. Be sure to warn them that the seafood is so fresh, it may jump off their plate if they dawdle over dinner. *44 Beachview Dr., Jekyll Island. (912) 635-3128.*

Souvenir Hunting

The Cinderella Shop

This pricey children's clothing store carries a gazillion Lily Pulitzer items for girls (through size 14), not to mention some good-looking duds for boys (through size 7). *5500 Abercorn St., Savannah. (912) 691-0109.*

Cinnamon Bear Country Store

Although the children's section is relatively small, there's still plenty to delight the younger generation with clever zipper pulls, finger puppets, stuffed animals, and cutesy jewelry. Multiple locations. *Old City Market, Savannah. (912) 232-2888.*

Go Fish
Whether your kids are looking for a cool fish sculpture to decorate their room or a funky T-shirt to decorate their bodies, they'll find it at this popular shop in the village. *203 Mallery St., St. Simons Island. (912) 634-5654.*

Jekyll Books and Antiques
Housed in a former infirmary for the rich and famous, this two-story treasure sells a few antiques (check out the ancient Coke bottles), but mostly books—both old and new. The children's book room is at the rear. *101 Old Plantation Rd., Jekyll Island. (912) 635-3077.*

Just 4 Funn Toys
This village kids' store is jam-packed with toys for kids of all ages. From Playmobil to Wild Planet, you're sure to find it here. *205 Mallery St., St. Simons Island. (912) 638-3866.*

Ocean Motion
Your preteens will find loads of cool duds at this village beachwear shop that specializes in popular names like Patagonia and JAMS World. Multiple locations. *1300 Ocean Blvd., St. Simons Island. (912) 638-5225.*

Universe Trading Co.
This warehouselike shopping stop is a cross between the world's funkiest garage sale and some honest-to-goodness antiques. Give each child a buck or two—you'll be amazed at what they'll come back with. *27 Montgomery St., Savannah. (912) 233-1585.*

Pedal your way through Callaway Gardens on the Discovery Bicycle Trail.

INTRODUCTION

Callaway Gardens and Columbus

COLUMBUS is a distinctive mixture of the new and old—filled with historic buildings now used in modern ways. The city is dotted with locations rich in history, including Civil War sites and textile mills. The Chattahoochee River runs through here, part of it edged by a 12-mile walking park called the Riverwalk, a picturesque place for families to bike, skate, jog, or stroll.

Although Columbus is the big city in this region, tiny Pine Mountain—home to well-known Callaway Gardens—is the main attraction. The downtown is small—only two stoplights, no Golden Arches or 7-Elevens—and Pine Mountain is full of opportunities for family fun. Whether your kids are into nature, sports, recreation, or just chilling out, Callaway Gardens has it all.

THE FamilyFun LIST

Callaway Gardens (page 231)

F.D. Roosevelt State Park (page 232)

Westville (page 231)

Wild Animal Safari (page 235)

FamilyFun **VACATION GUIDE**

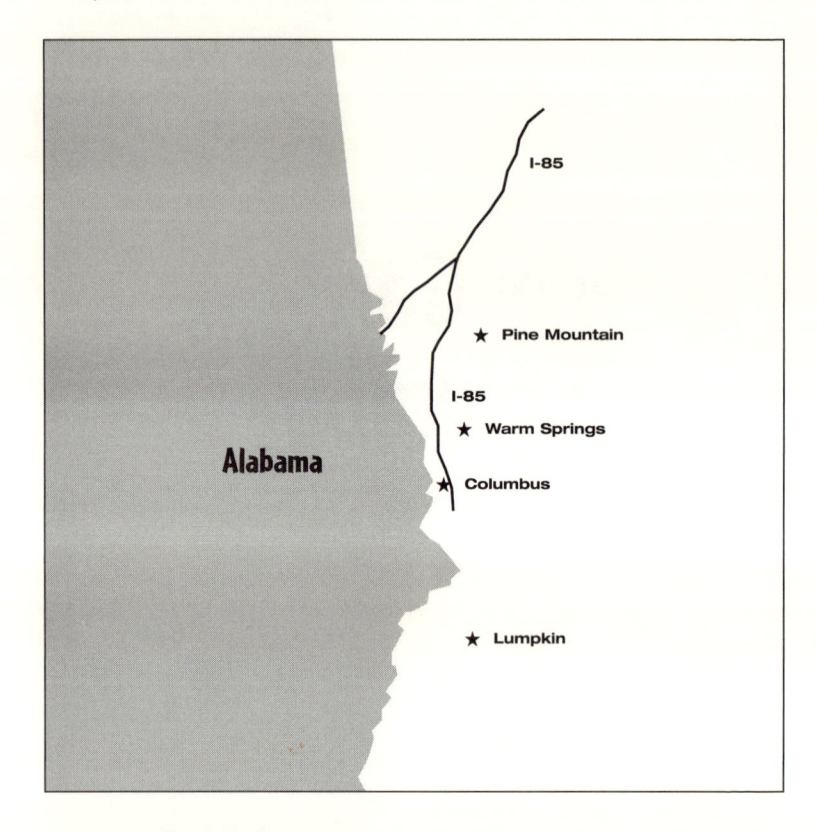

Map showing Alabama border with markers for Pine Mountain, Warm Springs, Columbus, and Lumpkin, with I-85 indicated.

Nearby Warm Springs is known for its sultry waters and therapeutic centers as well as its small-town charm. It is a bustling center of activity, offering visitors a healthy heaping of southern hospitality.

Families who visit the region will be rewarded with a vacation packed with relaxation and glimpses of times past. Sorry, kids: no amusement parks, T-shirt shops, or souvenir stands in these parts—just lots of natural attractions, nifty animals, and history that will hold your interest even if you've never really been into history. Most important, families who visit here have plenty of quality time to experience some memorable moments together.

CULTURAL ADVENTURES

Little White House
★★/$

President Franklin D. Roosevelt first came to the Warm Springs area in 1924 in search of warm-water treatments for his paralysis. The six-room Little White House he had built still looks much as it did the day he died here, April 12, 1945. A guided tour takes you through the home, plus gives you a look at FDR's two (now) antique cars. The little ones may not find it spellbinding, but your budding history buffs won't want to miss it. Nearly everyone gets a bang out of the outdoor walkway—made up of stones and flags from the 50 states. Can you find your state flag? *401 Little White House Rd., Warm Springs. (706) 655-5870;* www.attractionsamerica.com/ae_atlanta/atlanta_20.htm

Westville
FamilyFun ★★★★/$

Step back in time to the days of the '50s . . . the *1850s*, that is. With more than 30 authentically furnished pre–Civil War buildings, including homes, stores, and workshops, Westville has all the trappings of a functioning mid-18th-century town. A novel way to make American history come alive—you can hear the clang of the blacksmith's hammer; smell biscuits and coffee cooking on the hearth; try your hand at making candles, syrup, and soap; see where the townspeople worshiped, voted, and went to school; visit old-time gardens; and sample hearth-cooked food. *Located at the intersection of U.S. 27 and Georgia 27, Lumpkin. (888) 733-1850; (229) 838-6310;* www.westville.org

JUST FOR FUN

Butts Mill Farm ★★/$$
Let your youngsters discover the sights and sounds of a fully operational farm and gristmill at this restored 80-acre farm. Here, kids can get to know more than 120 farm animals in a safe and friendly petting zoo and then enjoy a hayride, carriage ride, or horseback ride (included in admission price). If fishing is your pleasure, the farm supplies the bait and tackle and the fish-filled pond—the rest is up to you. And don't let the kids miss the Wild West playground and the in-ground trampolines. *2280 Butts Mill Rd. (off U.S. Hwy. 27), Pine Mountain. (706) 663-7400.*

Callaway Gardens
FamilyFun ★★★★/$$

This unforgettable garden beckons you with its azalea-lined roadways and picturesque lakes. Nature lovers of all ages will not want to miss this spot, where nature has been transformed into lush exhibits, with the added attractions of walking trails, golf courses, retail shops, and restaurants. Plan on spending at least two days exploring the many facets of this 14,000-acre salute to Mother Nature. For more information, see "An Outdoor Wonderland" on page 233. *U.S. Hwy. 27, Pine Mountain. (800) 225-5292;* www.callawaygardens.com

FamilyFun VACATION GUIDE

MUST-SEE FamilyFun MUST-SEE F.D. Roosevelt State Park ★★★★/$

Right on Pine Mountain, this 9,047-acre park became known to Americans as the place where President Franklin Roosevelt went for physical and emotional comfort. Don't miss FDR's favorite picnic spot, Dowdell's Knob (located above Kings Gap). It's a perfect place for some downtime while you soak up the breathtaking view of the valley below. In addition to the riding stables (*see below*), families will especially enjoy hiking some of the South's most picturesque trails that run throughout the park. Make a day of it and take a dip in the park's mountain rock swimming hole. There's also fishing and boating (fee) on Lake Delano. Camping, too (see below). *2970 Georgia Hwy. 190 (across from the Callaway Gardens Country Store), Pine Mountain. (706) 663-4858.*

Hollywood Connection ★★★/$-$$

This is the perfect place for kids—and parents—to work off some excess energy. Youngsters ages 3 to 8 will enjoy the amusement area, with its miniature Ferris wheel, carousel, swings, train, and animal-house maze. Preteens won't know which to choose first—the video arcade, laser tag area, or skate center. Of course, everyone will have a blast at the indoor miniature golf course. When you're done playing, grab a bite at the Lieutenant's Diner, then catch a movie at the 10-plex. *1683 Whittlesey Rd., Columbus. (706) 571-3456.*

Providence Canyon State Park ★★★/$

Named for the historic church that sits on its grounds, Providence gives you a panorama of 1,100 acres of chasms, crevices, and canyons. Often referred to as Georgia's Little Grand Canyon, the park contains 16 canyons altogether. In the spring, 150 varieties of wildflowers bloom throughout the area. You and your kids can choose between hiking a three-mile loop, which features the park's main canyons, or a more adventurous seven-mile trail, where you can pitch your tent if you're backpacking. The park also has a playground, museum, and gift shop. Open seasonally; call ahead. *South of Columbus on Hwy. 39C, Lumpkin. (229) 838-6202.*

Roosevelt Stables ★★★/$$

Using the various trails winding their way through F.D. Roosevelt State Park, these stables offer families a choice of several excursions. If your riders are new to the saddle, you may want to start with the guided one-hour bridle trail ride, which follows a creek along the base of the mountain and is great for children. Families with kids over 7 who have been on a horse before might want

AN OUTDOOR WONDERLAND

Pine Mountain serves as the gateway to the 14,000-acre **Callaway Gardens** *(U.S. Hwy. 27; 800/225-5292)*, created as a beautiful, natural setting for a host of educational and recreational activities. The gardens that Cason Callaway opened to the public in 1952 have blossomed into a family-fun retreat with stunning floral displays year round, 63 holes of championship golf, fishing lakes, and an array of hiking and biking trails, just for starters.

No matter what you choose to do at Callaway Gardens, make sure your to-do list includes at least one hike along one of the many trails that wind through these gorgeous Georgia woods. Most trails range from 0.5 mile to 1.5 miles and offer an easy to moderate walk. Each trail has its own distinctive charm, so you may want to try more than one.

Callaway gives your family lots of ways to observe the beauty of nature. If your time is limited, make sure to visit the Cecil B. Day Butterfly Center, the John A. Sibley Horticultural Center, and the Pioneer Log Cabin. The Log Cabin is also where you'll find the beginnings of several hiking trails. Callaway Gardens highlights include:

Cecil B. Day Butterfly Center
Your kids will love wandering among a thousand tropical butterflies, as they fly freely through the air. North America's largest, glass-enclosed tropical conservatory, the Butterfly Center also features tropical plants and birds. A sure thumbs-up!

Discovery Bicycle Trail
The wide, paved path of this trail is perfect for both you and your kids. The bicycle route takes you past all of the Gardens' major attractions, so you can make a biking day of it while seeing all there is. Bicycles and helmets may be rented here.

Ida Cason Callaway Memorial Chapel
This chapel, reminiscent of 16th-century Gothic chapels, was constructed of natural materials and features six beautiful stained-glass windows depicting the southern forest in a progression of seasons. Kids will enjoy walking among the rocks that dot the nearby stream. Just remember: slippery when wet!

John A. Sibley Horticultural Center
Make sure your family visits this one-of-a-kind garden and greenhouse, which encompasses five acres of native and exotic plants within its tropical conservatory, rock-wall garden, sculpture garden, fern grotto, floral conservatory, and outdoor

garden. Turn this stop into a "who can spot the" game for your budding florists.

Mr. Cason's Vegetable Garden

This outstanding 7.5-acre garden brings to life the art of growing things. The southern setting for the PBS television show *The Victory Garden*, the Vegetable Garden has much more than vegetables growing in it. Other crops include fruits, herbs, and flowers, plus there's a composting area. Be aware, however, that little ones may find this a tiring walk during the summer heat, since there is very little shade.

Pioneer Log Cabin

Walk inside the door of this log cabin and take a peek at what life was like back in the good old days (mid-1800s). Authentic period-style furniture, tools, and household items fill the cabin, making you appreciate your modern-day conveniences. Interestingly, this pine cabin was constructed in the 1830s and occupied until the 1930s. The last folks to live in its two rooms were a family of 15—and you thought your minivan was cramped!

Robin Lake Beach

Few people come to the woods to go to the beach, but you can do that here. Reportedly the world's largest man-made, white-sand beach, it stretches a mile around the 65-acre Robin Lake. In addition to swimming and sunning, you can also enjoy miniature golf, table tennis, shuffleboard, volleyball, paddleboats, and rides on the Chickadee Choo Choo. And don't miss the spectacular Florida State University Flying High Circus, which performs eight shows (seasonal) weekly under the big top adjacent to the beach.

The Virginia Hand Callaway Discovery Center

Named for the cofounder of Callaway Gardens, this facility is also the visitors' center, with interactive kiosks and information on what's happening throughout the gardens' 14,000 acres. The center is located in the heart of the gardens.

to try the two-hour Thoroughbred Trail, which goes to the top of Pine Mountain, where you can view the lake and valley below. For those with a more adventuresome streak—or more experience—try an overnight trip and sleep under the stars—you won't forget it. Call ahead to be sure you can take the rides you want, but you generally won't need reservations for the day trips. Do reserve for the overnight rides—complete with an afternoon cookout. *Located inside the F.D. Roosevelt State Park, Pine Mountain. (706) 628-7463.*

Wild Animal Safari
FamilyFun ★★★★/$-$$

A drive on the wild side, this is an up-close-and-personal treat for the whole family. As you wind along a paved road through the park's 500 acres, you will be able to touch a giraffe, come face-to-face with American bison, and see many other animals from all over the world, including such creatures as a nilgia (a type of antelope), rhea (a bird resembling a small ostrich), and watusi (a breed of cattle). After your safari tour, visit Old McDonald's Farm, which is similar to a traditional zoo, with the requisite monkeys, tropical birds, and alligators. The zoo animals are penned; you walk through the zoo to see them. *1300 Oak Grove Rd., Pine Mountain. (800) 367-2751; (706) 663-8744;* www.animalsafari.com

BUNKING DOWN

Callaway Gardens
★★★★/$-$$$$

Here, families can choose from three different lodgings, designed to meet any pocketbook or lifestyle. Those on tighter budgets may want to try the Callaway Gardens Inn, with more than 300 guest rooms, as well as comfortable suites with extra touches. However, Callaway's Country Cottages and Mountain Creek Villas both offer a true home-away-from-home feel; they are individual houses, with fully equipped kitchens, fireplaces, and porches—some even have washer and dryer. For the ultimate, but pricey, family getaway, Callaway offers its

---

FamilyFun GAME

I Could Eat an Alphabet

Let your half-starved brood describe how hungry they are in this game, best played about half an hour before you make a pit stop for food. This version of the I'm Packing for a Picnic game begins when you announce "I'm so hungry I could eat an aviator" ("alligator," or "apple"). The next player adds on with a B word. She might say, "I'm so hungry I could eat an aviator and a bunny rabbit" ("belly button," or "baseball"). See if you can keep it up until your family is eating zoos, zippers, or zigzags.

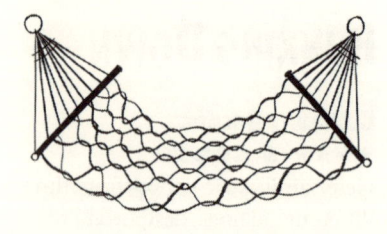

Summer Family Adventure, featuring lodging at country cottages or Mountain Creek Villas. Monday through Friday, youngsters can participate in a day camp supervised by members of the Florida State University Flying High Circus with other cool evening events. The package features seven nights' lodging for up to five people, all activities, admission to Callaway Gardens and Robin Lake Beach, and daily use of the Callaway Fitness Center (call for package rates). *Hwy. 27, Pine Mountain. (800) 225-5292;* www.callawaygardens.com

Columbus Hilton ★★★/$$

Built around the original Empire Mills Grist Mill, a red-brick mill that began operating in 1861, this hotel is ideally located: in the downtown historic district, walking distance from the Chattahoochee River, Columbus Civic Center, 1996 Olympic softball fields, and the Riverwalk. Extremely kid-friendly, the property also boasts a heated swimming pool, video arcade, and walking trail. *800 Front Ave., Columbus. (800) 524-4020; (706) 324-1800;* www.hilton.com

F.D. Roosevelt State Park Campground ★★★/$

Fully equipped cottages have stoves and refrigerators, all necessary cooking and serving utensils, towels, bed linens, and blankets; many even have porches, decks, and wood-burning fireplaces. (BYOF—bring your own firewood.) For those who *really* want to commune with the great outdoors, F.D.R. offers primitive campsites (no water spigots, rest rooms, or electricity) that are in more remote sections of the park; you can reach them only by hiking trail. *2970 Georgia Hwy. 190 (across from the Callaway Gardens Country Store), Pine Mountain. (706) 663-4858.*

Mountain Top Inn and Resort ★/$-$$

If you want to be a little more removed from the relative hustle and bustle of Pine Mountain, head into the woods of F. D. Roosevelt State Park to this secluded inn. Best bet here are the log cabins with whirlpool tubs. Families will also appreciate the pool, tennis courts, and hiking trails. *7288 Hwy. 190 and Winesgap Rd., Pine Mountain. (800) 533-6376; (706) 663-4719.*

Pine Mountain Club Chalets ★★★★/$

Nestled among the Georgia pines, these Alpine-inspired chalets feature plenty of runaround room—and lots of activities. There's a nine-hole miniature-golf course, basketball, shuffleboard, horseshoes, a children's playground, two swimming pools, and two tennis courts. What's more, many of the chalets overlook the lake, where you can also boat and fish. *14475 Hwy. 18 (across from Callaway Gardens), Pine Mountain. (800) 535-7622; (706) 663-2211.*

GOOD EATS

The Bulloch House ★★★★/$$
If you can't indulge yourself a little on vacation, when can you? If your budget can stand it, this is the place to indulge. Your kids will be wide-eyed at the hearty buffet of home-cooked southern specialties, including chicken, biscuits, and other yummy regional dishes amid the beauty of this plantation-style home. During the spring and fall, weather permitting, request a porchside table. Your entire family will love dining alfresco. *U.S. Alt. 27, Warm Springs. (706) 655-9068.*

Callaway Gardens Country Kitchen ★★★★/$$
One of the best ways to enjoy this restaurant is to *leave* it—after you've stocked up on a lot of kid-friendly food. This quaint restaurant, tucked inside the Callaway Country Store, offers a selection of dishes with down-home, country-style flavor. Order a box lunch and picnic in the splendor of nearby F.D. Roosevelt

A Travel Scrapbook

This suitcase-style scrapbook is just right for your child to pack with mementos of his vacation adventures — and it's a cinch to make.

Start with two cardboard report covers. Use one for the suitcase itself and one to cut out two U-shaped handles and two 1^1/$_2$- by 18-inch straps.

Attach one handle to the front of the suitcase by gluing the ends to the inside of the upper edge. Match up the second handle with the first one and glue it to the back side. Now close the suitcase and glue on the straps. Position the strap tops on the front of the suitcase 1 inch down from the upper edge, then wrap the straps around the back of the suitcase. Finally, fold down the strap ends so that they overlap the tops and attach stick-on, Velcro-type fasteners.

For a handy photo pocket, glue a large open envelope to the inner cover Then, fill the suitcase with manila folders for storing ticket stubs, brochures, and other souvenirs.

FamilyFun VACATION GUIDE

FamilyFun READER'S TIP

Terrific Task Masters

When our family goes on vacation, we assign each of our seven children an important task for the duration of the trip, one that will make each child an active part of planning. On a trip to Orlando, Florida, these were their assignments. Sylvia, age 15, navigator and accountant, kept track of mileage, maps, and money; TamiSue, 13, photographer, had to use two rolls of film a day; Joshua, 10, auto mechanic, pumped gas and checked oil and tire pressure; Bryan, 7, mailman, got postcards and stamps and mailed the cards kids write to themselves each day (see page 202); Libby, 7, dietitian, made sure the cooler was stocked; Andrew, 6, activities coordinator and music director, was solely in charge of the tape player; and Katie, 5, referee, settled all road disputes.

Wendy Lira, Alma, Kansas

State Park. The lunches feature such kid-favorite selections as fried chicken and ham or turkey sandwiches, plus coleslaw, sliced tomatoes, and cookies. *Hwy. 27 (across from the F.D.R. State Park entrance), Pine Mountain. (706) 663-2281; www.callawaygardens.com*

Country's Barbeque ★★★★/$

You can't (or certainly shouldn't) visit Georgia without getting some good stick-to-your-ribs barbecue, and this is the place to find it. Just how country is Country's? Well, a peek at its menu shows such southern favorites as scramble dogs, black-eyed peas, buttermilk, and goober pie. If you can't choose, order the conglomeration platter. You'll find PB&J and chicken fingers for your finicky eaters. Multiple locations. *6298 Veterans Pkwy., Columbus. (706) 660-1415.*

San Marcos Mexican Restaurante ★★★/$

Though modest in price, this restaurant has an extensive menu with more than 40 traditional Mexican dishes. Check out the perennial favorites—the chicken quesadillas and the queso (cheese) sauce are not to be missed. Mom or Dad (whoever's not driving) may want to splurge on a margarita, but, beware: the large margaritas are *really* large. *352 Main St., Pine Mountain. (706) 663-8075.*

SOUVENIR HUNTING

Callaway Gardens Country Store

You can find a little bit of everything at this cutesy country store: candles, old-fashioned candies, toys, cookbooks, and country decor galore. *U.S. Hwy. 27, Pine Mountain. (706) 663-2281.*

Day Butterfly Center Gift Shop

This shop is filled with children's toys, books, jewelry, videos, and home decor items—all with a "buggy" theme—making it a fun shopping stop for the whole family. For a really distinctive and long-lasting memento of your trip here, pick up a butterfly kit. *Located in the lobby of the Butterfly Center in Callaway Gardens, Pine Mountain. (706) 663-2281.*

The Discovery Shop

Here you'll find an intriguing collection of nature-related items for your home and garden. Youngsters will love the rain-stick kits, nature-craft kits, and sand gardens. *Located within Callaway Garden's Virginia Hand Callaway Discovery Center, Pine Mountain. (706) 663-2281.*

Kimbrough Brothers Company

Visit one of the few general stores still operating. Built in 1892, Kimbrough offers feed and seed, as well as clothing and gifts. Okay, so it may not offer all the bells and whistles that kids expect, but much of its merchandise makes it seem like a living-history museum. *44 Main St., Pine Mountain. (706) 663-2528.*

Warm Springs Village

This Victorian village features dozens of small retail shops ranging from antiques to the unique. Stroll through stores featuring handcrafted furniture, toys, quilts, collectibles, and more. Be sure to stop along the way and enjoy an ice-cream cone or pick up a sweet treat at one of the candy counters. *U.S. Alt. 27 and Georgia. Hwy. 85, Warm Springs. (800) 337-1927.*

The California sea lion is one of 250 species at Zoo Atlanta.

INTRODUCTION

Greater Atlanta

I N ONE WAY, Atlanta and its outlying communities exude a warm and fuzzy southern feel. At the same time, this capital city is fast-paced, sophisticated, and loaded with sights and sounds to delight both young and old. From the Civil War-related attractions of the Cyclorama and honest-to-goodness battlefields to the state-of-the-art world of CNN's 24-hour-a-day news operation, this town successfully blends the past with the present and future. Some people call it the Gateway to the New South. We'll let you decide.

Greater Atlanta is the perfect place to explore with your kids—to expose them to the significant historical happenings and excite them about the technologies of today and tomorrow. In addition, this major American city boasts some of the most high-tech, high-thrill places to visit, like Six Flags Over Georgia, White Water, and Stone Mountain.

Just as important as what there is to do here, the natives will make you feel right at home. Atlanta is a city

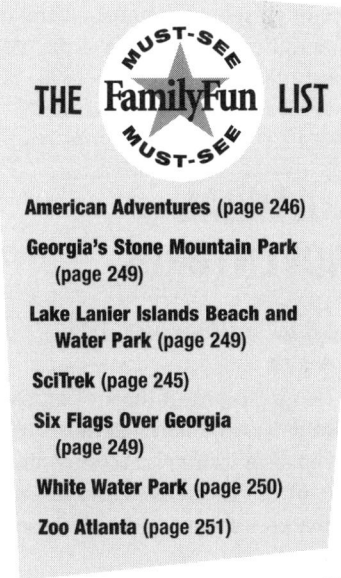

THE FamilyFun LIST

American Adventures (page 246)

Georgia's Stone Mountain Park (page 249)

Lake Lanier Islands Beach and Water Park (page 249)

SciTrek (page 245)

Six Flags Over Georgia (page 249)

White Water Park (page 250)

Zoo Atlanta (page 251)

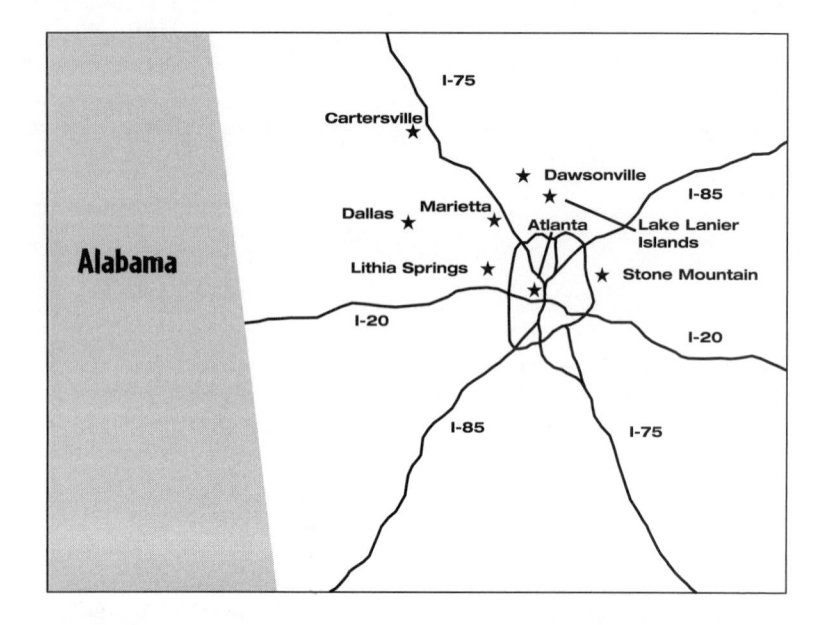

that has built its modern reputation on a warm welcome that reflects its legacy of southern hospitality. That attribute was one of the deciding factors when the Olympic Committee chose Atlanta as the site for the Summer Games in 1996. As they say in Atlanta, "Y'all, come!"

Cultural Adventures

Center For Puppetry Arts
★★★/$

Welcome to one of the area's most distinctive experiences in museum-going. Begin your visit by attending one of the theater's highly imaginative performances (usually based on classic tales like *The Tortoise and the Hare*), then head to the third floor to make your own puppet based on your favorite character from the show. The super kid-friendly museum, located in midtown Atlanta, displays one-of-a-kind creations such as the nine-foot-high Animatronics puppet named Trashcan Phoenix, the symbol of Atlanta. Don't miss the video of the late Jim Henson interviewing six of his favorite puppets from around the world—let's hear it for Kermit and Miss Piggy! You can visit the museum without attending the performance, but it's a great way to introduce kids to the world of theater, and grown-ups have fun, too. *1404 Spring St., Atlanta. (404) 873-3391;* www.puppet.org

CNN Studio Tour
★★★/$

It's not exactly showbiz, but the tour of CNN studios is glitzy enough to impress the entire family. Even the little ones will be entranced by the 37 monitors in the new Control Room Theater, all linked directly to CNN's main control room. Here they'll see firsthand how news broadcasts are produced, from receiving incoming satellite footage to various camera angles and graphics. Don't miss the special-effects area, where kids can learn secrets of the newsroom, such as the TelePrompTer and the weather reports' Blue ChromaKey System, then try their hand at the controls. *247 CNN Center, Atlanta. (404) 827-2300; www.cnn.com/studiotour/*

Etowah Indian Mounds
★★/$

If your kids fancy themselves experts at solving unsolved mysteries, Etowah is just the place to challenge their Sherlock Holmes skills. Archaeologists are *still* perplexed by these six earthen platform mounds, which date back to A.D. 1000 to 1500. Native Americans used these mounds for rituals, temples, and burials. Judging from the elaborate costumes and items buried here, these folks were somewhat like the Egyptian pharaohs (remind your kids of King Tut) in that they planned to "take it with them." A video explains what is known about

Southern Leaders, Atlanta Neighbors

Jimmy Carter and Martin Luther King, Jr.—two great southerners who helped shape our nation—both have midtown Atlanta museums and monuments in their honor. Carter, the 39th president of the United States, has his **library and museum** nestled in a serene hillside, complete with a Japanese garden *(441 Freedom Pkwy.; 404/331-3942)*. Inside, kids and parents can see a life-size replica of the Oval Office in the White House, and view a short film about President Carter's tenure as chief executive. Also interesting are gifts received from international heads of state and other memorabilia. Just down the road within a couple of miles, is the **Martin Luther King, Jr., National Historic Site** *(450 Auburn Ave.; 404/331-3920)*, a solemn tribute to the life of the slain civil rights leader. In a four-block area, this attraction includes King's birthplace, the Ebenezer Baptist Church where he preached, and a modern-day tribute, encompassing his gravesite and the Freedom Hall Complex with the Martin Luther King, Jr., Center for Nonviolent Social Change. Knowledgeable and friendly National Park Service hosts are on hand to answer questions.

FamilyFun **VACATION GUIDE**

Clap, Tickle, Tug

It's the sitting—and sitting and sitting—that gets to kids on the road. Get their belted-in bodies moving with this game of competitive copycat. The first player makes an expression or a movement, such as a hand clap; the next player repeats that movement and adds another; and so on. Kids will be pulling on their ears, sticking out their tongues, tipping back their heads, holding their elbows—and smiling! When a player forgets a movement, he's out. When everyone's out, start over.

these ancient peoples, and artifacts such as beads, seashells, and wooden objects are on display. Even more fun than learning about this sophisticated society is the trek up a wooden stairway to the top of a 63-foot-high mound. History will come alive here in a short visit, especially for your preteen crowd. Located about 40 miles northwest of Atlanta. *813 Indian Mounds Rd. S.E., Cartersville. (770) 387-3747; ngeorgia.com/parks/etowah.html*

Fernbank Museum of Natural History ★★/$

A 20-minute drive from downtown, this museum is decidedly over the top as kid-friendly museums go. Here you'll find spectacular exhibits on the history and environment of Georgia and a mind-boggling IMAX theater (fee) with movies that will have everybody riveted to the five-story, 72-foot-wide screen as sights and sounds (all 12,000 watts of it!) abound.

For the wee ones, don't miss the interactive play areas of Georgia Adventure, where they can go Velcro fishing, and Fantasy Forest, where they can experiment with flowers and pollination. An interactive exhibit called Sensing Nature helps explain scientific concepts like physics, and even has a five-foot "tornado in a bottle"—a glass case housing an ever-developing storm. Dino diehards will be on cloud nine when touring the museum's newest exhibit, which features a fully mounted skeleton of a gigantic 100-foot-long Argentinosaurus (this is the first museum in the world to showcase this gargantuan plant eater) and loads of other cool bones. *767 Clifton Rd. N.E., Atlanta. (404) 929-6300; www.fernbank.edu*

Jimmy Carter Library and Museum ★/$

Your school-age children can learn about our 39th president at this excellent museum (for more information, see "Southern Leaders, Atlanta Neighbors" on page 243). No admission charge for children under 16. *1 Copenhill Ave., Atlanta. (404) 331-3942; carterlibrary.galileo.peachnet.edu*

Martin Luther King, Jr., National Historic Site
★★★/Free

A comprehensive history lesson about the slain civil rights leader is an enriching experience for your school-age crowd (for more information, see "Southern Leaders, Atlanta Neighbors" on page 243). *450 Auburn Ave., Atlanta. (404) 331-3920; www.nps.gov/malu/*

Pickett's Mill ★★★/$

Civil War buffs or kids who like to play army will be thrilled with this battlefield that's been so well preserved that the 765-acre site remains much the way it was in 1864 when 14,000 Federal and 10,000 Confederate troops clashed during a one-night battle. Bringing to life the drama of this historic event are reenactors (men and women dressed in authentic period costume) who will help transform the battle into a real-time story, with "wounded" soldiers requiring amputations and other aspects of the past that your kids will be glad are past. (Call ahead for schedule.) Your family can walk down the same roads and see the earthworks constructed by the troops and will pass through the ravine where more than 2,000 soldiers died. Picnic sites and a visitors' center with exhibits and a film also help young ones understand this key Civil War battle. Pickett's Mill is about 30 miles northwest of Atlanta. *4432 Mt. Tabor Rd., Dallas. (770) 443-7850.*

SciTrek ★★★★/$
MUST-SEE FamilyFun MUST-SEE

One of the first and best hands-on museums in the area, this one still gives families adventures in the awesome world of technology and all that surrounds it. The 150 or so permanent interactive exhibit stations make it easy for kids and adults to understand why and how things work. By applying scientific and mathematical principles, kids can do things like lifting a race-car engine with one hand. Be careful what you say when you whisper at one of the exhibits—your friends can hear you loud and clear 80 feet away, thanks to the principle of sound focusing. Super fun for the 5-and-unders is the big sink area where they don waterproof aprons and experiment with water wheels, pipes, and other splashables. **NOTE:** The museum is on the edge of downtown, so take public transportation or drive if little ones are in tow. *395 Piedmont Ave., Atlanta. (404) 522-5500; www.scitrek.org*

FamilyFun VACATION GUIDE

World of Coca-Cola ★★★/$

Basically a big advertisement for the Real Thing, but what kid—or adult for that matter—doesn't like a sweet dose of soda pop? This downtown museum holds some nifty memorabilia and the like, but skip the movies about international imbibers and proceed directly to the old-fashioned soda jerk scene at the 1930s Barnes Soda Fountain. It's never "last call" at Club Coca-Cola, where kids can sample any or all of Coke's 20 different beverages. In this interactive part of the museum, you take a cup, place it under a room-size neon fountain that just happens to dispense sodas, and, as if by magic, your cup is filled. The brave at heart can proceed to the International Video Lounge and Tastes of the World for a sample of Coke products not available in the U.S. Hailing from Italy, "Beverly" is sure to make an impression—a bitter one at that—but others are quite tasty. *55 Martin Luther King, Jr., Dr., Atlanta. (404) 676-5151; www.thecocacolacompany.com*

JUST FOR FUN

American Adventures ★★★★/$-$$
MUST-SEE FamilyFun MUST-SEE

Here's *the* perfect place for the 12-and-under set to exceed their fun quota, while adults need not be overwhelmed by the scope of the park. American Adventures is a friendly, doable place, with old-fashioned thrill rides like a miniature roller coaster, Tilt-A-Whirl, scrambler, and bumper cars—almost like a flashback to the days of state fairs. Older kids will go for the go-cart race track and miniature golf while the younger generation will love the Foam Factory, a 40,000-foot extravaganza in a multilevel area where cushy balls are launched from more than 80 different blasters located on

DAY TRIP
A Water Wonderland

If you're looking to escape Hotlanta for a day with the kids, you'll find just the spot to cool off at **Lake Lanier Islands Beach and Water Park** *(6950 Holiday Rd., Lake Lanier Islands; 770/932-7200)*, less than an hour's drive from downtown. Your sun worshipers will adore this mile-long sandy white beach with water, water, everywhere, thanks to a recent $10-million improvement project. You'll find that the surf's definitely up at Surf Wave, a virtual surfing experience where you get your own board and test your skill on a simulated wave that could fool even a Beach Boy. Everybody, from little ones to adults, will adore the three-story-high FunDunker, with its water guns and other gadgets for spraying, not to mention the 1,000

the three-story towers. There are targets and turrets and baskets to dump on those below, and every few minutes, the crowd gets "foamed," that is, showered with the foam balls. You get a lot of fun with a minimum of hassle. Located next to White Water, its sister park. *250 North Cobb Pkwy., Marietta. (770) 424-9283.*

Atlanta Botanical Garden
★★/$

It might sound like the kind of place you'd take your grandmother instead of your family, but truly, the kids will dig it, pardon the pun. Besides its central location and breath of fresh air within the city, the garden boasts a Children's Garden, which offers interactive exhibits specially designed for youngsters 4 to 11. Choose from ponds, slides, a sandbox, and tree house, all as kid-friendly as the colorful caterpillar maze and air factory, which allows children to share carbon dioxide with the plants. Digging for dinosaur bones, getting warm and fuzzy with giant model bees, and witnessing the plant and insect cat-and-mouse game in a Bullfrog Pond and Soggy Bog will keep younger kids enthralled. All ages will enjoy the amphitheater programs on topics like the Okefenokee Swamp and Afrikan Traditions and Lore. It's an easy bus ride from downtown. *1345 Piedmont Ave. N.E., Atlanta. (404) 876-5859; www.atlantabotanicalgarden.org*

Atlanta Cyclorama
★★★/$

This attraction is truly one of a kind, and that's no exaggeration, because they just aren't painting panoramas the way they did in 1883, which is when this one was commissioned. The Cyclorama is a painting with three-dimensional figures (128 in all) depicting the Battle of Atlanta, when more than 12,000 soldiers were killed on the hot summer day

gallons of wet stuff that washes through the area every few minutes. Get as wet as you like, or pull levers that will douse those below as you walk through the giant water world. Also visit Wiggle Waves, specially designed for the under-four-feet-tall set with a miniwave pool and slides. Wild Waves, said to be Georgia's largest wave pool, will keep everyone cool. Sorry, no picnic coolers allowed, but plenty of dining options available. As if the beach and water park weren't enough to keep your kids entertained, other activities (fees) awaiting at this lake include horseback riding, golf, biking, hiking, and video arcade action. Lodging options here include fun and relaxing (but pricey) houseboat rentals that can be arranged at several places, including Harbor Landing *(770/932-7255).*

This Joint Is Jumpin'

Imagine kangaroos—more than the average tourist would see on a given day in Australia—hopping around in an 87-acre wildlife park about an hour's drive north of Atlanta. That's what's really happening at the **Kangaroo Conservation Center** *(222 Bailey-Waters Rd., Dawsonville; 706/265-6100;* www.kangaroocenter.com), where you and your kids (8 and older only) can board an old army truck and take a two-hour, safari-like tour and watch as joeys (baby kangaroos), their moms and dads, wallabies, burros, and species of exotic birds frolic in the wild—wild Georgia, that is.

Here's a great tidbit for show-and-tell: did you know that kangaroos can run at speeds of up to 55 miles per hour and jump 12 feet in the air? Guides/owners Debbie and Roger Nelson are full of neat facts, like that about the "roos" and their aviary family, which include a kookaburra and a Guenther's dik-dik. If you've never heard of these oddly named creatures, the Nelsons will happily fill you in; the kids can even get to feed them. Don't miss this one.

of July 22, 1864. Seated in the cool quiet of the amphitheater, kids will fall under the spell of days gone by as they watch from the vantage point of a revolving platform. The sights and sounds are so realistic that viewers actually feel part of the scene, which is 42 feet high and 358 feet in circumference. It's a great way to make history come alive for kids. Located next to Zoo Atlanta, just 15 minutes from downtown. *800 Cherokee Ave. S.E., Atlanta. (404) 658-7625.*

Centennial Olympic Park
★/Free

Sports buffs will want to check out this historic oasis right in the middle of downtown—a park created for the 1996 Olympics in Atlanta. Even without the festivals, concerts, or theatrical productions going on, the park's Fountain of Rings will provide plenty of easygoing entertainment, especially for the younger crowd. The interactive fountain invites kids (and hot adults) to frolic through the water, setting off new streams seemingly at every move. Check out the commemorative bricks that line the park and honor some famous people. Who's the first to spot former President Bill Clinton's brick? Children also have their own garden and playground for amusement, while adults can check out various Olympic memorabilia. *265 Luckie St., Atlanta. (404) 223-4412.*

GREATER ATLANTA

★ Georgia's Stone Mountain Park
FamilyFun ★★★★/$$

No matter how you look at it—from the bottom, from the top, or from the side—Georgia's Stone Mountain definitely lives up to its reputation as the eighth wonder of the world. The view from the top (more than 800 feet up) is a must—it's almost like the view from an airplane—and you can get there by foot or an exciting ride on an Alpine-like cable car. The hike might be a bit much for the under-5 set. If you prefer to go around rather than up, take the steam-powered locomotive and train that goes all the way around the mountain. Other kid-friendly activities include a swimming beach and water slide, petting zoo, and paddlewheel riverboat. Evening brings an exciting laser extravaganza, showcased alongside the dramatic carvings of Confederate generals, and best viewed from the expansive lawn—the perfect backdrop for a well-deserved picnic supper. (Picnic baskets and coolers are welcome—alcohol is not.) During the high season, costumed storytellers will fascinate your group with southern folklore and information. This place exudes true southern hospitality. Y'all, come! Located in the "burbs" of Atlanta, less than a 45-minute drive from downtown. *U.S. 78, Stone Mountain. (800) 317-2006; (770) 498-5690;* www.stonemountainpark.com

★ Lake Lanier Islands Beach and Water Park
FamilyFun ★★★★/$$$$

Water lovers, take note: there's a lot of wet stuff for fun and frolic to be found here. Just look at "A Water Wonderland" (see page 246) and you'll see what we mean.

★ Six Flags Over Georgia
FamilyFun ★★★★/$$$$

People from all over come here to excite, energize, and in the end, exhaust themselves on more than 100 thrilling rides, shows, and attractions. Especially popular are the "crazy eight"—different roller coasters that are guaranteed to turn you every which way but loose. The newest and most white-knuckled of them all is the Georgia Scorcher, one of the tallest (107 feet) and fastest (54 mph) stand-up coasters around. The wooden Georgia Cyclone is truly scary, what with its rattling wooden girders trembling as you race along at top speeds. Neither of these coasters is for the faint of heart. Prepare to get completely

---

FamilyFun SNACK

Cranberry-nut Snack Mix

Measure 2 cups raw sunflower seeds; 1 cup pine nuts; 1 cup raw pumpkin seeds; 1 cup sweetened, dried cranberries; and 1 cup raisins into a mixing bowl and stir with a wooden spoon. Makes 6 cups.

FamilyFun VACATION GUIDE

soaked if you ride Splashwater Falls, which may be *way* too much ride for the smaller children. This is a park where your post-stroller-age kids will get the most bang for the buck. (The little ones just become cranky and overwhelmed.) *7661 Six Flags Pkwy., Atlanta. (770) 739-3440; www.sixflags.com*

White Water Park
FamilyFun ★★★★/$$$$

This is an all-day, or even all-weekend splashing fun time, with suitable areas of the wet wonderland for all ages. The littlest ones will love playing in the shallow fountain, sliding down easy chutes, and the squirt gun area at Little Squirt's Island. Kicking it up a notch or two, your daredevils can test their nerve at the exciting, and to some, terrifying Cliffhanger, billed as one of the tallest free falls in the world. Try this one and get ready to be propelled 90 feet straight down, kind of like falling off a nine-story building, but into water. If you think this sounds extreme, just wait until you hear the choruses of "let's go again!" Another thumbs-up aspect of this park is that it allows multiple family members or friends to ride the same ride, such as the Run-a-Way River, where four rafters traverse a 735-foot water tunnel, complete with curves and dips for multiple thrills. The Atlanta Ocean is a wave pool for relaxing. All four sections deliver on their promise of a good time. An added bonus during the summer months are Dive-In Movies on Friday nights, when families can laze in tubes or lawn chairs and watch family-

DAY TRIP
Crossroads at Stone Mountain Park

This is the latest and greatest park adding to family fun in the South—and it's sure to be a hit with all age groups. Situated in the heart of beautiful Stone Mountain Park and only 16 miles east of downtown Atlanta, this is a place you'll want to give at least a couple of days. **Crossroads** is meant to teach kids (and adults, too) about life in the Old South. If the youngsters turn up their noses about learning, assure them that this is done in a fun and exciting (read: painless) way. The experience is different from visits to the antebellum mansions on other historic tours (although there is another mansion elsewhere in the park). This is an authentic, meticulous recreation of a small Georgia town, circa 1870. What makes it appealing to kids is that all of the various sites are working stations for actual artisans who showcase their particular crafts. There's a bakery and gristmill; a blacksmith shop; Tweedle's candle shop, where kids can make soft wax sculptures; and

friendly flicks. *250 North Cobb Pkwy., Marietta. (770) 424-9283;* www.whitewaterpark.com

Zoo Atlanta
MUST-SEE FamilyFun ★★★★/$$

Allow plenty of time for wandering here, where natural habitats shelter the exotic animals while giving you an unobstructed view of the critters. The most popular jewels in the crown here are the giant pandas Lunlun and Yangyang, ten-year residents of the zoo. A perennial favorite stop is the Ford African Rainforest, where your family can sit for a bit in a comfortable amphitheater, especially at feeding times (which are posted), and be entertained by the hilarious antics of the gorillas. No matter when you go, it seems there's always a baby gorilla driving its parents crazy. You'll probably have to ride the zoo-encircling train—it's no big deal, but the little kids always beg for a ride. The petting zoo is also a draw for the small set, but older children may want to head for the scary creatures in the World of Reptiles, which is full of slithery, slimy things. *800 Cherokee Ave., S.E., Atlanta. (404) 624-5600;* www.zooatlanta.org

BUNKING DOWN

Embassy Suites Centennial Park ★★★★/$$

A comfortable, somewhat upscale all-suite hotel, it's convenient to most every hot spot you'd want to see in downtown Atlanta—CNN Center is across the street, and so is the

---

the general store with everything from homemade ice cream (youngsters can pump the pedals that turn the large churns) to handmade crafts.

Your little ones will feel as though they're in heaven when they enter the Great Barn, a real dream for kids of all ages. From the gigantic rope nets for the younger ones to the super-slides and interactive games for the teens, this place will help them use up some of that excess energy. And if you crave something a little less "active" after the Great Barn, head on over to the Cotton Exchange for *Tall Tales*; it's a 3-D film with in-house special effects where you'll be transported to a South Georgia swamp!

This trip through history is set within **Historic Stone Mountain Park**, a 3,200-acre preserve at the center of which is the world's largest mass of exposed granite. It's an awe-inspiring sight seeing this behemoth—surrounded by pristine forests, lakes, and hiking trails—rising from the land. Activities are plentiful, so plan ahead. With so much to see and do, it's easy to get overwhelmed. *Hwy. 78 E. (770) 498-5710.*

World of Coca-Cola. A short drive will take you to SciTrek, Zoo Atlanta, and Six Flags. Spacious living and sleeping quarters, swimming pool, concierge service, free breakfast, and a nightly manager's reception with drinks and snacks make this attractive to families. *267 Marietta St., Atlanta. (404) 223-2300;* www.embassy_suites.com

Hilton Atlanta Northwest
★★/$-$$

This is White Water's official hotel, so you know it's close (about five minutes) to this kid-favorite water park and its sister attraction, American Adventures. Comfortable rooms, two swimming pools, and some White Water discount packages add to the appeal. *2055 S. Park Pl., Atlanta. (770) 953-9300;* www.hilton.com

SpringHill Suites Atlanta/ Six Flags ★/$

No more than three miles from Six Flags, this is a convenient place for families to wind down after a big day at the park. The suites offer plenty of room to spread out, and complimentary continental breakfast and an indoor pool help make this property a year-round winner. Sorry, no shuttle service to Six Flags. *960 Bob Arnold Blvd., Lithia Springs. (770) 819-9906;* www.springhillsuites.com

Stone Mountain Family Campground
★★★★/$

With so much to do within the park and surrounding areas, it's no surprise this campground is a family favorite. The wonderful waterfront campsites are close to a sandy beach and swimming area. Add to that a game room, playground, grocery store, and swimming pool for a fun overnight or two. *U.S. 78, Stone Mountain. (800) 385-9807; (770) 498-5710.*

> **THE COMPLIMENT**
> "You're a real peach" came from the tradition of giving the fruit to good friends.

GOOD EATS

Everybody's Pizza
★★/$

This chain of restaurants does a bang-up job catering to diners of all ages. The specialty of the house is pizza, with inexpensive and handmade pies made to order so little ones can "have it their way." Kid-sized handmade pasta (at half the price of an adult entrée) is delicious and a tad more exotic than the standard burgers and fries (although they're tasty, too). Good eats and the funky décor (when was the last time you saw a Harley suspended from the ceiling?) make this a good value and a good time. Multiple locations. *1593 N. Decatur Rd., Atlanta. (404) 377-7766.*

Mick's ★★★/$

A takeoff on the *Happy Days* diner idea, but a bit upscale, this place has a children's menu that is one of the most extensive around, offering something for the pickiest eater to the more sophisticated palate. It also probably serves the very *best* and biggest milk shakes in town, so go hungry! The more than 10 local branches are usually in a shopping mall or near a busy part of town. The only downside can be a long waiting list at peak times or on weekends. Unless you've got cranky ones in tow, it's worth the wait. Multiple locations. *2110 Peachtree St., Atlanta. (404) 351-6425.*

The Varsity ★★★★/$

Touting itself as the world's largest drive-in, this family-owned fast-food restaurant is an Atlanta favorite with old and young alike. Predating the Golden Arches, this place was founded by a hungry Georgia Tech student in the 1920s. While the menu has been updated to cater to the calorie conscious, the old favorites like chili dogs, greasy (but oh-so-good) onion rings, and smooth, sweet frosted orange drinks are the way to go. Families can park underneath the awning outside and honk their horns for curb service from friendly, sometimes entertaining carhops, or, for a more up-close dining experience, go inside, where glass picture windows reveal the bustling kitchen with its mountains of raw, sliced onions and more. Multiple locations. *Try the original location at 61 North Ave. near downtown Atlanta for the best atmosphere. (404) 881-1706.*

Souvenir Hunting

Phipps Plaza

Hands down, the celebrated strip of Peachtree just north of Buckhead offers some of the best shopping in the country. And it's not just for shopaholic Moms, either, though the presence of Neiman Marcus, Lord & Taylor, and Tiffany can make many grown women swoon. For little people, The Little Shop *(404/266-1577)* features tony apparel for the youngest fashion slave, while Abercrombie & Fitch *(404/233-8522)* will please older kids who have their teenage years on their minds. *3500 Peachtree Rd., Atlanta.*

Lenox Square

Directly across the street from Phipps Plaza is the crème de la crème of toy stores: FAO Schwarz *(404/814-1675)*, which keeps company with the intellectually stimulating Discovery Channel Store *(404/231-9252)*. *3393 Peachtree Rd., Atlanta.*

Enjoy the natural beauty of Smithgall Woods-Dukes Creek Conservation Area's 5,500 acre wilderness.

INTRODUCTION

North Georgia

NORTH GEORGIA offers a convenient, yet completely convincing getaway from the urban buzz of Atlanta to the south, and indeed, the rest of this rapidly growing state. You'll be only about an hour or so from the harried perimeter highway that circles Hotlanta, but you and your family will immediately sense cleaner air and a slower pace. The ancient blue mountains are a soothing sight—this entire outdoor wonderland promises some incredible natural fun.

North Georgia has rolling farmlands, crystal-clear streams and rivers, trails for wilderness hikes, and wildflowers galore. It's ideal for climbing mountains, riding tubes down rivers, rocking on front porches, and exploring the unusual towns and villages—and even a few ancient Indian mounds, still intact some 1,000 years after they were constructed.

Pack comfortable shoes, sunscreen, insect repellent, sweaters, and a picnic basket and blanket and

THE FamilyFun LIST

Appalachian Outfitters
(page 257)

BabyLand General Hospital
(page 257)

Charlemagne's Kingdom
(page 258)

Helen (page 260)

Smithgall Woods-Dukes Creek Conservation Area
(page 260)

255

FamilyFun VACATION GUIDE

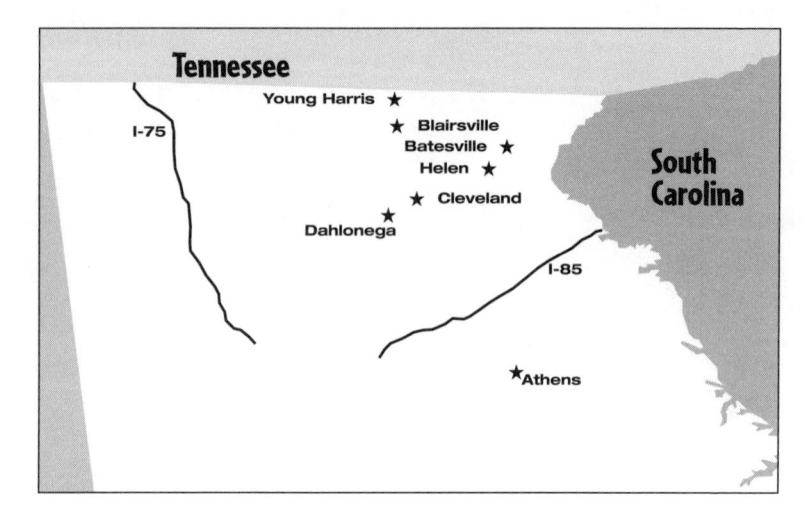

head for any one of the wonderful state parks where you can spend a day or a week—it's up to you. Every so often you'll run into a place you'll want to stop that people, not nature, made (check out the Bavarian village in Helen), a *totally* consumed college town (Dawgs rule in Athens!), and a chance for riches (there's gold in them thar hills in Dahlonega). Part of the appeal is definitely getting away from it all, but you'll still find things to do for families with kids of all ages.

CULTURAL ADVENTURES

Butts-Mehre Heritage Museum ★★/Free
Give in to the University of Georgia's Bulldog fever and visit this treasury of sports memorabilia, from videos to uniforms to photographs—even the Heisman Trophies awarded to famous Bulldogs Herschel Walker and Frankie Sinkwich are on display. Soccer buffs will be in seventh heaven when they enter the area that commemorates the heroic feats of the U.S. women's soccer team that won the hearts of millions during the 1996 Olympics, even a tribute to Mia Hamm, from the 2000 Olympics. Guess where the '96 soccer games were held? Right here in Athens! *1 Selig Circle, Athens. (706) 542-9036.*

Dahlonega Gold Museum ★/$
This imposing building on the square in Dahlonega is a state historic site filled with memorabilia of the town's rich mining past. Your older kids may appreciate getting

an up-close look at some of the gold coins (like the five-ounce gold nugget) from the $6 million worth coined here by the U.S. Branch Mint from 1838 to 1861. Although Mom and Dad will enjoy the 23-minute film on the history of mining, kids will have a real blast messing in the dirt and water as they pan at one of the mines. *On the public square, Dahlonega. (706) 864-2257;* www.dahlonega.org/museum/goldmuseum.html

JUST FOR FUN

Appalachian Outfitters
FamilyFun ★★★★/$$
MUST-SEE Trust this family-owned outfit to make your river experience a memorable one. Dahlonega's Chestatee River is surely one of the clearest, cleanest—and laziest—ways to get from point A to point B, and your kids will love the laid-back approach to experiencing the local scenery. Try the 3.5-mile Miner's Run and relax in your big inner tube as it encounters small shoals, rocky bends, and gentle currents. The lazy float lasts between three and four hours, perfect for kids 6 and up. If time is short, you can opt for the faster water trip (20 to 30 minutes). Bring the usual accoutrements: sunglasses, sunscreen, snacks, and drinks in unbreakable waterproof containers, and prepare for a good, wet time. Older and more experienced boaters may want to ask this friendly outfitter about canoe and kayak trips on the Chestatee and other nearby rivers. *24 N. Park St., Dahlonega. (706) 867-7116.*

BabyLand General
FamilyFun Hospital
MUST-SEE ★★★★/Free
It sounds almost too cute to be true, but yes, there is a real hospital that specializes in the delivery of dolls—but not just any dolls can be born (and adopted) here, only the special Cabbage Patch Kids. Housed in what was once a real doctor's clinic, the "hospital" is staffed by "nurses" in uniform and decked out with vintage incubators and baby paraphernalia. The self-guided tour begins in the Father's Waiting Room. There are thousands of "kids" at the hospital, all successfully birthed before visitors in the special Cabbage Patch delivery room; Mom is an animated soft-sculpted Cabbage. You can't help but smile when you hear the public address announcement, "There's a cabbage in labor! All staff

FamilyFun GAME

A Tougher Tic-tac-toe
   Make the classic game of tic-tac-toe a little more lively and a bit tougher with this one basic change: with each turn, a player can fill in the empty space of his choice with either an X or an O.

to delivery room, STAT!" Your kids' eyes will get saucer-sized when the newest kid makes its entrance, and adults will get a chuckle out of the play on words uttered by the attending nurse: like "imagicillin," "easyotomy," and "branch delivery." Afterward, your family can wander among the many rooms with the kids, stop by the gift shop, or if they choose, go the office to adopt a kid (entry is free: the dolls aren't!). Don't worry, there's no pressure to buy, only to smile and enjoy the experience. Even boys will warm up to this place. *73 W. Underwood St., Cleveland. (706) 865-2171;* www.ngeorgia.com/site/babyland.html

Brasstown Bald Mountain ★★/$

The highest spot in Georgia, its summit offers an awe-inspiring view of four states—Georgia, Tennessee, and North and South Carolina. The air gets a little thin this far up—nearly 5,000 feet above sea level. And that's not the only reason you may huff and puff—the trail is extremely steep, too. The heartiest youngsters can power on up, but for little ones and those out of shape, it's better to take the shuttle (fee) up the half-mile path. For a breather, or just some good information, check out the visitors' center, which has interpretive programs, slide shows, and exhibits on the area's fauna and flora. Pack a sweater for everybody—you may need them at the top. Open seasonally; call ahead for information. *State 180 Spur, Blairsville. (706) 896-2555; (706) 896-2556;* www.ngeorgia.com/travel/brasstown.html

Charlemagne's Kingdom ★★★★/$

Touted as the largest Alpine model railroad museum in the country, this fantastic miniature Germany is housed in a two-story barnlike building. Whatever your age, you'll be fascinated by the 400 feet of railroad tracks and loads of computerized trains, a sprawling display that features the tiniest of delightful details—from a miniature "motorcycle accident" on the highway to a castle of Mad King Ludwig, to mountains, circus tents, and handpainted figurines. Walk around the freestanding display several times; see if your kids can spot something new each time. Also, don't miss a view from the balcony. In addition, any time you come you can watch a hot-air balloon race in progress. And what visit to Germany would be complete without the sound of a glockenspiel? Make sure to time your visit so that you'll be here on the hour to hear the glockenspiel in the gingerbread house chime. Our kid-tested observations show that you'll have a hard time dragging the little ones away. For more about the charming village of Helen, see "An Alpine Adventure" at right. *8808 N. Main St., Helen. (706) 878-2200.*

Consolidated Gold Mines
★★/$$
More appropriate for the preteen set, this working mine offers a 45-minute tour, including a walk 250 feet into the massive underground tunnel network where you can see the original track system. Your guides are actual miners who have helped remove approximately 4,000 tons of dirt, debris, and ore from the mine, and they are happy to answer questions. The mine also features displays of the real equipment used back in the gold rush days of the 1800s, when the Dahlonega area was the nation's leading mining site and home to the U.S. Branch Mint. After you've seen it all, try your hand at panning here. You can skip the tour and pay just a few bucks for the panning fun. *185 Consolidated Gold Mine Rd., Dahlonega. (706) 864-8473.*

Crisson Gold Mine
★★★/$-$$
Expect a really good time at this Dahlonega mine where you can pan not just for gold, but gemstones, too. As the helpful owner explains, the gemstone search is instant gratification for the kids as they sift the dirt (really crushed rock from the nearby mine)—they're almost sure to find some kind of sapphire, garnet, or other semiprecious stone. Nearby charts help them identify their treasures, which they can take home in a little black bag. You'll have

An Alpine Adventure
The charming Alpine village of **Helen** is an attraction in itself. Remodeled in the 1970s, the entire town went from lazy, small-town obscurity to a tourist treasure when it completed its transformation to a Bavarian village. The architecture, restaurants, and hotels—not to mention gift and souvenir shops galore—all show off their best German-themed look and feel year round. The wild and woolly celebration known as Oktoberfest is celebrated here throughout the month of October, when throngs descend on the small village. (If you dislike crowds, plan your trip for another time.) This is something you won't see anywhere else in the area, or outside of Germany, for that matter. Kids will enjoy the sights and sounds of the glockenspiel clock, and parents can feast on German food and beer. There is an appealing but slightly tacky amusement area called **Alpine Amusement Park**, where you can stop in for some old-fashioned American fun on attractions like the 40-foot-high Ferris wheel, the arcade, and little rides for the kiddies. *419 Edelweiss Strasse, Helen. (706) 878-2306.*

fun, and who knows, you may get lucky—a 480-karat amethyst was found here not so long ago! Panning for gold takes a little more skill (and time), as amateur gold miners slosh the pans from side to side. Kids love to get down and dirty here, so it's a good idea to bring a change of clothes. Instructors will help you get started. They recommend that a family of four begin with a five-gallon bucket of both gold and gemstone "dirt." When the stamp mill is working, it makes quite a racket, but it's all part of the fun. You can pan indoors in the winter. *2736 Morrison Moore Pkwy. E., Dahlonega. (706) 864-6363.*

Helen
★★★/Free-$

For a touch of Bavaria in North Georgia, check out this charming town. For more information, see "An Alpine Adventure" on page 259.

Smithgall Woods-Dukes Creek Conservation Area
★★★★/Free

Parents who want their youngsters to experience first-hand the beauty of nature, unspoiled by man's intrusion, should head for these 5,500 acres of wilderness and wildlife. Acquired by the state in 1994, this was once the private estate of a Georgia conservationist. Here your kids are free to hike, bike, and fish amid the beautiful sights and sounds of Dukes Creek. On-site naturalists offer kids hands-on experience with pond and stream ecology while they're knee-deep in some of the best trout-fishing waters on earth. Wildlife habitat, mountain folklore, Native American artifacts, and archery are also part of the environmental education programs. (Call for activity schedule.) Camping is allowed (there's a fee), and an orientation program teaches youngsters how to use maps and compasses. *61 Tsalaki Trail, Helen. (706) 878-3087.*

The Tree That Owns Itself
★★/Free

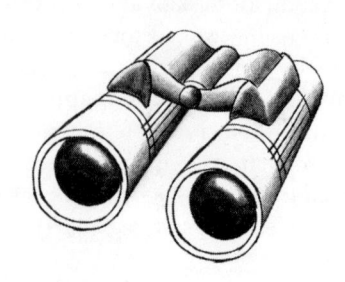

With these days of ever-rising real estate prices, you won't see another tree like this any time soon. The oak at the corner of Dearing and Finley Streets—and eight feet of space on all sides—was deeded to the city of Athens by University of Georgia Professor W. H. Jackson (he loved its shade). Though Jackson's original tree died in 1942, nature obligingly grew this masterpiece from one of its acorns. It's truly a peaceful canopy offering a shady place to rest a while—and a novelty (it's even been featured in *Ripley's Believe It or Not* that will make for great conversation back home. *Athens.*

Trackrock Archaeological Area
★/Free

If your family has a budding archaeologist, take a look at the preserved petroglyphs made by Native Americans in these parts thousands of years ago. These 52 acres offer a meandering walk during which you'll discover carvings resembling animal and bird tracks, crosses, circles, and human footprints. Turn your visit into a fun but educational outing by challenging your curious young ones to see who can be the first to spot some bird tracks. *To find the area, look for the historical marker just off U.S. Hwy. 19/129. South of Blairsville.*

Trackrock Stables
★★★/$$$

This is the place for city slickers and seasoned horse folks alike to indulge in a pleasant guided ride through the beautiful North Georgia mountains. The one-hour excursion is lazy and easy for families, while longer adventures allow experienced riders to go faster and farther along the streams and fields. No age restrictions, except common sense. Camping (including cabins; there's a fee) is good here, too, as are hayrides, fishing, and swimming. *4890 Trackrock Campground Rd., Blairsville. (706) 745-5252.*

BUNKING DOWN

Aunt Anne's Log Cabins
★/$-$$

Just one mile from downtown Dahlonega and an hour from Atlanta, Aunt Anne's is a handful of honest-to-goodness log cabins, each ideal for a family of four. The lofts are a real plus for kids, and one of the cabins has a mini upstairs decorated in a *Winnie the Pooh* theme. Parents will enjoy the hot tub just off the main bedroom and appreciate the handy kitchenettes and the cozy fireplaces. The front porch is a good place to chill out after a day of gold mining or tubing. *130 Lila Way, Dahlonega. (706) 864-9714.*

Best Western Colonial Inn
★/$

When your family plans to overnight in Athens, check out this family-friendly property that's just five blocks from the University. The heated pool and extensive complimentary breakfast buffet earn this place an easy thumbs-up. *170 N. Milledge Ave., Athens. (706) 546-7311.*

Brasstown Valley Resort
★★★★/$$

At this posh (but not snooty) Georgia Mountain resort, your family will enjoy more than the comforts of home—especially your sports-minded and outdoorsy youngsters. There's on-site lighted tennis courts, state-of-the-art exercise equipment, and an indoor/outdoor pool; and just a stone's through away are such minithrillers as white-water rafting and mountain climbing. It's one of the few properties to offer a summer kids' program where children ages 5 to 17 can (for a fee) experience wildlife hikes, storytelling, crafts, and pool Olympics. *6321 U.S. Hwy. 76, Young Harris. (800) 201-3205; (706) 379-9900.*

Cavender Creek Cabins
★★/$$

More than a place to rest your head, these cabins are perfect for kids who like to play in the crystal-clear creek or fish in the stocked pond. They can pan for gold in the stream, too (panning equipment and instruction are available). Cabins have fully stocked kitchens, and the lofts make this superpopular among kids. The spacious lodge has a common area with fireplace, pool table, and other games that guests may use. Clearly marked nearby hiking trails and the surrounding woods make this a real nature getaway. *200 Beaver Dam Rd., Dahlonega. (706) 864-7221.*

The Smith House
★★★★/$-$$

Genuine southern hospitality and authentic southern cooking are two very good reasons to stay here. Rooms at this welcoming wooden structure that's just off the town square are ideal for a family of four. You get a continental breakfast, there's an outdoor pool, and you can easily walk to shops and downtown. But quite possibly the property's main lure is its family-style dining room with its heavenly aromas of fried chicken, sweet ham, and homemade yeast rolls—guaranteed to draw young and old alike to the table. *84 S. Chestatee St., Dahlonega. (800) 852-9577; (706) 867-7000.*

Vogel State Park
★★★★/$

Even if you don't stay here, be sure to visit this park, with its camping and cottages managed by the Georgia Park Service. Your kids will love the pedal boats (fee); other sure-to-please activities include miniature golf (fee) and hiking on well-marked trails in the Chattahoochee National Forest and adjacent to the Appalachian Trail. A sandy beach is part of the package, as are grills and picnic areas. Because of the altitude, you may need light jackets and blankets even during the summer. It's especially popular when fall foliage peaks, so reserve early. *7485 Vogel State Park Rd. (U.S.19/129), Blairsville. (800) 864-7275; (706) 745-2628.*

GOOD EATS

Caruso's Ristorante Italiano
★★★★/$-$$

If you need a break from all that southern cooking, try this authentic, very good, and remarkably inexpensive Italian restaurant in the heart of North Georgia. Located right on the square, it features a children's menu—for those under 12—with such mouthwatering pasta dishes as spaghetti with meatballs and tortellini with tomato sauce, all for just a couple of dollars. Mom and Dad can feast on wonderful spinach tortellini or chicken Parmesan, just two of the outstanding dishes on the grown-up menu. *Mangia! 113 E. Main St., Dahlonega. (706) 864-4664.*

Charlie Williams' Pinecrest
★★★/$-$$

An Athens institution, this good ole' boy and girl eatery is in the piney woods, complete with an old mill nearby. The hearty menu includes such family staples as steak, chicken, seafood, and, of course, desserts. Other locations offer 'cue and stew (barbecue and Brunswick stew—southern staples). Multiple locations. *2020 Timothy Rd., Athens. (706) 353-2606.*

Gibson's Drive-In
★/$

Don't be put off by the somewhat rough exterior here—it's a gravel drive and shacklike building—because inside are some of the best burgers and fresh fruit milk shakes you'll find in these parts. The pool table next door is a draw, as are the video games, as long as you're not expecting high-tech stuff: Gibson's is more like a flashback to *Happy Days*. A hungry man can eat well for under $5. *Hwy. 76, Young Harris. (706) 379-3258.*

Hofer's Bakery
★★★/$

A fabulously tempting bakery (plus delicious lunch and dinner entrées) will more than satisfy your kids' hunger pangs. There's no children's menu here, but plenty of items that normally appeal to the 12-and-under set—like tasty German hot dogs and grilled cheese. The kids will like the exterior, too, with door handles shaped like pretzels and doors flanked by the figures of a peasant girl and baker boy. Inside, along with delectables like Sacher torte, is a hand-painted mural that traces the history of a cake from wheat seed to frosting. Good soups and omelettes are also on the menu here. *8758 Main St., Helen. (706) 878-8200; www.hofers.com*

Mayflower Restaurant
★★★★/$

This down-home eatery has been cooking up southern delicacies for more than 50 years, and students flock here to partake of its tasty treats. Downtown near the UGA campus, this is a perfect place for breakfast—eggs, grits, specialty omelettes, or lunch—for "meat 'n three," that is, an entrée like beef tips or turkey and dressing, plus two veggies, rolls, and tea. Plus, the sweet waitresses are as authentic as the home-cooked food. *171 E. Broad St., Athens. (706) 548-1692.*

Rick's
★★★★/$$

Though this quaint Victorian-home-cum-restaurant looks like a grown-ups only, white-tablecloth establishment, looks are deceiving. It is adamant in its welcome to kids—it even says so on the menu! Kids' choices range from peanut-butter-and-jelly sandwiches to chicken fingers and hot dogs, plus dessert and a drink for under three bucks. Check to see if "worms and dirt" (chocolate pudding with gummy worms) is on the menu the day you're there. The sunny front garden is a nice spot for catching your breath—maybe even rocking on the porch for a spell, like the locals do. *47 S. Park St., Dahlonega. 706-864-9422.*

Tuckers' Family Restaurant
★★★/$

Warm and welcoming, with its spacious dining room and extensive menu, Tucker's offers a buffet that will more than satisfy—yummy fried chicken, roast beef, and ham, plus all the fixins—and it won't cost you an arm and a leg! Kids can feast on their kind of food on the even less expensive children's menu—fried chicken, grilled cheese sandwiches, and burgers. *1657 Murphy Hwy., Blairsville. (706) 745-6474.*

Souvenir Hunting

Burton Gallery & Emporium

If your family likes one-of-a-kind arts and crafts, including wood carvings, folk art, and walking sticks, then visit this welcoming white house outside of Clarkesville. The prices are reasonable and the people who work there are super-friendly. *295 Cherokee Ridge Dr., Batesville. (706) 947-1351.*

The Fudge Factory

Right on the square, this shop beckons those with a sweet tooth to come and sample some of the many kinds of homemade cream and butter fudge, from chocolate to butter brickle crunch to rocky road. Awesome stuff! *8 Park St. N., Dahlonega. (706) 864-2256.*

Tekakwitha

You can bet that your kid won't leave this treasure trove of Native American arts and crafts empty-handed, so resign yourself to picking up some kind of jewelry, drum, pottery, moccasins, or even a Navajo rug. *338 S. Main St., Helen. (706) 878-2938.*

Wet Pets

Even if you're not up to traveling with one of the 2,000 imported Japanese goldfish here, kids can feed these beautiful creatures right from their hands. *1085 Mountain Cover Rd., Dahlonega. (706) 865-7190.*

A NATIVE VOCABULARY

THE MOUNTAINS and hills of North Georgia were long ago inhabited by various tribes of Native Americans, whose presence lingers only in the place names of the region. They all sound kind of odd to a youngster's untrained ear, but when you learn their meaning, they make perfect sense. For example:

Appalachian (Trail) Beginning just outside Blairsville this famous path stretches from Georgia all the way to Maine. Its name derives from a Creek word meaning "people on the other side." The name was first used by a Frenchman exploring this range—he picked up the Creek word *Apalachee* and applied it to the physical division of land and peoples that the mountain range created.

Chattahoochee (River) This mighty river starts in North Georgia (great for tubing upstream) and then finds its way south to metro Atlanta. The name comes from *Chatu-huchi*, a Creek word that means "marked rock" or "picture rocks," which refer to the pictograms found on rocks along the river. This river flows all the way through Georgia, Alabama, and Florida and joins the Apalachicola River to empty into the Gulf of Mexico.

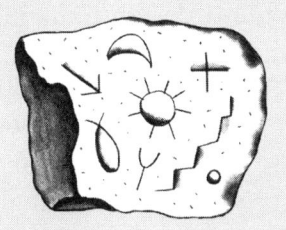

Cherokee (Native American) Another corruption of a Cherokee word *Tsa-ra-gi*. These Native Americans also called themselves *ani-uni-wa*, or "principal people." Cherokee County, Georgia, was formed in 1831 by the Georgia legislature to include what was then the Cherokee Nation.

Chestatee (River) This pristine river near Dahlonega (great for tubing) has a name that comes from a corruption of the Cherokee word *atsun-stati-yi*, meaning "firelight place." When the sunlight illuminates this crystal-clear flow, you'll see why the Cherokee thought of fire.

Dahlonega (Town) Choose from three theories on this name. One is that it comes from *Tahlonega*, which means "golden." The second is that it means "place of yellow money." The third version comes from the corruption of the Cherokee word *da-lon-ni-gei*, the Cherokee term for the color yellow. Anyway you look at it, these Native Americans realized something yellow and precious was in these parts—later proved by America's first gold rush, which took place here in the early 1800s.

South Carolina

THE NATURAL beauty of South Carolina extends in an unbroken line from its white sandy beaches to the green, rolling hills of the Blue Ridge Escarpment. You'll find fishing, hiking, camping, and birding in abundance here. Add to this action-packed list miles of pristine wilderness, plus an easy-livin' climate most of the year, and it's no wonder the state ranks among the top outdoor destinations in the country.

Along the coast, you will find an endless summer at the beach that's perfect for your family getaway, with swimming and roller coasting, dolphin watching, and fossil hunting.

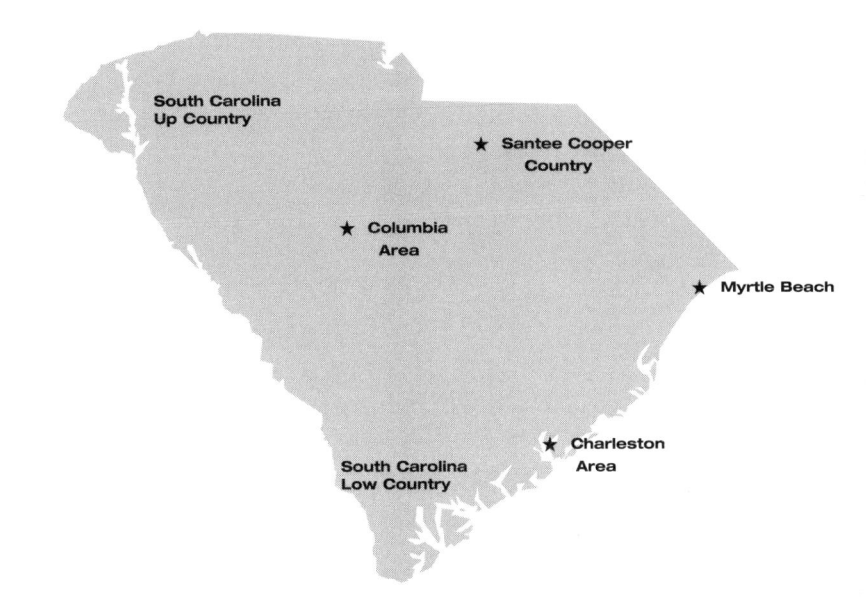

'Gators and egrets rise up and settle down as you paddle the Low Country's ACE Basin—one of the Nature Conservancy's designated "last great places on earth." The Palmetto Trails take you straight to the heart of nature, and your family will see spectacular vistas and wildlife around every bend.

And for a true look into yesterday, the antebellum days of the Old South are alive and well in Historic Charleston.

From the mountains to the sea, the Palmetto State is packed with the perfect mix of on- and off-the-beaten-track fun, and lots of smiling faces to make you feel right at home.

ATTRACTIONS
$	under $10
$$	$10 - $20
$$$	$20 - $30
$$$$	$30 +

HOTELS/MOTELS/CAMPGROUNDS
$	under $100
$$	$100 - $200
$$$	$200 - $300
$$$$	$300 +

RESTAURANTS
$	under $10
$$	$10 - $20
$$$	$20 - $30
$$$$	$30 +

***FAMILYFUN* RATED**
★	Fine
★★	Good
★★★	Very Good
★★★★	FamilyFun Recommended

Charleston's Broad Street is home to many historic antebellum mansions.

INTRODUCTION

Charleston Area

THIS MAGICAL, shining city by the sea has been drawing travelers for centuries with its stylish beauty and warm hospitality. No hurricanes, wars, or earthquakes have proven a match for the feisty town—known as well for its partying high rollers as its genteel southern manners. History comes alive for kids when they hear tales of Charleston's pirates, Native Americans, and blockade runners who kept the colonial town on its toes.

The old peninsular city, bounded by the Ashley and Cooper rivers, is a living example of Colonial America. Kids love exploring the colorful historic downtown by horse and buggy (petting the ponies, too) and cooling off under the famous pineapple fountain in Waterfront Park.

Many more wonderful attractions are just a quick, 10-minute drive across either of Charleston's rivers. The area West of the Ashley and the towns of James Island and John's Island lie across the Ashley; Mt. Pleasant, Sullivan's Island, and Isle of Palms, across the Cooper. Beaches where you can kick back and relax

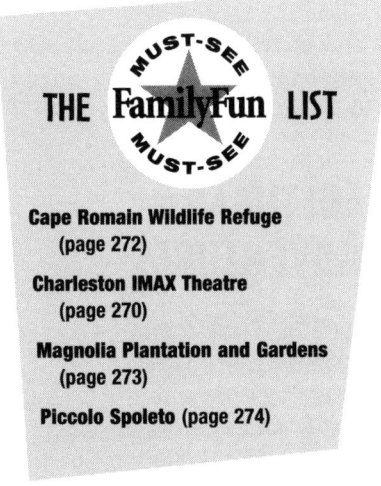

THE FamilyFun LIST

Cape Romain Wildlife Refuge
(page 272)

Charleston IMAX Theatre
(page 270)

Magnolia Plantation and Gardens
(page 273)

Piccolo Spoleto (page 274)

FamilyFun VACATION GUIDE

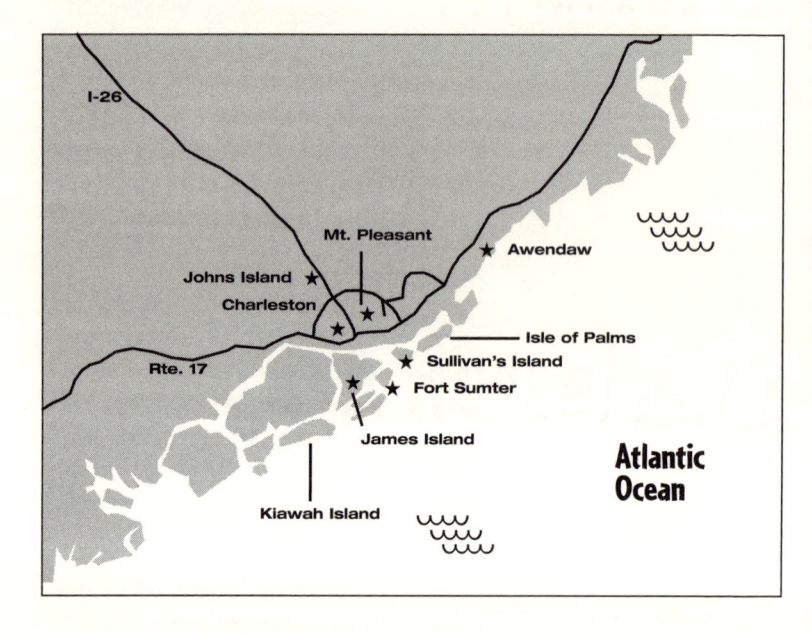

beckon from east of the Cooper, with lots of sandy shoreline for swimming, playing, shelling, and lazing under the sun. West of the Ashley, the old plantations whisper stories of wealth, power, and war. Their gracious antebellum homes and incredible gardens will take you—young and old alike—for an unforgettable trip back in time.

Cultural Adventures

Charleston IMAX Theatre
★★★★/$

Big and loud is one way to describe this beautiful theater on Charleston Harbor. The IMAX has a screen the size of a professional basketball court with a 12,000-watt sound system. It's the only one with 3-D capability in the Carolinas. The signature imported Italian leather seats—in an eye-popping brilliant turquoise—will keep kids comfy and cozy throughout the movies. IMAX shows include critically acclaimed titles such as *Dolphins*, *Everest*, and *T-Rex: Back to the Crustaceous*. Parents love the educational value of these programs; the kids love them because they're larger than life and lots of fun to watch. A snack bar serves up very reasonably priced frosty juices and sodas, popcorn, and candy. *360 Concord St., Charleston. (843) 725-4629;* www.charleston imax.com

South Carolina Aquarium
★★★/$$

Children will have a ball getting up close and personal with creatures of all kinds at this water wonderland. The aquarium does a whale of a job educating and entertaining youngsters of all ages and interest levels. Beautiful mosaics in the lobby floor trace the patterns of area riverbeds, and a free-standing aquarium filled with brightly colored schools of tiny fish is a sight to behold. Exhibits explore South Carolina habitats from the mountains to the sea. The wildlife of the mountain forest, piedmont, coastal plain, salt marsh, and Atlantic are all displayed in natural settings. Playful otters keep kids spellbound in the mountain stream exhibit, while sharks, rays, and sea turtles take the limelight in the ocean area. Watching the critters at feeding time will fascinate everybody. *100 Aquarium Wharf, Charleston. (843) 720-1990;* www.scaquarium.org

JUST FOR FUN

Angel Oak ★/Free
This extraordinary live oak is so humongous that it blocks the sky and dominates the landscape. It takes a moment or two before you realize you're standing under it and that all the surrounding foliage is, indeed, one massive tree. Although no one knows for sure, the best guess

Picnic Perfect

For those days when you and the kids are tired of restaurant fare and have the urge to picnic, here are some places that will make packing the perfect picnic a piece of cake:

EARTH FARE Beautiful baguettes, yummy cheeses, freshly ground peanut butter, and all sorts of energy-packed salads and pastas from the deli make this supermarket a sure bet. *74 Folly Rd. Blvd., Charleston. (843) 769-4800.*

HARRIS TEETER This market, housed in an old train station, carries many hard-to-find items and imports. Treat the kids to an Orangina, and if your family loves sushi, this is the place to find the best; it's prepared daily on the premises. *290 East Bay St., Charleston. (843) 722-6821.*

PUBLIX Simply the best fried chicken in town! Tender, juicy chicken fingers, too. The bakery breads and buns are fresh from the oven and above average as well, plus the deli makes a mean hoagie. *1000 Johnnie Dodds Blvd., Mt. Pleasant. (843) 856-3000.*

THE GREEN HERON GROCERY STORE This tiny grocer on Sullivan's Island is a great place to pick up sandwiches, a shaved ice, a *Hunley* T-shirt, and even some live bait. *2019 Middle St., Sullivan's Island. (843) 883-9474.*

is that this Low Country treasure is about 1,400 years old. That would put its birthdate at A.D. 600—around the time of King Arthur, the Anglo-Saxon invaders, and the Islamic Prophet Muhammad. (Great time for a mini history lesson.) Kids love circling the tree, weaving around branches that have sunken into the ground under their own tremendous weight. The largest limb is 89 feet long and more than 11 feet in circumference. To give you an idea of its girth, it takes a family of seven, standing with arms outstretched, to encircle the base of the tree. *3688 Angel Oak Rd., Johns Island. (843) 559-3496.*

Cape Romain Wildlife Refuge
★★★★/$$$

A great way to begin your vacation in the Low Country is to explore it by water. Charleston is surrounded by it, kids can't get enough of it, and your family can choose from lots of fun charters and boat tours. A local favorite is the pontoon boat to Bull Island, part of the Cape Romain National Wildlife Refuge. You can sit back for a relaxing 30-minute cruise while the kids keep track of the dolphins. Snowy egrets and blue herons rise up as the boat glides through mud flats and tidal marsh. Loggerhead sea turtles love these pristine waters, too, and build their nests along the 22 miles of protected beach. Watch closely—stingrays have been spotted here leaping from the sea. The boat drops you on the remote barrier island where you can picnic, organize an expedition, swim, or just soak up some sun. Your entire family will enjoy trekking for treasure on the unspoiled beaches, and bird-watchers have a field day in the maritime forest, where the occasional alligator can be found basking in a pond. Don't forget to fill your backpack with plenty of water, sunblock, and insect repellent. Tours can be arrranged through Coastal Expeditions, *514-B Mill St., Mt. Pleasant. (843) 884-7684; (843) 928-3368.*

Charles Towne Landing State Historic Site
★★/$

Carolina's first permanent residents sailed into the Ashley River and laid claim to this settlement in 1670. Today, more than three centuries later, your family can envision the humble beginnings of Charleston and the rigors of wild country life by way of several reconstructions that have been added to original artifacts—the colonial home, the blacksmith, and a carpenter's shop, to name a few. Kids love climbing aboard the *Adventure*, a full-scale replica of a 17th-century vessel, docked near the original fortifications that protected the town from attacks by sea. Youngsters also enjoy the natural habitat zoo, where bears, bobcats, and other indigenous animals prowl. The one-dollar tram tour is another pleasant way to get an overview of this historic site. *1500 Old Towne Rd., Charleston. (843) 852-4200.*

Isle of Palms County Park
★★/$

A whole string of cute, funky shops and eateries line the sand dunes of this park; it also is the only beach area on Isle of Palms and Sullivan's Island with a full range of facilities and lifeguards. You can rent boogie boards for the kids and beach chairs and umbrellas for the whole family. A play area and a volleyball court are nearby when your crew is ready for a break from water sports. Aprés swim showers and sheltered picnic tables with barbecues, as well as hassle-free parking, round out this terrific beach. *1 14th Ave., Isle of Palms. (843) 886-3863;* beach parks.com/isleofpalms.htm

MUST-SEE FamilyFun Magnolia Plantation and Gardens
★★★★/$$

The stately mansion at the end of the beautiful avenue of oaks is a vision of southern grace, with ancient paths meandering through gardens that are exploding with year-round color. (The plantation has been passed down through 12 generations of Draytons and remains in the family today.) Your kids will make a beeline for the little petting zoo, where they'll find a collection of animals typically found on the old plantations (billygoats, peacocks, and deer). They'll also love the nature train ride (fee), a guided 45-minute expedition through lush woods and around swampy ponds in search of alligators, turtles, herons, and egrets. Another fun tour takes you over flooded rice fields on a pontoon boat (fee), but save it for kids who can sit still for the 45-minute ride. You can stroll the gardens under ancient trees dripping with Spanish moss, and take in various plantation landmarks, including the famous long white bridge over Cypress Pond. You can rent canoes and bikes to get a closer look at nature, and kids really enjoy climbing the observation tower, where the sighting of an eagle's nest makes for an extra-special treat. *Rte. 4. Hwy. 61, Charleston. (800) 367-3517; (843) 571-1266;* www.magnoliaplanta tion.com

FamilyFun **VACATION GUIDE**

Piccolo Spoleto
FamilyFun ★★★★/Most events are free

The Piccolo puppets kick off the festivities each year for this citywide celebration of the arts—Charleston's official companion to the famous Spoleto Festival U.S.A. Piccolo Spoleto focuses on the best of local and southeastern artists from every discipline, with a much greater emphasis on cool kid things than its big brother. The whole city turns into a stage, as hundreds of performers delight crowds on the streets and in parks, restaurants, and churches—even on boats. Colorful booths and bandstands bring a carnival atmosphere to Marion Square, where kids can take in the sights, have their faces painted, munch on treats, and boogie to the music. The event runs from May 25 to June 10. *(843) 724-7305;* www.charleston.net/charlestoncity/piccolo.html

BUNKING DOWN

Comfort Inn ★/$-$$

This chain property is a parent's—and kid's—dream come true. Only two miles from the ocean, it also is near Mt. Pleasant's beautiful Towne Center, an open-air mall featuring all your favorite shops (Gap, Old Navy), plus the multiscreen Palmetto Grand Theater. Comfy rooms are equipped with refrigerators, microwaves, and other must-haves for a traveling family. The hot breakfast bar with kid-pleasers like eggs,

---

DAY TRIP
Living History

For those kids who haven't gotten their fill of history while in Charleston, this trip is just for you. **Fort Sumter**, located about three miles across the Charleston Harbor, was the site of the first Civil War battle in April 1861. The battle itself lasted 34 hours before the Union Army surrendered to the Confederate troops. (Amazingly, no one was killed.) For the next 22 months, the brave soldiers at Fort Sumter protected the city from Union siege. Although much of the fort has been destroyed over time, there are still some really cool ruins and replicas for kids to see. You'll want to spend a few minutes in the museum checking out the artillery, cannons, and other Civil War artifacts. Then it's outside for more cannons, historic flags—there are even three original shells still embedded in the fort wall. (Who's the first to spot them?) National Park Service rangers present an overview of the fort, and are available to answer questions.

At press time, a 30-minute narrated boat ride departing from the Charleston City Marina and Patriot's Point Naval and Maritime Museum

sausage, and grits is complimentary. An outdoor pool is waiting when your kids tire of the nearby waves of the Atlantic. *1130 Hungryneck Blvd., Mt. Pleasant. (800) 517-4000; (843) 216-0004; www.comfortinn.com*

Embassy Suites Historic Charleston ★★★★/$$

First a fort, then an arsenal, later the original site of The Citadel military school—today it has been restored and renovated to become one of the most charming properties in Charleston. Decorated with a West Indies flair (lots of mahogany, bamboo, and palms), it's a place where even your kids will notice the details—like the refined but funny monkey paintings in the lobby. Youngsters like having their own room in the suite complex, complete with TV, Nintendo, and kitchenette. The complimentary cooked-to-order breakfast and nightly beverage-and-snack-reception make even the youngest guest feel welcome. And, if that's not enough, the hotel is a block or two from the bustling visitors' centers where you can pick up a trolley or motor-coach tour of the city. *337 Meeting St., Charleston. (800) 362-2779; (843) 723-6900;* www.embassysuites.com

Holiday Inn Express Hotel and Suites ★★/$-$$

This is not your ordinary Holiday Inn Express—light, bright colors set a cheerful tone for everyone's stay at the ocean. The suites have pullout

transports visitors to Fort Sumter, followed by a one-hour tour of the fort. Departure points, schedules, and fees change; it's best to call ahead for information.

Continuing your history lesson, **Patriot's Point Naval and Maritime Museum** *($$; 40 Patriot's Point Rd., Mt. Pleasant; 843/884-2727)* is a mecca for those children eager to get an up-close-and-personal look at such awesome ships as the 880-foot long USS *Yorktown*, a retired aircraft carrier that served our nation during World War II and Vietnam. Upon arrival, make sure to pick up a brochure that will help guide your crew through a number of the ship's key sections, like the engine room, mess hall, bridge, and flight deck. Other onboard must-sees include the hands-on navy flight simulator, rotating guns, and nearly two dozen aircraft—all of which are guaranteed to get a huge thumbs-up from your preteen crowd. Got a question? Ask any of the friendly volunteers—many are retired shipmates from the *Yorktown* and love to share their experiences with kids. Rounding out this fun yet educational adventure is a cool submarine, destroyer, and a Coast Guard Cutter, which sank a U-boat during World War II.

sofas and amenities such as small kitchenettes, as well as views of the Atlantic. Kids can pop from the pool right into the ocean, and the whole family will love the funky beach-town atmosphere. The continental breakfast is complimentary. *1126 Ocean Blvd., Isle of Palms. (800) 465-4329; (843) 886-3003.*

James Island County Park
★★★/$

Modern vacation cabins overlook the beautiful Stono River and have fully outfitted kitchens and other kid-minded essentials like TVs and phones. Campers can choose from primitive camps, tent sites, and recreational vehicle sites with conveniences like full hookups, laundry facilities, grills, and ceramic bathhouses. The 643-acre park is a great place for the whole family to enjoy the outdoors, with boardwalks, fishing piers, and bike trails that hug the marsh. Kids can scale the heights of South Carolina's tallest outdoor climbing wall (fee), and have tons of fun at Splash Zone pool, one of the most popular water parks in the area (fee). *871 Riverland Dr., James Island. (843) 795-7275; www.ccprc.com/jicp.htm*

Kiawah Island Resort
★★★★/$-$$$

Kids have the best of both worlds at this remote island resort, starting with 10 miles of nationally acclaimed beach on the Atlantic Ocean and plenty of crystal-clear swimming pools to pop into. Kiawah's villas and luxury private homes, scattered throughout the island, are completely equipped and tastefully decorated. The resort offers a camp (fee) for kids ages 3 to 11, as well as a nature excursion program (fee), including marsh creek canoe trips, sea kayaking, birding, and bike tours. Special events like sand-sculpture contests, ice-cream socials, beach bashes, and "dive-in" movies make for lots of special moments for the whole family to share. *12 Kiawah Beach Dr., Kiawah Island. (800) 654-2924; (843) 768-2121; www.kiawahisland.com*

Middleton Inn at Middleton Place ★★★★/$$

This delightful inn overlooking the Ashley River is right on plantation row, with several major historical sites within a few miles. In fact, your family is as close to staying on a plantation as it gets—a five-minute walk across Azalea Hillside and the Half Moon Bridge gives you free daytime access to the Middleton plantation house and internationally acclaimed gardens. During Plantation Days, costumed guides give kids an inside look at what it took to run an antebellum plantation. At Christmastime you'll find carolers, Gullah storytelling, wreath-making classes, and lots of hot cider and cookies. King or queen rooms can accommodate a rollaway bed, and all have wood-burning fireplaces, floor-to-ceiling windows, plantation shutters, and gorgeous wooded or river views. A small refrigerator is filled with complimentary juices and snacks, and kids will love cooling off in the outdoor pool. Guided nature walks (fee) explore the river habitat of alligators and wading birds; other activities include basket making, kayaking, biking (fees), and lots of hammocks to kick back and relax in. *4290 Ashley River Rd., Charleston. (800) 543-4774; (843) 556-0500;* www.middletonplace.org

GOOD EATS

Blossom ★/$$
A high-energy eatery with a touch of art deco design and an exhibition kitchen is a feast for the senses for parents and kids alike. The bistro is casual enough for youngsters, who can watch as their pizza is crafted and popped into an oak-burning oven. Weather permitting, eat outside in the walled courtyard—a must-do, when in Charleston. The eclectic menu includes sophisticated pizzas, fresh pastas, lots of grilled seafood, and out-of-sight house-made desserts. *171 East Bay St., Charleston. (843) 722-9200.*

The Boathouse at Breach Inlet
★★★★/$-$$
Lolling on the decks overlooking the Intracoastal Waterway is a pleas-

> **FamilyFun TIP**
>
> **Wind Bags**
>
> Getting a homemade kite off the ground doesn't get much easier than this quick trick. First, tie together the handles of a plastic shopping bag with an end of a ball of string. Staple a few 2-foot lengths of ribbon to the bottom of the bag for kite tails. As you run, and the bag fills with air, slowly let out the string and the kite should begin to soar and dive.

ant pastime while waiting for dinner to arrive at this popular restaurant. (Look closely and you may spot a dolphin or two.) The kids' menu has some rather grown-up choices, like a petite-size filet or lobster tail—both of which get a thumbs-up from young diners. If yours are more traditional eaters, they can have mainstays like chicken fingers and pasta. The sleek nautical design of this casual eatery, beautiful sunsets, and terrific food keep it packed all the time, so make reservations a day or so in advance. *101 Palm Blvd., Isle of Palms. (843) 886-8000.*

California Dreaming
★★★/$$
The view of Charleston Harbor from this wide-open, casual restaurant is truly exceptional—your kids will be glued to the windows, and parents' cameras will be clicking, capturing photos of the busy water traffic. The

FamilyFun VACATION GUIDE

FamilyFun READER'S TIP

Scenic Views

I am always trying to make car travel more fun for my kids and easier on me. One idea that has worked very well is a picture scavenger hunt. I cut pictures out of old picture books, magazines, and catalogs and paste them on a piece of poster board. Then I punch holes in the two top corners of the poster, tie a piece of elastic between them, and hang the poster from the back of the front seat. Each time they see one of the items—an airplane, tractor, bicycle, or horse, for example—they place a sticker on that picture. My kids love this game so much that it entertained them throughout a recent 13-hour trip.

Lisa Reynolds, San Antonio, Texas

---

chicken fingers, quesadillas, and fettucine are wildly popular items with the younger set, and parents devour everything, from the restaurant's famous baby backs and prime ribs to the huge entrée salads; it's fine family fare. *1 Ashley Pointe Dr., Charleston. (843) 766-1644.*

See Wee Restaurant ★★/$$

After all that fresh island air and scouring for seashells, y'all will no doubt be in the mood for some serious seafood. Less than 30 miles from Charleston, you'll find this country-style dining place just across Highway 17, and Miss Mary's good home cooking is known for miles around. Kick back with a cool beverage and soak up some local color. McClellanville fishing boats supply the kitchen with fresh shrimp, flounder, mahi-mahi, whatever's biting. Burgers, grilled cheese, and scaled-down orders of fried shrimp keep the little ones happy. Top it off with a wedge of old-fashioned, made-from-scratch layer cake prepared by one of the local church ladies—yum. *4808 Hwy. 17 N., Awendaw. (843) 928-3609.*

Sticky Fingers ★★★/$$

This local favorite has some of the best sticky stuff around—and a kids' corner to keep them happy before and after the meal. Slide into a booth, take your pick of pork ribs, barbecue, grilled chicken, prepared just about any way you can imagine, and relax with a cool beverage. Multiple locations. *341 Hwy. 17 N. Bypass, Mt. Pleasant. (843) 856-9840.*

Vickery's ★★★★/$$

Funky and fun, this eatery has broken bits of crockery and 1950s ashtrays embedded in the walls—a decorating style guaranteed to catch your child's eye. It also has one of the best views of Shem Creek and its fleet of working shrimp boats, plus lots of decks for dining and exploring. The food has a Cuban flair, but fear not—the chicken fingers, grilled cheese, pasta, and burgers are definite kid pleasers. *1313 Shrimp Boat La., Mt. Pleasant. (843) 884-4440.*

Souvenir Hunting

Gwynn's of Mt. Pleasant
This unique, locally owned department store has a kids' corner with a library of fun movies for them to watch while parents get in a little quality shopping time. You'll find lots of smart clothing for the little ones and yourself, plus fine books, and always the very latest in must-have toys. *916 Houston Northcutt Blvd., Mt. Pleasant. (843) 884-9518.*

Sarah Anne's Ltd.
Located in Charleston's famous shopping district, this beautiful shop is packed with great things for your kids. Tea sets, dress-up costumes, arts and crafts, stickers, books—you name it, they've got it. *279 King St., Charleston. (843) 722-8675.*

Wonder Works
A toy store is an adventure in itself, and this is one of Mt. Pleasant's finest—but beware, your children may never want to leave. Lots of demos for hands-on experimentation make this a wonderful playground for kids of all ages, with everything from telescopes to T-shirts, Lava lamps, books, and the latest in collectibles. (This could be one expensive stop!) *280 W. Coleman Blvd., Mt. Pleasant. (843) 849-6757.*

Kids go wild for the mini golf, batting cage, and bumper boats at Frankie's Fun Park.

INTRODUCTION

Columbia Area

WIDE OPEN spaces, huge expanses of pine forest, and countryside dotted with cotton and tobacco fields all signal that you're in the South Carolina midlands. Within this landscape, the sand hills meet the piedmont and overlap, making for an interesting collage of coastal and mountain characteristics.

The capital city of Columbia survived the War Between the States, but only a few of its antebellum homes and buildings were left standing. The historic State House wears six bronze stars to mark hits from Sherman's cannons. The huge Italian Renaissance building—with its lofty galleries and rich appointments—is enough to impress the older kids in your crowd. They'll have fun, too, getting an up-close look at the inner workings of government.

The South Carolina National Heritage Corridor cuts through the heartland to the south of Columbia as it crosses the state. Aiken, the center of Thoroughbred Country, is among the historical and natural resources along this route, and a fun stop for young horse lovers.

THE FamilyFun LIST

MUST-SEE

Congaree Swamp National Monument (page 283)

Frankie's Fun Park (page 283)

Riverbanks Zoological Park and Botanical Garden (page 283)

FamilyFun **VACATION GUIDE**

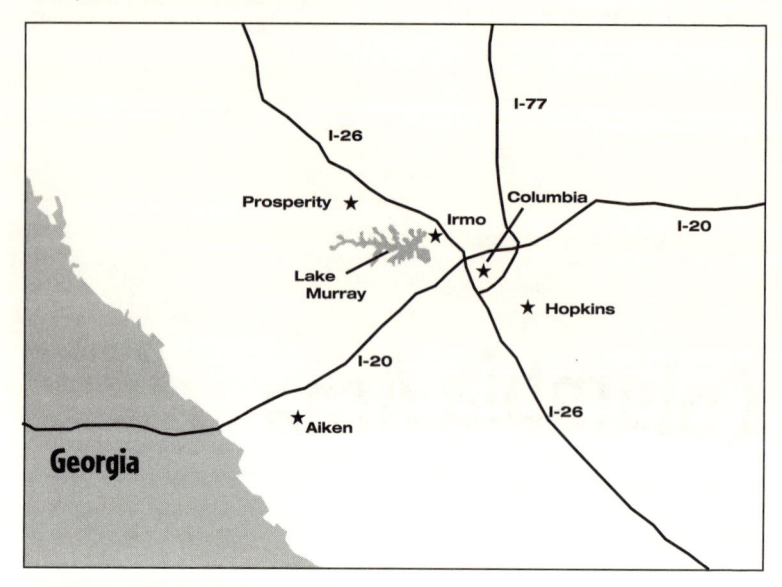

The waters of beautiful Lake Murray extend for 78 square miles. Numerous marinas and vacation-home rentals make it easy for your family to settle in for a sporting time along its shores. The lake is full of small wilderness islands. Many camping families pitch a tent, put a boat at one of the many public landings, and spend the night under the stars.

Cultural Adventures

South Carolina State Museum ★/$
The beautifully restored building that houses the museum was originally the world's first electric textile mill. Here, each floor has its own niche: art, natural history, science and technology, and cultural history—you name it, they've got it with enough neat stuff for kids of just about every age. The Stringer Discovery Center on the first floor is a totally touchable room that kids as young as 3 can enjoy. Exhibits include everything from Model T's to lasers, a walking piano, a working telegraph, and Lincoln Logs. The interactive sites really draw kids in—like an earthquake machine that simulates continental collisions with a movable puzzle of continents. One landing sports a 43-foot model of a giant white shark suspended from the ceiling—it's enough to give you goose bumps. *301 Gervais St., Columbia. (803) 898-4921;* www.museum.state.sc.us

JUST FOR FUN

Congaree Swamp National Monument ★★/Free

As you walk the trails of this ancient forest and a family of wild hogs scurries for cover, you may get the sense that you, too, are being watched here. This untouched place is the last intact stand of old-growth bottomland forest in the United States, and the home to deer, bobcat, snakes and other reptiles, birds, and waterfowl. It's enough to captivate every child's imagination. Little ones may spy a spider spinning a web, while the slightly older kids take in the awesomeness of a 160-foot pine nearly 300 years old. Most of the monument lies within the rich floodplains of the Congaree River. Everywhere you look, the genius of nature is at work—like the dead trees that furnish food and shelter for all eight species of woodpeckers found in the Southeast, including the endangered red-cockaded woodpecker. Once a month, you can take a free, guided boat tour (call ahead), or call the park visitor center for boat rental information. *100 National Park Rd., Hopkins. (803) 776-4396; www.nps.gov/cosw*

Frankie's Fun Park ★★★/$-$$$

Kids from far and wide come to Frankie's for a rip-roaring good time. In fact, word has it that many adults are regulars, too. It's an amusement park where kids can really be kids, and so can you, at least for a little while. Bumper boats and go carts (carts and tracks offer varying levels of difficulty—there's even a rookie cart for the 4-year-olds) give kids that behind-the-wheel thrill. There's a batting cage for your wanna-be pros, plus more challenges—thanks to laser tag and what seems to be a gazillion video games. *140 Parkridge Dr., Columbia. (803) 781-2342.*

Riverbanks Zoological Park and Botanical Garden ★★★★/$

This beautiful park nestled on the banks of the Saluda River is rated among the top 10 in the country. African lions, Amur tigers, and all kinds of monkeys are among the 2,000-plus animals in this awesome zoo. Moats, water, and light create an environment free of bars and cages for animals, and even the lushly landscaped paths are a treat to walk. A birdhouse features feathered friends from Africa and South America, and gorillas and elephants have recently been added to the growing zoo family. An 18-foot anaconda (way cool) and giant sea turtles take center stage in the Aquarium Reptile Complex. Crocodiles, king cobras, and poison dart frogs sun themselves in the misty tropical habitat. Gila monsters and iguanas hide beneath cacti in the desert gallery. Kids really get a kick out of watching the sea lions gobble up breakfast during feeding times. They also love the trams that shuttle you across the river into the spectacular botanical gardens. The park features an indoor fast-food restaurant and several refreshment stands, as well as picnic tables and a gift shop. Little ones can ride their favorite animals on the Endangered Species Carousel. *500 Wildlife Pkwy., Columbia. (803) 779-8717.*

Bunking Down

AmeriSuites
★/$

Kids and adults will love this property's proximity to Columbiana Mall; it's also less than 10 miles from Columbia's must-see attractions. Other family-friendly features like the hotel's outdoor pool, small but comfy suite setup with kitchenette, and free breakfast buffet make this an easy overnight choice. *1130 Kinley Rd., Irmo. (800) 833-1516; (803) 407-1560; www.amerisuites.com*

Dreher Island State Park
★★★★/$-$$

Your family will feel right at home in the park's beautiful, contemporary villas on the wooded shores of Lake Murray. Villas are completely equipped, have screened porches, balconies, and fireplaces, and even a color TV—something the kids will appreciate when they're not diving off the dock or out fishing. You can also take in the views from lakefront camping areas perfect for RVs or tents. Activities (fee) like waterskiing, fishing, boating, and sailing guarantee an unforgettable family vacation. Located about 30 miles from downtown Columbia. *3677 State Park Rd., Prosperity. (803) 364-4152.*

Embassy Suites Hotel
★★/$$

The suites here have all the usual amenities, including a small kitchenette. There's a comfy setting for dining on pizza and other kid-friendly dishes from the on-site restaurant. Growing youngsters with big appetites love the hotel's complimentary made-to-order breakfasts. Headed to the zoo? Leave your car behind—the property is just a short walk to this wildly popular attraction. *200 Stoneridge Dr., Columbia. (800) 362-2779; (803) 252-8700; www.embassysuites.com*

The Jumper House Bed and Breakfast
★★★/$

Kids just love jumping into cool and refreshing Lake Murray from their own little beach at this B&B. When they tire of that, they can frolic in the 30 acres of pretty countryside. The 1905 house contains four rooms, all charmingly restored, as well as three one-bedroom cottages. Youngsters can sleep on the comfy rollaway beds. A private dock with a boat ramp provides easy access to the lake. A continental breakfast is offered in the main house only. Cottages come with fully equipped kitchens. *Jumper Rd., Prosperity. (864) 445-2950; (803) 364-0742.*

Good Eats

Maurice's Gourmet Barbeque ★★★★/$

Known far and wide as the Piggie Park, this place announces itself with a neon flying pig two stories above the restaurant. The "yellow" barbecue, soaked in Maurice's own zingy, mustard-based Carolina Gold, with a side of slaw and hush puppies, is the main attraction. The kids' menu has smaller portions, as well as tenders, burgers, and hot dogs. The fresh fruit shakes and cobblers are terrific, so save room. *1601 Charleston Hwy., West Columbia. (800) 628-7423; (803) 796-0220;* www.mauricesbbq.com/restloc.htm

New Orleans Riverfront Restaurant ★/$$

Perched on the riverbank where the Congaree and Saluda rivers join, this casual place is a great spot to pop into after a trip to the zoo. Kids love the view, and they're keen on the burgers, ribs, and seafood. *121 Alexander Rd., West Columbia. (803) 794-5112.*

Perry's Back Porch ★★★/$

This charming eatery a few minutes from Lake Murray and the Jumper House bed-and-breakfast is a great place for a home-cooked meal when you're out in the country, far from the crowds. Mouthwatering meals like fried chicken, meat loaf, and country-style steak will please even your most finicky eater. The bakeshop has yummy sweets like old-fashioned lemon bars that will also delight the kids. *Main St., Prosperity. (803) 364-3556.*

Souvenir Hunting

State Museum Gift Shop

This humongous shop is packed with enough keepsakes of South Carolina that everyone in the family will find exactly what they want. *301 Gervais St., Columbia. (803) 898-4921.*

Zany Brainy

Children will find a zillion neat-o things in this multimedia kids' superstore. There's everything from Harry Potter magician hats and wands to Thomas the Tank Engine toys. Free events every day, too. *242 Harbison Blvd., Columbia. (803) 407-6230;* www.zanybrainy.com

For a quiet Myrtle Beach experience, grab your mask, snorkel, and flippers and search for sea creatures.

INTRODUCTION

Myrtle Beach

A BUSTLING BEACH scene (sand that stretches for 60 miles) and lots of family-oriented things to do make Myrtle Beach one of the most popular vacation spots on the East Coast. A quick stroll from the white sands of the Grand Strand (a great beach with lots of parking) and you're in the middle of town—amusement parks, restaurants, shopping, lots of people, and all sorts of things going on. This is the home of the famous Pavilion and Ripley's Aquarium. With 225 outlet stores, shopping families can indulge that passion. You can even take in a show at Broadway on the Beach while in town.

On Myrtle Beach's South Strand, you can find a more relaxed atmosphere at getaways like Surfside Beach. The old resort town of Pawleys Island is famous for its laid-back atmosphere. All you need here is a beach hat, several bathing suits, and a shovel and bucket to ensure a wonderful vacation with the kids.

THE FamilyFun MUST-SEE LIST

Alligator Adventure (page 288)

Carolina Safari (page 289)

Dixie Stampede Dinner and Show (page 289)

Myrtle Beach Pavilion Amusement Park (page 290)

Wild Water (page 291)

FamilyFun VACATION GUIDE

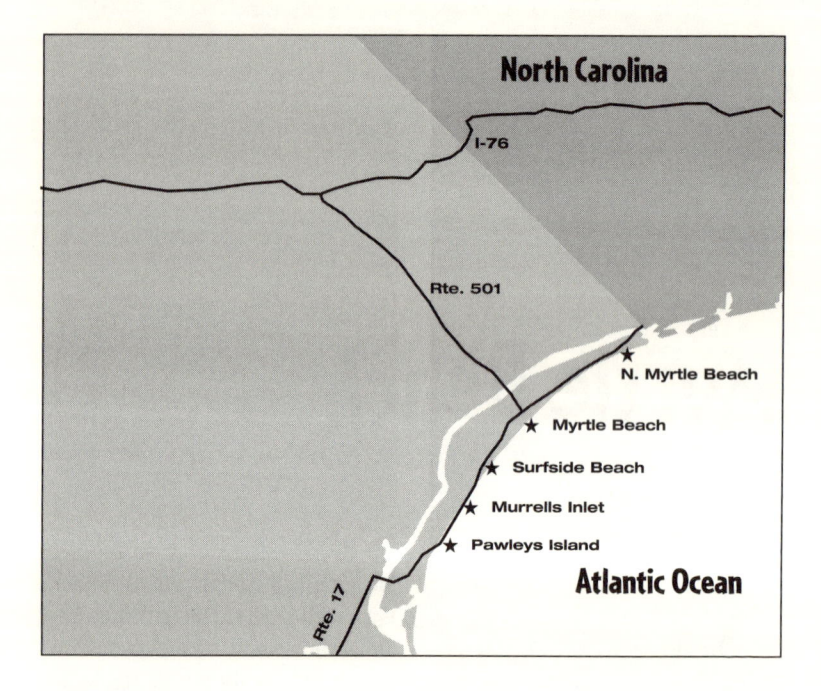

Cultural Adventures

Alabama Theater ★/$$$

The knockout shows staged here will blow you and your family away. Big-name stars and glossy, high-energy production numbers make this some of the best entertainment that will genuinely appeal to everyone from the youngest to the oldest family members. Youngsters get a kick out of the dance numbers and go bonkers over the house comedienne. From November to January, the Christmas special, a lavish arrangement of traditional Christmas classics, dazzles kids and adults with dramatic stage sets, special effects, and lighting. Free admission for kids 12 and younger on Monday and Wednesday from June to August. *Barefoot Landing, 4750 Hwy. 17 S., N. Myrtle Beach. (800) 342-2262; (843) 272-1111;* www.alabamatheater.com

Just for Fun

Alligator Adventure
FamilyFun ★★★/$$

Rare and exotic wildlife await in this highly acclaimed specialty zoo perched on the edge of marshland near the Intracoastal

Waterway. A series of boardwalks leads to the homes of hundreds of alligators, snakes and other reptiles, and birds. There are literally alligators everywhere—and kids just love it. This is one of the biggest facilities for reptile life in the world, with some rare and endangered species. Kids love the many live demonstrations, especially the one in which a handler demonstrates how rubbing the spot on its tummy will turn a 200-pound alligator into a sleeping babe. *4898 Hwy. 17 S., N. Myrtle Beach. (843) 361-0789.*

Carolina Safari
FamilyFun ★★★★/$$$$

Hop aboard a customized Jeep for a Jurassic Park–style tour—minus the dinosaurs. The year-round, three-and-a-half-hour ride takes you through swamps, open country, and more; it's the only tour of its kind in the area. Kids love hearing spine-tingling stories about pirates and ghosts, and actually seeing some of their haunts firsthand. The tour takes you to a 300-year-old rice field and the graveyard of strong-willed Alice Flagg. You'll drive along the Atlantic migratory path—a birder's paradise—and explore the salt marsh for alligators. There are plenty of pit stops, and kids can even hop out and explore a 15th-century Spanish-style castle. The roomy, customized, safari-style Jeep has a canopy top and roll-up sides, with plenty of space for car seats, strollers, coolers—and your crew. Tour buses will pick up passengers at most resorts. *Barefoot Landing, 4866 Hwy. 17 S., N. Myrtle Beach. (888) 497-5330; (843) 272-1177.*

Dixie Stampede Dinner and Show
★★★★/$$$$

This is probably the most fun your kids will ever have eating a meal. In Dolly Parton's Dixie Stampede, parents and kids get to eat with their fingers and watch a show at the same time. And what a show: it's a two-hour feast of live-action entertainment, amazing stunts, and world-class trick riding. The show begins in the Dixie Belle Saloon (nonalcoholic) with Australia's Electric Cowboy, and moves on to the dinner theater where a dazzling display of horsemanship and friendly competition between North and South begins. The four-course meal is a southern classic, with soup, biscuits, rotisserie chicken, barbecue pork, and an apple turnover. Kids love all the action and may even be enlisted in the chicken races. Closed January and early February. *8901-B Hwy. 17, N. Myrtle Beach. (800) 433-4401; (843) 497-9700;* www.dixiestampede.com

Dragon's Lair Fantasy Golf
★/$

Kids will probably like the smoke-breathing dragon here as much as the round of golf. The 18-hole

FamilyFun VACATION GUIDE

miniature-golf course meanders through darkened caves and castles, with medieval adventures around every corner. But the kids look forward most to the 30-foot dragon that rises out of the mountain every 20 minutes. *Broadway at the Beach. 1197 Celebrity Cir., Myrtle Beach. (843) 444-3215.*

Great American Riverboat Company ★★/$$

Here's a great way for the whole family to enjoy a little sight-seeing by boat. Float down the Intracoastal Waterway on an entertaining cruise aboard a replica of a side-wheel riverboat. A narrator talks up some of the local color during the 90-minute tour, and a lively band keeps the kids hopping. You can also opt for the dinner cruise. Cruises depart from a spot next to the Greg Norman Australian Restaurant. *Barefoot Landing, Myrtle Beach. (800) 685-6601; (843) 236-1700; www.mbriverboat.com*

MUST-SEE FamilyFun Myrtle Beach Pavilion Amusement Park ★★★★/$-$$

Nearly a century old, this seaside park is one of the leading attractions in the southeast. It's kid heaven, with 11 acres of roller coasters, thrill rides, go-cart tracks, and games. Kids and parents can cool off together on water rides like the Hydro Surge rafting adventure and Log Flume. The youngest set will like the more than a dozen kiddie rides, and older kids can do skill games, a video and pinball arcade, and shops. Plenty of snacks to be had. The park's newest attraction, The Hurricane, is a 110-foot double-looping roller coaster that reaches the force of three Gs—meaning your 6-year-old needs to be pretty brave to take on this challenge; there's also a minimum height requirement of 48 inches. The frame is a steel-and-wood construction, taking fans to new heights and giving them the classic ride that keeps them coming back for more. Open

Chill Out

Take a break from all those wild Myrtle Beach attractions for a couple of hours and get back in sync with nature at one of the most beautiful gardens in the south. An excursion to the fabulous **Brookgreen Gardens** (*$; 1931 Brookgreen Dr., Murrells Inlet; 843/235-6001; 843/235-6000 on weekends*) will give you and the kids a much-needed break (and fun) from the action—plus it's less than 30 minutes from Myrtle Beach. A magnificent, 250-year-old avenue oak is the garden's centerpiece, and sets that *Gone with the Wind* tone for your visit. The kids will love the shady canopy of huge trees and the equally huge preserve of pine, live oaks, myrtle,

Wild Water
FamilyFun ★★★★/$$

MUST-SEE This water park is a local favorite. Awesome mat slides rise 60 feet into the air, with kids flying down them head-first, feet-first, every which way. Your family can choose from more than 30 rides, including such thrills as Free Fall Dive Cliff, Head Rush, and Wipeout Wavepool. Wee Kids Water World is geared to the younger set, with two kiddie pools and a tree-stump slide. Small children can also ride with Mom or Dad on the popular tube slides. Relax a bit in the Lazy River or kick it up a notch in the Wipeout Wavepool that serves up a whole repertory of wave types. There's also an 18-hole miniature-golf course and go-carts for kids 3 and older. A food court tops off the fun with snacks like pizza, burgers, chicken, and ice cream. Wavepool open April to Labor Day; park open March through September. *910 Hwy. 17 S., Surfside Beach. (800) 833-9453; www.wild-water.com*

March through mid-October. *812 N. Ocean Blvd., Myrtle Beach. (843) 448-6456; www.mbpavillion.com*

BUNKING DOWN

Crown Reef at South Beach Resort ★★★★/$-$$

A 575-foot Lazy River ride will be the main attraction for the kids, while parents will appreciate the many kid-pleasing extras at this high-powered hotel. Knock-your-socks-off features include four restaurants, two game rooms, several indoor and outdoor pools, kiddie pools, and Jacuzzis. Kids are kept busy during the summer with organized activity programs (fee), and downtown Myrtle Beach is a quick, complimentary shuttle ride away. All rooms, suites, and efficiencies are oceanfront and have small kitchens with

and gardenia. Informal gardens, bursting with color, frame works created by prominent American sculptors. Brookgreen is a great way to give the whole family a little culture kick. The Garden Room for Children is a special place just for the young and young at heart, complete with a kid-size sculpture collection. In addition to the gardens, a tour aboard a 48-foot pontoon boat (fee) explores the freshwater creeks and abandoned ricefields bordering the Waccamaw River. The Trekker (fee) takes you on an off-road adventure in a 20-passenger vehicle for a glimpse of remote sites like the old rice mill tower and the bluffs overlooking the Waccamaw. Sorry, this rocky road experience is not recommended for kids 5 and under.

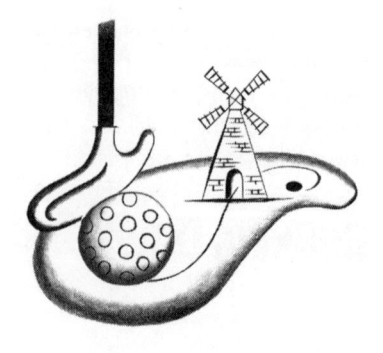

microwaves and stoves. *2913 S. Ocean Blvd., Myrtle Beach. (800) 405-7333; (843) 626-8077;* www.crownreef.com

Huntington Beach State Park
★★★/$

Away from the crowds of Myrtle Beach, this state park offers beautiful, unspoiled beaches with a good measure of things for families to do. Campers will find 184 sites within walking distance of the beach for RV and tent overnights. Kids can enjoy supervised programs that explore the alligators and sea turtles in their natural habitats, plus try beachcombing, kayaking (fee), and cast netting. Bathhouses and a concession stand for snacking are also welcome touches. *16148 Ocean Hwy., Murrells Inlet. (843) 237-4440.*

Sea Island Inn
★★★★/$

Tucked in a quiet residential neighborhood, this charming family-owned hotel offers oceanfront rooms, with comfortable sleep quarters and family essentials like a small refrigerator and microwave. Parents and kids will also appreciate a hassle-free meal in Sea Island's first-rate dining room. An old-fashioned game room (Monopoly and such), a beautifully landscaped pool, and a summer activities program for kids (some with fees) make this a good choice for families. *6000 N. Ocean Blvd., Myrtle Beach. (800) 548-0767; (843) 449-6406.*

GOOD EATS

Bullwinkles Family Food & Fun
★★★★/$

With indoor games, crawl toys, TVs, and stage shows, this is like a restaurant with a theme park inside. Kids make quick business of their favorite food and head to the fabulous play area to give Mom and Dad some time out. The kid-friendly menu includes everything from pizza and burgers to soup and sandwiches. Multiple locations. *1002 29th Ave., N. Myrtle Beach. (843) 626-3091.*

Hard Rock Café
★★★★/$$

South Carolina's only branch of this nationwide chain is a hot dining spot for kids of all ages. Youngsters love everything from the zany pyramid-shaped building to stargazing at the rock 'n' roll memorabilia, not to mention all the other wild and glittery stuff coming out of the walls and ceilings. A coloring book and crayons keep youngsters busy while they wait for their tasty hamburgers and fries. Multiple locations. *Broadway at the Beach, 1322 Celebrity Cir., Myrtle Beach. (843) 946-0007;* www.hardrockcafe.com

Johnny Rockets
★★/$

The waiters here break into 1950s songs while they dish out your food, and the kids just love it. Each table has its own jukebox to keep young toes tapping while waiting for such popular items as egg salad sandwiches (they're wonderful), chili, fries, out-of-this-world malts, and apple pie. *Barefoot Landing, 4712-A Hwy. 17 S., N. Myrtle Beach. (843) 361-0191;* www.johnnyrockets.com

Peaches Corner
★★★/$

Take a break from an outing at the Pavilion and treat yourself to some well-deserved nourishment at this nearby family-friendly eatery. Peaches serves up favorite kids' fare like hot dogs, burgers, and fries, as well as barbecue and catfish. After they snarf down the tasty food, you can bet your kids will be back at the Pavilion in no time. *900 N. Ocean Blvd., Myrtle Beach. (843) 448-7424.*

SOUVENIR HUNTING

Barefoot Landing
This shopping mall is in a picture-perfect setting with boardwalks and docks galore overlooking the Intracoastal Waterway. Regularly scheduled childrens' festivals during the summer, a turn-of-the-century carousel (fee), and a mega game arcade are mixed in with great shops like Kligs Kites, where you can find every type of kite imaginable. *4898 Hwy. 17S., N. Myrtle Beach. (800) 272-2320; (843) 272-8349;* www.ncnet.com/ncnw/mb-baref.html

Build-A-Bear Workshop
Master Bear Builders help kids choose, stuff, stitch, fluff, dress, and name their very own bear, frog, bunny, monkey, dog, or cat. *Broadway at the Beach, 1301 Celebrity Cir., Myrtle Beach. (843) 445-7675;* www.buildabear.com

Hammock Shops at Pawleys Island
This complex has more than 20 shops and eateries in a wonderful, forest-like setting. Kids love to watch the daily demonstrations by weavers of the famous Pawleys Island hammock. *10880 Ocean Hwy., Pawleys Island. (843) 237-8448;* www.pawleys.com

Explore Old Santee Canal Park by boardwalk, trail, or water.

INTRODUCTION

Santee Cooper Country

As YOU LEAVE the coastal cities and head inland, you'll find yourselves quickly charmed by the beauty of rural South Carolina. Single-lane roads cut through dense forests and small towns—you'll welcome the simpler, slower pace. Let a side road take you off the beaten track, where seemingly endless acres of cotton fields will amaze the kids.

Traveling south on Interstate 95 you cross a bridge that spans one of the narrower parts of Lake Marion; the lake seems to just go on forever. In fact, the Santee Cooper lakes are the largest in the state, and among the top five freshwater fishing sites in the world. Let your kids cast a line here—they're almost guaranteed a catch. The building of the lakes was the largest engineering feat of its time in the United States—your older children will find the story fascinating.

The surrounding lakes and forests are filled with fauna and wildlife that your kids probably won't have seen before. Still within the flat,

THE FamilyFun LIST

Cypress Gardens (page 296)

Fisheagle Adventure Tours (page 297)

Francis Beidler Forest in Four Holes Swamp (page 297)

Old Santee Canal Park (page 299)

Swan Lake Iris Gardens (page 300)

FamilyFun **VACATION GUIDE**

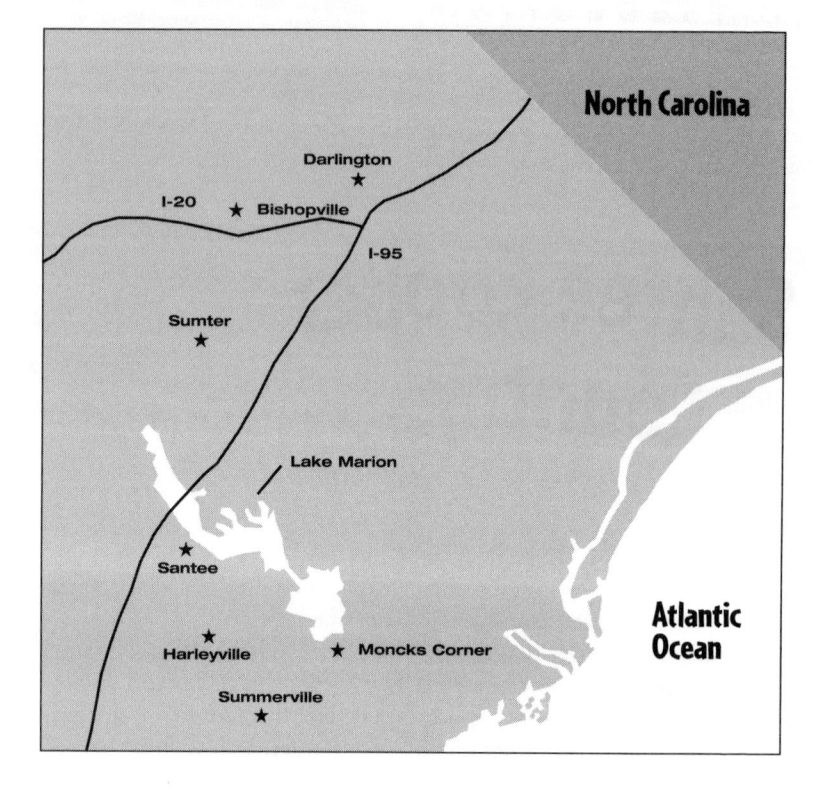

coastal plain, the trails are very kid-friendly—a great place for introducing young minds to the gifts of Mother Nature.

JUST FOR FUN

Cypress Gardens
FamilyFun ★★★★/$

These beautiful gardens are part of an old rice plantation, and they have enough to fascinate even the most hard-to-please kids. You can take your family in a sturdy bateau (flat-bottomed boat), with or without a guide, and explore the swamp and all the wonderful wild things that live within. Alligators, wood ducks, hawks, and herons are just a few of the critters you'll spot on your voyage. You'll walk the same paths on land as deer, raccoons, opossum, bobcat, and fox, which generally lay low till nighttime. Take a break at one of the several shaded picnic shelters, and then move on to the Butterfly House, where hundreds of colorful butterflies and nectar-eating birds flit freely among lush tropical foliage. Back outside, you can stroll the blossom-filled

SANTEE COOPER COUNTRY

gardens, but first visit the alligators hanging out near the bridge. Your little ones will love the aquarium and terrariums, filled with everything from freshwater fish to turtles. Closed December 23 through January. *3030 Cypress Gardens Rd., Moncks Corner. (843) 553-0515; www.aesir.com/charleston/cypress/welcome.html*

Fisheagle Adventure Tours ★★★/$$

Hop aboard a pontoon boat for a relaxing tour through the Santee Cooper waterways—they're cruises that the whole family is guaranteed to love. The Lake and Swamp Tour explores the mysterious swamps that cover this part of the state; within minutes you'll see that this is truly alligator-counting country, and home to lots of beautiful long-legged birds, too. And your kids won't believe the old cypress trees, literally growing out of the water. Older kids will enjoy hearing stories about the Native American customs, old moonshine stills, and past inhabitants who lived in the area around Lake Marion, South Carolina's largest lake. The Pinopolis Lock Tour winds along the historic Cooper River, taking you past flooded rice fields where a surprise—perhaps a jumping fish, a bird, an alligator—awaits around every bend. Plantation ruins stand out against the dense forests on this serene journey. But the part the kids will really get a charge out of is the vertical trip up the lock, with 12,000 gallons of water churning and rising around them. These waters are much cooler than the surrounding land and are mosquito-free. Tour schedules vary; call ahead. Open March through October. In Santee State Park, *305 State Park Rd., Santee. (800) 967-7739; (803) 854-4005; www.sctours.com*

Francis Beidler Forest in Four Holes Swamp ★★★/$

A 90-minute walk takes you back in time, into a place of ancient cypress groves and pre-Pleistocene swamps. The trail, right off I-26, is a barrier-free boardwalk, so children (even those in strollers) can see everything easily. Take your favorite wildlife field guide so that your kids can better become tuned in to nature. There's even a separate guide written just for kids

All About Alligators

What sounds do alligators make? During territorial standoffs, an alligator hisses and grunts at the competition. When a male wants to woo a female, he bellows or makes a coughlike sound: To alligators, these are the sweet sounds of love.

(available at the visitors' center) so they can have their own unique experience on the boardwalk. The hollow cypress tree is a big hit; children can climb into it from the walkway and peer out the top, pretending it's a gigantic ship's crow's nest. If your kids are over 6, try touring by canoe in spring and summer. Smaller children can enjoy the touch table in the visitors' center, where they can get a look at neat stuff like snakeskins, fox pelts, bones, and cypress "knees," and, for those who aren't worried about creepy-crawlies, some live specimens. Don't worry if you left your binoculars home—you can borrow them from the center. *336 Sanctuary Rd., Harleyville. (843) 462-2150; www.pride-net.com/swamp/*

Lake Moultrie Passage
★★/Free

The 24-mile hiking passage opened in 1996, and is the first official segment of the Palmetto Trail, which, when complete, will offer your family and other hikers a continuous path through South Carolina, from the mountains to the sea. The trail takes you into remote and beautiful country on a course that skirts Lake Moultrie's eastern and northern shores on roads along the lake's dike system. The southern trailhead cuts through a pine forest and up the earthen Pinopolis East Dike. Your troops get spectacular views of the lake at the top of this climb on one of the most popular trails along the Palmetto Trail, especially among mountain bikers. Young hikers will find the flat trail an easy challenge if done a little bit at a time as day hikes; there's lots of easy access (or egress) along the way. Owned and operated by the South Carolina Public Services Authority. *For entrance and trail information, contact Forestry & Undeveloped Lands, Santee Cooper Land Division, Moncks Corner. (843) 761-8000, ext. 5327.*

DAY TRIP
Culture–Painlessly

Has the rain spoiled your outdoor plans? No worries—today, museum mania kicks into high gear, first with a visit to **Darlington Raceway** and the **NMPA Stock Car Hall of Fame/ Joe Weatherly Museum** *($; 1301 Harry Byrd Hwy., Darlington; 843/395-8821).* Here you'll find the world's largest collection of authentic stock cars (including Bill Elliott's Million Dollar Bird), plus tons of cool racing memorabilia. The Hall of Fame features about 50 of racing's greatest stars, including Bill France and Davey Allison. Before leaving, check out Darlington's course, known in racing circles as the track too tough to tame. Home of the world-renowned Southern 500, Darlington is a pioneer in the world of NASCAR. *The speedway is located*

Old Santee Canal Park
FamilyFun ★★★/$

You can hike the wildlife-filled trails, canoe the old canal, and even view a replica of a submarine, plus much more at this, America's first canal. The interpretive center is a great place to begin your tour. A sign on a large wooden display table that says Please Touch! really sets the tone for your visit. Kids can get up close to bones, skulls, snakeskins, and lots of other artifacts. Dominating the center is a towering scale model of a live oak tree—so real-looking, you have to look twice. Your kids will love walking through this natural habitat—an exhibit filled with models of cool wildlife inhabitants. Beyond it, huge walls of glass let the outside in and set the stage for a spectacular view. In the surrounding swamps, marshes, and limestone bluffs you'll find some of the finest birding in the state, so pack the binoculars. With four miles of trails, seven wildlife observation blinds, and a little help from the handy bird list provided by the center, your little naturalists will have a field day. For a small fee, you can rent a canoe, paddles, and life jackets at the park's visitors' center. *900 Stony Landing Rd., Moncks Corner. (843) 899-5200;* www.santeecooper.com/recreation/santeecanal.html

The Pinopolis Lock
★/Free

There's nothing quite like sitting in a boat 75 feet below Lake Moultrie and watching as water gushes around you, slowly raising your craft to the top of the lock. The entire experience is an adventure—from the time you put your boat in the water to your arrival at the lock. Once there, you pull right up to the gate and use the handy telephone to call for a "lock operator," and, schedule permitting, a few minutes later—bingo, you're in! Boats of up to 150

about 70 miles northwest of Santee Cooper, just a few miles off I-95.

For something completely different with something for everyone, try the **South Carolina Cotton Museum** *(121 W. Cedar La., Bishopville; 803/484-4497)*. This small museum does a nice job depicting the different steps in the planting, growth, and production cycles of cotton. Your 5-and-unders will get a bang out of the mechanical mule whose ears and tail wiggle, while the preteens will have a gas punching the 500-pound bales of cotton. Along the way, there's an interesting replica of an early 1900s farmhouse, where the kids can see a full-size crop duster suspended from the ceiling, and an old-fashioned spinning machine. *To reach the museum from Darlington Raceway, take U.S. 401 south to I-20; follow signs (25 miles) to Bishopville.*

FamilyFun VACATION GUIDE

feet in length can pass through the lock, and several smaller boats can share this ride. The entire process takes from 20 to 40 minutes. It's best to call ahead to reduce waiting time; weekends in the summer are the busiest times. The lock does not operate during thunderstorms or when the waters are rough. (Non-boat owners, please see Fisheagle Adventure Tours information on page 297). Jefferies Generating Station. *463 Powerhouse Rd., Moncks Corner. (843) 761-8311, ext. 2611.*

Swan Lake Iris Gardens ★★★★/Free

Your budding naturalists will find the flocks of waterfowl here irresistible, especially when they find out feeding is allowed. This is the largest collection of swan species in the world. They're everywhere—gliding across the lake, roosting in the shade, or taking a casual stroll around the grounds. During your visit, you'll encounter the vocal trumpeter swan, a quieter cousin called the royal white mute, the black Australian with its bright red beak, and the whooper, to name a few. Towering cypresses border the lakeside paths, making it an interesting walk for all ages. Amid the great southern magnolias and fragrant yellow jasmine stand tall, slender stalks of Japanese iris. The flowers are especially beautiful during blooming season, which runs from mid-May through June. There's a concession stand with snacks and drinks, and food for the swans. Bring a picnic—tables are provided—there's a kids' playground with a vintage 1920 fire engine for your toddlers. *833 W. Liberty, Sumter. (800) 688-4748;* www.sumter-sc.com/iris.html

BUNKING DOWN

Clark's Inn ★★★★/$

The Clarks have been pleasing traveling families with warm, friendly hospitality since 1946 with touches that make you and the kids feel right at home. Rocking chairs and porch swings in the breezeways are almost as popular with the little ones as is the lushly landscaped pool. Suites come with two televisions and other family-friendly touches like a microwave, small refrigerator, and wet bar. There's also a restaurant (see page 301). *114 Bradford Blvd., Santee. (800) 531-9658; (803) 854-2141.*

Country Inn & Suites ★/$
An open entryway with a fireplace puts even the youngest guest at ease. Of course, so does the miniature putting green (next to the pool), which will surely help improve the par of all the little aspiring golf pros in your family. Microwave, small refrigerator, and complimentary continental breakfast make this a popular sleepover for families. Country Inn also holds a special place in the heart of boating enthusiasts since it's the only hotel in the area with boat hookups. *221 Britain St., Santee. (803) 854-4104; www.countryinns.com*

Hampton Inn ★★★/$
The sparkling pool tempts your kids through the lobby window—leaving no doubt as to what's on their first-to-do list. Suites have a pleasing look about them, and some have a wet bar in the small kitchenette and a Jacuzzi everybody will love. The continental breakfast is complimentary—and very substantial. After eating your morning meal here, plan on a light lunch. *9060 Old #6 Hwy., Santee. (803) 854-2444; www.hamptoninn.com*

Santee State Park ★★★/$
Everyone will love the way these cute, octagonal cabins are built on a wide pier extending right out over the water. Expect your kids to have a pole in the water before you're even up in the morning. The rustic lodgings have fully equipped kitchens. Or try a campsite if you feel like roughing it. The park is a natural for kids, with bike and nature trails, pedal boating, and fishing. There's also a nature center and a great gift shop that carries everything from a six-foot stuffed alligator to fishing rods and worms. And, of course, a freezer full of ice cream—sweets for the sweet. *251 State Park Rd., Santee. (803) 854-2408.*

GOOD EATS

Clark's Restaurant ★★★★/$$
This is a very comfortable eatery for families to relax in after spying on alligators or just lazing around the hotel pool at Clark's Inn. The cozy fireplace is nice in case the weather turns nippy. The fish on the menu is local (except for the flounder)—even the kids will find it tasty. Kids' meals—such as burgers and chicken tenders—come with fries, a veggie, and a scoop of ice cream. For those with a real sweet tooth, the hot fudge sundae or banana split will do the trick. *114 Bradford Blvd., Santee. (803) 854-2101.*

County Fair Restaurant ★★★/$
It's the only eatery in South Carolina devoted to "fair food," so step right up for a corn dog, sausage sandwich, or an unbeatable burger basket. Seasoned diners may go for

CONVERSATION STARTERS

Time on the road offers families the perfect opportunity to reconnect by having conversations that don't revolve around car pools, chores, or eating all your vegetables. If you have trouble switching conversational gears, try asking your kids these questions or similar variations. You can let them take charge sometimes, too, letting them ask you probing queries! Or you can turn this less-than-idle chat into a game by writing questions on slips of paper, placing them in a hat, and passing the hat—the question you pick out is the one you must answer, honestly. Make your queries silly or serious, but be sure they cannot be answered by just saying yes or no.

- If you could make up a holiday, what would it be and how would you celebrate it?
- What is the first thing you would do if you became president?
- Would you rather be a butterfly or a fish? Why?
- Do you think dogs are smarter than cats? Are dogs smarter than horses?
- What did settlers on the prairie have for breakfast 100 years ago? What will we be eating for breakfast in 100 years?
- If you had to lose one of your five senses, which would it be? Which one sense would you choose if you could only have one? Why?
- Would you like to have sonar like a bat, or be able to run as fast as a gazelle? Why?
- If you could choose five animal qualities for yourself from the animal kingdom, what would they be?
- What is the best book you've read recently, and why did you like it?
- What's the silliest thing you ever did?
- What will you do this summer?
- What's your earliest memory?
- What do you think the surface of the moon looks like?
- If you were going to write a book, what would it be about?
- What will you be doing in ten years?
- If you discovered a new island what do you imagine would be on it?
- What one thing would you change about school?
- Who is your hero and why?
- What should we surprise Mom with for her birthday this year?
- What is the best—and the worst—thing you have ever eaten?
- What is an item of international news that you have heard or read about in the past few months?

an all-beef hot dog topped off with sautéed peppers and onions, sauerkraut, and/or chili. The fries are fresh-cut and served with malt vinegar on the side, a local tradition (there's ketchup too). Funnel cakes, old-fashioned milk shakes, candy apples, roasted peanuts, and terrific homemade lemonade will capture the entire family's heart. County Fair even has a few rides, like a merry-go-round that the little guys will love. *1150 W. Liberty St., Sumter. (803) 934-8181.*

The Dock Seafood Restaurant and Bar ★★/$$

Top off your time at the Pinopolis Lock with a really good meal at this longtime local eatery. Set on the Tailrace Canal, it features wide windows that open onto terrific water views. Kids can experiment with a catfish filet or the tiny popcorn shrimp, and there's always chicken tenders or grilled cheese for a backup. *Hwy. 52 on Tailrace Canal, Moncks Corner. (843) 761-8080.*

Woodlands Resort and Inn ★★★★/$$

The opulence of the Old South awaits you just a few steps from the woodlands of Francis Beidler Forest. The dining room of this award-winning inn and restaurant features seating in a bamboo-enclosed courtyard where kids can explore while you treat yourself to a relaxing lunch. There's always pasta on the menu, and the chef will whip up a grilled cheese or hamburger to please the kids; the peach iced tea is a hit with everyone. A postluncheon game of croquet completes this not-to-miss sampling of southern hospitality. *125 Parsons Rd., Summerville. (800) 774-9999; (843) 875-2600.*

SOUVENIR HUNTING

Cypress Gardens Gift Shop

You and your little ones will love the alligator dollies—all dressed up and waiting for someplace to go. Lots of other critter stuff of all kinds, as well as glistening sun catchers in every shape and size, and nature-oriented books for younger and older readers both. *3030 Cypress Gardens Rd., Moncks Corner. (843) 553-0515.*

The Heritage Shop

The Berkeley Museum gift shop has neat stuff based on historical periods, like a soldier sketchbook for boys and one on period dress for the little ladies. You'll also find books on everything from the *Hunley* to Blackbeard, and Gullah spirituals on tape. *950 Stony Landing Rd., Moncks Corner. (843) 899-5101.*

Marshland stretches over many miles of the Low Country.

INTRODUCTION

South Carolina Low Country

SOUTH CAROLINA'S Low Country boasts some of the East Coast's most pristine waterways and abundant wildlife. Your family can enjoy both in just about every setting imaginable. Whether you opt for a full-service resort or pitch a tent by a creek, you'll find a way to suit your style.

Hilton Head Island is a marriage of natural beauty and human luxury. The largest of South Carolina's sea islands, it's loaded with places to go and things to do. Hotels, shopping, shows—every comfort and convenience that your little ones could ever dream of—are right here in a fairy-tale setting that blends into the surrounding subtropical foliage. This is a beautiful place to hop on a bicycle with the kids and explore the miles and miles of smooth bike paths.

As you head north along the coast, the tempo slows down, the lights are fewer and farther between, and you'll find entirely different charms. For a total getaway, check out Edisto Island. Life here is simple and unstructured: your kids can pole

THE FamilyFun LIST

Adventure Cove Family Fun Center (page 307)

Edisto Island Serpentarium (page 307)

Sea Pines EcoTours (page 308)

Wee Links (page 309)

FamilyFun **VACATION GUIDE**

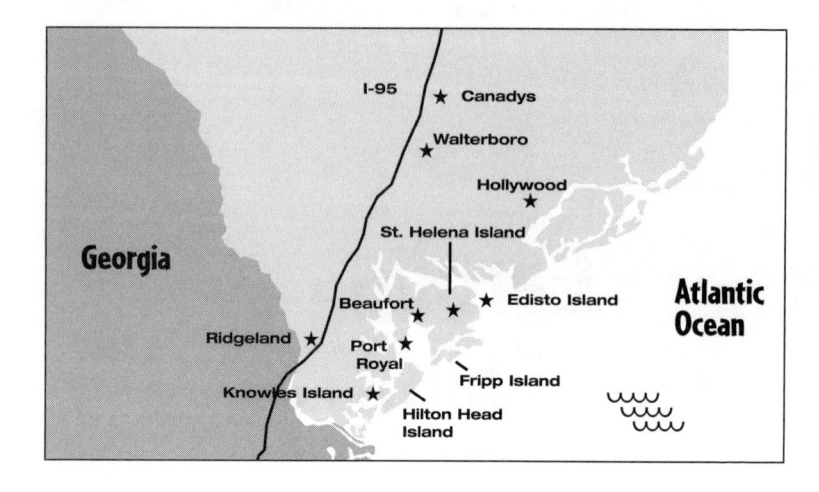

fish from a public dock or marvel at sea creatures from the deck of a tour boat. A handful of restaurants, a tiny shop or two—otherwise, you're on your own.

To the west lies Beaufort, a charming, antebellum city right on the Beaufort River. It's a must-see for kids who know their Colonial history and has a killer waterfront park they'll love when they've had their fill of history. Farther inland, saltwater and blackwater creeks wind through pristine wilderness areas where your naturalists can birdwatch, boat, and hike.

JUST FOR FUN

ACE Basin
National Wildlife Refuge
★★/Free

Take some time to lose the crowds and replace them with peace and solitude—well, except for the thousands of birds, fish, reptiles, and other wildlife that inhabit this incredible place. Your kids will feel like they're extras in a nature film, and you'll feel like you're in heaven. Imagine coasting silently over a pristine tidal marsh where you need only a field guide and binoculars to make your day complete. Kids fight over being the "lookout," sitting in the bow—the best place to spot alligators. The 11,000-acre refuge is part of one of the largest wetland ecosystems on the East Coast. The acronym ACE stands for Ashepoo, Combahee, and Edisto—the three rivers that converge in this protected area. Visit in the spring or the fall if you can, when the weather is best, and bird migrations are at their peak, as are the spectacular blooms. Summer is fun, too—but it's *hot;* be sure to take plenty of water, sunscreen, and insect repellent. For information about kayak rentals and guided tours, call Outpost Moe's *(843/844-2514)* or Tullifinny Joe's Outposts *(843/726-4545). 8675 Willtown Rd., Hollywood. (843) 889-3084;* acebasin.furs.gov

Adventure Cove Family Fun Center
★★★/$-$$$

This is a great place to go when a rainy day dampens your beach plans or you just need a few hours out of the sun. The giant indoor play world is packed with high-energy attractions for kids, and even a few surprises for Mom and Dad. Your little monkeys can work out on the jungle gym or drive their own bumper cars (kids have to be 7 and older to ride). If your kids are hooked on video games, the arcade will keep them busy for a while; if mini bowling is their thing, they've got that, too. Add in laser tag and a 3-D motion theater, and outside, a lighted driving range, batting cage, and two miniature-golf courses, plus several food concessions, and you've got a hassle-free place to let the whole family unwind. *Intersection of Folly Field Rd. and Hwy. 278, Hilton Head Island. (843) 842-9990;* www.adventurecove.com

Edisto Island Serpentarium
★★★★/$

Imagine all those creepy crawlers that kids can't seem to get enough

GULLAH

For many kids, an introduction to Gullah is not necessary—Public Television's Gullah Gullah Island has already taken care of that. The Gullah people and their culture are a colorful part of the Low Country—up and down the Carolina coast, the gentle sounds of the sea islands mingle with the lilting language of Gullah. It's a musical, spoken language, and a treat for the ear, when you're lucky enough to catch a wisp of its sing-song cadence.

These South Carolinians are descendants of Africans from Sierra Leone, Senegambia, and Liberia, who were brought here as slaves to work in the rice fields. The language they pieced together in their new home was not quite English, and not quite African, but a blend of the two.

The isolation of the sea islands has helped preserve their culture, and African influences may still be seen in crafts, cuisine, music, folk tales, and other traditions. If you and the kids are tuned in to it, you will catch glimpses of Gullah—like the ladies weaving sweet-grass baskets—wherever you go.

of—slithering around under one roof. South Carolina's only serpentarium, a beautiful, ecosensitive nature center overlooking Store Creek, is home to snakes—hundreds of them, and many of their reptilian cousins. Live shows throughout the day give kids a close-up look at these fascinating creatures—even a chance to touch and hold them. The alligator feedings draw big crowds in the afternoon. At the outdoor ponds, kids can spy on the alligators and turtles. Hours vary; call ahead for schedules. *1374 Hwy. 174, Edisto Island. (843) 869-1171.*

Hunting Island Lighthouse ★/$

This historic 132-foot lighthouse—the only one in the state open to the public—is an incredible place to get a bird's-eye view of the Low Country coastline. (It replaced the original structure, which Confederate soldiers destroyed in the face of an advancing Union Army during the Civil War. The building was later moved due to the advancing ocean.) The stairs to the top catwalk have 10 landings where you can catch your breath on the way to the top (most kids 4 and up can manage the climb just fine). Once there, you can see Fripp, Harbour, St. Helena, and Edisto islands—in all, it's a spectacular panorama. Located in Hunting Island State Park. *2555 Sea Island Pkwy., Hunting Island. (843) 838-2011.*

Sea Pines EcoTours ★★★★/$-$$$

Kids are natural explorers, and the barrier islands are a wonderland waiting to be discovered. Sea Pines Resort's Ecotours programs open up this world to families with a variety of programs—for example, the Beach Discovery tour shows children what keeps our beaches alive; on other ecotours you can hike, bike, fish, and go horseback riding. You'll probably spot a dolphin or two while you're beachcombing. At night, try the Forest Preserve Hayride—a thrilling search for alligators, deer, and other night dwellers under a sky ripe for stargazing. Join a moonlit search for loggerhead sea turtle nests while learning about these magnificent creatures and the Coastal Discovery Museum's Sea Turtle Protection Project. *100 N. Sea Pines Dr., Hilton Head Island. (800) 732-7463; (843) 363-4530.*

FamilyFun TIP

Eco Etiquette

Eating garbage is one of the leading causes of death in aquatic animals. Turtles, manatees, and other animals often mistake plastic bags for jellyfish. When snacking on the beach, make sure you throw away plastic bags and garbage, which can easily drift into the water.

Wee Links
FamilyFun ★★★★/$

Your aspiring golf pros can learn the basics or improve their handicap on a golf course that hasn't overlooked the younger set. As part of the Wee Links program, kids 10 and under get to play a real game (when accompanied by an adult) at three beautiful courses on Fripp Island—Ocean Point, Ocean Creek, and South Carolina National. Wee Links golfers play from special tees (set closer to the hole). Kids can also register for the Wee Links clinic (fee), a helpful lesson in the basics of the game and etiquette on the green. The pro shops carry hats, shirts, shorts, shoes, gloves—everything a budding linkster could want. Kid-size golf clubs are also available for rent. *Fripp Island Resort. 1 Tarpon Dr., Fripp Island. (800) 933-0050; (843) 838-1533.*

BUNKING DOWN

Beaulieu House at Cat Island ★/$$

This bed-and-breakfast offers tons of old-time charm in a dreamy island setting where youngsters can bike, hike, roller-skate, and just be kids. Minutes from Beaufort, the accommodations—like the cute carriage house with a small kitchenette—are just the right size for a family. The innkeeper's full breakfast will get everyone up bright and early with pancakes, Belgian waffles, and cheese blintzes. *3 Sheffield Ct., Cat Island. (843) 770-0303.*

Disney's Hilton Head Island Resort
★★★★/$$-$$$

A wonderland created in classic Disney style, this resort is tucked in a pristine marsh on a private island. The super-family-friendly accommodations include studios with small kitchenettes; the villas have full kitchens. If you want to kick back and relax, fine; you and your kids can do as much or as little as you like. If you feel more on the go, you'll find a seemingly limitless number of things to do—fun and educational. So whether you're up for meeting dolphins, exploring the night sky, cruising the waterways, or joining up with the Disney Discovery Club Programs (fees), plan on having a blast at this magical resort. *22 Harbourside La., Hilton Head Island. (800) 453-4911; (843) 341-4000; www.disney.com*

Edisto River Refuge
★★/$

Your kids won't believe their eyes when they see the tree-house-like cabin that's right out of Swiss Family Robinson. Imagine bunking down at night serenaded by frogs and owls in a place where egrets and wood storks, deer, raccoons, bobcats, otters, and wild turkey roam freely. The Edisto River Refuge is a privately owned wildlife refuge with swampland, ponds, and more than a mile of river frontage in which to explore and relax. The tree house is self-contained, with a small gas stove, gas lamps, and cooking utensils. (An outhouse and water are available.) You can also try one of the cabins. Carolina Heritage Outfitters. *Three miles off I-95. Hwy. 15, Canadys. (843) 563-5051.*

Fairfield Ocean Ridge Resort
★★★/$$

Edisto Island's only resort is like the island itself: extremely laid-back. Kids will love taking the trolley to the beach, splashing in one of several pools, or just hanging at the oceanside cabana. Mini-golf, volleyball courts, and a playground, plus an oceanful of comfy lodging options make this an unbeatable island retreat. Nearly all accommodation options require a two-night minimum. *1 King Cotton Rd., Edisto Island. (877) 296-6335.*

Fripp Island Resort
★★★/$$-$$$

A really awesome pool with misty caves, plus really neat golf buggies to buzz around in, make this oceanfront neighborhood resort a big hit with the kids. You and your family will enjoy the island retreat, which offers lots of kid-friendly lodgings—privately owned efficiencies, villas, and homes in all sorts of neighborhoods. Kids meet for special activities in a "tree house" activities center (seasonal, fee). Parents will like the dining, shopping, golf, and tennis at the doorstep. *250 Ocean Point Dr., Fripp Island. (800) 845-4100; www.frippislandresort.com*

Hunting Island State Park
★★/$-$$

Kids can roll out of their bunks right onto the beach from one of the oceanfront cabins on this wilderness island. Not really rustic, the cabins have TV and air-conditioning. Or you can try sites in the lush maritime forest that offer rustic camping. Don't be surprised if the deer and raccoons come for a closer look at *you. 2555 Sea Island Pkwy., Hunting Island. (843) 838-2011; www.huntingisland.com*

Palm Key Nature Get-Away
★★★★/$-$$$

Summer camp for both parents and kids best describes this place. The private island, overlooking miles of tidal marsh, is neat enough to get your kids up and out the door for fishing or paddling. You probably won't see them until they get hungry. Any family member so inclined can spend long, lazy days shrimping, crabbing, or reading a book; evenings are great for feasting on the day's catch and taking in the gorgeous sunsets. The 350-acre retreat has trails that meander through forests of live oak and pine, and egrets and wood storks glide past your deck. You can choose from self-guided or guided tours. Beautifully furnished cottages are fully equipped. *26 Coosaw Way, Knowles Island. (800) 228-8420; (843) 726-6468;* www.palmkey.com

The Westin Resort
★★★★/$$-$$$

Do your kids want to try their hand (or foot) at karate? Cooking? Eco-programs? Sand castle-building? At the Westin Resort (the northernmost resort on Hilton Head Island), the sky's the limit when your 5- to 12-year-olds participate in full- or half-day programs (fee) at Camp Wackatoo. The Awesome Adventures Beach Camp (fee) for kids 9 through 16 offers an incredible line-up of water sports—from kayaking and sailing to windsurfing and boogie boarding, with a few Low Country adventures like crabbing thrown in for good measure. Add to that package a fun-filled Kids' Night Out (fee), three cool pools, on-site family-minded restaurants like the Carolina Café (great breakfast and seafood buffets), a junior golf program, and miles of unspoiled beach. *2 Grass Lawn Ave., Hilton Head Island. (800) 228-3000; (843) 681-4000;* www.westin.com

GOOD EATS

Crabby Nick's Seafood House
★★★/$$

Nothing like a little magic to keep the young ones spellbound for a while. At Crabby Nick's, they'll stare in awe as Joseph the Magician performs tableside (Tuesday through Saturday). You'll find lots of kid-size seafood selections like broiled mahi-mahi, fried shrimp, and popcorn shrimp, as well as chicken strips and hamburgers—all served with healthful applesauce, fries, and cookies. *2 Regency Pkwy. off Hwy. 278, Hilton Head Island. (843) 842-2425.*

11th Street Dockside
★/$$

A fabulous dockside location and scrumptious kitchen creations make this a winner for the whole family. The popular kids' menu has li'l mates cheese pizza and a slice of homemade pecan or Key lime pie. And while Mom and Dad finish their dinner of Cajun catfish or a steamed crab pot, kids can keep amused watching the shrimp trawlers as they pass by. *1699 11th St., Port Royal. (843) 524-7433.*

Hilton Head Diner
★★/$-$$

This kid pleaser is on the island's main artery (U.S. 278) and super-close to Disney's Hilton Head Resort. They serve breakfast anytime—a promise you can take literally because it's open 24 hours a day. The kids' menu is filled with tasty entrées like macaroni and cheese or cheeseburgers. Tune lovers young and old will get a kick out of the individual juke boxes at each booth. Multiple locations. *Hwy. 278 at Yacht Cove Dr., Hilton Head Island. (843) 686-2400.*

The Old House Smoke House
★★★★/$$

After a day of paddling at Palm Key Nature Resort, this laid-back eatery is great. It's the only restaurant for miles, and you'll soon see why no other is necessary. The chickens out back will entertain the kids while the chef whips up Low Country fare like crab, shrimp, chicken, and rabbit. If your kids aren't quite ready for fried catfish or barbecued shrimp, they can choose from a menu with all the old standbys. *Hwy. 462 at Hwy. 336, Ridgeland. (843) 258-4444.*

Plums
★★/$

This cute waterfront café is perfect if you want to take a break while strolling downtown Beaufort. On the menu you'll find everything from a down-to-earth grilled catch sandwich to a funky grilled Gouda with artichoke garlic spread for the discerning diner. For their part, kids can have grilled cheese or PB&J on wheat, and plenty of milk shakes,

---

FamilyFun READER'S TIP

A Map of His Own

Whenever our family sets out on a road trip, my husband and I trace out the planned route for our 11-year-old son, David, and our 8-year-old daughter, Caytlin. Using AAA maps, I cut out the portion that pertains to our trip and glue it to a piece of cardboard. (Depending on how much area our journey will cover, I sometimes use both sides of the cardboard to display the map.) My husband highlights the roadways with a marker, then we cover the map with a sheet of clear Con-Tact paper. Besides being a big hit with the kids, the map is a ready reference for the driver. Although long stints in the car can be hard on kids (and adults), we have learned that when everyone is interested in following the route, the trip can be a special time spent together as a family.

Annette Payne, Santa Barbara, California

sundaes, and floats to brighten their day. *904½ Bay St., Beaufort. (843) 525-1946.*

The Shrimp Shack
★★★/$

Your hungry ones will appreciate the simple, no-fuss style of this local joint, just a short hop from Hunting Island. The tiny eatery has wooden tables that you can't mess up and the freshest seafood this side of heaven. Don't miss with the house specialty—a seafood platter, some red rice, and sweet potatoes. Kids can chow down on a small version or opt for chicken nuggets and hush puppies and all the usual fare. *Hwy. 21, St. Helena. (843) 838-2962.*

The Sunset Grille
★★★★/$$

Nothing beats a gorgeous sunset on the Edisto, and this is the perfect spot from which to enjoy it. From Memorial Day to Labor Day, the deck is hoppin'—and so are the kids—with a Jimmy Buffett–style band. The fresh seafood comes straight from the docks to your dinner plate and the smaller family members will go for the kids' menu. *3702 Docksite Rd., Edisto Beach. (843) 869-1010.*

Souvenir Hunting

Audubon Nature Store
Here, your young nature lovers are in their element with toys, games, books, puzzles, jewelry—even binoculars for spotting nature's finest. Just being there—cool music and visuals—is a lot of fun. *J-2 Village at Wexford, Hilton Head Island. (843) 785-4311.*

Chocolate Canopy, Ltd.
Kids love chocolates, especially these delightfully shaped darlings made fresh in the shop. Take home a box of alligators, seashells, perhaps a lighthouse or two. Here you're sure to find the perfect gift for the person who's looking after your pets and plants. *Crossroads Shop Ctr., Palmetto Bay Rd., Hilton Head Island. (800) 685-8123; (843) 842-4567; www.chocolatecanopy.com*

South Carolina Artisans Center
The dolls here are every little collector's dream come true, and the tons of other neat-o stuff created by South Carolina artisans will catch your eye—and your kids' spending money, too. *334 Wichman St., Walterboro. (843) 549-0011.*

**Capture memories of your time
in the Blue Ridge Mountains.**

INTRODUCTION

South Carolina Up Country

AS YOUR FAMILY heads west on I-26, the gentle grades of the midlands give rise to the rolling hills of the Carolina Up Country. The foothills of the Blue Ridge Mountains come into view, bringing with them the promise of many happy hours playing in the great outdoors. Wide-open country filled with beautiful lakes, waterfalls, and wildlife make this area a camper's paradise.

Traveling northwest, the beautiful Cherokee Foothills Scenic Highway winds through a lush landscape dotted with many beautiful state parks. Splashing in the cool mountain lakes is great fun for everyone, and the more sure-footed can play hopscotch on the rocks beneath the waterfalls. Simple pleasures like spotting a deer or roasting marshmallows over an open fire—you know, the makings of great vacation memories—are plentiful here.

Equipped with binoculars and field guide, kids who like to birdwatch will have a real field day here. South Carolina is major birding

THE FamilyFun LIST

Greenville Zoo (page 317)

Hollywild Animal Park (page 318)

Table Rock State Park (page 319)

Wildwater, Ltd. (page 319)

315

FamilyFun **VACATION GUIDE**

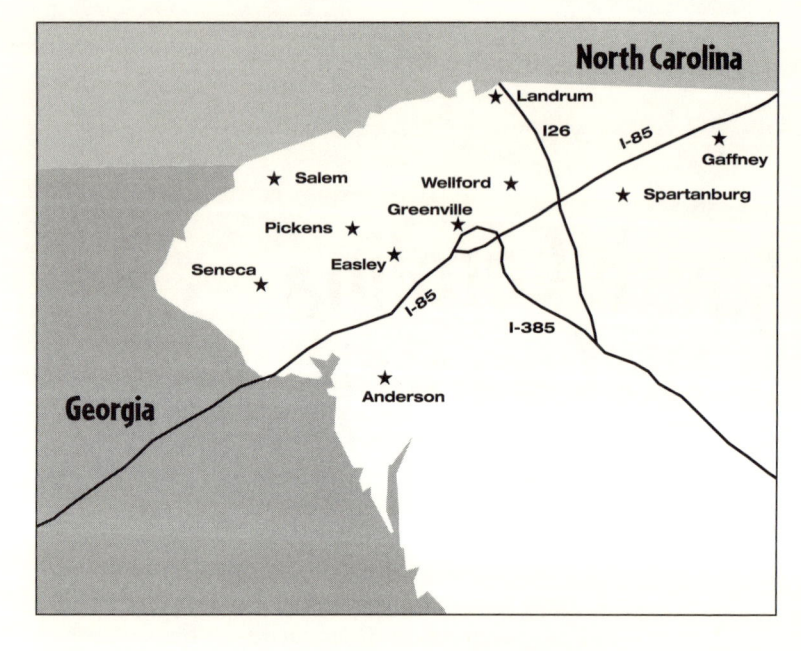

country, with over 40 percent of the species that live in the United States within its borders. The National Heritage Corridor begins in the northwestern part of the state; you'll travel through changing habitats, from the mountains to the sea. Know, too, that you are in peach country. South Carolina is the second-largest producer in the nation, meaning lots of peachy treats, ice cream, shakes, pies, and cobblers for everyone.

The cities of Greenville and Spartanburg are in the midst of a revitalization, and are fun to visit, with funky shops, great restaurants, and seasonal festivals and street parties that attract thousands of families every year.

CULTURAL ADVENTURES

Duke Power's World of Energy
★★/Free

Located off the Cherokee Foothills Scenic Highway on beautiful Lake Keowee, this nuclear power plant and its visitors' center at the Oconee Nuclear Station are great destinations for families with an interest in science. The self-guided tour is loaded with high-tech, hands-on, interactive exhibits that will put your kids' imaginations into high gear. The spectacular view, including the nearby nuclear reactors, will dazzle all. The site is one of only three in the nation to receive a certificate of merit from the National Wildlife Federation for exceptional stewardship of a natural habitat. *7812 Rochester Hwy., Seneca. (800) 777-1004; (864) 885-4600.*

JUST FOR FUN

Golden Creek Mill
★/$

Mills were once common sights all across the Up Country landscape, but few survive today. This old gristmill, built in 1825, still grinds up hominy, corn, and other grain. Kids of the electronic age will be fascinated as they watch the huge wheel turn, powered simply by the waters of a nearby stream. You can also stock up on grits and other culinary treats here; they're all made the old-fashioned way. The miller keeps the shelves stocked with an assortment of goodies like jams, jellies, pickles, and relishes. And check out the Unkers Salve—reputed to cure most modern-day maladies. *201 Enon Church Rd., Easley. (864) 859-1958.*

Greenville Zoo
FamilyFun ★★★★/$

The 15-foot Burmese python, big enough to swallow a grown-up, is guaranteed to elicit some "wows!" from everybody. The python is one of many slimy, cold-blooded creatures that hang out in the wildly popular reptile building;

Fly Time Scavenger Hunts

You end up with a lot of idle time when you travel by air. Scavenger hunts are an easy way to spend those hours calmly.

IN THE AIRPORT
You don't want anyone lost in the crowd, so set off in parent-child teams to find the following:
♦ A child holding a doll
♦ A person carrying four pieces of luggage
♦ An abandoned sports section of *USA Today*
♦ 4 pilots
♦ 2 courtesy carts

ON THE AIRPLANE
Find these items individually or together:
♦ Cars
♦ Railroad tracks
♦ A cloud
♦ Another airplane
♦ A mountain range below
♦ Someone speaking in a foreign language
♦ A father holding a baby
♦ A person in an apron
♦ Somebody sleeping
♦ A laptop computer
♦ A mustache
♦ A briefcase
♦ A Walkman radio
♦ A pillow and blanket
♦ Candy
♦ A blue tie

FamilyFun SNACK

Pretzel Twist

Give your kids a bag of traditional pretzels and challenge them to bite out every letter of the alphabet.

all of them will grab your kids' attention, big-time. A well-placed plate-glass window along the alligator pond lets you get close enough to count the scary reptiles' teeth without worrying that you'll become their lunch. But the real star of the zoo is Joy, a prize elephant and zoo resident since the 1970s. And then there are the big cats, the barn animals, and the flamingos. An oasis in the middle of town, the zoo strives to replicate a natural habitat for the creatures, and with its lagoons, waterfalls, and beautiful landscaping, is pretty people-friendly, too. In fact, it has been rated one of the top three community-based zoos in the country. There's a playground and walking trails for kids to work up a healthy appetite—and picnic tables nearby where you can satisfy it. *150 Cleveland Park Dr., Greenville. (864) 467-4300.*

Hatcher Garden and Woodland Preserve
★★/Free

With eight acres of gardens, ponds, and peace and quiet, stop here to take a break and let the kids stretch their legs. Stroll along the shaded paths that cut through magnolia-filled woods and lush natural gardens of daylilies and butterfly bushes. Chipmunks and squirrels munch at a feed station along with feathered friends. Challenge your kids by turning the visit into a game—who can identify the most flowers or spot the biggest animal? A gazebo, strategically placed benches, and picnic tables complete this idyllic setting. The preserve is open to the public every day of the year from dawn till dusk, compliments of 93-year-old philanthropist Harold Hatcher: he donated the property to a local foundation and still tends the gardens daily. *8 John B. White Sr. Blvd., Spartanburg. (864) 574-7724;* www.hatchergarden.org

Hollywild Animal Park
★★★★/$

Your kids will go wild over this zoo, where they can ride a miniature train, buy little bottles to nurse baby goats, and get up close and personal to the animals. Children are especially impressed when they hear that many of these precocious pets are stars—animal actors they've seen on TV or in the movies, like the zebra that played in an MTV music video, or the big cat that was the model for *The Lion King*'s Scar character. One of the most popular attractions in the park is the safari ride—a trip through 70 acres of "outback" where the animals roam free and come to investigate *you*. Giraffes, bison, ostriches, rhinos, elephants, camels, and deer are just some of the wild game patrolling the grounds. Kids can toss feed to the curious ones and spot the baby animals in the woods. Bring your own picnic basket or grab a bite at the snack bar. For lasting memories, there are lots of wild animal toys and games in the gift shop. Open March through October. *2325 Hampton Rd., Wellford. (864) 472-2038*; www.hollywild.com

Table Rock State Park
★★★/$

The Cherokees believed Table Rock Mountain was a great dining table in the sky for an enormous, mythological spirit, and the surrounding blue haze of mountain mist was the shadow of this Great Spirit. Kids enjoy the lore, and the mountain is an awesome sight as it looms into view above the Cherokee Foothills Scenic Highway. The park's wilderness trails and roads are family-friendly, with spectacular views of both Table Rock and Pinnacle Mountain, two of South Carolina's highest peaks. Kids love leaping off the diving boards into the park lake and then drying off on the sandy beach. The self-guided nature walks—color-coded according to level of difficulty—score major points with most young trailblazers—although the seven-mile (round-trip) hike up to the top of Table Mountain is moderately strenuous and may be too much for small tykes. Carrick Creek Trail, a two-mile, one-hour loop, is a fun, easy hike for families. The park is also a great place for kayaking, canoeing, fishing, and birding. You can rent boats and stock up on snacks and even groceries at the park store. Your hungry tribe will love dining at Table Rock, just as the Great Spirit did. There are picnic spots throughout the park, and the park restaurant is well known for its home-cooked southern fare, especially the trout and catfish. *158 E. Ellison La., Pickens. (864) 878-9813.*

Wildwater, Ltd.
★★★★/$$$$

A trip to the Blue Ridge foothills wouldn't be complete without a tour by water—white water, that is. It's a pure adrenaline rush that even the uninitiated can enjoy. You follow the course of the famous Chattooga, a national Wild and Scenic River, as it cuts through protected wilderness—meaning lots of natural unspoiled beauty with few folks around. It has been named one of America's top 10 rivers, and paddling it with your kids is an unforgettable experience. Whether you're an experienced rafter looking for a challenge or a first-timer, there's the right white water course for you. Excursions vary in difficulty and in length, from a few hours to two days.

The Scenic Mini Trip, a guide-assisted half-day outing, has just the right amount of thrills for kids as young as 8. Ice cream and hot showers await the troops back at the lodge, a circa 1915 country house with clean facilities and a service-oriented staff. Open March through mid-November. *1251 Academy Rd., Long Creek. (800) 451-9972; (864) 647-9587.*

BUNKING DOWN

Courtyard by Marriott
★★/$

Double doors in the two-room suite give Mom and Dad a bit of privacy and let the kids do their own thing. There's a pool in the courtyard and in-room movies for rainy days. Suites have small kitchenettes, plus the hotel restaurant serves breakfast. A host of nearby fast-food chains and a supermarket will take care of your family's other cravings. *110 Mobile Dr., Spartanburg. (800) 321-2211; (864) 585-2400;* www.marriott.com

Devil's Fork State Park on Lake Jocassee
★★★/$-$$

Whether you go for rustic simplicity or something a little ritzier, you'll find it at the variety of lakeside lodgings here. Families who aren't into roughing it may opt for the mountain villas, with decks that have a great view of Lake Jocassee, as well as fully equipped kitchens. Across the lake from the villas is a 59-site campground in a dense woods. Each campsite has water and electrical hookups, a picnic table and grill, and nearby rest rooms with hot showers. There are also 25 tent sites, all with elevated pads. *161 Holcombe Cir., Salem. (864) 944-2639.*

La Quinta Inn & Suites
★★★★/$

After your kids spend a few minutes in the glistening courtyard pool and Jacuzzi, they won't want to leave. This newer property has that sun-washed, south-of-the-border feel. Rooms are bright and airy with amenities like Nintendo, and the king suite extras include a small but handy kitchenette. The complimentary continental breakfast and location that's superconvenient to downtown make this property a family fave. *65 W. Orchard Park Dr., Greenville. (800) 687-6667; (864) 233-8018;* www.laquinta.com

Sunrise Farm Bed & Breakfast
★★★★/$-$$

The bright red barn of this country inn might come straight out of a storybook illustration. Surrounded by rolling hills and blossoming trees (in season), the farm is a kids' wonderland, complete with ponies, goats, and a pet pig named Muffin. Parents can relax and take in the panoramic views from the wraparound porch while the kids explore the farm. Choose from country-comfortable rooms in the circa 1890 farmhouse or comfy private cottages complete with kitchen and fireplace. A refreshment nook in the farmhouse contains a microwave, a mini fridge stocked with juice boxes and sodas, and a bottomless cookie jar. The full country breakfast is complimentary for farmhouse guests only. *325 Sunrise Dr., Salem. (888) 991-0121; (864) 944-0121; www.bbonline.com/sc/sunrisefarm/*

Table Rock State Park Campground and Cabins
★★★/$

Table Rock appeals to all outdoorsy-type overnight guests. Whether your family's up for pitching a tent in the wilderness of this spectacular mountainous park or wanting the comparative luxury of a real campsite or cabin, you'll find it here. The cabins are comfortable and outfitted with everything you need, including a full kitchen. *158 Ellison La., Pickens. (864) 878-9813.*

GOOD EATS

Beacon Drive-In
★/$

Opened in 1946, this is one of the few remaining drive-ins with curbside service. Although the kids will get a bang out of curbside, the real show is inside where the staff has been ruling the roost for 20 to 30 years, and their decades of experience make for a quick, tasty meal. Step up, order, and a few shouts later you've got a plate piled high with fixin's quicker than you can say "a double chili cheeseburger, side of fries, and sweet tea, please." They'll put just about anything on a bun—catfish, country ham, even bananas. Mom and Dad may go for a piece of cake or pie for dessert while the kids will have a blast checking out the 21 flavors of ice cream. It's a real slice of Americana. *255 John B. White, Sr., Blvd., Spartanburg. (864) 585-9387.*

Hare & Hound
★★★/$

This bright, casual eatery has lots of fun selections that go over big with kids and adults, too, from chicken quesadillas to lasagna and fish-and-chips. Homemade soups, hearty salads, burgers, and, the old standby, chicken strips, round out the menu. Don't forget to ask about the in-season pies—they're out of this world! *101 E. Rutherfordton St., Landrum. (864) 457-3232.*

Hickory Tavern
★★★/$$

Beamed ceilings and a cozy fieldstone fireplace make this a great place to unwind after spending some quality toy time at Imagination Station *(see below)*, which is right down the road from this popular Spartanburg eatery. Your hungry troops will chow down on fun finger foods like nachos, tenders, and wings. Preteens may go for the solid American fare—steaks, seafood, and salads. *143 Fernwood Dr., Spartanburg. (864) 591-3290.*

RJ Rockers Brewing Co.
★★★/$$

Depending on your personal beliefs, you might want to take the family to this stylish, upbeat eatery that holds Spartanburg's own microbrewery. There's lots of pub-style fare that may interest the kids—Buffalo wings, smothered fries, and cheese sticks, and the like. They'll also enjoy the extra legroom and laid-back style here. Grown-ups can try some serious food, like the half-pound Spartanburger marinated in house beer and topped with three cheeses, or a light pasta dish like the broccoli and pecan fettucines. To quote a kid: yum. *117 W. Main St., Spartanburg. (864) 583-3100.*

Trio ★★★★/$

This is a fun, casual eatery with just the right amount of pizzazz, a perfect stop when touring downtown Greenville. The menu includes over two dozen pastas and wood-fired pizzas, many of which can be modified to suit the tastes of young diners. Your budding connoisseur may want to try the pad Thai or the Mediterranean salad—all the dishes are made to order using fresh, seasonal ingredients. *21 N. Main St., Greenville. (864) 467-1000.*

SOUVENIR HUNTING

Cottage Books

Kids can browse the shelves of this quaint bookshop while Mom enjoys a latte and tasty pastry from the little café in the back. *109 E. Rutherford St., Landrum. (864) 457-2772.*

Imagination Station

Jam-packed with tons of terrific toys, this place covers the spectrum: from your basic Planetarium Projector and Thomas the Tank Engine to rocket radios and a vast collection of dolls, the sky's the limit at this fun shop. *1855 E. Main St., across from Hillcrest Specialty Shopping Center, Spartanburg. (864) 573-8800.*

PEACH COUNTRY: SETTING THE RECORD STRAIGHT

Most folks think of Georgia as the Peach State, but did you know that South Carolina actually holds the title of the Tastier Peach State? And not just tastier—it outranks its neighbor to the south in volume, too. South Carolina is the second-biggest peach growing state in the union (California actually ranks as number one, and should, technically, be called the Peach State, but no one has challenged these southern locales to date).

Nevertheless, Georgia has managed to cling to its peach-state notoriety. There was actually a time, back in the 1930s, when Georgia growers were really packing in the peaches, and probably did outrank the other peach-producing states. Locals began naming everything in sight after the popular fruit. Years went by, and production steadily declined, but the Peach State title stuck. To this day, though, license plates, streets, buildings, and shopping centers still take credit.

South Carolinians—and peach lovers everywhere—owe thanks to the boll weevil, the pesky bug that took a big bite out of the cotton industry, for pushing their state into peach production. Today, crops are grown in the Piedmont, Ridge, and Coastal Plain regions, with some of the sweetest fruit in the country coming from the south-central farmland of the Ridge, where good soil and just the right number of "chilling hours" make for peachy growing condition. There was a time when one county in South Carolina produced more fresh peaches than the entire state of Georgia.

Up Country cities such as Edgefield, Saluda, and Spartanburg are the state's leading peach-producing counties, with 200 million pounds and 30 to 40 varieties harvested each year. In fact, the succulent fruit is so revered in these parts that festivals are held honoring the regal Palmetto peach. There is also a water tower in Gaffney, South Carolina, called the Peachoid—a monument to the power of the Palmetto peach.

So, kids, read the signs on the license plates—but don't believe everything you read. When in comes to peaches, South Carolina rules!

North Carolina

ALTHOUGH WE HAVE only three chapters in our North Carolina section, don't be fooled into thinking that there's not much happening in the Tar Heel State. Quite the contrary. This trio of beauties—mountains, heartland, and coast—brings you some of the best family vacation experiences around.

North Carolina is blessed with some of the most majestic sights that nature offers. Whether it's the view from Grandfather Mountain's Mile High Swinging Bridge or a climb to the top of the awesome sand dunes at Jockey's Ridge State Park, there's

North Carolina Mountains

The Heartland

Coastal North Carolina

a real abundance of outdoor activities for all ages. Thanks to the spectacular vistas along the Blue Ridge Parkway, this is probably one of the few times that your kids will give a thumbs-up for—of all things—a Sunday drive!

The state's natural beauty is matched by its many cool attractions—from the entertaining and educational, such as Biltmore Estate (Asheville), Exploris (Raleigh), Old Salem (Winston-Salem), and *Battleship North Carolina* (Wilmington), to the wet and *wow*, such as Emerald Pointe (Greensboro) and Carowinds (Charlotte).

ATTRACTIONS
$	under $10
$$	$10 - $20
$$$	$20 - $30
$$$$	$30 +

HOTELS/MOTELS/CAMPGROUNDS
$	under $100
$$	$100 - $200
$$$	$200 - $300
$$$$	$300 +

RESTAURANTS
$	under $10
$$	$10 - $20
$$$	$20 - $30
$$$$	$30 +

***FAMILYFUN* RATED**
★	Fine
★★	Good
★★★	Very Good
★★★★	*FamilyFun* Recommended

You can run the distance of Wilbur and Orville's first flights at Wright Brothers National Memorial.

INTRODUCTION

Coastal North Carolina

THE COAST of North Carolina encompasses more than 300 miles of fun-filled family vacation getaways. And with cool names like Pleasure Island, Cape Fear, Kill Devil Hills, and Kitty Hawk, these places promise—and deliver—great times for kids.

Take the Cape Fear Coast, for example. Whether you're exploring the World War II vessel the *Battleship North Carolina*, the Michael Jordan Discovery Gallery at the Cape Fear Museum, or the Civil War battlefield at Fort Fisher, a stay at the Cape rates a high five from your troops.

Heading north, you'll join the tradition set by families who have been vacationing in the Outer Banks and the Cape Hatteras National Seashore seemingly forever. Home to the first English settlement, the first successful airplane flight, and the tallest

THE FamilyFun LIST

Battleship North Carolina (page 328)

Cape Fear Museum (page 330)

Coquina Beach (page 336)

Diamond Shoals Family Fun Park (page 337)

Jockey's Ridge State Park (page 338)

The Lost Colony (page 332)

North Carolina Aquarium— Roanoke Island (page 333)

Wright Brothers National Memorial (page 340)

FamilyFun **VACATION GUIDE**

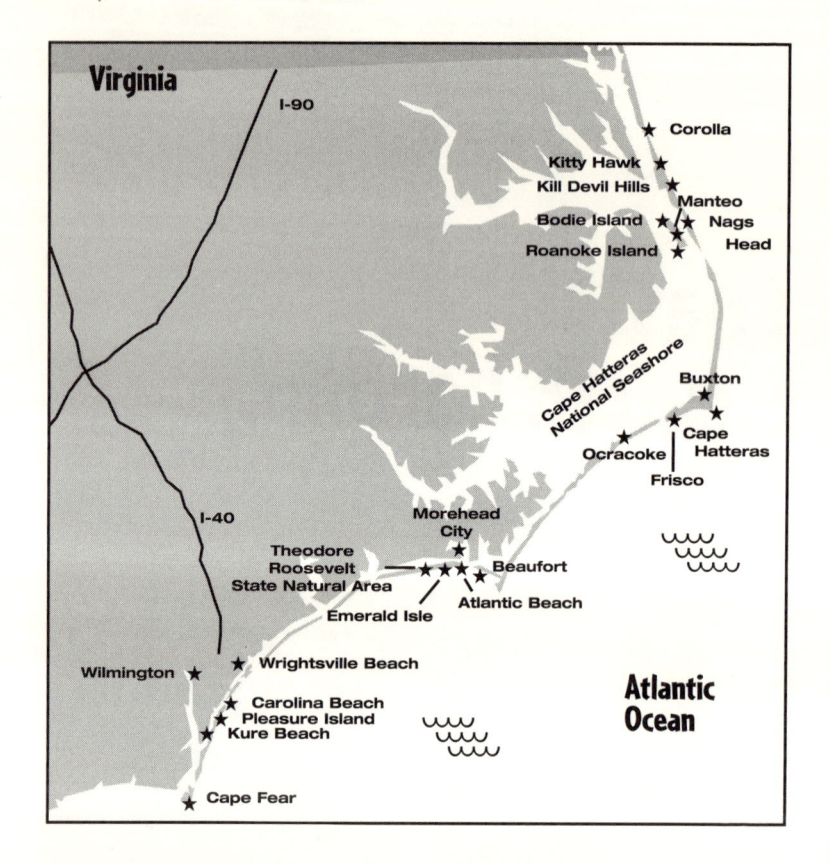

sand dunes on the East Coast, this area is also believed to be the final resting place for the infamous Edward Teach, a pirate affectionately known as Blackbeard. World-class fishing and hang-gliding, neat lighthouses to visit, and ferries to ride—all make for a memorable visit.

Along the way are cool aquariums, kid-friendly historic buildings, fishing piers, and miles of sun-drenched beaches just perfect for catching a few rays. Welcome to paradise—kid-style!

CULTURAL ADVENTURES

Battleship North Carolina
FamilyFun ★★★★/$

If your kids think a battleship is just a boat with a bunch of guns, they're in for a real surprise when they tour this planet-size World War II vessel, docked across the water from Wilmington's historic district. The ship—and its more than 2,300 residents—earned some 15 battle stars for superior performance; it was a floating home-away-from-home with such essentials as a hospital, post office, dentist, movie theater, and soda fountain. You can visit these areas and more during your self-guided tour of the historic nine-deck ship. Before you board, be sure to watch the 10-minute orientation film to get a good overview of the ship's proud history. Then it's off to the lower decks (or main or upper decks—your choice) where you'll zigzag through areas like the engine rooms (don't miss the pipe ID markings), galley and mess deck (get a load of the pumpkin pie recipe), berthing area (that's some bunk-bed system), and, of course, the way-cool defense mission control (coding, computer and radio rooms, and the ammunition magazines for storing the projectiles). Then move up to the main deck where you're immediately drawn to the 16-inch gun turrets and the Kingfisher float plane, which, in its six years of service, has traveled the equivalent of three times around the world. This deck also houses a series of museumlike displays, including a must-see exhibit called Through Their Eyes: State Veterans Remember WWII. The upper decks contain the captain's and admiral's cabins (quite a contrast to the lower quarters) and the bridge and chart house. **NOTE:** Although the lower deck is marked

Hey, Dune

One of the Outer Banks' lesser-known treasures is **Jockey's Ridge** *(Free; Hwy. 158/Croatan Hwy., Milepost 12; Nags Head; 252/441-7132)*, thought to be the tallest natural sand dune system on the East Coast. How old is this mega-dune? For once your kids' reply of "older than dirt" may be right on the money. During the Ice Age the grains were carried in by wind and storms from their original home—about 500 miles out to sea. Today, Jockey's Ridge shifts only a little bit each year—about 1 to 6 miles south to southwest. Other fun facts:

♦ Jockey's Ridge has about 6 million dump truckloads of sand on its 385 acres.
♦ These all-natural sand dunes stand about 110 feet tall.
♦ The dunes don't blow away because the northeast and southwest winds blow the sand back and forth.
♦ Sand temperatures can get up to 30° higher than the air temperature. (Shoes are a must!)
♦ The sand is mostly quartz rock.

with directional arrows, it is easy to get semi-lost down below. Don't let your kids roam freely through this area. Use caution throughout the ship when going up and down stairs—many are steep and can be slippery when wet. *Junction of Hwys. 17/74/76/421, Wilmington. (910) 350-1817; (910) 251-5797;* www.battleshipnc.com

Beaufort Historic Site
★/$

The third-oldest town in North Carolina, Beaufort has a wealth of history to entertain and educate your family. For starters, check out the one-hour guided walking tour through some buildings and furnishings from the 1700s and 1800s. If your kids complain about their chores back home, they'll be eternally grateful after they hear about some of the daily tasks assigned to young Beaufortites at that time (pay close attention to the tale about the cottonseeds). Of special kid-appeal is the upscale Bell House, where items like a bird-shaped pincushion, toys, and a music storage box are sure to catch their fancy. Also check out the apothecary and doctor's office, featuring a ton of artifacts used in early medicine (such as a fainting couch and yucky-looking leeches), and the county jail, containing two cells, the keeper's quarters, and a few instruments of punishment, 18th-century style—ouch! If you're traveling with little ones, consider the double-decker bus tour of the town's historic district that runs several times a week—it's less tiring, and a bit more exciting, than hiking through town. *130 Turner St., Beaufort. (800) 575-7483; (252) 728-5225;* www.beaufort_nc.com

Cape Fear Museum
MUST-SEE FamilyFun ★★★/$

Nearly every sports fan can recite a couple of Michael Jordan's record-breaking statistics, but few know that Wilmington is where MJ spent his formative years. This museum in the city's historic district houses a display of Jordan memorabilia—his Little League baseball team photo from 1971, the stub from his first paycheck, and a Tar Heels uniform from his college days at North Carolina. The display is on the way to the adjacent Michael Jordan Discovery Gallery, jam-packed with cool, interactive displays about the area's three distinct ecosystems. Other world-class exhibits here include a mega-model of Wilmington's waterfront in 1863 and a narrated, illuminated, and nearly animated diorama of the Civil War

FamilyFun READER'S TIP

Fledgling Photographers

Last summer, I put an extra flash in our vacation. Instead of having grown-ups be the only photographers, I bought each of our five children, whose ages range from 7 to 19, a 24-exposure disposable camera and let them snap their own pictures. The kids loved it, and we were able to see our vacation through their eyes. Plus, since they were inexpensive cameras, I didn't worry about them being dropped or lost. For very little money, these simple cameras brought our family a lot of smiles.

Kathi Kanuk, Chardon, Ohio

battle of Fort Fisher. Along with some top-notch traveling exhibits, the second floor houses 29 meticulously hand-carved bride figures of important historical women. *814 Market St., Wilmington. (910) 341-7413.*

Fort Fisher
★/Free

One of the last remaining strongholds for the Confederacy was at Cape Fear's Fort Fisher, where troops worked tirelessly to keep the port of Wilmington open as a supply route for the region; in the end, more than 2,000 soldiers died in battle here. Although only a fraction of the original fortification stands today, your kids—mostly the 9-and-older set—will still get a charge out of this history lesson. Begin at the visitors' center, where several displays and a brief presentation equip your troops with a helpful overview of the fort. Outside, the self-guided tour takes you alongside the mega-mounds to the rear of the fort and up the steps to Shepherd's Battery. Not only is the view great, but the battery's once-powerful cannon (reconstructed) is sure to capture your imagination. During the summer, costumed guides bring Fort Fisher to life with exciting demonstrations and colorful tales of battle and blockade running. *U.S. 421 S., Kure Beach. (910) 458-5538.*

Fort Raleigh National Historic Site & Elizabethan Gardens
★★/Free-$

Here's the perfect place to learn about the trials and tribulations of the first two British attempts to settle in America. First, the bad news: these events occurred in 1585 and 1587, so the only remains are some earthworks that probably were part of the original fort. Now, the good news: the visitors' center (free) within Fort Raleigh offers a treasure trove of information that kids will eat up—promise. The 17-minute film is a must-see to better understand the likes of Sir Walter Raleigh, John White, and Virginia Dare. Stay after the show for a lively chat and a weapons demo with a park ranger. The center also displays some ornate armor and other painful-but-not-practical weapons from a bygone era. Also within the grounds are the Elizabethan Gardens (fee), a living memorial to the English colonists. These fragrant gardens—exploding with herbs, roses, rhododendron, and other familiar and not-so-familiar flowers, bushes, and trees—are best appreciated on a self-guided tour (don't forget the insect repellent). Put your kids in charge of the leisurely walk. Who's first to spot the ancient fountain, statue of Apollo, or the centuries-old oak tree? Take it slow, stopping every so often to admire the butterflies and bugs along the way—you won't be disappointed. About three miles north of Manteo. *Hwy. 64/264, Roanoke Island. Fort Raleigh Visitor Center: (252) 473-5772. Elizabethan Gardens: (252) 473-3234;* ww.nps.gov

> **A SHARK WILL** pick up the smell of blood in the water, even if it's just one drop of blood within one million drops of water.

The Lost Colony
FamilyFun ★★★/$$

Chronicling the struggles and successes of the first English settlers in America, this is the oldest and longest-running outdoor drama in the United States; the original plan called for it to run only one season in 1937 in commemoration of the 350th anniversary of the birth of Virginia Dare, the first English child born in America. Today, more than three million people—many of whom are children—have experienced this two-and-a-half-hour presentation. The show appeals on many levels—especially to young audiences. They love the music, the costumes, the dancing, and the excitement of a live stage, but also the Indians' weird war paint, the mysterious changing of the backdrops and scenery, the sudden explosion of fireworks, and the exciting swashbuckling antics and gunfight between John Borden and Simon Fernando that make this one a keeper. *The Lost Colony* is most appropriate for children ages 6 and up. Although there's a brief preshow, the action doesn't begin until 8:30 P.M., making it a late night—especially for your younger set. **NOTE:** The seats are fairly comfortable; but a dollar or two more will buy a cushion—it's worth it. Also, you're a stone's throw from Roanoke Sound, so lather up with insect repellent. Open only June through August. Located in the Fort Raleigh Historic Site, about three miles north of Manteo. *Hwy. 64/264, Roanoke Island. (800) 488-5012; (252) 473-3414;* www.thelostcolony.org

North Carolina Aquarium—Pine Knoll Shores ★★/$

An ideal rainy-day destination, this facility is one of three coastal aquariums operated by the State Department of Environment and Natural Resources. The aquarium's Coastal Gallery displays sea life that kids find fascinating—the stingray, sea horse, nurse shark, and moray eel—in tanks as large as 3,000 gallons. The touch tank is always a big draw, and friendly volunteers are on hand to instruct families how to properly—and painlessly—pick up the slippery crustaceans. The Living Shipwreck exhibit is another popular stop; kids love the colorful reef fish that hang out in the wreckage; the gargantuan loggerhead and sometimes-hard-to-spot moray eel are faves, too. Don't leave before checking out the small snake exhibit and half-mile salt-marsh trail that winds through an area that's home to a variety of birds and animals. *Five miles west of Atlantic Beach in the Theodore Roosevelt State Natural Area. S.R. 58N. (252) 247-4003; www.ncaquariums.com*

MUST-SEE FamilyFun North Carolina Aquarium—Roanoke Island ★★★/$

Expanded (actually doubling in square footage) in 2000, this aquarium now boasts the largest saltwater tank—285,000 gallons—and most specimens—2,000—in the state. The facility holds tons of way-cool stuff, like the Seuss-inspired Fish I Am exhibit, but number one on your kids' greatest-hits list has got to be the exhibit called Graveyard of the Atlantic. This mega-display features the state's largest ocean tank, which houses the remains of the recreated USS *Monitor* shipwreck (the *Monitor* was the Union contender in the first battle of "ironclads," or armored ships, in the Civil War). The one-third-scale replica (the actual ship is resting about 16 miles off Cape Hatteras) is so realistic that even the reef fish try to snack off it every once in a while. Kids love checking out residents like the loggerhead turtles, rays, and, what most go bonkers over, the sharks (there are three types). Several times a day trained divers enter the gargantuan tank and interact with some of the residents. It's an encounter your kids won't forget. Although most people skip it, the small, outdoor whale exhibit is a

---

FamilyFun TIP

Call Ahead

Besides scouting resources at your library, call or write to city chambers of commerce and state tourism boards for information about your destination. Let your kids make lists of the things they hope to see and let each child pick one activity to do each day (parents have veto power over monster truck rallies, of course).

fun way to wrap up your aquarium adventure. *374 Airport Rd., Manteo. (252) 473-3493; www.ncaquarums.com*

North Carolina Maritime Museum ★★/Free

A great white shark that weighs more than 2,000 pounds graces the lobby, the entryway has a collection of tiny shells (we're talking an inch or less) displayed on a kind of lazy Susan—and you've only just begun your exploration of this first-rate seafaring spot. Supercool artifacts from the recent recovery of what is presumed to be the infamous pirate Blackbeard's flagship, the *Queen Anne's Revenge* (it was lost near the Beaufort Inlet in 1718), are standouts. Other attention-getters include some small, shallow-water boats, a display of early outboards, a collection of coastal marine tanks, and an odd-looking "life car," used in the early 1900s to rescue boaters in distress. *315 Front St., Beaufort. (252) 728-7317; www.ah.der.state.nc.us/sections/maritime*

Wilmington Railroad Museum ★★/$

All aboard for a good time! Railroading was Wilmington's chief industry for more than a century, and this small, fun-packed museum commemorates its contributions to the local scene. The first floor displays include a working Lionel train set and a ticketing office complete with a telegraph set for sending messages. (Don't leave until everyone gets a turn at sending a message via Morse code.) Even the

---

DAY TRIP

Cape Capers

If your kids have never felt the salty spray and open winds from the deck of a ferryboat, let them taste one of life's greatest small pleasures on the crossing from Hatteras to Ocracoke. Best of all, it doesn't cost you a cent. But before you get in line at the ferry dock, make two stops along the way that will enhance this special day of family fun even more: the **Cape Hatteras Lighthouse** (*Off S.R. 12, Buxton; 252/995-4474*) and **Frisco Native American Museum** (*S.R. 12, Frisco; 252/995-4440*).

From Nags Head, it's an easy 50-mile drive along the pristine Cape Hatteras National Seashore to this popular lighthouse. Considered the state's most famous landmark, Cape Hatteras is the tallest lighthouse in the country, standing 208 feet from the bottom of the foundation to the peak of the roof. But don't take our word for it: Climb the 268 steps to the top and see for yourself.

Then head for the tiny but jam-packed Frisco Native American Museum. Don't expect to find hands-on exhibits here. Instead,

children's menu from the 1940s (it's part of the dining car display) should get a laugh (or yuck!) from your pint-size conductors. Level two may be the hands-down favorite, with its network of working model trains that chug through tunnels, neighborhoods, beaches, downtowns, and even construction sites. The second floor also houses the children's corner, with train-themed videos, toys, and cushions for weary youngsters and parents. The fun continues outside in the rail yard with a full-size caboose and real steam locomotive. Upon entering the museum, make sure each of your kids picks up a scavenger-hunt list. At the end of the visit, turn in the completed form for a special surprise. *501 Nutt St., Wilmington. (910) 763-2634; www.wilmington.org/railroad/*

JUST FOR FUN

Cape Fear Riverboats
★★★/$-$$

A sightseeing cruise is a fun alternative for touring the mysterious waters of the Cape Fear Coast. For an earful (and an eyeful), hop on either the *Captain Maffitt* (45-minute narrated ride) or the *Henrietta III* (90-minute narrated ride) for a whale of a good time learning about the old and the new Wilmington. If your youngsters seem bored at the prospect, don't worry—the yawns stop fast when your boat approaches a real, live cargo ship and the tiny but powerful tugs do their thing. It's quite a sight. Colorful tales like the one about the bridge tender and the

you'll see a world-class collection of Native American artifacts that's sure to impress your youngsters. Weapons, musical instruments, pottery, baskets, beadwork—it's here.

Next stop is the **Hatteras Inlet Ferry Dock**, about 10 miles from the museum off S.R. 12. During the summer, ferries depart at least every 30 minutes for the 40-minute crossing to Ocracoke. Once the ferry has pushed off from the dock, kids love to run out on deck to check out the view; there's also an enclosed upper cabin. Before you know it, you're on solid ground in Ocracoke where there's a ton of dining options, like **The Pelican Restaurant** *($-$$; Silver Lake Dr.; 252/928-7431)*, and shops, like **Books To Be Red** *(School Rd.; 252/928-3936)* and **Island Ragpicker** *(Hwy. 12; 252/928-7571)* to check out. **Teach's Hole** *(161 Back Rd.; 252/928-1718)* features a fun Blackbeard exhibit (fee), plus loads of pirate memorabilia for sale. (The infamous pirate, whose real name was Edward Teach, was killed at Ocracoke in 1718.) Then it's back to the ferry dock, a short ride, and, before you know it, it's land ho again!

BACKSEAT GAMES

In the privacy of your own car, you can laugh as loud as you want or shout out the answers to questions. So don't hold back when you play these games — laugh, yell, or sing your hearts out. The ideas are well suited to driving, as they don't involve writing.

THE CAR NEXT DOOR
Invent stories about people in the car next to yours. What do you think they do for work? What's their favorite food? Where do they go on vacation? Get into lots of details, such as whether they snore loudly or are afraid of spiders. Give them names, hobbies, pets, and so on.

BUZZ
This is a team effort to try to reach 100 without making a mistake. Take turns counting, beginning with one. Every time you get to a number that's divisible by seven (7, 14, 21, . . .) or has a seven in it (17), say "Buzz" instead of the number. If one person forgets to say "Buzz," everyone has to start over. If this is too hard, say "Buzz" for every number divisible by 5. If you want a real challenge, try Fuzz Buzz. Say "Fuzz" for every number with a three in it or that's divisible by three, and "Buzz" for every number with a seven in it or that's divisible by seven.

---

origin of the name Cape Fear will keep your kids amused along the way. Named after one of the Confederacy's most successful blockade runners, the *Captain Maffitt* is a converted World War II open-air navy boat. Docked at the foot of Market Street, it also serves as a river taxi to and from the *Battleship North Carolina*. The *Henrietta III* is the state's largest riverboat; it's docked at the foot of Dock Street—board early and head for the top deck, bow end, for the best view. In addition to the regular sightseeing excursion, the *Henrietta III* offers specialty cruises, including lunch, dinner, and moonlight sailings. **NOTE:** Open April to December; schedules vary, so call ahead. *Downtown Wilmington. (800) 676-0162; (910) 343-1611; www.cfrboats.com*

Coquina Beach
FamilyFun ★★★/Free

If your kids (and you) need a day of downtime, this Outer Banks beach is the perfect place. It's far enough from the tourist throngs to give you the peace and quiet you need, but close enough so that you're not wasting precious time (only about 10 minutes from Nags Head) to get there. A superwide beach, decent waves, lifeguard (seasonal), clean dressing rooms, plus a shaded picnic area provide a quiet haven. Coquina is also home to the remains of the *Laura A. Barnes,* a coastal schooner that ran aground just north of this beach in 1921. The shipwreck now rests on the beach in a roped-off area where your kids can check it out when they need an ocean break. Don't forget to pack a few beach toys and a boogieboard or two. *Located off Hwy. 12, about 8 miles south of Hwy. 158.*

Diamond Shoals Family Fun Park
★★★★/$-$$$

For one-stop entertainment—miniature golf, an arcade, a water park, and then some—this place in the heart of the Outer Banks has it all. The water park includes three cool slides, ranging from a thrilling, enclosed body slide to a less intense open flume tube ride with twists and turns that the entire family (ages 3 and up) can enjoy. Kids love the park's Water Wars stations, the newest rage in water-balloon fun (perfect for dueling siblings!). After a few hours at the water park, try your hand at a round of golf at Diamond Shoals' 36-hole putting course made of real grass. Remember, this one is not equipped with bunkers or borders that help contain your ball, so it's a bit more challenging, especially for the younger golfer. If your kids like going to the batting cage back home, just wait till they get a load of this: a slugger's dream, it's an actual batting "stadium" where hits can sail some 250 feet to the fence. An action-packed arcade and paddleboat rides round out this family-friendly attraction. **NOTE:** Times vary—water park: open Memorial to Labor Day; golf and batting cage: open March or April to Thanksgiving. *2010 S. Croatan Hwy./Hwy. 158, Kill Devil Hills. (252) 480-3553.*

Horse-Drawn Carriage Tour
★★/$

With kids in tow, it can be a real challenge to tour a town's historic section—especially in places like Wilmington, where the "preserved" district boasts more than 230 blocks of vintage structures. Don't despair: thanks to a gentle horse, comfy buggy, and a friendly guide, the answer to your dilemma is just a couple of dollars away with a memorable tour experience operated by Springbrook Farms. Lasting about 40 minutes, the ride showcases some of the finest and most unusual architecture in old Wilmington. (Can you find the house with the supertall door? Extra-wide door? Even a door-less balcony?) The drivers, who are naturals with kids, are full of factoids, like the difference between the black and brown plaques that grace the entryways of many of these old mansions. A fun and educational ride. *Water and Market Sts., Downtown Wilmington. (910) 251-8889.*

Fort Fisher State Recreation Area
★★/Free

After a visit to the Civil War encampment at Fort Fisher (see page 331), you'll probably want to cool off with a swim. There's no better—or closer—place to do it than this uncrowded, family-friendly beach almost directly across the road from the fort. Besides having a refreshing swim in the Atlantic, your kids are bound to find something interesting as they explore the four-mile sandy shoreline. Turtle Talk and Shell Stroll are two of the free nature programs (seasonal) that the park has for your young naturalists. Clean dressing rooms and seasonal snack bar and lifeguards make this beach a must.

U.S. 421 S., Kure Beach. (910) 458-5798; ils.unc.edu/parkproject/jori.html

Jockey's Ridge State Park
★★★★/Free

With dunes that range from 80 to 120 feet in height (depending on the weather), Jockey's Ridge is the tallest natural sand dune system in the eastern United States. It is an incredible sight, especially when hang gliders and kite flyers do their thing. Although it takes about 30 minutes to walk to the summit, it's worth the hike—unless you're traveling with 5-and-unders who may poop out halfway up. At Jockey's Ridge, your kids can fly a kite across the same skies as some of the world's most famous pilots—like Orville and Wilbur Wright. Don't leave until your troops (Mom and Dad, too!) have rolled down the dune; it's not nearly as treacherous as it sounds, and the free-fall feeling is spectacular. If one parent needs to stay

---

FamilyFun READER'S TIP

She Shows Seashells

My family loves to spend our vacations at the beach. We always collect many seashells that we think are pretty enough to frame so that we can make them part of our annual summer photo collage. Once we get home, Danielle, 9, and Tiffany and Stephanie, 7-year-old twins, pick out their favorite shells and glue them on the edge of an 8- by 10-inch frame. We cut up vacation photos and assemble the collage, then attach labels to caption the pictures. We hang the pictures proudly every year.

Lorene Hall, Starke, Florida

behind with the wee ones (or is just too tuckered out), Jockey's Ridge Overlook is a great place to view the dunes (plus it's less than a five-minute walk from the visitors' center). **NOTE:** This sand really cooks, so shoes are a must when hiking the dune. Because of the intense heat, the best time to enjoy Jockey's Ridge is after 5 P.M., once the sand has started to cool down. For more facts on the dunes, see "Hey Dune," page 329. *Hwy. 158/Croatan Hwy. Milepost 12, Nags Head. (252) 441-7132.*

Jungle Rapids Family Fun Park
★★★/$-$$

Where to go first—the go-carts, the arcade, the playground, the water park? Inside, the 100-plus games arcade has excitement for all ages—from games like Milk Bessie and Wack-a-Doodle-Doo for your 3- to 5-year-olds to Top Skater and Radikal Biker for the almost-teen set. Next stop? There's fun galore at the humongous indoor playground, or a big thumbs-up at the alien invader-themed laser tag arena. The Grand Prix Go-Kart Track is a quarter-mile of good times, and its "two-seaters" let even your 3-year-old experience the mini thrills—as long as a licensed driver is behind the wheel. If all that excitement makes you build up a sweat, never fear—Jungle Rapids' million-gallon wave pool, volcanic mountain water slide, speed slides, and kiddie splash pool bring instant relief—big smiles, too! **NOTE:** The water park is open Memorial Day through September. *5320 Oleander Dr., Wilmington. (910) 791-0666;* www.junglerapids.com

Nag's Head Fishing Pier ★★/$

The Outer Banks boasts some of the greatest fishing holes around, and the waters at this 760-foot pier are no exception. Whether your anglers are dropping their lines for flounder, cobia, king, mackerel, or blues, don't be surprised if they pull up a winner here—especially since the many friendly fishermen around are happy to dole out helpful advice. For a really cool time, try your hand at night fishing. Except in winter, it's open 24 hours a day. The tackle shop stocks everything the vacationing fishing family would ever need, and the on-site restaurant will cook and serve up your catch with all the fixings. *3335 S. Virginia Dare Trail, Nags Head. (252) 441-5141;* www.nagsheadpier.com

---

FamilyFun ACTIVITY
Keep a Trip Journal

On a canoe trip to a new spot, pretend that your family is recording a great expedition, in the spirit of Lewis and Clark, and imagine that you've discovered the place. Have people take turns recording their feelings, plus the weather and wildlife sightings.

FamilyFun VACATION GUIDE

Wright Brothers National Memorial
MUST-SEE FamilyFun MUST-SEE ★★★★/$

A history lesson plus a shining example of "if at first you don't succeed, try, try again," this Outer Banks site shows your kids firsthand how persistence, guts, and just plain old hard work really can pay off. Although most youngsters will want to breeze through the visitors' center, do pause long enough to listen to one of the short, regularly scheduled programs conducted by one of the knowledgeable park rangers. You'll walk away with a tad more insight into what the Wrights were up against in their aeronautical struggles and achievements, plus be able to check out the cool life-size reproductions of their 1902 and 1903 gliders. Then head outdoors to see just how far Orville and Wilbur successfully flew their power-driven airplane on December 17, 1903. Large markers indicate the distance achieved during those first four flights. If your kids are like most, expect them to run all the way down to the fourth marker, some 852 feet away. Time their run with your watch, and compare it to Wilbur's famous 59-second flight. Don't leave without visiting the 60-foot granite monument that's perched on top of the 90-foot Big Kill Devil Hill. The monument marks the site of hundreds of glider flights the Wrights made before the first powered flights. Parking lots on the east and west sides of the memorial provide easy access—*do not* try to walk all the way from the

Light the Way

One is red, one is white, another is horizontally striped, and the fourth diagonally striped. What are they? The Outer Banks lighthouses, probably the most well known—and certainly the most visible—landmark of the Tar Heel State. Parents and kids both love to explore the exhibits and the towering structures, even if a couple of them are tough climbs (see below) and can be conquered only with lots of stamina. Cape Hatteras (in Buxton) and Currituck Beach (in Corolla) lighthouses are open for climbing; Bodie Island (off Hwy. 12) and Ocracoke (Ocracoke Island) only offer exhibits and information.

If you're headed to either the lighthouse at Cape Hatteras or Currituck Sound, don't take the climb lightly—especially with toddlers in tow.

SOME SCALING TIPS:
Leave the backpacks and other paraphernalia in the car. Stairways may be narrow and steep, and somewhat difficult to maneuver, especially with extra baggage. If you insist on taking the camera (everyone

famous landing strip to the top. *Croatan Hwy./Hwy. 158. Milepost 8, Kill Devil Hills. (252) 441-7430; www.nps.gov/wrbr*

Bunking Down

Blockade Runner Beach Resort and Conference Center ★★★/$$

The name of this oceanfront resort holds great promise—and the place really delivers: Your kids can actually sail to a deserted island on a pirate ship. It's all part of the property's Sandcampers Treasure Hunt, which offers morning, afternoon, and evening programs for mini pirates, ages 5 to 12 (fee). The pirate ship adventure is Saturday only, but your kids can try lots of other fun activities throughout the week. If your troops are nearing their teens, they may opt for a windsurfing lesson through the Blockade's sailing center (fee) across the street in Wrightsville Sound. The complimentary breakfast buffet gets everyone's day off to a good start. Mom and Dad, the guest rooms are comfortable treasures, too. *275 Waynick Blvd., Wrightsville Beach. (800) 541-1161; (910) 256-2251.*

Carolina Beach State Park and Campground ★/$

This 1,773-acre park is on a triangle of land known as Pleasure Island, which lies between the Atlantic Ocean and the Cape Fear River. The family camping area is nestled in a

does) make sure you've got it securely attached to your person.

Drink plenty of water before the climb. Sorry, no food or drink is permitted.

Children must be able to walk on their own. In other words, forget carrying your tykes to the top; although there may be rest spots along the way, when in doubt, don't try it. Most of the visitors' centers have enough to amuse your 3-year-old until Dad and the rest of the crew make it to the top. Take your smallest outside and see if you can spot the rest of the family high above. Children younger than 12 must be accompanied by an adult.

Moms, this is not the place to make a fashion statement. Heels higher than 1½ inches are not permitted.

Pace yourself. A small observation deck at the top affords an awesome view, sure to generate a high five or two from your young climbers. Be aware that this isn't appropriate for young kids (or adults) who have a fear of heights.

forestlike area of towering pines and oaks, comfortably shading the 83 tent and RV sites on even the hottest of summer days. An easy walk through any or all of the park's five hiking trails connects you with Mother Nature's finest array of plant life. In fact, this park is within an exclusive 75-mile radius that's home to the colorful and captivating Venus's-flytrap. Don't miss exploring the half-mile Fly Trap Trail where you're sure to encounter this devilish carnivore. The visitors' center offers plenty of info about the area's many kid-friendly—and free—nature programs, like Webs of Wonder and Reading Animal Signs. You can also fish (fee) and boat. Insect repellent is a must here! *Dow Rd. Off U.S. 421, Carolina Beach. (910) 458-8206.*

Colony IV Motel ★★★★/$

A mom-and-pop oceanfront property on North Carolina's Outer Banks is one of the greatest family vacation values this side of the Atlantic. But price isn't the only standout feature. Add to that the number of comfortable lodging options (impressive for a small property)—efficiencies, standard rooms, and two nice cottages—convenient location (less than one mile from the Wright Brothers Memorial and Jockey's Ridge State Park), and tons of free on-site fun stuff (miniature golf, large playground, and outdoor pool). You can stoke up on the free doughnuts, juice, and coffee each morning in the office. Open March through October. *405 Virginia Dare Trail. Rte. 12, Kill Devil Hills. (800) 848-3728; (252) 441-5581.*

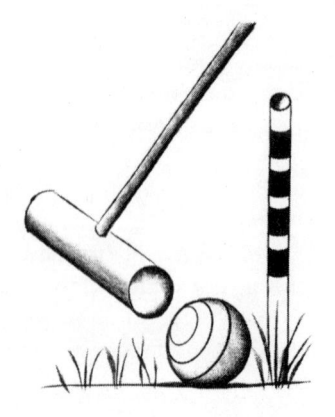

Frisco Campground, Oceanside ★★/$

If your family is looking to rough it during your Outer Banks vacation, you'll find no better overnight digs than at this campground, part of the National Park Service network. Although it lacks some of the bells and whistles you get elsewhere, it's one of the few campgrounds that has "sand dune" lodging—where you're literally bunked in between the dunes. Located just five miles south of the Cape Hatteras Lighthouse, the campground has 127 tent and RV sites, all of which offer spectacular views of the Atlantic. Sorry, no utility connections. **NOTE:** Depending where your campsite is, the walk to the ocean may be a bit of a hike. But the property's uncrowded, lifeguarded (seasonal), and expansive beach make the trek well worth it. Interpretive programs and a nearby store for provisions add to this seasonal campground's family-friendly appeal. *S.R. 12, Cape Hatteras National Seashore. (800) 365-2267; (252) 473-2111.*

Holiday Inn SunSpree Resort Wrightsville Beach
★★★★/$-$$

Whether you're greeted by this resort's outgoing parrot or one of its friendly staff members, expect the property to rank high among your North Carolina favorites. All rooms have microwaves and refrigerators and most offer views of the ocean or the Intracoastal. The SunSpree's KidSpree vacation club (ages 4 to 12) offers a whale of a selection of fun-filled activities like tie-dyed art (fee), scavenger hunts, and water balloon contests. The fun continues several evenings a week with dinner and way-cool things like Nintendo 64 showdowns and live sea animal encounters (fee). Little tykes will delight in the Saturday Kids Cartoon Breakfast (fee) or the tuck-in by Gabby, the resort's costumed parrot mascot (fee). Beach playground, video arcade, plus indoor and outdoor swimming pools round out the amenities at this popular Cape Fear Coast property. *1706 N. Lumina Ave., Wrightsville Beach. (877) 330-5050; (910) 256-2231.*

Holiday Trav-L-Park Resort
★★★★/$

There are almost too many pluses to name when recommending this camping mecca on what's called the Crystal Coast, some 25 miles south of Beaufort, North Carolina. For starters, a full-time entertainment director amuses, educates, and energizes kids young and older with a jam-packed schedule of daily activities during the summer. Saturday night concerts, Naskart speedway, outdoor pool, and a well-stocked recreation hall/game room add to the fun. An informal worship service is also held weekly during the summer. You can choose from 375 grassy tent and RV sites (with full hookups), and although the sites themselves lack shade and privacy, no one seems to mind. Closed mid-December to mid-February. *9102 Coast Guard Rd., Emerald Isle. (252) 354-2250.*

Residence Inn Landfall
★★/$-$$

Although this inn tends to attract business travelers, it's also the perfect place for vacationing families—especially those looking for a mix of convenience, affordability, and ample kid-favorite features. The apartment-style property is less than two miles from popular Wrightsville Beach and less than 15 miles from the loads-to-do Historic Wilmington district. The suites' fully equipped kitchens make meals a snap—as

FamilyFun VACATION GUIDE

does the property's free grocery-shopping service. A large outdoor pool, basketball and volleyball courts, and complimentary deluxe continental breakfast earn this friendly property an extra thumbs-up. *1200 Culbreth Dr., Wilmington. (800) 331-3131; (910) 256-0098.*

Sheraton Atlantic Beach Resort
★★★/$-$$

Your kids will find lots to do here: Fishing (from an awesome 600-foot private pier), swimming (indoor and outdoor pools), small game room, and in-room Nintendo (fee) are served up daily, rain or shine, and, in summer, there are free children's activities programs. A small amusement park directly across the street will entertain both young and older children. Parents' conveniences include microwaves and refrigerators in the rooms. *2717 W. Fort Macon Rd., Atlantic Beach. (800) 624-8875; (252) 240-1155; www.sheraton.com*

GOOD EATS

Alleigh's ★★★★/$$
Restaurant/entertainment complex/sports bar/jazz and blues club—it's all that and more; mostly it's a fun night out for families, especially those with kids ages 7 and up. Most families choose to eat either in the main dining room or the popular sports bar, which is close to the mega-game area. After your kids chow down on a quick but filling meal from the restaurant's junior menu (cheeseburger or chicken tenders are sure to please), accompany them to the epicenter of fun: a game arena featuring more than 120 interactive attractions. The virtual reality gaming section is sure to capture your preteens' fancy, especially the roller coaster and life-size skateboard encounters. Power cards—actually debit cards good for any purchase of food, drinks, games, or souvenirs—serve as the official currency here. Remember, *you* have to decide how much you're willing to spring for before you set the kids loose with it! *4925 New Centre Dr., Wilmington. (910) 793-0999.*

Big Al's ★★★★/$
With items from the kids' menu like Twistin' (spaghetti), Lil' Surfer (fish sticks), or the Lil' Bopper (burger), don't be surprised if your family wants to eat every meal at this friendly joint. Make sure to save room for the mile-high dessert called Wipe-Out—you'll need three or four spoons to finish off this sweet treat. In addition to a good meal, your family can have a ball playing

> **NORTH CAROLINA'S** state vegetable is the sweet potato. The state is the largest producer of that veggie in the nation.

in the game room, checking out the tons of Coke memorabilia, or grooving on the dance floor. **NOTE:** Be prepared to wait for a table. If you're ravenous, try grabbing a couple of stools at the counter; same good food, just a few steps closer to the bustling and friendly kitchen. *100 Patty La., Hwy. 64/264, Manteo. (252) 473-5570.*

The Cottage
★★★★/$$

Upscale dining doesn't automatically mean a no-kids zone. In fact, quite the opposite at friendly restaurants, like this one in Carolina Beach, part of the Cape Fear Coast. Comfortable touches like the rocking chairs and the swing out front make your kids feel at ease from the get-go—so does the outdoor deck dining where you can all enjoy the cool sea breezes. The children's menu offers some all-time faves like fish sticks and chicken tenders with ranch dressing (yum) and two buttered noodle options. Young pasta aficionados will give high marks to menu's unique mix and match of yummy homemade sauces and noodle types, especially the *quattro formaggi* (four cheeses—similar to an Alfredo sauce) or *farfalle* (bowtie pasta). Portions are large, but the kitchen will gladly oblige with a lunch-size portion and lower price at dinnertime for the kids. *Buon appetito! 1 North Lake Park Blvd., Carolina Beach. (910) 458-4383.*

Italian Bistro
★★★/$-$$

A great shopping break, this Italian eatery in Wilmington's retail district's Wood Seed Building offers yummy fried ravioli appetizers. They're lighter than fried mozzarella sticks, but will still curb your hunger while you're waiting for the entrées. Consider bypassing the extensive menu and ordering a few individual pizza slices, especially for the kids. The slices are humongous, order sparingly. *319 N. Front St., Wilmington. (910) 762-1222.*

Kitty Hawk Pizza
★★/$

With no cutesy name or funky décor—though a few pizzas do have the kind of weird names kids love—this place has friendly service and tasty pie, prepared just about any way you want it. Try the wacko spe-

---

FamilyFun TIP

A Beachside Shower

Everybody loves spending a fun-packed day at the shore until it's time to climb back in the car, still sticky and sandy, for the ride home. Here's a quick way for your backseat travelers to freshen up before hitting the road. Fill two or three clean plastic milk jugs with water and leave them in the car while you swim. When you're ready to leave, the water will be warm enough for a soothing rinse.

cialty pizzas like the One-Eyed Purple People Eater or Bacon Cheeseburger in Paradise. Your best kid-bet is the pizza buffet, with a sampling of pies (all made with Kitty Hawk's homemade dough), available at lunch and dinner except on Friday and Saturday night. The doggi dog and chick 'n' chips are also notable contenders. *3730 Croatan Hwy./Hwy. 158, Kitty Hawk. (252) 261-3933.*

Pizzuti's
★★★★/$$

Treat your family to some wonderful Italian cooking—and we're not talking pizza here. Instead, introduce their young palates to homemade pastas, intriguing veal dishes, or the more familiar chicken, but with an Italian twist. They serve half portions and prices for the younger set. And if your kids aren't quite at the gourmet level, the kitchen obliges with fettucine Alfredo, chicken Parmesan, or chicken tenders. Don't pass up the pannecotta for dessert. *201 W. Fort Macon Rd., Atlantic Beach. (252) 222-0166.*

Sanitary Fish Market and Restaurant
★★/$$

Strange name, good food! In 1938, Sanitary opened its doors in Morehead City (across the bridge from Atlantic Beach) with the promise of cleanliness and neatness—a commitment that still holds true. The place has been enlarged many times and now seats a gazillion people (600 at a time!). Order first, then they'll bring you one of the restaurant's signature items—the Tar Heel Hush Puppy—a wormy-looking creation that is *um-um* good. Hungry youngsters won't be disappointed with the shrimp or cheeseburger. Before you leave, have your children look at the photographs on the lobby wall to see if they recognize any of the famous diners. Closed December and January. *501 Evans St., Morehead City. (252) 247-3111;* www.morehead.com/sanitary

Water Street Restaurant
★★★★/$-$$

A former peanut warehouse is now home to one of Wilmington's most popular riverfront eateries. Your kids will love the fried shrimp and shoestring fries from the children's menu. More daring diners can order a cup of seafood chowder; its blend of shrimp, scallops, clams, fish, and veggies is a real showstopper. The funky interior (can you spot the eagle, pig, Indian, and tiger?) and the small aquarium in the back help kids pass the time while Mom and Dad finish their meals. Most evenings bring live blues, jazz, or other musicians to the restaurant's center stage. The town's Sundown Shindig on the River, held a couple of nights a week in the summer, makes Water Street's sidewalk café the place to be. *5 S. Water St., Wilmington. (910) 343-0042.*

Souvenir Hunting

Donna Designs
Not only does this shop carry adorable jewelry, hair accessories, purses, and clothing, during the summer, you can spring for ten bucks (per person) and let the kids try a paint-your-own-fish-printed-T-shirt session. Fun for Mom and Dad, too. *Jockey's Ridge Crossing, Croatan Hwy./Hwy. 158, Milepost 13, Nags Head. (252) 480-3930.*

Kitty Hawk Kites
Water balloon launchers, vortex mega howlers, stunt kites, parafoils—you name it, this store's got it. It's also the place to go for gear for hang gliding, kite surfing, kayaking—anything outdoorsy. Multiple locations. *Jockey's Ridge Crossing, Croatan Hwy./Hwy. 158, Milepost 13, Nags Head. (252) 441-4124; www.kittyhawk.com*

Poodle's Island Wear
Bright colors, funky fish, and big flowers abound on this shop's casual shirts, shorts, dresses, and swimsuits. Also colorful jewelry, zany picture frames, and *Dawson's Creek* memorabilia (the show is filmed in Wilmington). *18 S. Water St., Wilmington. (910) 763-4523.*

Top Toad
Sure, a load of clever frog memorabilia fills this cute shop, but it's the neat-o shirts that really steal the show. With killer T-shirts emblazoned with slogans like "just chummin" and "got fish?" you can expect to drop some dough here. Located in the Granary Building at the Cotton Exchange. *362 Nutt St., Wilmington. (910) 763-6494.*

The Toy Boat Toy Store
Whether you're adding to your collection of Bendos or Steiff bears, you'll find it in this fun kid's shop on the Manteo waterfront. The dress-up section—cool boas and pirate paraphernalia—has great small-fry appeal. *200 Sir Walter Raleigh St., Manteo. (252) 473-6171.*

Zoo
Kids have a heyday in this Noah's ark of a store that's stuffed with furry pals, puppets, even purses, all fashioned after animals. Appropriately, it's in the Bear Building at the Cotton Exchange. *321 N. Front St., Wilmington. (910) 815-3410.*

Exhibits like rat basketball make Discovery Place one of the nation's top science museums.

INTRODUCTION

The Heartland

NESTLED BETWEEN North Carolina's mountains and coast is the bustling heartland of the Tar Heel State. It's also called the Piedmont, referring to the gently rolling hills that gracefully intersect with such booming cities as Charlotte, called the Queen City after its namesake Queen Charlotte, and Raleigh, the state capital.

Here, instead of waterfalls and lighthouses, you'll find skyscrapers, big-time universities, and most important, a load of must-see, family-friendly attractions. Where the mountains and coast built their vacation reputations on nature and history, the Heartland serves up some of the most incredible—white-knucklers, even—man-made attractions, on the planet. And, speaking of things celestial, you'll find a couple of knock-your-socks-off

THE FamilyFun LIST

Discovery Place (see page 356)

Emerald Pointe Water Park (see page 357)

Exploris (see page 350)

Greensboro Children's Museum (see page 351)

Museum of Life and Science (see page 352)

North Carolina Museum of Natural Science (see page 353)

North Carolina Zoological Park (see page 356)

Old Salem (see page 353)

Paramount's Carowinds Theme Park (see page 359)

FamilyFun **VACATION GUIDE**

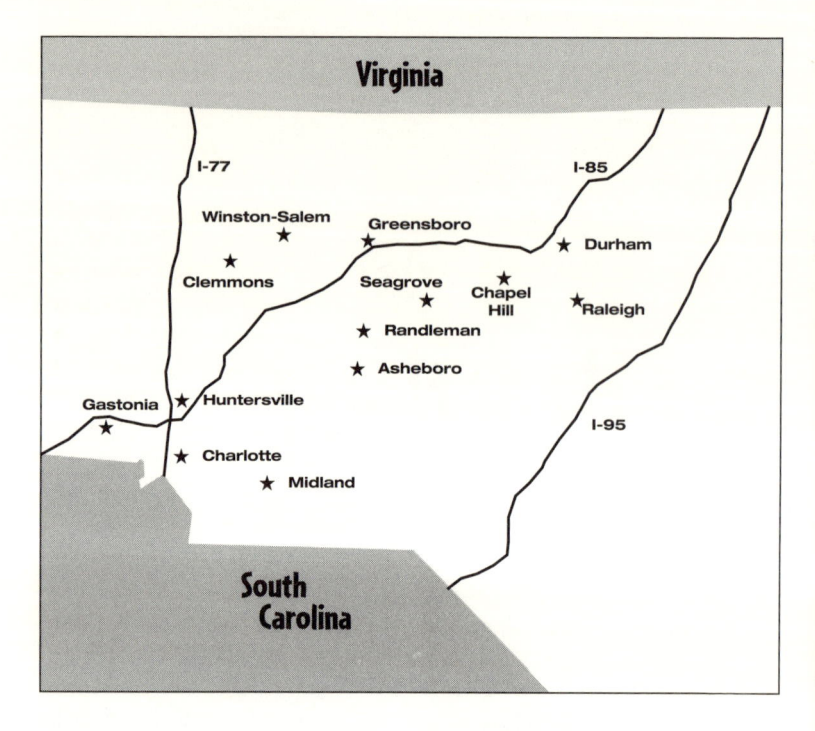

Virginia

- I-77
- Winston-Salem
- Greensboro
- Durham
- Clemmons
- Seagrove
- Chapel Hill
- Raleigh
- Randleman
- Asheboro
- Gastonia
- Huntersville
- I-95
- Charlotte
- Midland
- I-85

South Carolina

planetariums in friendly places like Gastonia and Chapel Hill.

Your hard-core thrill seekers will be in their element in this region thanks to such crowd pleasers as Paramount's Carowinds, Charlotte's supercharged action park that features a round of stomach-swirling roller coasters, and Emerald Pointe, an awesome water park with something of fun for every wave level.

The heartland also is home to an unbeatable lineup of top-flight museums and hands-on attractions; with monikers like Exploris, Sci-Works, Discovery Street, and Busy Street, they are sure to convert your kids into exhibit-lovers.

Cultural Adventures

Exploris ★★★★/$
Most kids think that all museums are about facts—history and science. Exploris focuses on people, and examines the concerns (like the environment) and interests (like communication) that we share as a world. A museum for all ages, at this place, which is like a mini-United Nations, younger tykes will enjoy simple activities like dressing the international traveler or weaving at the loom (on the first

350

THE HEARTLAND

floor), while the 8- to-12-year-olds will enjoy the imaginary bus ride that will transport them to exotic faraway lands, like Dakar, Senegal, and Surabaya, Indonesia. Although the Living in Balance area (rear area, first floor) may be a bit over your 6-year-old's head, they'll still get the message, loud and clear, of the need to protect the fragile environment. Upstairs, Many Voices is all about communications and cooperation. Sure to please is the totally weird-looking—and wired—TV man who helps you connect to more than 40 live television broadcasts throughout the world. At several stops, visitors young and old are encouraged to write down their thoughts on certain issues, which are then posted for all to see. The world-class exhibit One Voice: From the Pen of Anne Frank reveals the effects of the Holocaust as seen through this 13-year-old's eyes; it's a must-see for all ages. Before leaving the second floor, spend some time in Tradeworks, where your kids can play the stock market (well, kind of), sample (smell) the spice trade, and get a look-see at which countries mass-produce those athletic sneakers (hint: it's not necessarily the U.S.A.). A quick stomp on the suspension bridge and a reflective moment or two at the looking in/looking out window makes for a grand finale. If time permits, take a load off at Exploris's new IMAX theater. *201 E. Hargett St., Raleigh. (919) 834-4040;* wwwexploris.org

Greensboro Children's Museum
★★★★/$

If your youngsters are under 10 and like lots of hands-on activities, they'll love this supercharged, superfun museum. An ATM machine for kids? Maestro for a day? Architect, doctor, actor? Almost anything is possible here. At this museum you can actually design your dream home on the computer and then build it with a working crane, blocks, and bricks. Budding broadcasters get honest-to-goodness scripts to read with the aid of TelePrompTers, while wanna-

---

FamilyFun READER'S TIP

It's in the Cards

My family loves to travel, and I have found a wonderful way to preserve our vacation memories. First, we buy postcards at all the different locations we visit. On the backs, I jot down the highlights of the trip or funny things that happened while we were there. After we have returned home, I laminate all the postcards, punch holes in the top left corners, and put them all on a ring clip. It's exciting to see all of the places we have been.

Stefanie Wirths, Camdenton, Missouri

FamilyFun SNACK

Gobbledy Gook

4 cups oat or crispy rice cereal, 1 cup chopped peanuts, 1 cup raisins or chopped, dried prunes or apricots, 1 cup sunflower seeds, 1 cup chopped pretzels, 3 tablespoons margarine, melted (optional)

Place all ingredients in a 2-quart plastic bag, seal, and shake until well mixed.

---

be disc jockeys can try their hand at the radio control panel. A full-size fire truck, police car, NASCAR race car—even a real DC-9 cockpit—are all just a touch away. *220 N. Church St., Greensboro. (336) 574-2898; www.gemuseum.com*

Morehead Planetarium ★/$

Your young stargazers will be about as close to seventh heaven as they can get with a visit to this planetarium on the north end of UNC's Chapel Hill campus. The experience can be as simple or complex as you want to make it. If time is limited, head for the Copernican Orrery, reportedly the largest working orrery (start the learning before you leave by getting the kids to look "orrery" up in the dictionary) in the world. The five-minute narrated program teaches youngsters how the planets rotate in relation to the sun. Several of the wall displays in the surrounding hallways answer such questions as what causes night and day, why the moon changes shape, and how big the planets are. For lucky families with more time, the planetarium schedules a great lineup of kid-friendly shows. Presentations might include Earth, Moon, and Sun (grade three and up), Once Upon a Universe (grades K-three), and Winnie-the-Pooh and the Golden Rocket (preschool-grade one). *250 E. Franklin St., Chapel Hill. (919) 549-6863; www.morehead.unc.edu*

Museum of Life and Science ★★★/$

Look out: This place is bugged—big time! Whether you want to learn more about the exotic death's head roach, goliath bird eater, or even the run-of-the-mill ladybug or beetle, you'll find it all at this museum's Insectarium. The use of zoom cameras, video macroscopes, and specialized audio equipment gives your budding scientists an intimate encounter with some of the creepiest creatures around. If bugs bug you, move a couple of steps away to the Magic Wings Butterfly House, home to some 1,000 graceful creatures. On your way in, grab an ID card so you'll know who's who in this winged wonderland. For a real treat, ask a staff member for help in getting one to land on one of your kids. Don't miss the Emerging Wonders Room, where hundreds of adult butterflies emerge from their chrysalises. (Ongoing demonstrations like spider feedings and butterfly releases happen throughout the day; ask at the admissions desk for the schedule.) Before returning to the main building, let the kids run off steam at Loblolly Park, where they can make music with drums and bells, experiment with some far-out water pumps, and play hide-and-seek through cool tunnels, bridges, and forts. Back in the main building, there are loads of wow-type permanent adventures, like walking through a 15-foot-high "tornado" and checking out Neil Armstrong's space suit (the real one), and traveling exhibits—like How Things Work, a recent show that explored the mechanics of everyday gadgets. All in all it's a cultural blastoff. *433 Murray Ave., Durham. (919) 220-5429.*

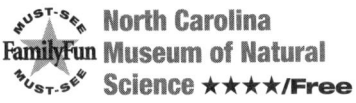

North Carolina Museum of Natural Science ★★★★/Free

Nature lovers of all ages will appreciate this museum, which takes you back to the early days of North Carolina's natural treasures—bald cypress trees, panthers, butterflies, and much more. Resist the temptation to head right for the third floor (that's the most way-cool place). The first floor is also home to loads of interactive activities, including the state's watery wonders like the yellowline arrow crab, sea cucumber, and the wide-mouthed goosefish. Except for the Coastal Overlook area on the next level (don't miss the suspended sperm whale named Trouble), you can breeze through the second floor to find your way to the highlight of the museum, on the third floor. Here's where you'll find things older than dirt—like the Terror of the South (*Acrocanthusaurus dino*—the world's only one) and an awesome fossil lab where your kids can watch the staff actually working on restoring dinosaur bones. Encourage your kids to ask questions: These people know their stuff and explain it in easy-to-understand lingo. The top floor offers you a relaxing spot for a snack or drink before you make the final foray into the arthropod zoo. Be prepared to come face-to-face with some live, squeal-producing bugs like a hissing cockroach, bird-eating scorpion, and a giant millipede. For a great photo op, have your kids stick their heads inside one of the (make-believe) insect heads. *11 W. Jones St., Raleigh. (919) 733-7450; www.naturalsciences.org*

Old Salem ★★★★/$$

The past returns at Old Salem, the popular living-history town that accurately represents daily life in this Moravian community from 1766 to 1840. Begin your visit with the short orientation film in the visitor center. Then, with the aid of a superhelpful guide map (pass on the hassle-prone audio tour), you're off to explore nearly 20 points of interest, most of which line Main Street. Costumed guides demonstrate the behavior, chores, and hobbies of the Moravian people in the late-18th and early-19th centuries. Guaranteed kid favorites are the Shultz Shoemaker Shop (where you can really order a pair of custom-made shoes), the Tavern (where George Washington took a snooze), and the Single Brothers House (where you smell spices in the kitchen or watch the cabinetmaker or tailor in action). Kids will find plenty of other cool hands-on stuff to try along the way—like writing with quills or molding pewter flatware. (Weekly activity schedules are available at the visitor center.) Housed in the Frank L. Horton Museum Center, the Children's Museum (fee) is another must-see if your children are between the ages of 4 and 9. This stop may serve as a welcome diversion halfway through your visit to Old Salem. *924 South Main St., Winston-Salem. (888) 653-7253; (336) 721-7300*; www.oldsalem.org

RIVER OTTERS sometimes let loose a yucky smell when they are startled or threatened. So be careful not to sneak up on one.

Richard Petty Museum ★/$

With heroes like Richard Petty hailing from North Carolina, it's no surprise that auto racing has become one of—if not *the*—most popular noncollegiate sport in the Tar Heel State. It's only fitting that this tasteful tribute to the man who has started more races, logged more miles, taken more checkered flags, and won more Winston Cup championships than any other driver has or probably will in a lifetime, is a favorite family destination. Don't expect a glitzy showroom with room after room of memorabilia. Instead, the homey museum, about 20 miles south of Greensboro, is one huge room that features loads of trophies, awards, photos, and awesome race cars driven during The King's 35-year career. Also on display are Petty's most prized possessions—hundreds of gifts from his die-hard fans. The friendly staff will make you feel right at home—even if you don't know anything about racing. Don't leave without watching the video of Petty's life; it's a heartwarming story of what matters most... family, fans, friends, and the fury of racing. *Level Cross exit off U.S. 220 South, 311 Branson Mill Rd., Randleman. (336) 495-1143.*

Schiele Museum of Natural History and Planetarium ★★★/$

This learning center—located less than 30 minutes from Charlotte—has an eclectic collection: you'll encounter Native Americans, stars, moose and elk, fossils—even saber-toothed cats—all under one roof. The center offers loads of displays (the huge stuffed animals are incredible), dioramas, and drawers of stuff sure to engage, educate, and entertain most children, especially those over 5. The gallery featuring the North American Indian steals the show for most youngsters as it provides a glimpse into 12 tribal groups from five regions. Encourage your kids to listen to the recordings of the Native Americans as they describe their rich cultures. How are they different? What are their similarities? Although the planetarium programs change throughout the year, examples of kid-friendly shows include The Planet Patrol and Quest for Planet X. Outdoors, there's a farm where seasonal interpretive programs illustrate life in this region in the mid- to late-1700s. Don't miss the nearby Catawba Village, where youngsters love the tree-bark house and the council house with the turtle-shaped fire ring. Let your kids try their hand at grinding corn with the various implements. A friendly guide is available during June and July. *1500 E. Garrison Blvd., Gastonia. (704) 866-6908;* www.schielmuseum.org

SciWorks ★★★/$

From the science of racing and the mysteries of our solar system to the river otter and other animals native to North Carolina, you'll find it all at this popular Winston-Salem attraction. SciWorks is a science center, planetarium, and 15-acre environmental park all rolled into one. Inside, the Foucault pendulum is a big draw; its 250-pound brass bob seems to mesmerize with each steady swing. Your preteens will be in their element at the Nintendo racing stations, while younger race fans love the nearby roller-racing track. Other fun areas—especially for the 8-and-under-crowd—include DentalWorks (experiment with semireal instruments on a model mouth), Touch Tank (lots of hermits and horseshoe crabs), and the Science of Music (try "Jingle Bells" on the walk-on piano). On Saturdays, the planetarium has several showings of programs like Bear Tales, Dinos, and In My Backyard. Call ahead for the planetarium's weekday schedule. After your visit, check out the friendly barnyard residents and the nearby otters and deer that live behind the science center. *400 W. Hanes Mill Rd., Winston-Salem. (336) 767-6730;* www.sciworks.org

FamilyFun **VACATION GUIDE**

JUST FOR FUN

Busy Street ★★/$
Imagination, creativity, and curiosity all converge at this wonderful hands-on bonanza of fun in Durham's Shoppes at Lakewood. Specially designed for children 7 and under, Busy Street does a bang-up job of raising youngsters' imaginations a notch higher. Most of the exhibits are developed around popular careers like doctor, policeman, fireman, chef, and musician—all of which come with really cool activities like the sliding pole at the fire station, big drums and bongos at the music shop, and an X-ray room at the community emergency room. After a long day at the "job," youngsters love to congregate at the Busy Street diner or grocery store. Pack a picnic and dine alfresco at Busy Street's outdoor courtyard. *2000 Chapel Hill Rd., Durham. (919) 403-3743.*

Discovery Place
FamilyFun ★★★★/$
MUST-SEE This fun-filled science and technology center in the heart of Charlotte's uptown district contains such discoveries as liquid nitrogen ice cream; it also displays the nation's largest anatomically correct model eye. Your preschoolers will go bonkers in Kidsplace, where they can splash, build, smell, and

---

DAY TRIP
Lions and Tigers and Gold Nuggets, Oh My!

If your family is looking to escape the big city life of Charlotte for the day, you can go for the gold in the morning and cuddle with a chimp after lunch. Your journey begins about 30 miles northeast of Charlotte at the **Reed Gold Mine State Historic Site** *(9621 Reed Mine Rd., Midland; 704/721-4653)*, home to the first documented gold find in the United States. In 1799, young Conrad Reed found a 17-pound yellow rock in Little Meadow Creek. The 12-year-old carried it home where his family, figuring it was just a big old rock, used it as a doorstop. Three years later a jeweler purchased it for $3.50 (about one-tenth of 1 percent of its true value) and the rest, as they say, is history. With more than a million dollars in gold recovered each year, North Carolina led the nation in gold production—until 1848 when the California gold rush exploded. Today, your kids will have a blast (plus it's free) touring some of the restored underground tunnels and interesting visitors' center, and even trying their hand at panning.

Next stop is the **North Carolina Zoological Park** *(4401 Zoo Pkwy.,*

THE HEARTLAND

climb through a load of activities sure to stimulate their imaginations. Permanent exhibits like the Life Center include such hands-on activities as the stretch machine and chin-up bar. While in the Life Center, check out the outside and inside of the gargantuan eyeball. Traveling exhibits like Beakman's World on Tour and Sesame Street are first-rate, too. About midday look for the show-and-tell demos, with such wacky and entertaining programs as rat basketball (don't miss this one) and the Amazing Who-Genie Show. And, not to be outdone, the IMAX and Planetarium theater mesmerizes audiences with incredible movies, laser shows, and some pretty remarkable stargazing. *301 N. Tryon St., Charlotte. (800) 935-0553; (704) 372-6261;* www.discoveryplace.org

MUST-SEE FamilyFun MUST-SEE Emerald Pointe Water Park
★★★★/$$

The perfect place to cool off for the whole family, this water wonderland just outside of Greensboro is great for everyone from aquatic daredevils to swimmers who dog-paddle happily. Thunder Bay, the park's signature attraction and big-time favorite, releases three-foot-high waves every three minutes or so. (Unlike many wave pools, this one separates the "boarders" from the "nonboarders" to reduce the

Asheboro; 800/488-0444; 336/879-7000), located about 60 miles from the Reed Gold Mine. Though off the beaten track, this zoo offers your family one of the most incredible outdoor experiences this side of—well, nearly anywhere. Even though the park is divided into only two areas—the African and North American habitats—it's humongous; be prepared to do a lot of walking. (Free trams and shuttles help get you around, but you may have to wait 20 minutes or so for a ride.) Africa, at more than 300 acres, is home to zebras, elephants, porcupines, meerkats, and rhinos, to name a few; to see it all requires the greatest amount of foot power, so begin your zoo adventure here. The African Pavilion (its outdoor viewing venue is sure to please) and the renovated Forest Aviary (bursts of color and blossoms, especially in the spring) are showstoppers. The trek to North America may be a bit much by this time; this is when the tram or shuttle is most welcome. The Sonora Desert, home to tarantulas, roadrunners, and vampire bats, is a big favorite with the kids. Other stops along the way are Rocky Coast (polar bears, seals, and puffins), and the Touch and Learn Center (farm animals, garden, and orchard), especially appealing if you're traveling with youngsters under 6.

> **Homemade Travel Desks**
>
> Laps are great for lots of things, but writing and drawing are not among them. Keep art projects from collapsing all over your child by making a custom-fitted travel desk out of a sturdy cardboard box. First, while she is seated, measure the height and width of her lap. Now, cut a half-moon big enough to comfortably fit over her legs on two opposite sides of the box and remove the bottom flaps.
>
> If you have time, you can paint the box to dress it up and staple or glue smaller accessory boxes or envelopes to the sides for storage. You can also flip it over to store paper and other travel games inside when it's not in use.

chance of getting clobbered with a board.) Thrill seekers are in their element at Dare Devil Drop, a high-speed slide that drops 76 feet down a watery chute, and at Twin Twisters, a totally enclosed chute ride of more than 350 feet of twists and turns. The Blue Streak, Slidewinder, and 360°, a trio of enclosed action slides, are very popular among moderate scream seekers. And count on young splashers spending hours in the kiddie pools and tube slides at Happy Harbor and Splash Island. Open Memorial Day to Labor Day. *3910 S. Holden Rd., Greensboro. (800) 555-5900; (336) 852-9721;* www.emerald pointe.com

Latta Park and North Carolina Raptor Center ★★/Free

Here's just the place to let your kids run off some steam—especially if they've been cooped up in the car or inside at a museum for a couple of hours. This county-operated park, located just north of Charlotte, offers a load of great family activities, including boating (fee) and fishing on Mountain Island Lake (sorry, no swimming), guided horseback riding (fee), and 18 miles of easy-to-moderate hiking trails. Stop in at the friendly visitors' center to pick up literature to help you plan your outing. Don't leave without touring the outdoor Raptor Center (fee), one of the country's most extensive collections of birds of prey. All of the birds on display have been injured and cannot return to their natural habitats. On weekends, several presentations throughout the day help visitors better understand these predators. *5225 Sample Rd., Huntersville. (704) 875-6521.*

MUST-SEE FamilyFun MUST-SEE North Carolina Zoological Park ★★★★/$$$$

Zoom over to this big (like 300 acres!) zoo for an animal encounter that will delight the whole family. For more information, see page 356.

MUST-SEE FamilyFun MUST-SEE Paramount's Carowinds Theme Park ★★★★/$$$$

You'll need a full day (at least) to do justice to this theme and water park. Located about 10 miles south of Charlotte's booming uptown, the 100-acre attraction literally straddles the border of North and South Carolina; in fact, the supercharged coaster Thunder Road actually takes you through both states on your harrowing ride. The park's signature ride is TOP GUN, the biggest, tallest, fastest, and baddest one around. So bad, in fact, that you should probably watch a few rounds before you allow your 8-and-ups on this track (forget about younger kids). Same advice applies for the two wooden coasters (Thunder Road and Hurler), plus the 50-mph stand-up thriller called Vortex. The Flying Super Saturator combines high flying on a suspended coaster track with gushing geysers around every turn. This Nickelodeon attraction is wildly popular, so expect long lines during peak season. Other thrillers include the Drop Zone Stunt Tower, James Bond: A License To Thrill, and Frenzoid. Don't worry: your less bold fun seekers will find plenty to do, too, starting with water rides like Rip Roarin' Rapids and Powder Keg Flume and moving to Animation Station, featuring the favorite Scooby-Doo's Ghoster Coaster, and Laser Tag Arena. When you've tired of the rides, there are a ton of shows, carnival-like games (with huge stuffed animals as prizes), and stores (including the $2-and-under shop). Think you're done? Included in the admission price is an added bonus—a 12-acre, action-packed water park, with body slides, a river raft ride, a wave pool, and a splash factory—a three-story water jungle gym for the wee ones. Open April through mid-October; water park closes in September. *5225 Carowinds Blvd., Charlotte. (800) 888-4386; (704) 588-2600;* www.carowinds.com

Primate Center
★★/$

Animal lovers will delight in touring this center, Duke University's haven for some of the most unusual-looking lemurs, lorises, and bushbabies you'll see anywhere. Although the primary function of the center is the research and study of more than 300 primates, the establishment does offer several one-hour guided walking tours (daily) to raise public awareness and understanding of these animals. A visit here is a wonderful learning experience for youngsters older than 7. Super-knowledgeable tour guides do a great job educating, explaining, and encouraging questions about such residents as the blue-eyed black lemur with its piercing eyes, the wild-haired Sanford lemur, and the annoyingly loud black-and-white-ruffed lemur. **NOTE:** Before you head out to the Primate Center, call ahead to reserve space on the tour—no walk-ups accepted—and because most of the tour is spent outdoors, tours are not held during stormy conditions. To see the primates in their most active state, avoid a midday tour when many of them are napping. *3705 Erwin Rd., Durham. (919) 489-3364.*

Pullen Park
★/Free

Whether you want a carousel ride (fee), dip in the indoor pool (fee), pedal boat ride (fee), or just a good old romp on the playground, you'll find it here. Top off your visit with a picnic lunch from the on-site concession stand. *520 Ashe Ave., Raleigh. (919) 831-6468.*

Wafting the Eno
★★/$

You'll find some of nature's best-kept secrets on this gentle water adventure near Durham. This is *not* for the family seeking a wild and woolly ride through raging rapids. Instead, it's a two-hour kayak float led by River Dave, Durham's resident field naturalist, who's been leading these encounters since 1989. Part education, part personal reflection, part entertainment, the wafting experience focuses on observing, exploring, and discussing the hows and whys of the Eno River and its environs. All ages are welcome and no experience is necessary. Bring a little bit of horsepower (since someone has to paddle the two-person kayak) and a heaping helping of curiosity. In addition to the one or two floats offered during the day, a two-hour moonlight wafting is very popular. Regardless of your preference, reservations are an absolute must. Open mid-March to mid-November. *5101 N. Roxboro, Durham. (919) 471-3802.*

THE HEARTLAND

BUNKING DOWN

AmeriSuites Arrowood ★/$
Located just an exit or two away from the thrills and chills of Carowinds is this superaffordable mini-suite-type property. Although there's no on-site restaurant (many nearby), this clean and friendly hotel offers a complimentary breakfast buffet that's sure to please most kids, and an outdoor pool, fun and relaxing after a day at Carowinds. Ask about special Carowinds rates. *7900 Forest Point Blvd., Charlotte. (800) 833-1516; (704) 522-8400;* www.amerisuites.com

DoubleTree Guest Suites ★★/$-$$
This Durham property is the perfect haven for the business traveler who has the good fortune to bring the family along. While Dad or Mom go off to meetings (this place is located in the heart of the Research Triangle Park area), the kids will have a blast swimming, bicycling, playing basketball, or romping on the playground. There aren't any organized kids' programs, so whoever's not doing business in the boardroom is the designated baby-sitter. There are even paddleboats for a race or two around the lake. With the property's two-room-suite setup, there's lots of space for the whole crew. *2515 Meridian Pkwy., Durham. (919) 361-4660;* www.doubletree.com

FamilyFun GAME

A Is for Armadillo
This is a terrific game to play with preschoolers. More populated areas yield more interesting results. The leader picks a letter and announces it to the other players, who then join the leader in competing to find three things (both in and out of the car) that start with the designated letter. Choose A, for example, and you might spot an armadillo, an automobile, and an apple. The first person to succeed gets to choose the next letter.

O. Henry Hotel ★★/$$
Named after the famous short-story writer and Greensboro native, this centrally located property is a favorite for both business and vacation travelers. Family-friendly features include complimentary breakfast, video games, outdoor pool, and shuttle service to the nearby 80-store shopping center. *624 Green Valley Rd., Greensboro. (800) 222-2222; (336) 854-2000.*

Paramount's Carowinds Campground ★★★★/$
If your troops love camping, this popular place is outdoor nirvana. With about 200 campsites, seasonal swimming pool, miniature-golf course, and game room, the reason for its popularity quickly becomes obvious. Although you're within a

few minutes' walk of the popular theme park, a free shuttle transports you to the entrance. Another plus: Campground guests get discounted admission tickets to the park. *14523 Carowinds Blvd., Charlotte. (800) 888-4386; (704) 587-9116; www.carowinds.com*

Raleigh Marriott Crabtree Valley ★★★/$-$$

Whether it's the tasty pizza being served up in the hotel's pub-type restaurant, comfy guest rooms, splash time in the swimming pool, or a heaping helping of culture and fun at any of the nearby museums, you can't go wrong with an overnight at this property off of one of the city's main drags. For your shopping-fanatic, the upscale Crabtree Valley Mall is directly across the street. *4500 Marriott Dr., Raleigh. (800) 228-9290; (919) 781-7000; www.marriott.com*

Super 8 Motel ★★/$

This property is located near the popular SciWorks attraction in the northwest-end of Winston-Salem. Kids will like the motel's indoor pool—and the tasty continental breakfast; Mom and Dad will love the superaffordable rates. Although no restaurant is on-site, you'll have plenty of eateries to choose from within a block or two of the motel. *200 Mercantile Dr., Winston-Salem. (800) 800-8000; (336) 714-8888; www.super8.com*

Tanglewood Park ★★★★/$-$$

With so many attractive lodgings to choose from at this 1,200-acre park that's less than 15 miles southwest of Winston-Salem, you'll need a family powwow to reach a decision. There are tent and RV campsites, rustic cottages, and a lodge apartment, all perfect for vacationing families. During the day, enjoy the park's many recreational activities (fees), including fishing, boating, horseback riding, tennis, and golf. *U.S. 158, Clemmons. (336) 778-6370.*

GOOD EATS

Alfred & Charlie's BBQ House ★★★★/$

Youngsters can pig out on nearly any of their favorite meals here for less than three bucks. Even though barbecue is the signature item (and for good reason), some kids may shy away from trying the tasty sandwich from the Piglet Platter Menu and opt for the good old standby corn dog or grilled cheese. They—and you—won't go wrong either way. *815 S. New Hope Rd., Gastonia. (704) 864-4446.*

Big Ed's City Market Restaurant ★★★/$

Dessert for breakfast? It almost tastes that way when you start your day with an oversize, sweet, thick hotcake at this downtown Raleigh restaurant. Although breakfast is served anytime, specials like chicken and dumplings and unlimited lemonade are sure to please even the pickiest of eaters come lunchtime. The décor is rural Americana, with lots to look at until the food arrives. A superfriendly staff makes the experience even sweeter. *220 Wolfe St., Raleigh. (919) 836-9909.*

Boardwalk Billy's ★★/$-$$

This lakefront hangout, behind the Hilton Hotel in northeast Charlotte, is ideal for families: Peanut shells on the floor, a plastic tablecloth and roll of paper towels on each table, and an outgoing waitstaff create an at-home atmosphere—and the food's good, too. The cheeseburger basket and fries is a big favorite; but if your youngsters have really worked up an appetite, consider splitting an order of Billy's famous ribs—they're messy and sloppy, but oh-so-good! Multiple locations. *8933-2 JM Keynes Dr., Charlotte. (704) 503-7427.*

Bullwinkle's Family Food 'n' Fun ★★★★/$

If you're looking for good eats and family-style entertainment under one roof, check out this loud-but-fun, moose-and-squirrel-themed restaurant less than 15 miles from downtown Raleigh. With a 25-plus game arcade, light-sound-and-water shows, and a rock-climbing wall tempting your kids from the get-go,

Bandanna Sit-Upon

True camp crafts are traditionally the kind you can use in the woods — a water jug, a sling for hauling wood, a candle lantern, or this camp pillow. Made from two bandannas, the sit-upon fits into a kid's pocket, ready to fill with grasses and leaves whenever she needs a soft place to sit for a spell.

What you'll need: Two bandannas, embroidery floss or yarn, embroidery needle, adhesive Velcro tab, and soft grasses, leaves, or moss.

How it's done: Place one bandanna on top of the other and stitch them together on three sides. On the open side, attach a Velcro tab to make a simple closure (experienced sewers might like to make a basic button-and-hole closure instead). To fill the pillow, gather the softest grasses, dead leaves, and moss you can find, carefully broken into pieces small enough that they won't pierce the fabric; backyard grass clippings work well, too. At day's end, just shake out the filling and fold up the sit-upon for the next day's adventures.

Camp Crafter's Tip: You can stitch around the very edges of your bandannas or one inch in from the edges. A whip- or running stitch works fine, but if your child likes sewing, she can try a more decorative pattern or even embroider her name on one edge.

it shouldn't be too hard to get them to finish their meal. Casual fare like burgers, dogs, and PB&J triangles make dining here a breeze. Multiple locations. *1040 Buck Jones Rd., Raleigh. (919) 319-7575.*

Elmo's Diner ★★★/$

Known for its classic diner fare served up in a friendly, casual atmosphere (we're talking 1950s-style leather booths and stool-lined counters), this place will satisfy the "I'm hungry" desires of almost any family member. Your kids can start the day with an order of yummy banana pancakes or try a big burger and fries for lunch or dinner. It's a popular spot, located close to Duke's east campus. **NOTE:** Save room for the homemade desserts, such as Eno River mud pie and chocolate chip cheesecake—they're incredible! Multiple locations. *776 Ninth St., Durham. (919) 416-3823;* www.elmosdiner.com

Good Ol Days ★★★★/$-$$

Chrome, Formica, and poodle skirts set the stage for a fun and tasty meal at this 1950s-style eatery in Charlotte—if you're lucky, your family will get to sit in one of the vintage auto booths. Yummy burgers and hot dogs will delight the young ones, especially when they're served in a cute cardboard car container. For dessert, don't pass up the "cup of dirt" that's loaded with ice cream and a ton of other goodies. Flavored Cokes and the best shakes in town are just two of the superstars from the fountain. *3351 Pineville-Matthews Rd., Charlotte. (704) 543-4100.*

Herbie's Place ★★★/$

To satisfy all types of appetites at any time of day, head for this round-the-clock place where you can get a hot dog, T-bone steak, or ham and cheese on rye 24 hours a day, seven days a week. That said, Herbie's kids' breakfast of bacon, eggs, grits, and toast really does hit the spot. Sit at the counter and let your youngsters watch the beehive of activity in the kitchen. Simple fare, friendly waitstaff, and affordable prices—families can't beat this place. We forgot to mention the diner's namesake—an old VW beetle that's crashed head-on into the building. Ya gotta love it. Multiple locations. *3136 Battleground Ave., Greensboro. (336) 288-8896.*

Mama Dip's ★★/$-$$

This haven for delicious southern cooking offers something for everyone. For youngsters, it may be knowing that basketball star Michael Jordan dined here during his college days. (However, don't expect any MJ memorabilia.) For Moms and Dads, it's the barbecue or chicken and dumplings, and, of course, Dip's famous pecan pie. Kids can dig into the banana pudding. *405 W. Rosemary St., Chapel Hill. (919) 942-5837;* www.mamadips.com

Pottery–Then and Now

CLAY: FOR YOUR CHILDREN, it was one of their first toys. For parents, this creative turn of events marked the start of a collection of a gazillion hand-created-just-for-you thingamajigs, the beginning of a series of lifelong keepsakes. For the tiny community of Seagrove, the pottery capital of North Carolina—if not the entire United States—the good, rare earth continues to be the lifeblood of nearly 100 practicing potters, some of whom are eighth- and ninth-generation artisans. If you're planning a visit to the North Carolina Zoological Park (see page 356), Seagrove is not far (it's about 10 miles from Asheboro; 85 miles from Raleigh; and 95 miles from Charlotte). A craft-filled place where time seems to have stood still, it's well worth a stop. During the 18th century, area potters crafted simple, functional wares like plates, churns, crocks, jars, and jugs, all of which were sold from covered wagons that traveled throughout the Tar Heel State. Slowly but surely, word of the fine pottery spread, and by the 1900s, families would come to Seagrove to stock up on clay essentials, decorative pieces, and gifts.

Today, thousands of youngsters and their families explore the area's winding country roads, stopping along the way to watch the many potters at work—and maybe purchase a piece or two. **The North Carolina Pottery Center** (*250 East Ave., Seagrove; 336/873-8430; www.ncpotterycenter.com*) showcases the work of local and state artisans, including pieces dating back to the early settlers of the region. Youngsters enjoy watching the pottery demonstrations and voting for their favorite piece. Most potters take great delight in welcoming young visitors into their shops and studios. In fact, don't be surprised if your child is invited to take a turn at the wheel. If you're planning a visit, call ahead since schedules vary. Here are just four of the many potters of Seagrove who love to share their knowledge and skills with children (in addition, a handy guide of the area potters and their specialties is available free at the Pottery Center):

HOLLY HILL POTTERY
625 Fork Creek Mill Rd., Seagrove.
(336) 873-7300.

LUCK'S WARE (Fifth-generation potter) 1606 Adams Rd., Seagrove.
(336) 879-3261.

SMALL WORLD POTTERY
1385 Fork Creek Mill Rd., Seagrove.
(336) 873-8966.

TURN AND BURN POTTERY 124 East Ave., Seagrove.
(336) 873-7381.

PieWorks ★★★★/$-$$$

Pizza is always a good bet with kids, and this place—with more than 150 toppings—will bring out the creative chef in everyone. How's this for tasty but unusual starters: sauces like spicy chili and garlic butter; cheeses like brie, mascarpone, and cheddar; veggies such as artichoke hearts and fresh spinach; meats and seafood ranging from Cajun andouille, ostrich, and rattlesnake sausages to hot dogs, crab, and shrimp; and the truly nutty, including almonds, pine nuts, sunflower seeds, raisins, and chocolate chips. If you can't figure out your own toppings, choose one of the restaurant's combinations. Best bets: Spaghetti Works, the Rosemary Roast, and the All-American Hot Dog Pie. Don't skip dessert: try FruitWorks, a cold pizza with sweetened cream cheese and fruits. The atmosphere is casual and kid-friendly. This dizzying array of choices will make your next trip to the local pizza place seem downright dull. Multiple locations. *3700 Lawndale Dr., Greensboro. (336) 282-9003.*

Twin City Diner ★★★/$-$$

Lunch or dinner at this diner on the outskirts of downtown Winston-Salem is just what the family ordered. The black-and-white checkered floor, lunch counter and stools, and cushy booths set the tone. Chicken fingers from the children's menu are the hands-down favorite, but the selections also include a healthful grilled chicken breast. If your kids are into stuffed potatoes, the appetizer menu showcases several great combinations. Finish off the meal with the hot fudge brownie pie—you won't be disappointed. *1425 W. First St., Winston-Salem. (336) 724-4203.*

SOUVENIR HUNTING

Concord Mills

A total of some 200 shops, carnival-type rides, and restaurants all converge at this mega-mall near Charlotte. Your preteens will love cool shops like Sun & Ski Sports, an interactive specialty retailer (don't miss the in-line skate track), plus Bugle Boy and Banana Republic Factory Stores. An indoor amusement park (Jeepers) and stock-car racing simulators (NASCAR Silicon Motor Speedway) are only two of the mall's super-charged entertainment options for kids. *I-85, Concord Mills Blvd. (877) 626-4557; (704) 979-3000.*

Morgan Imports

From the funky to the classical, this home-furnishings shop is one that even kids will take a liking to. Candles, unusual holiday ornaments, pillow buddies—even a kid-size tepee—are among some of the 40,000 items from all over the world on display at this popular retailer in Durham's historic Brightleaf District. *113 S. Gregson St., Durham. (919) 688-1150;* www.morgan.city search.com

Sally Huss Gallery
The bright, bold "happy art" of this famed west coast artist's T-shirts, sweatshirts, prints, clocks, and watches will no doubt bring a smile to your daughter's face, plus a few "please oh please moms" if you even think of leaving empty-handed. *Magnolia Marketplace, 9650 Strickland, N. Raleigh. (919) 833-0809.*

Shrunken Head Boutique
Don't be fooled by the hippie-type name (it's been around since 1969). This shop carries every item of UNC/Chapel Hill (Michael Jordan's alma mater) memorabilia ever imagined—and then some. Kids have loads of Tar Heel stuff to choose from: basketball jerseys (free imprinting of first or last name), boxer shorts, hair scrunchies, backpacks, jean jackets, and pom-poms. *155 E. Franklin St., Chapel Hill. (919) 942-7544;* www.shrunkenhead.com

T. Bagge Merchant
A visit to Old Salem is not complete without a stop at this friendly gift shop facing the Square on Main Street. Here's the place for old-fashioned toys and games like nine pins (miniature bowling), rolling hoops (looks like a wooden Hula Hoop), marbles, tricornered hats, sewing kits, and a ton of other cool stuff. *626 S. Main St., Winston-Salem. (336) 721-7387.*

Toys & Co.
This cheery toy store (at the Friendly Shopping Center) delights young shoppers with loads of must-have merchandise—from sturdy scooters (the collapsible kind) and radio disc jockey sets to a well-stocked doll section and extensive line of cool play hats. *Intersection of Friendly and Wendover Aves., 627 Friendly Center, Greensboro. (336) 294-1114.*

Ninety-five percent of Great Smoky Mountains National Park is forested.

INTRODUCTION

North Carolina Mountains

GRACEFUL waterfalls, majestic mountain peaks, raging rivers, and mysterious caverns are just a few of nature's handiworks that await your family around every bend in western North Carolina's mountain region. Although the better-known places like Grandfather Mountain and its Mile High Swinging bridge are well marked and easy to find, sometimes your best bet is to stop where you see other cars have pulled off the road. Hop out, grab the camera, and go exploring. Encourage your kids to be on the lookout for the incredible—they'll certainly find it here.

If you think that life moves a tad slower around these parts, you're right. To best enjoy it, you should slow down, too. The area's fun-filled but lazy hayrides, folktales, and Indian lore lose much of their

THE FamilyFun LIST

Biltmore Estate (page 370)

Chimney Rock (page 372)

Fontana Village (page 373)

Grandfather Mountain (page 375)

Great Smoky Mountains National Park (page 376)

The Health Adventure (page 372)

Linville Caverns (see page 375)

Oconaluftee Indian Village (page 376)

Unto These Hills (page 379)

Western North Carolina Nature Center (page 380)

FamilyFun VACATION GUIDE

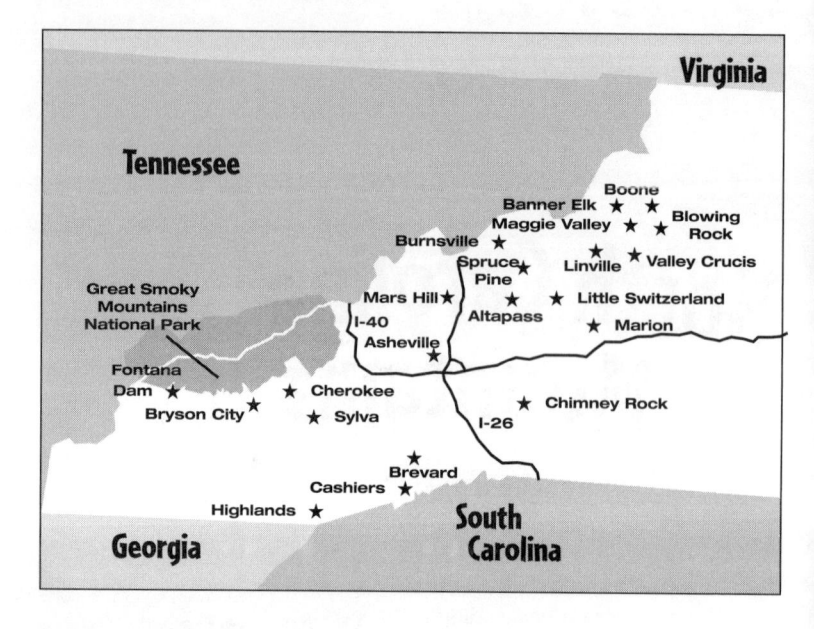

excitement when kids are champing at the bit to move on to the next stop. Speaking of slow, don't plan on zipping speedily along these winding mountain roads. Some of them may be treacherous, especially at night and during foggy or stormy conditions. Another valuable tip for the driver or navigator: what appears to be a short distance on the map may sometimes take two or three times longer than normal highway driving. Not a problem: just pack your patience and plan accordingly.

The reward for that patience is tons of way-cool, kid-friendly activities. Whether you're checking out how the rich and famous lived at the Biltmore Estate, riding the Red Devil roller coaster at Ghost Town in the Sky, or watching a Cherokee Indian weave a basket at the Oconaluftee Indian Village, the North Carolina mountains make for an ideal family vacation.

CULTURAL ADVENTURES

Biltmore Estate
FamilyFun ★★★★/$$$$

Adults aren't the only ones who enjoy this incredible place: young sightseers can have a blast at the Biltmore—if you plan your visit from a kids' point of view. The key is not touring the gazillion rooms on all four floors, but to narrow your options and focus on what's of most interest to kids—primarily the main

370

floor and basement levels. Also, make sure to purchase *A Young Person's Guide* at either the Gatehouse Gift Shop at the main entrance or at any of the shops in the stables next to the house. (The 50-plus page paperback sells for about $8 and points out the Biltmore's special treasures for youngsters, and the pictures, games, and puzzles come in handy on your trip home.) Encourage your family to look all around the rooms because some of the neatest elements are in easy-to-miss places like above a door or fireplace or way above, like the ceiling. Hands-down favorites on the main floor include the dining hall (how would you like to set *that* table for dinner?), the billiard room (can you find the secret passageways?), and the library (do you see the rabbit and rooster?). Take a quick look at a bedroom or two upstairs and then head to the *piece de resistance*: the basement! Hard to believe that the Halloween Room was part of the prewedding festivities for Vanderbilt daughter Cornelia and husband John Cecil. (Can you spot "Batman"?) Expect young eyes to pop when you reach the recreation area, complete with a bowling alley, swimming pool, and early-day fitness center. The 75 acres of colorful gardens make for a nice stroll. And don't pass up the bass pond and nearby waterfall as you drive out. Depending on whether you think wineries are suitable places for your kids to visit, this can be a fun time for kids since the tour passes by the machinery and stone tunnels used to store the wine. The winery frequently hosts children's activities such as grape stomping and cork bobbing. Any equestrians among you may visit the Biltmore Estate Equestrian Center for guided rides (fee) several times daily. We give this place a big thumbs-up. *U.S. 25 (three blocks north of I-40), Asheville. (800) 543-2961; (828) 274-6333;* www.biltmore.com

Emerald Village ★★/$

Western North Carolina, a haven for gem mining, boasts one of the best in-depth mining experiences we know of. It's Emerald Village, which has both a mining museum (lots of old-time, mysterious stuff that kids love) and a gemstone mine across the road. Kids find this museum cool, not necessarily because of what's on display, but because of its neat location: right in the middle of a series of underground mines, including the Bon

Ami mine. (You know, the cleaning product with the baby chick for its logo? Same one.) The museum has no official guide, so be sure to take the literature that identifies such weird-sounding contraptions as the slusher scraper and electric mule. After a tour of the museum (it shouldn't take long), head across the street to where the action really is: the fresh water flume where everyone in your family is guaranteed to find a gem. Gem bucket prices range from a few bucks all the way up to the $500 barrel. Don't laugh: someone actually found a 350-karat star garnet in one of them. Friendly and skillful artisans are around to answer questions and to cut and mount your special gems. Open April through October. *McKinney Mine Rd. and Crabtree Creek Rd., Little Switzerland. (877) 389-4653; (828) 765-6463;* www.emeraldvillage.com

The Health Adventure
FamilyFun ★★★★/$

Don't let its nondescript (and maybe off-putting to kids) name deter your family from visiting. Once inside, your kids will agree that this hands-on kid place in downtown Asheville is pretty cool. A gentle slide down the lion's tongue or whipping up a tasty meal in the play kitchen will get your preschoolers revved up in the center's first floor PlaySpace gallery. Across the hall meet TAM, a life-size transparent anatomical model that lights up and "explains" lots of neat things about the human body. Here, you'll also meet a cool dude named Tom, an anatomical mannequin puzzle. Turn the activity into a game for your children—who can reassemble Tom in under a minute? In ScienceSpace, check out the energy-generating bicycle and billboard-size magnet wall, while in nearby NutriSpace you'll learn about proper eating and dental habits. (There's even a three-foot-long toothbrush that kids can use to practice the proper brushing methods on some supersize molars.) Upstairs there's always a traveling exhibit that's interactive, a tiny-tiny gift shop (who can resist the adorable doctor's jacket for your wanna-be MD?), and other hands-on galleries that creatively approach critical topics such as smoking, AIDS, and driver safety. *2 S. Pack Pl., Asheville. (828) 254-6373;* www.healthadventure.com

JUST FOR FUN

Chimney Rock
FamilyFun ★★★/$$

From the top of this humongous granite monolith, your kids can see for what seems to be about a gazillion miles (actually it's about 75 on a clear day). Although several paths lead to the summit, your family's best bet is via the elevator, which gets you there—some 26 stories and 32 seconds later—

A GOOD EGG Hard-boiled eggs are a perfect road food if you peel them first, wrap them in plastic, and chill them. Here's a foolproof recipe: Place eggs in a saucepan and cover with water. Bring to a boil, reduce heat, and simmer 15 minutes (add 2 minutes if eggs are straight from the fridge). Plunge eggs into cold water. Keep in the cooler or eat within two hours.

painlessly. The temperature at the top is a lot cooler; on some summer days the difference can be 40 degrees. Once at the top, it's just about 40 steps to the awesome—and often photographed—vista. Rather than opt to take the elevator back down, why not savor the scenery with an easy hike down through the outcroppings; the path links up with the Forest Trail, ending at the foot of the 404-foot Hickory Nut Falls, truly one of the state's most spectacular natural wonders—its sheer drop is twice that of Niagara Falls. If your kids are still raring to go, check out the 30-minute Woodland Walk, where you'll discover loads of flowers just waiting to be captured by your 9-year-old's new camera. Get a copy of the free brochure designed specifically to enhance kids' exploration of the walk. A nature center and loads of picnic places round out a visit to this privately owned and operated mountain attraction that's about 25 miles southeast of Asheville. *U.S. 64/74A, Chimney Rock. (800) 277-9611; (828) 625-9611; www.chimneyrock.com*

Fontana Village
FamilyFun ★★★★/$-$$
MUST-SEE It's not really a village, but we promise it's a really first-rate destination. Curious about this *FamilyFun* favorite? Turn to page 374.

Forestry Discovery Center ★★/$
Once home to the country's first forestry school, this center is part of the Cradle of Forestry in America in the Pisgah National Forest. The hands-on learning center is in historic buildings where crafters demonstrate once common skills like weaving and toy making. Your kids will find out what goes on under an oak tree and in a mountain stream, while parents will be grateful that the troops aren't getting dirty or soaking wet in the process. A simulated helicopter ride lets youngsters find out what it's like to put out a forest fire from the air. The hands-down favorite, however, is the scavenger hunt. Children search through the center for forestry facts, and, ultimately, win a

prize. There are also the usual educational movies and hiking trails. *Ranger station: 1001 Pisgah Hwy., Brevard. (828) 877-3130; (828) 884-5713.*

Ghost Town in the Sky
★★/$$
Perched on the top of Buck Mountain in Maggie Valley, this park mixes the lure of an old Wild West town with the thrills of a modern amusement park. Your kids get quite a few choices—including how to get from the bottom of the mountain to the top. Whether you opt for the incline, chair lift, or van, expect a breathtaking 10-minute ride. The park is divided into several areas, with a few rides featured at nearly every stop. If your kids are seasoned thrill seekers, these rides may be too tame. Beginning screamers, though, should watch a few times before jumping on a ride. The white-knuckle crowd will definitely want to take a few spins on the Red Devil, a roller coaster full of dives, loops, and swings around the mountaintop. Other "grippers" include the Black Widow and Sea Dragon (talk about a view!). For your munchkins, Ghost Town offers a handful of super mild-mannered rides and games in Kiddieland. Ghost Town itself is a late 1800s western town complete with an hourly shoot-out on Main Street and a cancan show at the Silver Dollar Saloon. (Although it's a bit hokey, kids eat up the gunfight action. But since the gunshots can be startling to younger viewers, watch it from the wooden boardwalk.) The Country Music Show and Indian Dances performance, which take place seven or eight times a day in the Fort Cherokee area, is an ideal place to take a breather.

It Takes a Village

If you want to escape the mind-numbing pace of everyday life, **Fontana Village** *(Hwy. 28N, Fontana Dam; 800/849-2258),* at the largest dam east of the Mississippi, is just the place.

This is definitely not a day trip or even a single overnighter; plan to spend several days, at least. One reason is that there is so much to do here, the other is that it takes so long on those scenic, but slow-moving back roads (about a 90-mile drive from Asheville) just to reach the place. Once you arrive, you'll quickly see that it was well worth the trek.

There actually are too many things to do here, but here's a start: craft classes, hiking, swimming, zooming down the water slides, fishing, miniature golf, water skiing, tennis, horseback riding, historic tours, and square dancing (some fees apply). There are nightly marshmallow roasts and regularly sched-

NORTH CAROLINA MOUNTAINS

Open May through October. *U.S. Hwy. 19 North, Maggie Valley. (800) 446-7886; (828) 926-1140; www.smokymountainland.com/ghosttown.htm*

MUST-SEE FamilyFun Grandfather Mountain ★★★★/$$

Get ready for the view of a lifetime at this privately owned and operated mountain extravaganza just one mile south of the Blue Ridge Parkway near Linville. Although the swinging bridge is Grandfather's signature feature, don't rush there and rush out again. Urge your family to be patient and slowly drink in all that this natural beauty has to offer. Drive about half a mile from the entrance and you'll reach the animal habitats—home to bears, otters, eagles, and deer. This up-close-and-personal venue is an ideal photo op site—especially when the bear cubs are frisky and playing with nearby mama bear. Not to worry—the bears are in an open area, a natural habitat separated from visitors by a fence. A nature museum may strike kids as semi-interesting, especially the life-size statue of Mildred the Bear and an exact replica of the tree trunk with Daniel Boone's famous "killd a bar" message. Another half-mile drive (with some relatively steep inclines) takes you to the summit and the Mile High Swinging Bridge—the highest swinging footbridge in America. Here, you're more than a mile above sea level and surrounded by the awesome expanse of the southern Appalachians. Even on a sizzling afternoon, you may need a sweater. Bring lunch; picnic areas abound at Grandfather. Or you can order fried chicken to go at the nature museum's restaurant.

uled softball games. A weekly activity schedule helps everyone keep track of all the goings-on.

Nearby are places where you can go white-water rafting. And do stop at the **Fontana Dam** visitors' center: The tour (fee) takes you inside the dam to see how it works, and your kids will learn some fascinating facts about the history of the dam's construction. In fact, you'll learn that Fontana Village actually started out as a housing area for the workers building the dam. The village also has two restaurants, a general store, a gift shop, a service station, and an ice-cream parlor.

The **Inn at Fontana Village** offers several comfortable and affordable lodgings ($-$$), including cottages with kitchenettes. There's also a campground ($), with full hookups and tents for year-round camping. Rates at the inn take a big dip in the fall and winter, but quite frankly, Fontana Village is primarily a summer resort, as the activities essentially dry up after Labor Day.

Grandfather's 12 miles of hiking trails range from the supereasy to the extremely challenging. Family-friendly trails, especially for the novice hiker, include Woods Walk for the nature seeker (.4 mile through a hardwood forest) and Black Rock Nature Trail for the view seeker (1 mile, self-guided trek showcases 35 natural features and incredible vistas). Pick up the free Grandfather Mountain Trail Map and Backcountry Guide at the main entrance. *U.S. 221 and Blue Ridge Pkwy., Linville. (800) 468-7325; (828) 733-4337.*

Great Smoky Mountains National Park ★★★★/Free

There's no finer place to commune with nature in these parts than at this immensely popular park, whose mountains are named for the smoky blue haze that clings to their sides. The Great Smoky Mountains National Park is a "two-stater," with half of it in North Carolina and half in Tennessee. A drive along the park's main artery, Newfound Gap Road, will take you up and down through peaks and valleys, often revealing breathtaking vistas. Be sure to stop at one of the park's visitors' centers at Oconaluftee (south entrance—in North Carolina), Cades Cove (midway, west), and Sugarlands (north entrance—in Tennessee) and pick up some of the fact-filled maps and pamphlets. They will help you find some of the many don't-miss trails, waterfalls, and landmarks. Since this is a forest filled with animals (bears and such), the pamphlets also provide valuable wildlife safety tips. Begin at Clingman's Dome, the highest peak in the Smokies and one that offers spectacular sunsets; you can also get to the Appalachian Trail from this area. Cades Cove—about 35 miles southwest of Clingman's following the park road—is probably the most popular area for visitors. You and your kids can hike the trails and see waterfalls, ride horseback, explore the gristmill, take hayrides, and check out the historic buildings. Cades Cove also has a great family-friendly campground (fee), complete with rest rooms (no showers), bicycle rentals, a store, and an excellent Junior Ranger program. If you make only one stop in the forest, make it here. The wildlife viewing alone is worth the drive and will delight everybody. The park contains several other tent and RV campgrounds. *Hwy. 441, just north of Cherokee. (865) 436-1200;* www.nps.gov/grsm/

Linville Caverns ★★★★/$

Rich in stalactites and stalagmites, this limestone cavern is a few miles off the Blue Ridge Parkway between Linville and Marion. Set deep inside Humpback Mountain, in 1862 (during the Civil War) it was a hideout for deserters from both armies. Today it's one of the area's most popular natural attractions, thanks to some incredible limestone formations, not to mention animals like the seasonal Eastern Pipisrelle bat. Tours depart every five minutes and last about half an hour. Guides do a super job, using informative and colorful stories and factoids to appeal to a broad range of age groups. Listen closely as your guide points out such iciclelike formations as the wedding scene, tobacco leaves, alligator, and Niagara Falls. **NOTE:** With the exception of one area, this place is a hands-off zone: It's against the rules to touch the formations. Be aware that the caverns are dimly lighted and may be a bit scary for a 3-year-old. A constant year-round temperature of 52° F. may require a light jacket. South on U.S. *221, Marion. (800) 419-0540; (828) 756-4171; www.linvillecaverns.com*

Oconaluftee Indian Village
★★★★/$$

There's no better way to really understand and appreciate the Cherokee way of life than to view it firsthand. Stop at this place perched on a hill above the town of Cherokee and take guided walks of the village (they depart every few minutes), a 60-minute tour with Cherokee craftspeople and lecturers. The beadwork area is one of the most intriguing open-air shelters on the trail. Here you can watch as artisans swiftly and expertly weave colorful beads into belts and other items. Your kids won't find a potter's wheel at the pottery shelter—instead watch as a Cherokee with seasoned hands shapes the rich clay into bowls and pitchers. Kids will also enjoy demonstrations in the arts of basket weaving, arrowhead chipping, and use of the blowgun (talk about extreme accuracy). This is a good opportunity for you to encourage your children to probe, question, and comment on the various skills being demonstrated. Visits to the Ceremonial Grounds and Council House are lively, educational, and full of stories. Open May through October. *Drama Rd. off U.S. 441 North, Cherokee. (828) 497-2111; (828) 497-2315.*

The Orchard at Altapass
★★/$

Although you may have trouble finding this place, keep trying—a few extra minutes of scouting for the little brown sign on the Blue Ridge Parkway is well worth it. You'll note right away that The Orchard at Altapass offers much more than apples (but be sure to sample a few of the heritage apples like Grimes Golden, Transparent, and King Luscious, depending on the season). What the whole family will like best, though, is the 45-minute hayride that follows the path of the Revolutionary War mountain soldiers and then takes you through the orchard itself. The friendly and knowledgeable wagon master holds kids spellbound with tales of the area's Great Flood, the Revolutionary War's Overmountain Men, and the hard-working folk who first settled here. **NOTE:** The only downside to this place is the limited schedule for the hayrides: weekend afternoon schedules feature many rides, but weekday jaunts are less frequent; call ahead. Weekends at Altapass also bring foot-stomping, hand-clapping live music to the mountains with free afternoon concerts. This place rocks, but in a friendly, upbeat way. Open Memorial Day through October. *Near Spruce Pine at Milepost 328.3 at Orchard Rd. (888) 765-9531; (828) 765-9531; www.altapassorchard.com*

DAY TRIP
Fab Falls

About an hour's drive southwest of Asheville is the heart and soul of waterfall country. In fact, **Transylvania County** alone is home to more than 250 waterfalls and 200 miles of clear mountain streams. Although a family vacation *designed* around these natural wonders may be a bit much for your youngsters, several hours of exploration can be pure delight. **NOTE:** Be aware that waterfall deaths occur every year. Regardless of how breathtaking the view, waterfalls are dangerous and should be approached with extreme caution. Discuss the ground rules, and the potential hazards, with your kids—before you get out of the car and start exploring.

Since it's impossible to list all of the not-to-miss falls, here are five to whet your family's appetite:

Whitewater Falls With the upper fall measuring 411 feet and the lower fall at 285 feet, this scenic treasure is higher than Niagara Falls and is the tallest in the eastern U.S. An easy walk of less than a half mile round-trip offers a great view. *N.C. 281 near Cashiers. (828) 526-3765.*

Horsepasture River Falls Although this breathtaking series gives you some of the coolest waterfalls in the region, it's probably best explored by kids ages 5 and up. With the exception of Driftwood Falls, you've got a moderately challenging 1.5-mile

NORTH CAROLINA MOUNTAINS

Tweetsie Railroad ★★/$$$
This western-themed amusement park between Boone and Blowing Rock has been the place for down-home family fun for mountain guests and local folk since 1953. Your younger kids (soon-to-be-teens may find it a tad hokey) will get a bang out of Tweetsie, especially Number 12, the narrow-gauge, coal-fired steam locomotive that chugs around a three-mile loop, passing awesome scenery and encountering an unexpected ambush. Main Street is full of cowpokes, cancan girls, and toe-tappin' revues. Don't pass up a sample of the World Famous Tweetsie Railroad fudge at the General Store. It's the perfect thank-you gift for the friend who's feeding the pets back home—or for you. Carnival-type rides, an arcade, gold panning, and a petting zoo round out the good times here. Open May through October. *U.S. 321, Blowing Rock. (800) 526-5740; (828) 264-9061; www.tweetsie-railroad.com*

MUST-SEE Unto These Hills
FamilyFun ★★★★/$$
One of the nation's most popular and longest running outdoor performances (2000 was its 51st season) is *Unto These Hills*, on

hike to reach Umbrella Falls, the first of several beauties. Keep on trekking to the awesome and thunderously loud Rainbow Falls, a 200-footer that easily lives up to its name. Leave the Stairway Falls, the final wonder in the series, to the veteran adult explorer. *On N.C. 281 near Cashiers. (828) 526-3765.*

Dry Falls This beauty offers a truly special treat—a behind-the-scenes view of the majestic waterfall. You've got to work for it, though, with a one-mile trek through some moderately challenging terrain. Beware: depending on water levels, which change on a regular basis, you may get soaked. *On Hwy. 64 near Highlands. (828) 526-3765.*

Connestee Falls This twin-fall masterpiece, both cascading about 110 feet down, requires only a few steps to drink in its wonder. According to Indian lore, Princess Connestee leaped to her death over these falls when her English husband returned to his people. *On U.S. 276 near Brevard. (828) 885-2610.*

Sliding Rock If you're looking for a place to cool off after touring a waterfall or two, Sliding Rock is just the place, provided that you're older than 7. Here you can actually "ride" the waterfall down 60-foot slippery drop into a 55-degree, six-foot-deep natural pool. Lifeguards are on duty during the summer. Small fee for parking. *On U.S. 276 near Brevard. (828) 877-3265.*

stage in summer at the Mountainside Theater in the Oconaluftee Indian Village. The lively show brings to life the history, triumphs, and struggles of the Cherokee Indians from 1540 to the Trail of Tears in the late 1830s. Don't be surprised if your kids cheer, laugh, hum—maybe even cry—along with the cast of more than 130 actors and actresses (including some very talented youngsters) during the two-and-a-half-hour drama. Family favorites are likely to be scenes featuring the eagle dance, wedding ceremony, and Battle of Horseshoe Bend. **NOTE:** *Unto These Hills* is best experienced by children ages 6 and up. The darkness, gunshots, fire, and killing (including a firing squad) may frighten younger children. Showtime is around 8:30 P.M. (preshow around 8 P.M.), making it a rather late night. That said, it still gets a big thumbs-up in our book. Bug spray and sweatshirts will come in handy before the night is over. Tickets available by phone or at the box office on *Drama Rd. off U.S. 441 North, Cherokee. (704) 497-2111;* www.dnet/ ~cheratt

Western North Carolina Nature Center ★★★★/$

Not a zoo and more than a petting farm, the Nature Center gives you a chance to see some familiar creatures, like deer and goats, and some not-so-familiar ones, like cougars and black bears. One of the most fascinating and novel areas is the hands-on Nature Lab; here your kids may get a chance to pet a snake, see a brown recluse spider (one of the deadliest arachnids in the world), or look at a butterfly's wing under a microscope. The petting area is always a big hit. Other activities, such as puppet shows and cow milkings, happen throughout the day. Don't overlook the gift shop, which offers a selection of animal and insect toys at very reasonable prices. *75 Gashes Creek Rd., Asheville. (828) 298-5600;* http://wildwnc.org

Bunking Down

Bear Den Campground
★★/$

Here's the place to enjoy an outdoorsy type of lodging with conveniences of home (or at least a good motel) in fully equipped cabins. On-site you'll find a game room, lake swimming, fishing, paddleboats, plus everything you'll need for a rousing game of basketball, volleyball, or badminton. A trading post sells groceries, ice, and supplies. In addition to the creek-side cabins, Bear Den offers a handful of really rustic cabins and 144 campsites for tents and all types of RVs. **NOTE:** Remember, you'll be sleeping at an elevation of 3,000 feet, so you may need an extra sweater or blanket. Open April through October. *Located* directly off the Blue Ridge Parkway at milepost 324.8, Spruce Pine. (828) 765-2888; www.bear-den.com

Clear Creek Guest Ranch
★★★★/$$$$

Set in the Pisgah National Forest, this all-inclusive guest ranch features such western essentials as horses, hayrides, square dancing, and rodeos (it's a real taste of the Old West). The guest quarters are decorated in a rustic ranch style, complete with outside porches and rocking chairs. Meals, which are included in the rates, are served family style and feature lots of grandma's favorites. The kids will love the cowboys-and-Indians feel of the ranch, right down to the tepee. Kids' activities (on-site activities covered in room rate) include horseback riding (instruction is also available), nature hikes, fishing, hayrides, and even a trip to a local gem mine. Open April to Thanksgiving. *100 Clear Creek Drive, U.S. Hwy. 80 South, Burnsville. (800) 651-4510.*

Earthshine Mountain Lodge
★★★★/$$$$

Built on the site of a 100-year-old homestead, this is the ideal getaway for families who want to return to the basics—and we're not talking precomputer or television. Here, your family is transported back some 150 years, to the Appalachian frontier—a time when pressing cider, making candles, hiking, and trail blazing were the stuff of everyday life. Creature comforts aren't entirely absent, though: the property has 13 family units, each with private bath, and most with a neat *Little House on the Prairie*–style loft for your young farm hands; three meals a day are included in the room rate, as are all activities except horseback riding and wall climbing. Your kids get to sample a taste of those bygone days through the lodge's children's program, where families have a blast learning about all of the above, plus animal care, organic gardening, and the ancient games, dances, and ways of the Cherokees. (Kids under 6 must be accompanied by an adult.) Water games and a water slide, a visit to the barnyard to feed the animals, and story time around the campfire add to the fun. *Located about 11 miles from Brevard, off U.S. 64. (828) 862-4207;* www.earthshinemtnlodge.com

High Hampton Inn
★★★★/$$$-$$$$

If you're ready to splurge, this is the place. Reminiscent of a lodge in the

FamilyFun GAME

Word Stretch

Give your child a word challenge by asking her to make as many words as she can from the letters in a phrase such as "Are we there yet?" or "When will we be at the zoo?"

FamilyFun **VACATION GUIDE**

WHOOSH!

Western North Carolina offers some of the best winter snow skiing around, thanks to its snowmaking technology, the region's awesome terrain, and the ski professionals who aim to please—regardless of your skills. Many of the resorts here have expanded their lineup to include snowboarding, snow tubing, and ice skating as fun winter activities.

	PEAK	SLOPES	LIFTS	VERTICAL DROP	SKI ACRES
Appalachian Ski Mountain	4,000 feet	9, including 2 beginner	9	365 feet	22

Special features: Ice-skating rink, nursery, French Swiss ski college; smaller operation lends itself to family feeling. Open mid-November to mid-March. *940 Ski Mountain Rd., Blowing Rock. (800) 322-2373.*

Cataloochee Ski Area	5,400 feet	10, 25% beginner	4	740 feet	15

Special features: first ski resort in North Carolina (1961); snowboarding park; kids ski free program. Open mid-November to mid-March. *1080 Ski Lodge Rd., Maggie Valley. (800) 768-0285; (828) 926-0285.*

Hawksnest	4,819 feet	13, 30% beginner	5	669 feet	42

Special features: Night Hawk skiing until 2 A.M. (weekends), snowboarding park, tubing park. Open mid-November to mid-March. *2058 Skyland Dr., Banner Elk. (888) 429-5763; (828) 963-6561.*

Ski Beech	5,506 feet	15, 30% beginner	10	830 feet	100

Special features: highest ski resort in eastern North America; snowboarding section, snowtubing run; ice-skating rink; child-care services. Open mid-November to mid-March. *1007 Beech Mountain Pkwy., Beech Mountain (near Banner Elk). (800) 438-2093; (828) 387-2011; www.skibeech.com*

Sugar Mountain	5,300 feet	20, 40% beginner	8	1,200 feet	115

Special features: snowboarding park; 700-foot snowtubing run, child-care services. Open mid-November through March. *1009 Sugar Mountain Dr., Banner Elk. (800) 784-2768; (828) 898-4521; www.skisugar.com*

Wolf Laurel	4,650 feet	15, 3 beginner	2	700	54

Special features: snowboarding park, twin snowtubing runs, popular with snowboarders; on-site lodging. Open Thanksgiving to mid-March. *Rte. 3, Mars Hill. (800) 817-4111; (828) 689-4111; www.wolflaurel.com*

Catskill Mountains (only this one is in the small, quaint town of Cashiers), this all-inclusive resort is perfect for a family getaway. The inn has 117 rooms and a selection of cottages. The service here will make you feel like a millionaire, the surroundings are comfortably rustic, not stuffy. The property is only a few steps from a golf course, practice range, tennis courts, lake, children's play area, and the start of several kid-friendly walking trails. The inn also hosts a series of summer programs (fee) for children ages 2 to 11; there's a special gathering area for teens. Kids can try arts and crafts, donkey-cart rides, movies, swimming, and a lot more. And, while the rates are a bit pricey, they do include all three meals and afternoon tea. Another bonus: there is no tipping. *1525 Hwy. 107, Cashiers. (800) 334-2551;* www.hamptoninn.com

Great Smokies Holiday Inn SunSpree Resort ★★/$-$$

With an indoor soccer center right on the property, expect your soccer fanatics to shout *"goal!"* when you check in to this chain property that's only a quick five minutes from downtown Asheville. A daytime and evening children's program (fee) offers your kids games, arts and crafts, and sports, with dinner thrown in for a couple of bucks on Friday and Saturday nights. Add to those kid-friendly amenities two outdoor pools, tennis, and golf, all on-site, and you can't go wrong. *1 Holiday Inn Dr., Asheville. (800) 733-3211; (828) 254-3211;* www.sunspree.com

Grove Park Inn Resort & Spa
★★★★/$$-$$$

Family friendly and also refined and elegant, this place makes everyone feel at home. Expect your kids to be in awe over the resort's mammoth granite boulders, massive fireplaces, portrait and celebrity galleries (including Mickey and Minnie), and, of course, Major Bear—the property's resident mascot. Guest rooms are classically decorated, and many have incredible views of the mountain, golf course, or city. The children's programs seem to be non-stop daily (seasonal, fee), plus special event weekends, including such awesome activities as playground boot camp and fitness force. *290 Macon Ave., Asheville. (800) 438-0050; (828) 252-2711.*

Hidden Valley Campground and Waterpark
★★★/$

Although tons of cool excursions are in the area (gem mines, trails, caverns), don't be surprised if your children are content to play here all day. Hidden Valley's kid-friendly features include a three-loop water slide, gigantic swimming pool, fishing lake, paddleboats and canoes, miniature golf course, and game room. (Although a few of these activities carry a nominal fee, you won't blow the vacation budget at this campground.) Parents will appreciate the handy general store, snack bar, and shaded tent sites with grill, picnic table, and fire ring. Pull-through sites—some of which are lakefront—come with a picnic table and fire ring, but no grill. Open April through October. *1210 Deacon Dr., Marion. (828) 652-7208.*

Holiday Inn Cherokee
★★/$

This friendly property is just minutes away from Cherokee's mustsee Oconaluftee Indian Village and other nearby places to visit. The large outdoor and indoor pools, playground, and game room give it definite kid appeal, and the relatively low rates score high with the grown-ups who are paying the tab. Another plus: if you're going to see the popular outdoor drama *Unto These Hills*, the hotel provides free shuttle service for guests. *Hwy. 19 South, Cherokee. (828) 497-9181; www.hicherokee.com*

Mount Valley Lodge ★/$
Near the gateway to the Great Smoky Mountains National Park and Ghost Town in the Sky is this small motor lodge that offers simple rooms at incredibly low rates. Mount Valley's game room, miniature-golf course, and outdoor pool offer ample amusement for the entire family before turning in for the night. *2550 Soco Rd. U.S. Hwy. 19, Maggie Valley. (800) 942-0966; (828) 926-9244.*

Switzerland Inn
★★★/$-$$

Resembling a tiny Alpine village, this inn offers families a perfect respite from the city, plus a view that will knock your socks off. Choose from a variety of comfortable lodgings, including a cool A-frame with a sleeping loft. Although the inn's lobby is large, its inviting fireplace, couches, and game tables give it a warm, cozy feeling. An outdoor pool, delicious complimentary breakfast buffet, some neat shops nearby, and an outgoing staff make this perfect for the whole family. Open May through October. *Located midway between Asheville and Blowing Rock, Milepost 334 on the Blue Ridge Pkwy., Little Switzerland. (800) 654-4026; (828) 765-2153.*

GOOD EATS

Cheeseburger in Paradise
★/$

As its name implies, cheeseburgers are the specialty of the house at this supercasual restaurant in Blowing Rock. (In fact, you can order the eye-popping one-pounder—the largest burger this side of anywhere.) Family favorites include the Big

Dawg (quarter-pound hot dog) and the "almost world-famous wild wings" (with heat variances from mild to more-than-fiery). For a view of the quaint shopping area, request an upstairs porchside table. *U.S. 221 and Main St., Blowing Rock. (828) 295-4858.*

Dan'l Boone Inn Restaurant
★★/$-$$

Okay, so Daniel didn't really eat here. He did, however, pass through the area in 1773 while moving his family to Kentucky. The food—a hearty breakfast (weekends only) of scrambled eggs, sausage, and stewed apples, or lip-smacking good fried chicken or country-fried steak with all the fixings for lunch or dinner—is served up family style; no one leaves this popular restaurant hungry. *130 Hardin St., Boone. (828) 264-8657.*

J. Arthur's
★★★★/$$-$$$

If you're ready to splurge and want something upscale yet casual, this is the place. Here, kids are made to feel especially welcome—from the sign out front and their very own kids' corner in the lobby to an extensive children's menu and courteous waitstaff. This restaurant knows how to cater to families in style. Chicken tenders with all the trimmings are the hands-down favorite, but your hungry preteens may want to order the prime rib. If you have a youngster with a more sophisticated palate, let him or her sample the gorgonzola salad. Our tasters loved it. *Hwy. 19/Soco Rd., Maggie Valley. (828) 926-1817.*

La Paz
★★★★/$

Large, loud, and friendly, this Mexican restaurant located in the Biltmore Village shopping area will take your not-yet-gourmets beyond grilled cheese. The Little Chile Pepper menu offers mucho for the younger set. Tacos, nachos, Mexican pizza, or the "coyote corn dog" are surefire favorites. Spices are mild; portions are huge. Multiple locations. *10 Biltmore Plaza, Asheville. (828) 277-8779.*

Maggie Valley Restaurant
★★/$

In business since 1952, this no-frills diner serves up first-rate, down-home southern specialties like meat loaf and fried golden brown chicken fingers. If your nearly-teens overslept, don't worry: Breakfast, adolescent-style (buttermilk biscuits and gravy, perhaps?), is served all day here. *2804 Soco Rd./Hwy. 19, Maggie Valley. (828) 926-0425;* www.mtvalleylodge.com

Moose Café
★★★★/$

Right on the grounds of the bustling Western North Carolina Farmer's Market, this southern darling serves up some of the freshest, most scrumptious dishes in the South (north, east, or west). Stroll the bustling market, then grab a table at the Moose and order a breakfast that even your most finicky youngster will love (just try passing up the mouthwatering biscuits and apple butter). Although there is a children's menu—including a vegetable platter that even our test kids adored—the fried chicken, meat loaf, and pork chops are real showstoppers for lunch or dinner. Work off your meal with a visit to the Biltmore Estate (see page 370)—it's right next door. *570 Brevard Rd., Asheville. (828) 255-0920.*

Rocky's Grill and Soda Shop
★★★/$

For parents, lunch at Rocky's is like a step back to the early days of rock 'n' roll—hence the name. For kids, this downtown Brevard eatery is a cool place to check out the relic of a juke box, keep a hula hoop swinging, and wolf down a little mountain burger and chips. For dessert, the thick chocolate shake or a scoop of super-duper (swirls of yellow, blue, and pink vanilla ice cream) may be just the right finish for both young and less young diners. *36 S. Broad St., Brevard. (828) 877-5375.*

Spear's BBQ and Grill
★★★/$$

Whether you're here for the Friday or Saturday night buffet, the smoked-on-premises BBQ, or the fried shrimp platter on the kids' menu, you'll love this mountain eatery. Finish off the meal with a big bowl of blackberry cobbler and scoop of ice cream—you'll need at least two people to finish it. *U.S. 221 North and NC 183, Linville Falls. (828) 765-2658.*

Sunset Café
★★/$

Frankfurter fanatics will be in their element when they chow down on the "Dogzilla" or "Super Dog" at this lunch-stand-style restaurant in the heart of Blowing Rock's quaint shopping district. The café also serves a variety of really good breakfast sandwiches and bagels. There's only a table or two for seating; a better idea is to take your food and head across the street to Memorial Park, where you'll find benches and picnic tables. *1117 Main St., Blowing Rock. (828) 295-9326.*

FamilyFun GAME

Raindrop Race

On a rainy day, each player traces the course of a raindrop down the car window. The first drop to reach the bottom wins.

Tee Pee Restaurant
★/$-$$
Down the street from the Oconaluftee Indian Village, this popular Cherokee mainstay serves French toast sticks and bacon for breakfast and chicken strips with crinkle fries from the kids' menu for lunch or dinner. Lunch and evening buffets offer special pricing for children, too. *Hwy. 441 North, Cherokee. (828) 497-4610 or (828) 497-6025.*

SOUVENIR HUNTING

Dancing Bear Toys
This Asheville toy store gives new meaning to the term hands-on with its many demos, play tables, even a dress-up section where kids (adults, too) have been spotted trying on the boas, froufrou skirts, and pirate hats. Kid-friendly musicians, authors, and naturalists from the area are on hand every once in a while to share their talents with young shoppers. Multiple locations. *144 Tunnel Rd., Asheville. (828) 255-8697;* www.dbeartoys.com

Mast General Store
Let your kids roam around the old-fashioned candy department at this ancient (opened for business in 1883) general store. Wax bottles, Necco wafers, root beer barrels, and Boston baked beans are just a sampling from the 500-plus supply of sweet treats. Toys, outdoor apparel, housewares, too. Multiple locations. *Hwy. 194, Valley Crucis. (828) 963-6511;* www.mastgeneralstore.com

Once Upon a Time
Biltmore Village is home to this wonderful children's shop, which features really cool specialty toys, books, and clothing. Along with the staples, look for unusual and stimulating products like car-crazed Rush Hour, create-your-own-tune Music Blocks, and the out-of-the-box Anti-Coloring Book. Clothes are casual and upscale, with a few dress-up ensembles for that special occasion. *7 All Souls Crescent, Asheville. (828) 274-8788.*

Oz
This tiny shop is a jam-packed wonderland full of old-fashioned windup toys, Wizard of Oz memorabilia, and even some unusual metal lunch boxes and purses. A large inventory of metal cars, trucks, and specialty mobiles delight all vehicle buffs. *1077-1 Main St., Blowing Rock. (828) 295-0770.*

Qualla Arts and Crafts Mutual
Indian-owned, this huge craft cooperative sells wonderful baskets, pots, masks, jewelry, and beadwork, much of it made locally. The certificate of authenticity tells you you're getting the real thing. Located at the entrance to the Oconaluftee Indian Village. *Hwy. 441, Cherokee. (828) 497-3103.*

RIDING THE RAPIDS

Most white-knuckle seekers will agree that few if any thrills dreamed up by people come close to matching the heart-pounding exhilaration of white-water rafting. And there are no better places to test the waters than on several of the waterways that run through Western North Carolina. The bolder, more experienced rafting family may want to try out the Nantahala or French Broad Rivers (both are class II–III rapids), while novice families may be more comfortable on the Tuckaseigee River (class I–II rapids). Although advanced rafters might rent the equipment and go on their own, most will want to link up with an outfitter that sends a trained guide within a raft or two of yours.

Here's is a sampling of well-established, seasonal outfitters who all promise a memorable ride for the entire family:

Adventurous Fast Rivers Rafting ($$) In business since 1979, Fast Rivers offers a boatload of exciting rafting options on the Nantahala River, about 10 miles outside of Bryson City. Guide-assisted trips range from a full river excursion (about 3.5 hours) to a "taste of the river" outing (about 1 hour). All participants must weigh 60 pounds or more. Open March through October. *14690 Nantahala River, U.S. 19 West, Bryson City. (800) 438-7238; (828) 488-2386.*

Blue Ridge Outing Company ($$$-$$$$) If your kids aren't quite old enough for the raging waters, try this company that caters to the young family. Minimum age is 4. Guide-assisted trips last about three hours on the Tuckaseigee—a kinder, calmer river that still serves up a thrill or two when you least expect it. This outfitter, who's been around since 1988, even offers free storytelling a couple of mornings a week in the summer. Open mid-May through mid-September. *Hwy. 74, between Bryson City and Sylva. (800) 572-3510; (828) 586-3510.*

Nantahala Outdoor Center ($$-$$$$+) In business since 1972, this veteran rafting business offers trips on the Nantahala and French Broad Rivers—plus a handful of other waterways outside of North Carolina. (The French Broad is about 25 miles north of Asheville and runs through the Pisgah National Forest.) Guide-assisted half-day (with/without lunch) and full-day (with lunch) adventures feature some real oh-my-goshers along the way. Minimum age: 8. This outfitter's guide-assisted ride on the Nantahala is a thrill seeker's paradise and lasts about 3.5 hours. All participants must weigh 60 pounds or more. Nantahala season: March through October; French Broad season: April through October. *Call for directions. (800) 232-7238; (828) 488-6900;* www.noc.com

Southern Waterways ($$-$$$) It's one thing to tour the Biltmore on foot, but why not kick it up a notch and experience it by water? In business since 1992, Southern Waterways offers a number of packages, including a popular seven-mile float trip through The Biltmore and nearby environs on a very tame section of the French Broad River. **NOTE:** This isn't a rapids ride, but more like a lazy three-hour float in a canoe, raft, or kayak with some small waves that even the very young can safely enjoy. The only restriction is that all participants must weigh at least 35 pounds. Open April through October. *521 Amboy Rd., Asheville. (800) 849-1970; (828) 232-1970.*

Wildwater LTD—($$$$) Entering the white-water rafting arena in 1988, this friendly operator not only offers an exciting experience on the Nantahala like others in the area (plus a few out-of-state rafting excursions), it kicks it up a notch with an all-day raft and rail excursion with the Great Smoky Mountains Railway. The fun begins with a two-hour train ride through the Smokies (including lunch onboard), and then it's into the river for a guide-assisted adventure on the Nantahala—about seven hours. All participants must weigh at least 60 pounds; it's a long trip for younger kids anyway. Open April through October. *Call for directions. (800) 451-9972; (828) 488-2384.*

Index

A

accommodations (bunking down), 24–29
B&Bs (bed-and-breakfasts), 25
campgrounds, 26
condos, 25–26
cottages, 25–26
farm stays, 25
Florida
  Florida Keys and the Everglades, 153–157
  the Northeast, 50–52
  Orlando and the Space Coast, 65–68
  Sea World Orlando, 65–68
  South Florida, 137–141
  Southwest Florida, 164–165
  Tallahassee and the Florida Panhandle, 191–193
  Universal Orlando, 65–68
  Walt Disney World, 65–68
  the West Coast, 175–177
Georgia
  Augusta and Middle Georgia, 208–209
  Callaway Gardens and Columbus, 235–237
  greater Atlanta, 251–252
  North Georgia, 261–262
  Savannah and Coastal Georgia, 221–224
hostels (for the family), 26
hotels, 24
inns, 25
lodges, 24
motels, 24
North Carolina
  the Coast, 341–344
  the Heartland, 361–362
  the Mountains, 380–381
prebooking information, 23, 25, 27, 35
price rating guide ($) for, 7
resorts, 27
South Carolina
  Charleston area, 274–277
  Columbia area, 284–285
  Low Country, 309–311
  Myrtle Beach, 291–292
  Santee Cooper Country, 300–301
  Up Country, 320–321
using the Web for, 35, 37
Adventure Cove Family Fun Center (Hilton Head, S.C.), 307
Adventure Landing Daytona (Daytona Beach, Fla.), 46
Adventureland's Pirates of the Caribbean (WDW Resort, Orlando, Fla.), 100
Adventures Unlimited Outdoor Center (north of Milton, Fla), 188–189
Africa-Kilimanjaro Safari (WDW Resort, Orlando, Fla.), 119
Ah-Tah-Thi-Ki Museum (between Naples and Ft. Lauderdale, Fla.), 146–148
air travel, 16, 17
  with children
    car seats for safety, 176
    checklist, 17
    games/special activities, 203, 236, 317
    reservations on the Web, 35–36
Alligator Adventure (Myrtle Beach, S.C.), 288–289
Alpine Adventure, An (Helen, Ga.), 259, 260
Amazing Adventures of Spider-Man, The (Universal Studios, Orlando, Fla.), 91
Amelia Island's Main Beach (Fernandina Beach, Fla.), 49
American Adventures (Marietta, Ga.), 246–247
Appalachian Outfitters (Dahlonega, Ga.), 257
Atlanta (greater Atlanta), 241–253
accommodations, 251–252
background information, 241–242
cultural adventures, 242–246
day trips: Lanier Islands and Beach Park, 246–247
  Stone Mountain Park Crossroads, 250–251
"just for fun" attractions, 246–250
map, 242
"must-see" list, 241
restaurants, 252–253
souvenir hunting, 253
audio books (aid to travel), 18, 21
Augusta and Middle Georgia, 199–211
accommodations, 208–209
background information, 199–200
cultural adventures, 200–206
day trip: Fleet River Outdoor Center, 204–205
"just for fun" attractions, 206–208
map, 200
"must-see" list, 199
restaurants, 209–211
souvenir hunting, 211

B

B&Bs (bed-and-breakfasts), 25
BabyLand General Hospital (Cleveland, Ga.), 257–258
Back to the Future: The Ride (Universal Studios, Orlando, Fla.),87
Bahia Honda State Park (Bahia Honda Key, Fla.), 148–149
Battleship *North Carolina* (Wilmington, N.C.), 328–330
Billy Swamp Safari (between Naples and Ft. Lauderdale, Fla.), 146–148
Biltmore Estate (Asheville, N.C.), 370–371
Bowmans Beach (Southwest Fla.), 161–162
Brookgreen Gardens (Murrells Inlet, S.C.), 290–291
Busch Gardens Tampa Bay (Tampa, Fla.), 171, 180–183
restaurants, 183
roller coasters and other rides, 180–182
shopping, 183
bus travel, 21–22

390

INDEX

C

Callaway Gardens and Columbus, Georgia, 229–239
accommodations, 235–237
background information, 229–230
Callaway Gardens (Pine Mountain, Ga.), 231, 233–234
cultural adventures, 230–231
"just for fun" attractions, 231–233
map, 230
"must-see" list, 229
restaurants, 237–238
souvenir hunting, 238–239
Camp Minnie-Mickey: Festival of the Lion King (WDW Resort, Orlando, Fla.), 118
campgrounds/camping, 26–27
campcrafts, 363
resources for tent and RV camping, 38–39
canoe/kayak trips (Adventures Unlimited Outdoor Center, Fla.), 188–189
Canoe Outfitters of Florida, canoe trip with, 133
Cape Fear Museum (Wilmington, N.C.), 330–331
Cape Hatteras Lighthouse (Nags Head, N.C.), 334
Cape Romain Wildlife Refuge (Mt. Pleasant, S.C.), 272
Captain Nemo's Pirate Cruise (Clearwater Beach, Fla.), 171–172
car travel, 16–19
with children
audio books, 18, 21
games/special activities, 20, 38, 39, 65, 93, 111, 136, 150, 162, 179, 210, 221, 225, 237, 239, 244, 257, 277, 302, 312, 336, 345, 361, 381, 386
road map/road atlases, 16, 39
road trip survival kit, 19
travel insurance, 28
See also rental car; RVs
Caribbean Gardens (Naples, Fla.), 162, 169
Carolina Safari (N. Myrtle Beach, S.C.), 289
Cat in the Hat, The (Universal Studios, Fla.), 94
Charlemagne's Kingdom (Helen, Ga.), 258
Charleston (S.C.) area, 269–279
accommodations, 274–277
background information, 269–270
cultural adventures, 270–271
day trip: Fort Sumter and Patriot's Point Museum (Civil War history), 276–277
"just for fun" attractions, 271–274
map, 270
"must-see" list, 269
picnic preparation sources, 271
restaurants, 277–279
souvenir hunting, 279
Charleston IMAX Theatre (Charleston, S.C.), 270
children
air travel with (checklist), 17
audio books, 18, 21
car seats for safety, 176
car travel—games/special activities, 20, 38, 39, 65, 93, 111, 136, 150, 162, 179, 210, 221, 225, 237, 239, 244, 257, 277, 302, 312, 336, 345, 361, 381, 386
creating a travel scrapbook, 237
designing special map, 313
dining with
games to play while waiting, 54, 101, 136
solving the "picky eater" problem, 24
games/special activities, 203, 236, 317
healthy snacks for the road, 45, 105, 225, 249, 352, 373
keeping trip journal, 339
packing checklist and, 32
planning the trip with, 12–13, 14, 15, 333
preventing motion sickness, 18
travel kit for, 19, 27
Chimney Rock (Chimney Rock, N.C.), 372–373
Cirque du Soleil (WDW, Orlando, Fla.), 122
clothing, packing checklist, 32
Coastal North Carolina, 327–347
accommodations, 341–344
background information, 327–328
cultural adventures, 328–335
day trip: Cape Hatteras and Outer Banks lighthouses, 334–335, 340–341
"just for fun" attractions, 335–341
map, 328
"must-see" list, 327
restaurants, 344–346
souvenir hunting, 347
Columbia (S.C.) area, 281–285
accommodations, 284–285
background information, 281–282
cultural adventures, 282
"just for fun" attractions, 283–284
map, 282
"must-see" list, 281
restaurants, 285
souvenir hunting, 285
Columbus, Georgia. *See* Callaway Gardens and Columbus, Georgia
condos, 25–26
Congaree Swamp National Monument (Hopkins, S.C.), 283
Coquina Beach (Outer Banks, N.C.), 336–337
coral reefs, 53, 81
cottages, 25–26
Crossroads at Stone Mountain Park (Stone Mountain, Ga.), 250–251
Cypress Gardens (Moncks Corner, S.C.), 296–297
Cypress Gardens (Winterhaven, Fla.), 173, 177
waterskiing at, 177

D

Darlington Raceway (Darlington, S.C.), 298–299
Daytona USA (Daytona Beach, Fla.), 47
DeLeon Springs State Recreation Area (near Orlando, Fla.), 64
Diamond Shoals Family Fun Park (Kill Devil Hills, N.C.), 337
Discovery Cove (Orlando, Fla.), 80

391

INDEX

Discovery Place (Charlotte, N.C.), 356–357
Disney-MGM Studios (WDW Resort, Orlando, Fla.), 105–110
  restaurants and snack spots, 107, 109
  shopping, 109–110
Disney Quest (WDW Resort, Orlando, Fla.), 122
Disney's Animal Kingdom (WDW Resort, Orlando, Fla.), 117–121
  restaurants and snack spots, 120–121
  shopping, 121
Disney's Vero Beach Resort (Vero Beach, Fla.), 139
Dixie Stampede Dinner and Show (N. Myrtle Beach, S.C.), 289

E

Edison Ford Winter Estates (Ft. Myers), 161
Edisto Island Serpentarium (Edisto Island, S.C.), 307–308
Emerald Points Water Park (Greensboro, N.C.), 357–359
Epcot (WDW Resort, Orlando, Fla.), 110–117
  restaurants and snack spots, 115–117
  shopping, 117
E.T. Adventures (Universal Studios, Orlando, Fla.), 88
Everglades National Park (Florida City, Fla.), 149–151
Exploris (Raleigh, N.C.), 350–351

F

family hostels, 26
family travel Website, 34
farm stays, 25
FASTPASS (easy access to Disney attractions), 98
F. D. Roosevelt State Park (Pine Mountain, Ga.), 232
fireworks displays (WDW Resort, Orlando, Fla.), 122
first-aid kit, 33
Fisheagle Adventure Tours (Santee, S.C.), 297
Flint River Outdoor Center (west of Macon, Ga.), 204–205, 206

Florida
  background information, 40–41
  price guide ($) to attractions, accommodations, and restaurants, 41
  ratings guide (*) to attractions, 41
  See also Florida Keys and the Everglades; Northeast Florida; Orlando and the Space Coast; SeaWorld Orlando; South Florida; Southwest Florida; Tallahassee and the Panhandle; Universal Orlando; Walt Disney World Resort; West Coast of Florida
Florida Keys and the Everglades, 145–157
  accommodations, 153–155
  background information, 145–146
  cultural adventures, 146–148
  "just for fun" attractions, 148–155
  map, 146
  "must-see" list, 145
  restaurants, 155–157
  souvenir hunting, 157
Florida Panhandle. *See* Tallahassee and the Florida Panhandle
Fontana Village (Fontana Dam, N.C.), 373, 374–375
food
  authentic "Florida cuisine," 155
  cooking breakfast and/or lunch, 31
  healthy snacks for the road, 45, 105, 225, 249, 352, 373
  picnic preparations, sources for (Charleston, S.C.), 271
  See also restaurants
Fort Clinch State Park (Fernandina Beach, Fla.), 47–48
Fort Discovery's National Science Center (Augusta, Ga.), 201–202
Fort Pulaski (Savannah, Ga.), 215
Fort Sumter (Charleston, S.C.), 276–277
Francis Beidler Forest in Four Holes Swamp (Harleyville, S.C.), 297–298

Frankie's Fun Park (Columbia, S.C.), 283
Frisco Native American Museum (Frisco, N.C.), 334–335
Fun Spot Action Park (Orlando, Fla.), 60–61

G

games/special activities
  air travel and, 203, 236, 317
  car travel and, 20, 38, 39, 65, 93, 111, 136, 150, 162, 179, 210, 221, 225, 237, 239, 244, 257, 277, 302, 312, 336, 345, 361, 381, 386
  in restaurants, 54, 101, 130
Georgia
  background information, 196–197
  price guide ($) to attractions, accommodations, and restaurants, 197
  ratings guide (*) to attractions, 197
  See also Augusta and Middle Georgia; Callaway Gardens and Columbus; Greater Atlanta; North Georgia; Savannah and Coastal Georgia
Georgia Agrirama (Tifton, Ga.), 202–203
Georgia Sports Hall of Fame (Macon, Ga.), 203
Georgia's Stone Mountain Park (Stone Mountain, Ga.), 249
Crossroads at Stone Mountain, 250–251
Grandfather Mountain (Linville, N.C.), 375–376
Grandon Park (Key Biscayne, Fla.), 132–133
Greater Atlanta. *See* Atlanta (greater Atlanta)
Great Explorations (St. Petersburg, Fla.), 170
Great Smoky Mountains National Park (Cherokee, N.C.), 476
Green Meadows Petting Farm (Kissimmee, Fla.), 61–62
Greensboro Children's Museum (Greensboro, N.C.), 351–352
Greenville Zoo (Greenville, S.C.), 317–318
guided tours, 29

INDEX

Gulf World (Panama City, Fla.), 189
Gullah language of South Carolina Low Country, 307

H

Harbor Branch Oceanographic Institution (Ft. Pierce, Fla.), 138–139
Health Adventure, The (Asheville, N.C.), 372
Heartland of North Carolina, 349–367
  accommodations, 361–362
  background information, 349–350
  cultural adventures, 349–355
  day trip: Reed Gold Mine and North Carolina Zoological Park, 356
  "just for fun" attractions, 356–360
  map, 350
  "must-see" list, 349
  pottery center of the state (Seagrove), 365
  restaurants, 362–366
  souvenir hunting, 366–367
Hollywild Animal Park (Wellford, S.C.), 318–319
hostels for the family, 26
hotels, 24, 25
  prebooking information, 23, 25, 27, 35
  working with consolidators, 35
  See also accommodations

I

IGFA Fishing Hall of Fame and Museum (Dania Beach, Fla.), 128–129
Incredible Hulk Coaster (Universal Orlando, Fla.), 91
inns, 25
insurance, travel, 28
Islands of Adventure (Universal Orlando, Fla.), 90–95
  roller coaster rides, 125

J

Jacksonville Zoo (Jacksonville, Fla.), 48–49
J. N. "Ding" Darling National Wildlife Refuge (Sanibel, Fla.), 163
Jockey's Ridge State Park (Nags Head, N.C.), 338–339
John D. MacArthur Beach State Park (North Palm Beach, Fla.), 133–134
John Pennekamp Coral Reef State (Key Largo, Fla.), 151
Journey to Atlantis (SeaWorld Orlando, Fla.), 78–79
Jurassic Park River Adventure (Universal Orlando, Fla.), 92–93

K

Kennedy Space Center Visitor Complex (Merritt Island, Fla.), 58–59
Key West's Shipwreck Historeum (Key West, Fla.), 148
Kid City (Tampa, Fla.), 170–171
King Richard's Medieval Family Fun Park (Naples, Fla.), 163–164
Kraken (SeaWorld Orlando, Fla.), 79

L

Lake Lanier Islands Beach and Water Park (outside Atlanta, Ga.), 246–247, 249
Lexahatchee River, canoe trip on (Palm Beach area, Fla.), 133
lighthouses on the Outer Banks (coastal N.C.), 340–341
Linville Caverns (Marion, N.C.), 376–377
Lion Country Safari (Lexahatchee, Fla.), 134
lodges, 24
Lori Wilson Park (Cocoa Beach, Fla.), 62
Lost Colony, The (Roanoke Island, N.C.), 332

M

Magic Kingdom (WDW Resort, Orlando, Fla.), 99–105
  restaurants and snack spots, 103–104
  roller coaster rides, 124
  shopping, 104–105
  transportation, 99
Magnolia Plantation and Gardens (Charleston, S.C.), 273
map(s)
Florida
  Florida Keys and the Everglades, 146
  the Northeast, 44
  Orlando and the Space Coast, 58
  SeaWorld Orlando and Discovery Cove, 76
  South Florida, 128
  Southwest Florida, 160
  Tallahassee and the Florida Panhandle, 186
  Universal Orlando, 84
  Walt Disney World Resort, 98
  West Coast, 170
Georgia
  Augusta and Middle Georgia, 200
  Callaway Gardens and Columbus, 230
  greater Atlanta, 242
  North Georgia, 256
  Savannah and Coastal Georgia, 212
North Carolina
  the Coast, 328
  the Heartland, 350
  the Mountains, 370
South Carolina
  Charleston area, 270
  Columbia area, 282
  Low Country, 306
  Myrtle Beach, 288
  Santee Cooper Country, 296
  Up Country, 316
Marinelife Center (Juno Beach, Fla.), 133
Martin Luther King, Jr., National Historic Site (Atlanta, Ga.), 243
medical matters
  first-aid kit, 33
  preventing motion sickness, 18
Men in Black Alien Attack (Universal Studios, Orlando, Fla.), 87–88
Miami Seaquarium (Miami, Fla.), 135
Mote Marine Aquarium (City Island, Fla.), 174
motels, 24, 25
motion sickness, preventing, 18
Museum of Arts and Sciences (Macon, Ga.), 204–205
Museum of Discovery and Science (Fort Lauderdale, Fla.), 130–131

393

INDEX

Museum of Life and Science (Durham, N.C.), 352–353
Museum of Science & History (Jacksonville, Fla.), 45
Myrtle Beach, SC, 287–293
  accommodations, 291–292
  background information, 287
  cultural adventures, 288
  "just for fun" attractions, 288–291
  map, 288
  "must-see" list, 287
  restaurants, 292–293
  souvenir hunting, 293
Myrtle Beach Pavilion Amusement Park (Myrtle Beach, S.C.), 290–291

N

National Museum of Naval Aviation (Pensacola, Fla.), 187–188
National Presidents Hall of Fame (Clermont, Fla.), 60–61
NMPA Stock Car Hall of Fame/Joe Weatherly Museum (Darlington, S.C.), 298–299
North Carolina
  background information, 324–325
  price guide ($) for attractions, hotels, and restaurants, 325
  ratings guide (*) to attractions, 325
  See also Coastal North Carolina; Heartland of North Carolina; North Carolina Mountains
North Carolina Aquarium—Roanoke Island (Manteo, N.C.), 333–334
North Carolina Mountains, 369–389
  accommodations, 389–384
  background information, 369–370
  cultural adventures, 370–372
  day trip: waterfall country, 378–379
  "just for fun" attractions, 372–380
  map, 370
  "must-see" list, 369
  restaurants, 384–387

skiing resorts (and other winter activities), 382
  souvenir hunting, 387
  white-water rafting, 388–389
North Carolina Museum of Natural Science (Raleigh, N.C.), 353
North Carolina Pottery Center (Seagrove, N.C.), 365
North Carolina Zoological Park (Asheboro, N.C.), 356–357, 359
North Georgia, 255–265
  accommodations, 261–262
  background information, 255–256
  cultural adventures, 256–257
  "just for fun" attractions, 257–261
  map, 256
  "must-see" list, 255
  restaurants, 262–264
  souvenir hunting, 264
  vocabulary of the natives, 265
Northeast Florida, 43–55
  accommodations, 50–52
  background information, 43–44
  cultural adventures, 44–46
  "just for fun" attractions, 46–50
  map, 44
  "must-see" lists, 43
  restaurants, 52–54
  souvenir hunting, 55

O

Oconaluftee Indian Village (Cherokee, N.C.), 377
"off-season" travel, 28–29
Okaloosa Pier (Ft. Walton Beach, Fla.), 190
Okefenokee Swamp Park (Waycross, Ga.), 216–217, 219
Old Salem (Winston-Salem, N.C.), 353–354
Old Santee Canal Park (Moncks Corner, S.C.), 299
One Fish, Two Fish, Red Fish, Blue Fish (Universal Orlando, Fla.), 94
Online Travel (Perkins), 34
Orlando and the Space Coast, 57–71
  accommodations, 65–68
  background information, 57–58

cultural adventures, 58–59
  day trips: DeLeon Springs State Recreation Area, 64
  National Presidents Hall of Fame (Clermont, Fla.), 60–61
  "just for fun" attractions, 60–64
  map, 58
  "must-see" list, 57
  restaurants, 68–71
  souvenir hunting, 71
Orlando's Theme parks
  background information, 72–73
  price guide ($) for attractions, accommodations, and restaurants, 73
  ratings guide (*) for attractions, 73
  See also Discovery Cove; SeaWorld Orlando; Universal Orlando; Walt Disney World Resort
Outer Banks lighthouses (coastal N.C.), 340–341

P

packing
  checklist, 32
  helping the children with, 358
Palm Beach, Fla., outdoor attractions, 133
parades (WDW Resort, Orlando, Fla.), 121–122
Paramount's Carowinds Theme Park (Charlotte, N.C.), 359
Patriot's Point Naval and Maritime Museum (Mt. Pleasant, S.C.), 277
pets, traveling with, 48
Pets Ahoy (SeaWorld Orlando, Fla.), 79
Piccolo Spoleto (Charleston, S.C.), 274
picnics, sources for picnic preparation (Charleston, S.C.), 271
planning the trip
  getting there
    air travel, 16, 17
    by bus, 21–22
    by car, 16–19
    by rental car, 22–23
    by RV, 20–21
    by train, 19–20
  involving the children in, 12–13, 14, 15, 333

INDEX

money-saving tips, 12, 19, 28–31
"off-season" travel, 28–29
package deals, 29–30
ordering travel essentials by mail, 153
packing, checklist, 32
assisting the children, 358
pets, traveling with, 46
preparing the itinerary, 13–15
price guide ($) for attractions, accommodations, and restaurants, 7
rating guide (*) for attractions, 7
researching your destination, 14
theme-park outing dos and don'ts, 108
using city and state tourism boards, 333
using the Web, 12, 31–37
weather, 13, 18, 112
pottery center of North Carolina (Seagrove, N.C.), 365

R

rafting, white-water, for the family (North Carolina mountains), 388–389
Reed Gold Mine State Historic Site (Midland, N.C.), 356
rental car, travel by, 22–23
resorts, 27–28
restaurants ("good eats")
dining with children
games to play while waiting, 54, 101, 136
solving the "picky eater" problem, 24
Florida
authentic "Florida cuisine," 155
Busch Gardens, 183
Florida Keys, 155–156
the Northeast, 52–54
Orlando and the Space Coast, 68–71
SeaWorld Orlando, 80
South Florida, 141–143
Southwest Florida, 166–167
Tallahassee and the Florida Panhandle, 193–195
Universal Studios, Orlando, 89–90
Universal's Islands of Discovery, 94–95

WDW Resort
Disney-MGM Studios, 107, 109
Disney's Animal Kingdom, 120–121
Epcot, 115–117
Magic Kingdom, 103–104
the West Coast, 178–179
Georgia
Augusta and Middle Georgia, 209–211
Callaway Gardens and Columbus, 237–238
greater Atlanta, 252–253
North Georgia, 262–264
Savannah and Coastal Georgia, 224–226
money-saving tips, 31
North Carolina
the Coast, 344–346
the Heartland, 362–366
the Mountains, 384–387
price guide ($) for, 7
South Carolina
Charleston area, 277–279
Columbia area, 285
Low Country, 311–313
Myrtle Beach, 292–293
Santee Cooper Country, 301–303
Up Country, 321–322
Riverbanks Zoological Park and Botanical Garden (Columbia, S.C.), 283–284
road maps/road atlases, 16, 39
road trip survival kit, 19
Robbie's (Islamorada, Fla.), 151–152
Rock 'n' Roller Coaster Starring Aerosmith (WDW Resort, Orlando, Fla.), 107
roller coaster rides (Orlando, Fla.), 124–125
RVs, travel by, 20–21
camping information for, 38–39

S

St. Andrews State Recreation Area and Campground (Panama City Beach, Fla.), 190–191
St. Augustine Alligator Farm (St. Augustine, Fla.), 49–50
St. Lucie Nuclear Power Plant (Hutchinson Island, Fla.), 138

St. Simons Trolley Tour (St. Simons Island, Ga.), 220
Santee Cooper Country (S.C.), 295–303
accommodations, 300–301
background information, 295–296
day trip: Darlington Raceway and South Carolina Cotton Museum, 298–299
"just for fun" attractions, 296–300
map, 296
"must-see" list, 295
restaurants, 301–303
souvenir hunting, 303
Savannah and Coastal Georgia, 213–227
accommodations, 221–224
background information, 213–214
cultural adventures, 214–215
day trips: Okefenokee Swamp Park, 216–217
Tybee Island, 222–223
"just for fun" attractions, 218–221
map, 214
"must-see" list, 213
restaurants, 224–226
souvenir hunting, 226–227
SciTrek (Atlanta, Ga.), 245
Sea Pines EcoTours (Hilton Head Island, S.C.), 308
Seagrove, N.C., 365
Seaside (between Panama City and Pensacola, Fla.), 190, 194–195
SeaWorld Orlando (Orlando, Fla.), 75–81
accommodations, 65–68
restaurants, 80
roller coaster rides, 125
shopping, 80
Shamu Adventure Show (SeaWorld Orlando, Fla.), 79
Shamu's Happy Harbor (SeaWorld Orlando, Fla.), 78
Shipwreck Island Water Park (Panama City Beach, Fla.), 190
shopping. *See* souvenir hunting/shopping
Siesta Beach (Siesta Key, Fla.), 175
Six Flags over Georgia (Atlanta, Ga.), 249–250

395

INDEX

skiing resorts (North Carolina mountains), 382
Smithgall Woods-Dukes Creek Conservation Area (Helen, Ga.), 260
South Carolina
background information, 266–267
price guide ($) for attractions, hotels, and restaurants, 267
rating guide (*) for attractions, 267
the "real" Peach State, 323
See also Charleston area; Columbia area; Myrtle Beach; Santee Cooper Country: South Carolina Low Country; South Carolina Up Country
South Carolina Cotton Museum (Bishopville, S.C.), 299
South Carolina Low Country, 305–312
accommodations, 309–311
background information, 305–306
Gullah language in, 307
"just for fun" attractions, 306–309
map, 306
"must-see" list, 305
restaurants, 311–313
souvenir hunting, 313
South Carolina Up Country, 315–323
accommodations, 320–321
background information, 315–316
cultural adventures, 316–317
"just for fun" attractions, 317–320
map, 316
"must-see" list, 315
restaurants, 321–322
souvenir hunting, 322
South Florida, 127–143
accommodations, 137–141
background information, 127–128
cultural adventures, 128–132
day trip: oceanographic research laboratory and nuclear power plant, 138–139
"just for fun" attractions, 132–137

map, 128
"must-see" list, 127
restaurants, 141–143
souvenir hunting, 143
Southwest Florida, 159–167
accommodations, 164–165
background information, 159–160
cultural adventures, 160–161
"just for fun" attractions, 161–164
map, 160
"must-see" list, 159
restaurants, 166–167
souvenir hunting, 167
souvenir hunting/shopping. *See* "souvenir hunting" as sub-entry under main headings
Space Coast, FL. *See* Orlando and the Space Coast
sponges, diving for/harvesting, 171, 172–173
Summer Waves (Jekyll Island, Ga.), 220
Sun Splash Farm (Daytona Beach, Fla.), 50
sunset celebrations (Key West, Fla.), 152
Swan Lake Iris Gardens (Sumter, S.C.), 300

T

Table Rock State Park (Pickens, S.C.), 319
Tallahassee and the Florida Panhandle, 185–195
accommodations, 191–193
background information, 185–186
cultural adventures, 186–188
day trips: Adventures Unlimited Outdoor Center, 188–189; Seaside (beach town), 194–195
"just for fun" attractions, 188–191
map, 186
"must-see" list, 185
restaurants, 193–195
souvenir hunting, 195
Tallahassee Antique Car Museum (Tallahassee, Fla.), 188
Tarpon Springs (Clearwater-St. Petersburg area, Fla.), 172–173
Teddy Bear Museum of Naples (Naples, Fla.), 161

Theater of the Sea (Islamorada, Fla.), 153
theme park outings dos and don'ts, 108
toiletries, packing checklist, 32
Tomorrowland's Buzz Lightyear's Space Ranger Spin (WDW Resort, Orlando, Fla.), 103
Tomorrowland's Space Mountain (WDW Resort, Orlando, Fla.), 102–103
tours, guided, 29
train travel, 19–20
travel
Online Travel (Perkins), 14
See also air travel; bus travel; car travel; RVs, travel by; train travel
travel agents, using, 16
travel insurance, 28
travel scrapbook, created by children, 237
Twilight Zone of Terror, The (Disney-MGM, WDW Resort, Orlando, Fla.), 107
Tybee Island (east of Savannah, Ga.), 220, 222–223

U

Universal Orlando, 83–95
accommodations, 65–68
background information, 83–84
Islands of Adventure, 90–95
restaurants, 94–95
shopping, 95
map, 84
"must-see" list, 83
Universal Studios, 84–90
restaurants, 89–90
shopping, 90
theme-park outing dos and don'ts, 108
Unto These Hills (North Cherokee, N.C.), 379–380
U.S. Astronaut Hall of Fame (Titusville, Fla.), 59
Victoria's Carriages and Trail Rides (Jekyll Island, Ga.), 220–221

W

Walt Disney World Resort (Orlando, Fla.), 97–125
accommodations, 65–68
background, 97–98
Blizzard Beach, 123

INDEX

Cirque du Soleil, 122

Disney-MGM Studios,
105–110
restaurants and snack spots, 107, 109
shopping, 109–110
Disney Quest, 122
Disney's Animal Kingdom, 117–121
restaurants and snack spots, 120–121
shopping, 121
Epcot, 110–117
restaurants and snack spots, 115–117
shopping, 117
FASTPASS (easy entrance to Disney attractions), 98
fireworks displays, 121
Magic Kingdom, 99–105
restaurants and snack spots, 103–104
shopping, 105
transportation, 99
map, 98
"must-see" list, 97
parades, 121
roller coaster rides, 124
theme-park outing dos and don'ts, 108
Typhoon Lagoon, 123
waterfall country (Transylvania County, N.C.), 378–379
Water Mania (Kissimmee, Fla.), 62–63
water skiing (Cypress Gardens, Winterhaven, Fla.), 177
weather, 13
in Florida, temperatures (average) in major cities, 112
the Internet and, 18
Web, the,
accommodation bookings on, 35, 37
family travel Website, 45
planning the trip and, 12, 31–37
pros and cons for using, 31–34
Wee Links (Fripp Island, S.C.), 309
West Coast of Florida,
169–183
accommodations, 175–177
background information, 169–170
cultural adventures, 170–171
day trip: Tarpon Springs, 172–173
"just for fun" attractions, 171–175
map, 170
"must-see" list, 169
restaurants, 178–179

souvenir hunting, 179
Western North Carolina Nature Center (Asheville, N.C.), 380
Westville, Ga., 231
White Water Park (Marietta, Ga.), 250–251
white-water rafting for the family (North Carolina Mountains), 388–389
Wild Adventure (Valdosta, Ga.), 207–208
Wild Animal Safari (Pine Mountain, Ga.), 235
Wild Water (Surfside Beach, S.C.), 291
Wildwater, Ltd. (Long Creek, S.C.), 319–320
Wonders of Life's Cranium Command (WDW Resort, Orlando, Fla.), 112
Wonders of Life's Test Track (WDW Resort, Orlando, Fla.), 112–113
WonderWorks (Orlando, Fla.), 63
Wright Brothers National Memorial (Kill Devil Hills, N.C.), 340–341

Z

Zoo Atlanta (Atlanta, Ga.), 251

PHONE NUMBERS/WEBSITES

PHONE NUMBERS/WEBSITES

OUR ITINERARY

OUR ITINERARY

TRAVEL BUDGET

TRAVEL BUDGET

TRAVEL JOURNAL

TRAVEL JOURNAL

TRAVEL JOURNAL